THE FRENCH STRUGGLE
FOR THE WEST INDIES

~ Nellis M. Crouse ~

THE FRENCH STRUGGLE
FOR THE WEST INDIES

1665-1713

1966

OCTAGON BOOKS, INC.

New York

CONTENTS

ILLUSTRATIONS

THE FRENCH STRUGGLE
FOR THE WEST INDIES

THE GREAT WEST INDIA COMPANY

DURING the second half of the seventeenth century the history of the West Indies is marked by the struggle between Great Britain and France for supremacy. Besides these two nations there were also two others which played a minor part in the conflict: Spain and the United Netherlands. Spain, we might say, played a passive part. Her position was naturally a defensive one. Ruler of the Spanish Main, Mexico, and the Greater Antilles (save Jamaica), she was content to enjoy her wealth unmolested and had by this time consented to the presence of strangers in what she once regarded as her own particular domain. The Dutch were traders. Their colonial possessions in this part of the world were insignificant; nor had they any desire to increase them. They wished merely to enrich themselves by exchanging their merchandise for the agricultural produce of the islands. The struggle for colonial possessions was therefore reduced to the French and the English settlers who occupied that part of the West Indian archipelago known as the Lesser Antilles, or Caribbee Islands, and sometimes called by the English the Leeward Islands. England also owned Jamaica. The conflict was directed by the home governments; in fact the West Indian struggle was but a reflection of the series of wars raging in Europe at this time, the colonists lining up with or against each other according to the wars or alliances of the mother countries. Thus we have English against Dutch and French, French against Spaniards, French and Spaniards against English, and various other combinations. On the whole the colonists apparently gained little by these wars. Their conquests were frequently used at the conference table as pawns in the great game of European politics and world empire; and a hard-won territory was often returned to the original owner in exchange for some concession in another part of the world.

In the year 1664, when King Louis XIV organized the great West India Company to administer his dominions in the New World, the French controlled the most valuable part of that West Indian archipelago known as the Caribbee Islands. From the little colony founded on the shores of St. Christopher (St. Kitts) in 1624 by the enterprising pioneer Belain d'Esnambuc they had spread northward and southward until, forty years later, they could lay an effectual claim to Martinique, Grenada, St. Lucia, Mariegalante, Guadeloupe and its dependencies, St. Martin (which they shared with the Dutch), St. Eustatius, St. Bartholomew, and St. Croix. They also had a hold on the little islet of Tortuga off the northern coast of San Domingo, whose settlers presently spread to the western part of the larger island in the section known today as Haiti. St. Christopher, parent colony, was shared with the English, who occupied the middle portion, while the French held the northern and southern extremities.

Great as was the potential wealth of these islands—wealth consisting principally of vast sugar cane plantations, which were gradually replacing the tobacco fields that in earlier times had been the mainstay of the settlements—the backers of the various colonizing enterprises had never made a great success of their ventures. In fact, they had frequently suffered heavy losses. The Company of St. Christopher, hastily organized by Cardinal Richelieu in 1626 to meet the needs of D'Esnambuc's embryo colony, collapsed after a hectic career of nine years and was followed by the more formidable Company of the Isles of America. The new company succeeded in exceeding the scope of its predecessor's activities; under its auspices Martinique, St. Lucia, Grenada, and Guadeloupe were added to the French Crown. But in the end it fared no better than the first company, for the governors appointed to rule its island possessions ran matters much their own way, defied the corporation's representative, and looked first of all to their own interests. Despairing of ever making a success of its venture, the company at last decided to sell its various properties to the men who ruled them and to let these governors manage the business to suit themselves. Thus in 1649 Guadeloupe with its adjacent islets and Mariegalante passed into the hands of Charles Houël and his brother-in-law, Jean de Boisseret d'Herblay, and two years later Jacques Dyel du Parquet acquired Martinique, St. Lucia, and Grenada (which he presently sold to Jean Faudoas, Comte de Cérillac), while St. Christopher and the little islands to the north of it were bought by the Knights of Malta, whose representative, Philippe de Lonvilliers de Poincy, had ruled there for several years.

An interested spectator of the vicissitudes of the colonizing companies was Jean-Baptiste Colbert, King Louis's able minister, who during the years when the proprietary governors ruled the islands devoted himself to studying the general colonial situation to see if some policy could be formulated that would enable the government, or at any rate the French nation, to draw a substantial revenue from its outlying possessions. The cause of the trouble was not hard to find; it had, in fact, been known for several years and was simply that the Dutch monopolized the trade with the French Caribbee Islands. Ever since the days when D'Esnambuc founded his colony on St. Christopher these enterprising merchants had been supplying the French settlers with everything they needed in the way of merchandise, taking in payment their crops of sugar and tobacco. For this purpose they had established trading posts— one could hardly call them colonies—at St. Martin, St. Eustatius, Tortola, and, farther south, on the island of Curaçao and on the mainland in the Guianas. Here they had storehouses well stocked with everything their customers might need. They also maintained agents at such Spanish settlements as Maracaibo and La Guayra, for their business was by no means limited to trade with French buyers. In addition to this they had built warehouses in the principal French colonies for the convenience of the trade, everything the planter needed was to be found in these stores—clothing, tools, wines, and meats. Prices, it is true, were higher than in France, and the margin of profit was great, running sometimes as high as 100 percent, but even so the Dutch could undercut the French.

It is no doubt because of this system [wrote the historian Father du Tertre, who lived for several years in the islands] that the Dutch can give better bargains than our Frenchmen, even when offering merchandise which they have purchased in France, and that notwithstanding the losses they suffer at various times, having lost by storm sometimes as many as twenty-five or thirty ships in one year, they never failed us and always furnished the islands abundantly with everything needed by the inhabitants.[1]

The Dutch, it must be admitted, controlled at this time the carrying trade of Europe. They owned, roughly, three-quarters of all the vessels engaged in the transportation of goods and were to be found everywhere, in the ports of France as well as in those of other countries. They were in the habit of sending out about one hundred ships a year to the French Caribbee Islands alone. In comparison with this, France could muster barely two hundred merchantmen in seaworthy condition to carry her entire foreign and domestic trade. Moreover, the Dutch vessels were far cleaner and in better sanitary condition than those of the French, so that even Frenchmen who had occasion to visit the West Indies would journey overland to Dutch ports to take passage in them. The West Indian business was immensely valuable to the Netherlands, particularly to the town of Flushing, whose merchants felt they had a sort of proprietary interest in the French islands, referring to the colonists as "our planters." On one occasion, when a rupture between France and Holland seemed imminent, they even offered them the rights of Dutch bourgeois and furnished them with insurance policies on their properties written by Dutch firms.

What was the cause of all this? Why did the French merchants allow the traders of a rival power to carry off their business under their very noses? The general reason is to be found in the attitude of well-to-do Frenchmen toward trade at the time Colbert came into power. Trade was not considered the proper career for a gentleman. Well-born people who hoped to count for something in the world gravitated toward the Court, where political favors were dispensed and social position could be secured. Those who were sons of tradesmen and who, one might suppose, would be the ones to carry on their fathers' calling, left the counting houses, as soon as they could afford to do so, in order to improve their position. To make matters worse, the parents themselves were only too glad to help their children advance beyond the status of tradesmen by sending them to colleges where they could secure an education in

[1]Du Tertre, *Histoire générale des Antilles*, II, 462.

literature and science, but were kept in complete ignorance of matters pertaining to business. Thus prepared for life, the young tradesman's son, if he had no particular aptitude for applying the knowledge he had acquired and was well supplied with funds, was likely to spend his time in gaming and idleness. In Holland the reverse was true, for there commerce was held in high esteem and youths were trained for the career of merchandising in the practical school of experience. [2]

So much for the general reason, the one that explains the low state of French commerce at that time. But for the West Indies in particular we find that the root of the trouble was the excessive duties imposed by the French government on the products of the Caribbee Islands imported into France, plus, of course, the paucity of French ships. On sugar there was a duty of 40 percent, that is, the commodity sold for thirty livres a hundredweight and carried a duty of twelve livres. The customs also levied a tax of 50 percent on tobacco and 240 on ginger. In contradistinction to this the State Generals levied a uniform rate of only five sous a hundredweight on all these commodities. This favorable state of affairs enabled the Dutch to import raw sugar and tobacco from the French West Indies, treat it in their refineries and factories, and reship it to the Baltic ports and even into France, at a good profit. Faced with such competition, the French merchant was helpless; he could do nothing until his government took a more liberal view of the situation by repealing the laws which put him at such a disadvantage. [3]

The problem of securing this valuable trade exclusively for France was one which Colbert now proposed to solve. There happened to be in France a man named Antoine Le Febvre de la Barre, erstwhile intendant of Bourbonnais, now a captain in the Corps de la Marine, who had become greatly interested in the stories he had heard of the capture by the Dutch of the former French colony of Cayenne in Guiana and was determined to regain it for the French Crown. His enthusiasm pleased Colbert, who discussed the matter with his master the King, with the result that he was soon able to advise La Barre to form for this purpose a company which his Majesty would aid with men, money, and ships. La Barre

[2]Mims, *Colbert's West India Policy*, pp. 5–6. [3]*Ibid.*, p. 54.

needed no further encouragement. He immediately brought together a group of twenty men, who raised the required capital of
200,000 livres. Thus was formed the French Equatorial Company. [4]

It also happened at this time that a report reached Colbert that
chaotic conditions in Martinique had caused upward of a thousand
colonists to leave the island in disgust. [5] Here, then, was an oppor-.
tunity to intervene in the affairs of the West Indian possessions.
Selecting an able, experienced officer named Alexandre de Prouville,
Marquis de Tracy, he appointed him lieutenant-general of the
archipelago and provided him with a royal commission, dated
November 19, 1663, authorizing him to restore order, assert the
authority of the Crown, and make the people obey him. Though
the extent of the powers granted covered all the American colonies,
Canadian as well as West Indian, the King was pleased to make
an exception of Cayenne, where La Barre was to be in supreme
command. Only if military maneuvers were necessary was De
Tracy to exert his authority at Cayenne, and then for only as much
time as was needed for its conquest. With this trifling exception the
Marquis was given what amounted to viceregal powers, powers
far greater than had ever been accorded a mere governor-general
of the West Indies, for De Tracy was authorized to do as he pleased
in the Caribbee Islands. It was an exceptional mark of royal confidence, and De Tracy fully lived up to the trust reposed in him.

An expedition was arranged to transport both these men with
their followers to the West Indies. To Charles Colbert du Terron,
a relative of Jean-Baptiste, who among his many duties, had charge
of equipping the King's vessels, was given the task of organizing
the enterprise. The fleet assembled at La Rochelle was a small one.
The flagship was a handsome man-of-war of eight hundred tons,
mounting fifty guns, named the "Brezé," on which both De Tracy
and La Barre embarked. Accompanying her were the warship
"Terron," two flutes, a flyboat, and a frigate. The soldiers selected
to go with the expedition were the pick of four crack regiments,
and together with the passengers, of whom there were a few, they
numbered between twelve hundred and fifteen hundred men. They
were commanded by Sieur Vincent, a man who later became
governor of Grenada.

[4] *Compagnie de la France Equinoctiale* was the correct title.
[5] Clément, *Lettres . . . Colbert*, III (Part 2), 387.

The fleet set sail on February 26, 1664, and arrived at Madeira three weeks later. From there the vessels proceeded to the Cape Verde Islands and then directly across the ocean to Guiana, which they reached on the eleventh of May. The first objective of the expedition was the colony of Cayenne, situated on an island very near the mainland of what is now French Guiana. On anchoring here De Tracy sent an officer with a summons of surrender to the Dutch governor, Guerin Spranger. Unable to cope with such a powerful force, Spranger saw the folly of even attempting to resist it and gracefully offered to yield the island to the French for a down payment of 21,850 florins for his own extensive plantations. This matter settled, De Tracy bade farewell to La Barre and proceeded to Martinique in the "Brezé," attended by the "Terron" and an imposing retinue.

M. de Tracy's arrival at St. Pierre, capital of Martinique, was most impressive; even the English, when the news reached them, spoke of it as something worthy of notice. It seemed to them that the new representative of the King of France, with "thirty gentlemen for his guard" and a fifty-gun man-of-war to attend him boded ill for England. "In fine," wrote Governor Francis Willoughby of Barbados, "the dispute will be whether the King of England or of France shall be monarch of the West Indies, for the King of Spain cannot hold it long, and this is the first year's entrance of the King of France on his own account." Furthermore, Lord Willoughby added, he had just received word from the French governor of St. Christopher that King Louis stood ready to buy England's interest in that island and in adjacent islands now possessed by France to which England might have some claim, for His Majesty was sending a viceroy with men and ships to secure his own interests in them.[6]

While he was engaged in settling the local problems of Martinique, De Tracy was startled by the news that the English were stirring up trouble in St. Lucia. For several years the colony of Barbados had suffered from overcrowding and had been obliged to bear the loss of some sixteen hundred people, forced to migrate to other less populous islands such as Guadeloupe, Martinique, and Mariegalante. The loss of so many people was a source of

[6]*Calendar of State Papers, Amer. & West Indies, 1661–68*, No. 823.

annoyance to Governor Willoughby, who decided to seize St. Lucia, now occupied by only a small French settlement, and to plant a colony there that would take the overflow from Barbados. This plan, when it became known in Martinique—as it soon did— brought forth a spirited protest from the governor of Martinique, Jean Dyel de Clermont, who at once wrote Willoughby setting forth the French claims to the island and threatening to maintain them by force of arms if necessary. This attitude brought an equally spirited rejoinder from the British governor, who enclosed in his letter a copy of the famous Carlisle Patent, granted by King Charles I in 1627, in which that monarch gave his faithful henchman the Earl of Carlisle, St. Lucia together with the other islands named in the document. Each side having thus proved to its own satis-faction the rightfulness of its claims—though neither succeeded in convincing the other—Governor Willoughby proceeded to business.

There happened to be at this time in the island of Dominica, stronghold of the Carib nation, a half-breed named Thomas Warner, natural son of Sir Thomas Warner, first English governor of St. Christopher, and a Carib woman. This man was a person of considerable ability who had far more of the white man than the Indian in his mental make-up. After Sir Thomas's death his widow, who looked upon her stepson as a perpetual reminder of her hus-band's infidelity, compelled the poor fellow to work on her plan-tation at St. Christopher with her slaves. From this servitude he managed to escape to the mountains, where he joined a band of fugitive blacks; but he was soon recaptured and sent back to the fields, this time in irons. Here he was found by Edward Warner, the legitimate white son of Sir Thomas, who, moved by com-passion for his dark-skinned half-brother, obtained his release. Far from mollifying Mrs. Warner, this did but increase her hatred of the man, who now felt obliged to leave the island if he would be safe from her anger. He therefore made his escape to Dominica, where his superior intelligence soon made him a leader of the Caribs. Here he came under the notice of Lord Willoughby, who thought he had found in the half-breed an instrument which he could use to gain control, first of Dominica, then of St. Lucia. England and France, by virtue of a treaty signed by the colonials of both nations in 1660, had agreed to leave Dominica and St. Vincent to the Indians and to refrain from sending their people to plant colonies there. St. Lucia, which was claimed by both nations, was not included in the agreement, but since the French colony there was small and the Caribs numerous, Willoughby engineered a plan to get them on his side. To do this he first induced Warner to make a journey to England, where he was made much of and presented at Court. Then, on April 16, 1664, he was given a commission naming him governor of Dominica for England. This done, Willoughby purchased from the Caribs their claims to St. Lucia, using Warner as an intermediary, on the theory that since the island belonged rightfully to the savages a deed from them signed by Governor Warner, himself more or less one of them, would be a convincing token of legal ownership.

In June, Lord Willoughby prepared to colonize his newly acquired possession. He fitted out an expedition of fifteen hundred men, placed them in five vessels, two of which were armed with thirty-six guns each, and sent them forth accompanied by six hundred Carib warriors in seventeen canoes under the leadership of Warner, who, as the British representative, felt bound to support all British claims. On reaching St. Lucia, they found the small French colony under Governor Bonnard, a kinsman of the Du Parquet family. It was defended by an apology for a fort, manned by a garrison of fourteen men and equipped with a few guns. There was nothing for Bonnard to do but bow to the inevitable, and he promptly surrendered, with the understanding that he should be transported to Martinique with his men, munitions, and supplies. The English commander did send him back to Martinique, but he kept the property.

When the Marquis de Tracy heard this news, he promptly ordered Governor de Clermont to dispatch a ship to recover the property, and at the same time he wrote a letter to the English colonel in command asking him by whose orders he had taken the island. Somewhat frightened by the French governor's tone, the Englishman returned the guns and some of the equipment he had confiscated and also wrote Clermont a letter in which he tried to exculpate himself by saying he had captured St. Lucia by order of his king. On hearing this, De Tracy informed Colbert of the situation, expressing the hope that he would bring pressure on the British government to restore the island to its rightful owners, and he also sent word to Lord Willoughby that he had taken this step, suggesting at the same time that the English evacuate the place pending the decision of the home governments. Alarmed at the thought of losing his newly acquired colony, Willoughby hastily wrote Henry Bennet, Earl of Arlington, warning him of the demands soon to be made upon the Crown and urging him to persuade King Charles II not only to refuse to give up St. Lucia but also to send reinforcements to help his colonists in their attempts to resist the impending encroachments of the French on the British West Indian possessions. The Marquis de Tracy, however, did not push the matter any further, and the English were left in peaceful possession of the island. In the course of time various misfortunes overtook the colony, and in January, 1666, the pitiful remnant of the original settlers abandoned it, thus allowing the French to recapture it without striking a blow.[7]

One of Colbert's principal objects in founding the West India Company was, as we have said, to forge an instrument that would enable him to replace the Dutch traders in the Caribbee Islands with those of French nationality. The problem was a ticklish one— one that could not be solved over night—for the paucity of French merchantmen made it impossible for the colonists to relinquish immediately their trade relations with the Dutch. Some one must supply their needs until the newly formed company could acquire a sufficient merchant marine to take care of its West Indian business. Colbert, unfortunately, seems to have missed this point. Overanxious to end a state of affairs which was enriching a rival nation at the expense of France, he attempted to stop at once all Dutch activities in the French Islands. For this purpose he secured from the King an edict forbidding trade with the men of Holland for a period of six months, on the specious plea that an epidemic was raging in Amsterdam. De Tracy received the order in the latter part of June, and of course he had no other choice but to see that it was published and obeyed throughout the archipelago.

News that the Dutch were to be excluded from the islands was received with deep regret by the planters. For years they had re-

[7]Du Tertre, *Histoire générale des Antilles*, III, 81–90; *C.S.P., America & West Indies, 1661–68*, Nos. 565, 1657.

garded these enterprising traders as the men who would supply
their wants and take in exchange the surplus of their plantations.
Many Dutchmen had taken up residence in the French islands,
where they owned valuable properties, especially sugar mills,
which they had been instrumental in developing. Moreover, it
soon became apparent that in the immediate future there would
be no one to replace these traders. The vessels which the company
was to send over did not arrive at once; and even when a few did
put in an appearance, everyone saw that it would take considerable
time to replace the fleet of sixty to eighty vesesls which had arrived
from Holland each year. To add to the confusion, a bumper crop
was now expected, which must be transported to France without
too much loss of time if a profit was to be realized. M. de Tracy
wrote frantically to the directors, pointing out that if the company
was to take up where the Dutch had left off it would be necessary
to send over 3,000,000 livres worth of merchandise, a sum far in
excess of what the directors could raise. Thus serious want, though
though not actual starvation, stared the colonists in the face.

By this time the directors were fully cognizant of the situation
and of the need for prompt action if they expected to wean the
inhabitants away from their reliance on the Dutch traders. The
company by this time had sufficient funds to finance a respectable
fleet of merchantmen and was ready to send over its own representative to replace M. de Tracy, who had orders to proceed to Canada
when his task in the West Indies was ended. This representative
was to be, not a governor-general appointed by the king, but an
agent of the company in supreme command of its possessions, who
may be described as the "Intendant," a title by which Father du
Tertre refers to him. For this position they selected Sieur de
Chambré. In addition to the intendant, the company also needed
governors for the various islands—governors who, though named
by the directors, would receive their commissions from the king.
In their selections for these posts, as in the case of M. de Chambré,
they were particularly fortunate. For Martinique they chose an
able officer who had spent twenty-five years in the military service,
during which time he had been a captain in the Marine, commander of Calais during its governor's absence, and later governor
of the city of Cardonne. He bore the imposing name of Robert le

Frichot des Friches de Clodoré and was given his commission in October, 1664. For Guadeloupe a commission was obtained for M. du Lion, who had already been temporarily appointed by the Marquis de Tracy, while Jacques Boisseret de Téméricourt was placed over Maiiegalante, thanks to the influence of his mother, who received this right for him when she sold her interests to the company. MM. de Chambré and de Clodoré sailed in December, 1664, with a fleet stored with merchandise, and arrived at Martinique the following February.

Upon the arrival of these gentlemen the Marquis de Tracy proceeded to induct M. de Clodoré into office as governor of the island and representative of the West India Company. This done, he turned his attention to the appointment of a lieutenant-governor. The directors had selected for this post one Jean Duchêne and had sent him out with Clodoré, but it so happened that De Tracy had already appointed François Rolle de Loubière, a popular citizen much respected by the colonists. To avoid unpleasantness, the Marquis decided to divide the island between them. To Loubière he assigned the section lying south of a line drawn due east from St. Pierre, while Duchêne obtained the part lying north of it. Thus was Martinique supplied with a governor and two lieutenant-governors. Among the more prominent citizens of the island at this time were François le Vassor, captain of St. Pierre, Philippe de la Vallée, captain of the *quartier*, or district of Case Pilote, and the former governor of Grenada, Louis de Valmenière. [8] After the induction of Clodoré, De Tracy proceeded to Basseterre, [9] capital of Guadeloupe, where he proclaimed the company the legal proprietor of the island and read the royal commission confirming the appointment of Du Lion as governor. Pierre Hencelin, brother-in-law of former Governor Houël, was installed as commander of Fort St. Charles, the fortification protecting the town. His work done, De Tracy bade farewell to his friends and, embarking in the month of April (1665), set sail for Canada.

[8] François le Vassor de la Touche, Philippe le Vayer de la Vallée, and Louis Caqueray de Valmenière, to give them their full titles.

[9] The name of Basseterre was also that of the capital of St. Christopher. Care must be taken not to confuse these towns with the term *Basseterre* which was applied to the western or leeward side of all islands. *Capesterre* was the name given to the windward side.

Scarcely had the Marquis disappeared over the horizon when the Martinicans received a surprise visit from the Dutch admiral Michel Adriaanzoon de Ruyter, who anchored his fleet on the first of May in the roadstead of St. Pierre. Less than three months earlier the war, known as the Second Dutch War, had broken out between England and Holland, and this expedition had been sent to the West Indies to see what it could do. De Ruyter had met a fleet of forty English merchantmen at Barbados, escorted by a few men-of-war, and had fought them in a terrific battle under the guns of Bridgetown, capital of the island. He succeeded, according to his report, in battering most of the vessels and damaging a great part of the town. He could even have captured the city had he wished to do so; but, mindful of his instructions not to take too many risks, he abandoned his prize and sailed off, satisfied with the damage he had done. Yet according to an English account he sailed away after a heavy engagement "in the confusedest manner possible."[10]

On arriving at Martinique, De Ruyter sent a boat ashore with a letter to Governor de Clodoré requesting permission to land and take on supplies. The request was promptly granted, and the following day the admiral landed with his staff and was taken to the Governor's mansion, where the party were regaled with a sumptuous banquet, a courtesy which was promptly returned by De Ruyter on his flagship. As further proof of friendship, Clodoré permitted the burial of several "gentlemen volunteers" who had fallen in the battle off Bridgetown, and with his officers he attended the obsequies which were "conducted according to the custom of Holland." Before leaving, De Ruyter took on an ample supply of wood, water, wine, flour, meat, and other necessities, giving in exchange six hundred pounds of gunpowder, badly needed by the French. Then he set sail and proceeded to Nevis, where he captured several English ships. He would also have made an attack on the British section of St. Christopher, had not the French governor, mindful of the treaty of amity that existed between the French and the English colonists of the island, urged him to forego this pleasure.

The English were not slow to get their revenge for Barbados.

[10]C.S.P., *America & West Indies, 1661–68*, No. 980.

Sir Thomas Modyford, governor of Jamaica, deputed Colonel Edward Morgan to raise an expedition for a series of attacks on Dutch possessions. Morgan got together a ruffianly, mutinous gang of 650 buccaneers, bribed them into a semblance of obedience by promises of ample loot, and put them on board a fleet of nine vessels under Theodore Cary, Thomas Morgan, and himself. On the seventeenth of July they assembled at Montserrat, where they procured some boats for landing purposes. Proceeding thence to St. Eustatius, they were able with only half their force to capture the place with very little effort. Though the casualties were negligible, "the Lieutenant-General [Edward Morgan] died, not with any wound, but being ancient and corpulent, by hard marching and extraordinary heat fell and died, and Colonel Cary took command of the party upon himself by the desire of all." When the fort surrendered, quarrels over the booty began. The buccaneers refused to stir before a distribution had been made to their satisfaction. While they were quarreling a small English vessel arrived with some seventy men and was sent to capture the little volcanic cone of Saba, a few miles from St. Eustatius, a feat performed without striking a blow. Altercations at last grew so bitter that it was impossible to undertake anything more against the Dutch possessions, and the mutinous gang finally departed, leaving Thomas Morgan as governor of the two islands.[11]

Within the next few months Chambré took possession of all the remaining islands in the French domain. At St. Christopher, erstwhile property of the Knights of Malta, Governor Charles de Sales, who had ruled for the Order since the death of De Poincy, was confirmed as governor for the company on the third of December. The ceremony, similar to the ceremonies at Martinique and Guadeloupe, was carried out with a marked lack of enthusiasm on the part of the inhabitants, who, like their fellows on the other islands, were hostile to the rule of the corporation. The majority of the gentry absented themselves deliberately from the formalities in order to avoid the necessity of taking the oath of allegiance, an action which caused Chambré to refuse them the ratification of their ancient privileges. Governor de Sales saw fit to take the oath under protest lest he might prejudice the rights of the Order

[11] *Ibid.*, No. 1088.

in case the company did not pay for the islands the full amount stipulated in the contract. Shortly after this he held long conversations with Chambré, questioning the wisdom of curtailing the privileges granted the gentry by the Knights and sanctified by custom, with the result that the latter signed an agreement permitting a continuance of these privileges. Another important question was the right of merchants to trade with their English neighbors according to conditions set forth in a recent treaty. This, of course, infringed on the company's monopoly of trade; but Chambré, in view of the poor service given by the corporation, modified the prohibitory regulation insofar as to permit the purchase from the English of articles which were not available in the company's warehouses.

De Sales, now governor of all the possessions formerly held by the Order, sent Sieur de Guéry to take possession of the lesser islands in the name of the company. De Guéry proceeded first to St. Croix, where M. de Bois, who had governed there in the name of the Order for several years, surrendered his position and was at once reinstated in it as a governor under M. de Sales. Within a week De Guéry had visited St. Bartholomew and St. Martin, whose rulers acknowledged without protest the suzerainty of the West India Company.

❧ II ❧

THE FRENCH WIN THE FIRST ROUND

A DRASTIC CHANGE now took place in the relations between France and England, a change destined to mar the peaceful conditions in the West Indian colonies. The war between England and the Netherlands, known as the Second Dutch War, which broke out in February, 1665, was the cause of the rupture. By an agreement signed in 1662 the French king had obligated himself to come to the help of the States General should they be attacked by the English. When the occasion arose, Louis was for some time reluctant to fulfill his obligations, and the matter was allowed to drift; but at last, fearing the Dutch and the English might patch up a peace between them which would bring no good to France, he signed, on January 26, 1666, a declaration of war against his island neighbor. News of this outbreak of hostilities was no great shock to the West Indian colonists; in fact they had anticipated just such an eventuality and, despite the frantic, last-minute efforts to maintain peace at St. Christopher, were already flocking to their standards when the official notice reached them.

At this time the English held four islands of the Leeward group, and to the south of them the island of Barbados, lying out in the Atlantic Ocean. The old Carlisle Patent which covered these islands was issued in 1627 by Charles I to the earl of that name, and twenty years later was leased by Carlisle's son to Lord Francis Willoughby of Parham. After many vicissitudes, during which he lost control of his property at the time of the Protectorate, Willoughby had the good fortune to have his title confirmed by Charles II, and he at once betook himself to Barbados. Here he proceeded by means of deputy governors to exercise his authority over the four islands of the Leeward archipelago listed in the patent, as follows: for Nevis, Governor James Russell; Antigua, John Bunckley; Montserrat, William Osborne; St. Christopher, William Watts. The British also owned the great island of Jamaica, captured by Cromwell's expedition in 1655 and now governed by Thomas Modyford.

`A few days before King Louis signed the declaration of war governors De Sales and Watts had met to renew the old treaty of amity between the colonists of St. Christopher that had kept the peace for forty years. This treaty, first drawn up in 1627 by the original settlers, Belain d'Esnambuc and Sir Thomas Warner, provided for a division of the island between the two nations, outlined the rights and obligations which each had toward the other, and, most important of all in the present crisis, embodied an article guaranteeing that in case of a war between the home governments the colonists would not attack each other unless specifically ordered to do so by their sovereigns, and even then the attacking party would give notice of its intention to begin hostilities. As it had been the custom to renew this treaty upon the accession of a new governor or upon change of ownership, it was deemed appropriate to make another renewal now that the West India Company had taken over the island. A new treaty was accordingly drawn up, by which, among other things, the attacking party was required to give seventy-two hours notice. It was signed by the governors on January 20, 1666, and ratified in behalf of the company by M. de Chambré on the same day.

Though the document was signed by Governor Watts, it needed the ratification of his superior, Lord Willoughby. Watts kept putting off suggestions to send the treaty to Willoughby, until at last Chambré became impatient and left for Martinique, where he poured his suspicions into Governor de Clodoré's ear. As a result of their conference the two men decided to send an ambassador to Lord Willoughby asking him to advise them of his intentions and also to give an answer to certain complaints previously made about some outrages committed upon French property by English buccaneers. For this purpose they selected Julien le Cordelier du Blanc, Major of Guadeloupe, and sent him forth with the proper credentials.

Du Blanc arrived at Bridgetown, Barbados, in due course of

time and was at once ushered into the presence of Governor Willoughby. His lordship received the French envoy cordially and listened with great patience to all his complaints about the English freebooters and to his claims for damages for their depredations as well as to his request for an early ratification of the treaty. When the Frenchman had completed his harangue, Willoughby assured him of his willingness to make amends for any wrongs committed by his people and also expressed his desire to live at peace with his French neighbors even though war should break out between the two Crowns. He therefore suggested to Du Blanc that he retire for a few days to think the matter over and put in writing any plans he might have for establishing pleasant relations between the two peoples. To tell the truth, Willoughby had been advised some time before of the probability of an early declaration of war and was anxious to lull the French into a false sense of security in order to perfect certain plans he was making with Governor Watts for the seizure of French St. Christopher. For this reason he wished to nurse Du Blanc along; to keep him in suspense as long as possible in order to gain time. When the interview was over, he invited his guest to a sumptuous banquet and caused him to be given the best suite of rooms in the town's principal inn, where during the course of his stay he was visited by the leading persons of the island.

A few days later Lord Willoughby notified Du Blanc that he was ready to receive his report. As on the previous occasion, the French envoy was escorted to the executive mansion and was received by the Governor in person, who took him by the hand and placed him next to him at table. After an excellent repast Du Blanc presented the document he had drawn up embodying a plan for maintaining peace between the two nations in the West Indies. This document, a brief one, contained three points which he hoped might serve as bases for a treaty of amity: (1) in case of war, if the government of one nation ordered an attack on the other, the attacker should give a month's notice instead of the seventy-two hours provided by the treaty; (2) both parties should unite in suppressing robbers and buccaneers; (3) the treaty of 1660, guaranteeing Dominica to the Caribs, should be observed, and neither party should attempt to seize the island. Du Blanc also requested the

Governor to urge Modyford of Jamaica to join in the agreement.

Lord Willoughby suppressed a smile as he read the paper, so naïve were the suggestions. Feigning to be impressed with them—for at all costs he must gain time—he answered that a decision could not be reached at once, as such important matters demanded mature reflection, so he set a date at which Du Blanc should return for his reply. Meantime the envoy was free to roam about the island and enjoy himself. When the appointed day arrived, Du Blanc was again conducted to the Governor's residence where he was received with the usual marks of consideration and was now asked to show a copy of the King's edict establishing the West India Company and the credentials giving him authority to execute a treaty. Why these were not asked for at the first interview is not stated. Perhaps Willoughby did not think of them; but now, when Du Blanc handed them to him, he requested further time for examining them and dismissed his guest with a promise to send for him in three days. The three days passed and many more of them. Lord Willoughby was obliged to postpone his appointments because unexpected business always arose to demand his immediate attention. Meanwhile Du Blanc was feted, invited from house to house, and urged to prolong his stay indefinitely. At last realizing that all this was but a ruse to gain time, he sent the Governor notice of his intention to return to Martinique at once. Seeing he was no longer able to retain the envoy, Lord Willoughby sent for him and handed him two letters, one for Clodoré, the other for Chambré, and bade him Godspeed, but he did not ratify the treaty. Du Blanc was back at St. Pierre by the twelfth of March.

The gist of these letters could hardly be considered satisfactory from the French point of view. Indeed, on hearing Du Blanc's report the two officials saw clearly that he had been led along by the wily English governor so that the French, lulled into a feeling of security, would neglect military preparations, thus making it possible for the English to strike without warning. Willoughby, in his letter, appeared to agree with Chambré's complaints regarding the outrages perpetrated and promised to inflict punishment on the guilty parties. But he pointed out that English law forbade the condemnation of an accused person without a hearing and that in order to comply with the demands of justice it would be necessary to appoint a commission to make an investigation and take testimony. As to the treaty recently signed at St. Christopher, he professed complete ignorance of its merits and refused to commit himself until he had obtained the opinion of his advisers. He pointed out, however, and with considerable truth, that he could do nothing about Jamaica, since that island was independent of his authority. The important feature of Willoughby's communication was his refusal to accept the suggestion of Du Blanc to allow a respite of one month instead of seventy-two hours before beginning hostilities. On this point the Governor needed no advice and was quite willing to act on his own initiative.[1]

If Lord Willoughby hoped to pull the wool over French eyes, he was doomed to disappointment; for a week after Du Blanc's return a ship anchored off St. Pierre bringing two letters to Governor de Clodoré, one from the King, and one from Colbert, dated the second and the sixth of February, respectively, which advised him of the official declaration of war by the King of France. In these letters both the King and his minister stressed the importance of remaining at peace with the English in the West Indies if it were possible to do so. Clodoré, realizing how slim were the chances of obeying this injunction, at once passed the news on to De Sales, at the same time warning him to prepare for the worst. He also seized this occasion to offer military assistance to St. Christopher if it should be needed. This island was, of course, the most exposed to danger. It was small and easily accessible from all sides, and also the French had to face the English colonists already there. Fortunately the fortifications were in good condition; the men in excellent spirits. M. de Chambré went in person to Guadeloupe, where he made similar suggestions to Governor du Lion.

At Martinique, Clodoré had some sixty guns ready for use, which he placed at various points where an enemy could easily disembark. More than twenty batteries and redoubts were quickly constructed. A startling innovation was also introduced into the service. The Governor made a selection of the toughest negroes on the island and enrolled them into companies under a ferocious black named François Fabulé, who had shown his ability as a leader several months before, when he threatened a slave insurrection

[1] Du Tertre, *Histoire générale des Antilles*, III, 282–96.

against the whites. He was given a sword, a uniform, and a plumed hat as insignia of his rank and told to have his men ready in case of an attack. Unfortunately these warriors never had a chance to show their mettle, and opinions remained divided as to their merits as soldiers.

Governor du Lion did not lose any time in putting Guadeloupe in a state of defense. He built a powerful battery at Rivière aux Herbes and ordered the guns in Houël's famous residence of Houël-mont, near Basseterre,[2] to be brought down and set up in strategic spots where they could fire successfully on an enemy attempting to land in this locality. Mariegalante was sadly in need of ammunition and would have fared badly had not one of those ubiquitous Dutch traders been able to supply two hundred pounds of gunpowder. Governor Vincent considered discretion the better part of valor, for he had only sixty men capable of bearing guns, and he ordered a general retreat into the mountain fastnesses of Grenada.

Meanwhile the English were preparing for aggression. St. Christopher was considered the weak spot in the French possessions, and Governor Willoughby, as head of the British colonies, had received orders some time before to be ready to attack it as soon as war was officially declared. The colonists themselves were eager for the fray. Proposals were made by certain planters to urge the King to order Willoughby to raise one thousand men in Barbados, six hundred in Montserrat, three hundred in Antigua, and one thousand in Nevis, who should be transported to St. Christopher where they would join a force made up of all the inhabitants capable of bearing arms. Then he could proceed to seize the French portions of the island.[3] These proposals were never carried out, at least in the manner suggested by the planters, but the governors made elaborate arrangements to coöperate in the taking of St. Christopher. Proof of this was found, so Du Tertre tells us, in a collection of letters discovered on the person of Governor Watts, who was slain in the first campaign. According to this correspondence Governor Russell, of Nevis, promised to do his level best to aid in every possible way. He sent Watts notice of the declaration of war by King Charles the instant he received it and

[2] Refers to town of Basseterre, capital of Guadeloupe, not to the *Basseterre* section.

[3] *C.S.P., America & West Indies, 1661-68*, No. 1156.

followed it up with a contingent of four hundred men. In addition to this valuable aid, seven boatloads of buccaneers fresh from Jamaica were sent to St. Eustatius ready to go into action. This little army, numbering 260 men, was presently brought to St. Christopher by its leader, Colonel Thomas Morgan, and landed at Old Road Town, capital of the English colony. [4]

As soon as he had received his copy of the declaration of war Governor Watts forwarded it on the eighteenth of April to M. de Sales at Basseterre, [5] a Colonel Lawrence acting as the messenger. After delivering it, the Colonel requested the French governor to observe the articles of the recently signed concordat providing for the preservation of peace between the two colonies. Anxious to maintain peaceful relations, De Sales agreed to this, provided, of course, the English kept their part of the bargain. But he did not altogether trust his neighbors, since he had before him the report of a Frenchman, just escaped from Nevis, who had seen the military preparations being made there by Governor Russell. Three days later De Sales saw these reinforcements coming across the water from Nevis and landing at Palmetto Point. He acted quickly. The alarm was sounded, and the troops at Basseterre were ordered to assemble along the Pentecost River, which formed the boundary line separating the English from the southern French section. Before attacking, however, he felt it would only be fair to send an emissary to Governor Watts to hear what he had to say about the reinforcements and to remind him of Colonel Lawrence's request for peace. Somewhat nettled at this attitude and the bad faith it implied, Watts referred De Sales to the seventy-two-hours clause in the treaty, pointing out that the time limit had expired and that he had notified the French governor three days ago of the declaration of war on the part of the English government; while to the argument put forth that he had asked for peace through Colonel Lawrence he replied bluntly that he must serve his king. De Sales, therefore, had no choice but to meet force with force; and this he now proceeded to do.

Governor de Sales's forces, because of the territorial division of the island, were separated into two groups, one in the northern

[4] Du Tertre, *Histoire générale des Antilles*, IV, 7–10.
[5] As in the case of Guadeloupe, the French capital of St. Christopher was named Basseterre.

part, the other, by far the larger of the two, in the southern section. Between them lay English territory. The southern frontier
line ran from the mouth of the Pentecost River across the island
to the Cayonne River on the northern side, near which lay the
French settlement of that name. The northern line began at Pointe
de Sable and extended up over the mountains to an indentation in
the northern shore known as Sandy Bay. De Sales had stationed
his men at three of the four corners of the quadrilateral thus formed,
as being the key points to his defense, since the interior of the
island was mountainous and the expected attacks were bound to
take place along the coast. At Pointe de Sable he had a detachment of 350 men commanded by Robert Lonvilliers de Poincy,[6]
who acted as governor of the district, while two hundred under
Dominique des Vergers de Sanois held the corner at Sandy Bay.
Cayonne had no regular force to defend it. De Sales himself was at
Basseterre with about eight hundred men, face to face with the
English forces across the Pentecost River.

It was Governor Watts's plan to leave one thousand men to
guard the frontier between his territory and Basseterre and to
proceed with twelve hundred, including Colonel Morgan's buccaneers, to Pointe de Sable, where he expected no difficulty in dis-
posing of Lonvilliers's little army; then he would march to Sandy
Bay and crush Sanois. After this it would be an easy matter to
march on Cayonne, defeat the colonists there with the help of the
fifteen hundred men of Capesterre, and then invade Basseterre and
destroy the main French army.

Since Watts expected the French to remain on the defensive
because of their inferior numbers, De Sales determined to launch
a surprise attack and thus make up by aggressiveness what he
lacked in numerical strength. He proposed to take the bulk of his
army and make a tour of the island in the reverse direction from
that planned by Watts. His first objective was Cayonne where a
considerable English force was stationed. It was composed entirely
of the local militia of Capesterre, unsupported by any troops from
Nevis or elsewhere. Just what its numbers were is impossible to
say. De Tertre tells us there were some fifteen or sixteen hundred

[6]Nephew of former Governor-General de Poincy. We shall call him Lonvilliers to distin-
guish him from his famous uncle.

men in this region, of whom five hundred were at Cinq Combles (Nicholas Town), situated halfway between the northern and the southern frontiers of the English section. Thus there were not more than one thousand men at Cayonne to oppose De Sales's somewhat smaller force. If successful, De Sales intended to push on to Sandy Bay, then to Pointe de Sable, hoping to defeat the enemy with the help of the French forces stationed there. With this in view he sent two messengers, one by sea, the other by land, to Lonvilliers and Sanois, ordering them to time their attacks with the march he proposed to make on Cayonne. The messengers were captured, but the two commanders had the gumption to act on their own initiative when hostilities began. That De Sales considered the situation serious and the outcome doubtful he showed by dispatching to France the ship "Oranger" with the wives and children of the leading officials and planters, who took with them much of their portable property. Later we shall have occasion to deal with the arrival of this vessel in France.

It was Monday, April 21, 1666,[7] when De Sales placed his eight hundred men along the banks of the Pentecost River, where they could be readily seen by the English. This he did to deceive the enemy into thinking he intended to keep the army there for the defense of Basseterre. When darkness fell, the Governor gave orders to fall in, and, leaving a hundred men or so to keep the fires going and give the general impression that he was still encamped there, he led his men across the island to Cayonne. The march was a short one. Two hours after breaking camp the little army found itself at Cayonne, where the men spent the balance of the night resting or seeking spiritual preparation for the coming conflict from the Jesuit Fathers who accompanied them as chaplains. Governor de Sales in particular invoked the blessing of his great-uncle, the famous St. Francis de Sales, whom he had selected as the patron saint of the expedition.

At daybreak the Governor drew up his army for battle. He divided his men into two nearly equal columns in order to attack the enemy at two separate points. One of these columns, the one which was to form the left wing, he commanded himself, while the

---

[7]The dates we shall give are New Style according to the Gregorian Calendar then used by the French. The English records give the Old Style.

other was intrusted to his second-in-command, the Chevalier de Saint-Laurent, whom he designated as his successor should he fall on the field of battle. [8] From his division of 350 men he detached a group of fifty to form the vanguard of shock troops, which he placed under an officer named Urbain Guillon. The latter distinguished himself during the day by his bravery and leadership. The little army was followed by a band of 120 Negroes carrying torches for the purpose of setting fire to the plantations in English territory.

The line of demarcation between the French and the English territories at this point ran through the Ravine of Cayonne, whose slope was gentle on the French side, steep and rugged on the other. The two columns advanced side by side with a short interval between them and attacked their objectives almost simultaneously. Urbain Guillon, leading the shock troops of De Sales's division, met two English companies at the head of a defile through which his men were obliged to pass. When they came within range of the enemy's van, supported as it was by the main body, they received a terriffic volley that stopped them in their tracks. Shaken by the blast, the French returned it with interest, while Guillon charged the British formation on the flank and managed to break through the defile into the open ground beyond it. The English first gave way, then broke and ran, hotly pursued by the French, sword in hand, who made a great slaughter among the fugitives, with little loss to themselves.

Meanwhile Saint-Laurent attacked on the right, where he met with stiffer resistance. His line of approach lay through a much narrower and steeper ravine, where he was stopped by a heavy fire that drove back his van and threatened to throw his entire command into confusion. Dismounting, he put himself at the head of his troops, rallied them with his voice, and led them again through the defile. This was all that was needed. Once the French had come to grips with the enemy, they hurled themselves upon them and soon duplicated De Sales's feat of putting them to flight. But the English forces rallied. Joining a company held in reserve, they took their stand by a church situated a quarter of a league to the rear, where they awaited the French. De Sales now brought

[8]This is denied by Labat in *Nouveau voyage aux isles de l'Amérique*, II, 90.

together the two columns under his own command and advanced
on his foes. As in the previous encounter, the English stood up
fairly well under fire giving back volley for volley. But when the
French charged them with their swords, they broke ground and
were soon flying in great disorder toward the mountains north of
Cayonne. The French started off in hot pursuit, led by the gallant
Guillon and followed by the band of Negroes, who, encouraged by
the promise of plunder, freedom, and a white wife,[9] used their
torches with telling effect. They amused themselves by setting
fire to the crops of sugar cane, houses, barns, and personal property
of the wretched inhabitants. English accounts, written shortly
afterward, are loud in their complaints of the atrocities committed
by these blacks and also by the soldiery. A Mrs. Jordan, so runs
the story, "a gentlewoman of good reputation," was forced back
into her home with her small children by some soldiers, who
promptly set fire to the building and burned it to the ground
together with the occupants.[10] Thus killing and burning, the
French made their way across the English territory until they
came to the Hamilton River.

De Sales now perceived that he was approaching another body
of English troops and made his preparations accordingly. Crossing
the ravine formed by the Hamilton, he first called a halt to rest
his men, exhausted by the monring's battle and the march of the
previous night. Then, after a brief moment's respite, he gave the
order to fall in and marched to the settlement of Cinq Combles.
Here he found the enemy ready for him. The forces consisted of four
hundred fresh troops, which as yet had seen no action, and these
were concealed behind bushes lining the sides of a defile through
which the French must pass. It was here the French met with an
irreparable loss. Caught in the ambush prepared for them, they
had barely recovered from the first shock when one of the Governor's
most trusted officers, a valiant soldier named Roland le
Gendre de Saint-Amour, taking with him a small detachment of
cavalry, charged the enemy's flank, only to find himself cut off
from the main body of the French and surrounded by the English
forces. Seeing his predicament, De Sales called for volunteers and
rushed forward to his rescue. The English quickly closed in on

[9]*C.S.P., America & West Indies, 1661–68*, No. 1212.   [10]*Ibid.*, No. 1220.

him, and the Governor, finding himself outnumbered, made a brave attempt to break through the encircling lines. The odds were against him, and after a few minutes of desperate fighting he was brought down by two musket shots.

The death of Governor de Sales was a terrible blow to the French. For a few moments they stood irresolute; then Saint-Laurent, whom De Sales had appointed to succeed him in just such a contingency, sprang to the front and implored his men to join him in avenging the death of their commander. Heartened by the appearance of such a capable leader, the soldiers rallied and were presently driving the enemy back beyond the ravine. From then on it was a rout. The English fled headlong, and those who escaped the French fury took refuge in the thick underbrush on the hillsides or gained the fastnesses of the inland mountains.

The route to the northern frontier was now open, and the French, gathering up the remains of their beloved leader, proceeded on their way to join their confederates, who stood ready under the command of Vergers de Sanois to defend the northern section of the French possessions. Upon crossing the frontier, Saint-Laurent found Sanois with a force of about 250 men already under arms awaiting the orders of Governor de Sales, which, owing to the capture of the messenger sent from Basseterre, had never reached him. Here we shall leave the two little armies fraternizing together, while we turn our attention to the events that were taking place at the English headquarters in Old Road Town.

When the morning of the twenty-second dawned, the troops stationed at Palmetto Point near the Pentecost River learned how they had been tricked. Before they had recovered from their surprise they saw, far away in the direction of Capesterre, the fire and smoke of the burning plantations, and toward eight o'clock their worst fears were confirmed by the appearance of the first fugitives from Cayonne, who staggered into camp covered with wounds. When news of this was brought to Governor Watts, he at once sent word to a detachment he had placed near Pointe de Sable to be ready to attack. The men at Palmetto Point were ordered to stand fast and under no circumstances to move until ordered to do so. Sending for Colonel Morgan, the Governor, while still clad in gown and slippers, received him at his house.

He laid before the astonished colonel a fantastic plan by which he (Morgan) was to march with his buccaneers and a part of the regular army to Pointe de Sable, or wherever the fighting was likely to break out, and give battle. Meanwhile the Governor would enter Basseterre, where he would seize, during the French army's absence, the families, slaves, and property of the enemy, a proceeding which would soon bring De Sales to terms. The suggestion filled the doughty buccaneer with rage. He was eager to fight, but expected Watts to do his share also, and he had no intention of letting such a onesided scheme go through. He demanded that the Governor accompany him at once to the northern part of the island, where the enemy was awaiting them, and, placing his pistol at his superior's breast, called him a coward and threatened to shoot him on his threshold if he did not at once give the order to advance. Thus compelled by *force majeure* to yield, Governor Watts assembled his troops and started off for Pointe de Sable, accompanied by Morgan and his buccaneers. After Watt's death his handling of this situation drew forth a perfect avalanche of criticism, all the more bitter, perhaps, because he was no longer alive to defend himself. He was blamed by some for the loss of the colony and upheld by others.

Meanwhile Colonel Charles Reymes, who commanded some four hundred men in the northern section, had come to grips with Sanois's detachment. Early in the morning he had taken the French by surprise, for the messenger sent by De Sales to Sanois had never reached his destination. The engagement, however, was a brief one, for the French, despite their numerical inferiority were fully able to hold their own, and after a brief struggle Reymes and his men were sent scurrying over the mountains to rejoin Governor Watts, leaving eighty-four dead and a number of wounded. This was the pleasant news that greeted Saint-Laurent's men when they arrived at Sandy Bay after the battle of Cinq-Combles.

When they reached Sanois's camp, Saint-Laurent's men threw themselves down to rest. They had marched half-way around the island, fought two pitched battles, and were in no condition to join Lonvilliers at Pointe de Sable until they could get some food and sleep. It was while they were resting here that a messenger suddenly rode into camp with the startling news that Governor

Watts and his men had arrived at Pointe de Sable. The distance to Pointe de Sable was fully three leagues, too long a march for the leg-weary troops of Saint-Laurent, so he ordered Sanois to hasten at once to the support of Lonvilliers, knowing full well how small was the latter's force compared to the full might of the English army Watts was now leading against him. Taking with him a body of picked men, Sanois proceeded to carry out his instructions; but scarcely had he got under way, when a second messenger appeared with news of the defeat of the English and the death of their leader.

This battle proved to be the decisive action of the campaign. The day before, that is, on the twenty-first, Lonvilliers, who had evidently learned of De Sales's plan of campaign, had drawn two companies from Pointe de Sable and ordered them to the Capesterre sector. There they were to coöperate with De Sales's unit swinging over from Cayonne. Fortunately, during the night, before the maneuver could be carried out, one of Lonvilliers's captains, Bernard Lafond de l'Esperance, learned from a spy about Governor Watts's plan to attack Pointe de Sable. He at once sent word of this to Lonvilliers, who countermanded his previous orders and led the companies back to the Pointe himself. There he drew up his entire army, numbering some 350, in battle formation. Father Boulogne, sole ecclesiastic in that region, dressed himself in uniform, mounted a horse, and rode before the battalions, exhorting the men to fight for their homes and families, and assuring them that they were also fighting for the Faith, since the English were heretics.

Early in the forenoon of the twenty-second the English, fourteen hundred strong, appeared. Coming over the brow of a hill, they paused at the summit to survey the situation and saw before them the diminutive French army. As there was little in what they saw to inspire any misgivings, since they outnumbered the French four to one, Watts and Morgan set to work with the greatest confidence to win what they believed would be an easy victory. They began operations by sending some slaves to fire a field of sugar cane between the two armies, hoping that the French would break ranks, rush forward to save their property, and fall into an ambuscade they had prepared for them. But Lonvilliers, who saw through the scheme, had no intention of letting his men get caught in such a trap and ordered them to hold their ground. The English now took up their position around a large house, the property of one of their planters, which was separated from the French lines by another field of cane. This was an unfortunate move, for when the wind shifted to the north, blowing directly toward them, Lonvilliers set fire to the cane. He then sent out a score of volunteers under cover of the smoke, who crept forward undetected, set fire to the building, and returned to their lines without losing a man. The success of this action enraged the English leaders, who now decided on a direct attack, confident of crushing the French with their superior numbers. Morgan led the van with his buccaneers, who had been thoroughly primed with whiskey. Lonvilliers saw the maneuver and made ready for it by placing L'Esperance's company in ambuscade behind a hedge of brushwood. When Morgan's men advanced, they were greeted by a volley that broke their ranks. Rallying, they attacked again, and for half an hour the battle raged, until a handful of the English broke through the hedge and engaged two other companies, wounding M. de Lonvilliers fatally. Another small group of freebooters, having worked their way along the hedge, managed to reach the compound belonging to L'Esperance, which consisted of a large house surrounded by the usual outbuildings. Here the French had mounted a cannon on a farm wagon and loaded it to the muzzle with grapeshot. When the buccaneers rushed forward, the gunner touched a match to it and stopped them in their tracks. L'Esperance's men were now joined by the other companies, and they all opened such a fire on the freebooters that these desperados were only too glad to retreat, bearing with them their mortally wounded commander, Colonel Morgan. Of the 260 who had marched so gaily into battle, only seventeen left the field unhurt.

Astonished at the resistance offered by such a small body of men, Watts determined to take a hand in the business himself. He decided to surround the French in their compound with his greatly superior forces and to silence the gun if he could do nothing else. Leaving his main body to face the embattled enemy, he advanced with a few officers and some volunteers toward the house by a little side path, in order to reconnoiter the terrain prior to order-

Combat de la Pointe de Sable.

BATTLE OF POINTE DE SABLE

ing a general assault. L'Esperance, who now commanded the entire French army, saw him coming and detached a squad of marksmen to check him. When he came within range, they fired. The effect was disastrous. Watts and four of his officers fell, as did most of the volunteers. The entire English force now attacked, and the battle centered around L'Esperance's compound. The French ensconced behind the house sustained a terrific fire for more than two hours, which they continued to return until their powder was exhausted. Then, sword in hand, they rushed out from the protection of their rampart and charged with such fury that the English broke and fled to a fort situated in their territory about a quarter of a league away. But the disorder was so great that instead of rallying there—which they could easily have done—they paused only long enough to spike their guns, then fled ignominiously to Old Road Town, where they vented their rage against the Governor by pillaging his home.[11]

The campaign ended with the French in complete control of St. Christopher. The losses among the leaders on both sides had been heavy. Of the French, a son of M. de l'Esperance and three captains fell on the field at Pointe de Sable, while M. de Lonvilliers died a month later, and Governor de Sales, as we have said, was killed in Capesterre. The English lost Governor Watts, his wife's cousin Mr. Darcy, and Colonel Morgan, who was taken to Nevis, where he presently expired. When news of the victory reached France and the flags captured from the enemy were presented to the King, there was great rejoicing among the directors of the West India Company. To show their appreciation for the services the Chevalier de Saint-Laurent had rendered, they secured from His Majesty his appointment as successor to Charles de Sales and presented him with one thousand écus as a token of their gratitude.

On the English side the reactions were far different. Governor Watts, now that he was dead, became the object of much vilification for his alleged cowardice, and Colonel Reymes came in for his share of the general abuse. The Governor's wife, who fled to

[11]The best account of this campaign is in Du Tertre, *Histoire générale des Antilles*, IV, 21–40. Le Febvre de la Barre, *Relation de ce qui s'est passe dans les isles et terre-ferme de l'Amérique*, Vol. I, chap. viii, also gives valuable information. Some English letters in *C.S.P.*, *America & West Indies, 1661–68* (Nos. 1204, 1212, 1214, 1220) give a little data, but they are vague and contradictory. The number of men engaged vary in the different accounts.

Nevis, was cruelly received. The authorities there blamed the outcome of the whole unfortunate business on her husband and frankly
told her they hoped he was in hell by this time. From here she made
her way as soon as possible to Barbados, where she was given a
more sympathetic reception by Lord Willoughby. He tossed aside
the story of Watt's cowardice and in his letter to the King placed
the blame squarely on the shoulders of the planters, whose conduct
in battle, he found, contrasted unfavorably with that of Watts,
who at least had led a charge and lost his life in action. But Watts
was dead, and it was easy to blame him for the debacle, especially
after his quarrel with Morgan. The real marplot was, in all probability, Colonel Reymes, ably assisted by certain planters who were
anxious to save their property when they saw the French getting
the upper hand. While Watts was leading his troops at Pointe de
Sable, Reymes refused to assist. He stood on one side with four
hundred men, assuring his followers he would secure favorable
terms from the French when they had completed their conquest of
the island. The day after the battle Saint-Laurent was preparing
to follow up Lonvilliers's victory by marching on Old Road Town
when Reymes, in behalf of the English troops (which numbered
all told some sixteen hundred in addition to the thousand stationed
at Palmetto Point), appeared before him to discuss terms of surrender. A treaty was promptly drawn up and as promptly signed
by both parties on the twenty-third of April. By its terms the English agreed to surrender their forts, arms, and munitions; all
vagabonds were to be driven from the island, while persons who
elected to remain could do so on condition that they take an oath
of allegiance to the King of France and the West India Company.
Englishmen who did not choose to stay could sell their real estate
to the French and leave with their slaves and personal property.
Liberty of conscience was granted, provided Protestant worship
was conducted in private.

Saint-Laurent now led the army to Old Road Town, where he
took possession of Fort Charles with appropriate ceremonies.
Here he learned of the sudden exodus of a number of settlers, who
had left for Nevis as soon as they heard of the French victory. The
unfortunate Mrs. Watts had been hurried on board a vessel to
protect her against the infuriated buccaneers, who blamed their

defeat on her husband's pusillanimity. She escaped; but a ship which had taken on board four hundred slaves, whose owners had fled or been killed, was stopped and forced to disgorge its human cargo. Under the terms of capitulation these people could not leave the island, since the property of persons who had decided to leave St. Christopher could only be removed after the owners had made an orderly liquidation of their plantations. By virtue of the clause forbidding public Protestant worship, the Roman clergy felt themselves entitled to take over the four churches then standing in English territory. The one at Old Road Town was renamed St. Louis, Roi de France; another, near the Pointe, St. Jean-Baptiste; a third, at the Pentecost River, Ste. Therèse; a fourth, probably the one at Cayonne, St. François de Sales. [12]

Although he now held the entire island, Saint-Laurent still felt insecure. There were under him a large number of English people some of whom could, according to the treaty, remain there, permanently. Others who wished to leave could not be removed at once, since they retained the right to dispose of their holdings, and this could not be done over night. Their large numbers made them dangerous, for Lord Willoughby was sure to make some attempt to recover the island as soon as he learned of the disaster that had overtaken his fellow countrymen. In this predicament Saint-Laurent naturally turned to Martinique and Guadeloupe for assistance. Guadeloupe, being the nearest, was the first to receive his letters. When his messenger arrived at Basseterre he hurried ashore to awaken M. de Chambré with the joyful news of the French victory and the anxious call for help. Chambré hastened to Governor du Lion, and the two at once went into action. The Intendant made ready three large vessels anchored in the roadstead, while the Governor made the rounds of the various guardhouses, ordering on board whatever men he could find there. Fortunately De Sales had asked for reinforcements several days earlier, and preparations to send them were already under way—in fact one ship had just been dispatched. A little fleet soon weighed anchor and set sail, with Chambré on the flagship, arriving at St. Christopher within twenty-four hours. A few days later Clodoré arrived

[12]For capitulation and terms see Du Tertre, *Histoire générale des Antilles*, IV, 45–47. For treatment of Mrs. Watts see *C.S.P., America & West Indies, 1661–68*, No. 1206.

with a contingent from Martinique. Saint-Laurent received his colleagues with unbounded enthusiasm, then like a good Christian led them to church, where a *Te Deum* was sung to give thanks for the victory.

French colonists now began to assemble at St. Christopher from the outlying islands for the sake of protection. Some were already there, brought by De Sales in order to strengthen his forces. The governors felt it would be wise to bring them all in, since Lord Willoughby would be sure to launch an attack against the weaker outposts. Vessels were accordingly dispatched to St. Bartholomew and St. Martin, and they presently returned with a large number of settlers. The governor of Mariegalante, however, felt quite capable of taking care of himself. Du Bois of St. Croix not only equaled his self-confidence but also used the ship sent him to lead an expedition against the little English island of Anguilla, whence he presently returned with three prisoners and two pieces of ordnance to recompense him for his trouble.

Saint-Laurent and Chambré proceeded to put St. Christopher in a state to resist any possible attack. Within a week after Reymes's surrender they had gathered together all the available carpenters, masons, and blacksmiths, who in a short time erected seven or eight batteries in various positions, while the rank and file dug trenches wherever a landing might be made. The fortifications taken over from the English were also strengthened, and some sixty to eighty cannon no longer in use were unearthed and mounted in the batteries.

To minimize the danger of internal disorder in case of a siege, the officials ordered and carried out the eviction of the English colonists in accordance with the treaty. Five or six hundred vagabonds were quickly expelled, and this was followed by the exodus of eight hundred Irish people who were sent, for the most part, to St. Bartholomew. This done, the rest who elected to leave were deported as soon as they settled their affairs, for the French adhered scrupulously to the terms of the treaty, giving each settler ample opportunity to dispose of his real estate; some four hundred transfers were recorded. They were also permitted to remove their merchandise, furniture, jewelry, plate, and money, as well as some of their slaves, and to facilitate transportation three ships were sold to the wealthier planters and three others loaned for the use of those who could not afford to pay for them. Even the English, so Du Tertre tells, were satisfied with the treatment they received. The amount of property thus taken from St. Christopher was estimated at well over one million francs; the number of persons who left the island, at about eight thousand. The first to leave went to Nevis (to which, as a matter of self-protection, Saint-Laurent sent only noncombatants), to Montserrat, and to Antigua; when the inhabitants of these islands felt they had enough refugees, Jamaica, Virginia, Bermuda, and even Newfoundland each received a share.[13]

Before news of the French victory reached Barbados, Governor Willoughby had begun plans for sending an armada to protect St. Christopher. There happened to be in the harbor of Bridgetown a fleet of thirty merchantmen fully loaded and ready to sail for England. These he commandeered, and, placing six hundred soldiers on board, he dispatched them under command of his nephew, Henry Willoughby, with orders to proceed first to Antigua, where he could pick up additional men, and after touching at Montserrat and Nevis for the same purpose, to press on to assist St. Christopher. The younger Willoughby set sail, but at Antigua he learned of the surrender of Reymes, "which struck such terror into the merchantmen, that each one betook himself to his own course, and left him [Willoughby] and his soldiers on the island."[14]

Governor de Clodoré now conceived the idea of attacking Nevis. The time for such a move, he thought, was propitious, for on perusing letters seized on various captured vessels he had learned of Lord Willoughby's illness as well as of the fate of the recent Barbadian expedition, and he also knew that the British could hope for no immediate help from England, whose fleet was needed in home waters to keep the Dutch at bay. Anchored at Martinique in the Cul de Sac Royal was a large number of good-size vessels, just the sort for an effective naval expedition. They were five ships belonging to the company, totaling thirteen hundred tons and mounting 140 guns, and a like number of Dutch ships, aggregating one thousand tons with an armament of eighty guns. Clodoré

---

[13]A petition drawn up two years later by some disgruntled English colonists complains of their having been stripped of their possessions and otherwise abused. *C.S.P., America & West Indies, 1661–68*, No. 1629. [14]*Ibid.*, No. 1273.

therefore called a council of war on the thirtieth of May to discuss
the project. He offered to raise five or six hundred men to go under
his personal leadership, and in order to obtain the coöperation of
Guadeloupe he even offered to share the command with Governor
du Lion. Thus, with his help and with the addition of whatever
men he could find at St. Christopher, he could increase his army to
about sixteen hundred—a sufficient number, he thought, to insure
the success of the undertaking. After Nevis, the capture of all the
other English islands (save Barbados) would be a simple matter.
Every one was enthusiastic about the plan, and it had, no doubt,
a good chance of success; but Chambré and Du Lion pointed out
that they had been commanded to undertake nothing of this kind
without express orders from the company, and besides this news
had just been received that La Barre would presently sail from
France with a powerful fleet. Saint-Laurent also declined, on the
ground that he needed all his men to handle the English at St.
Christopher. The expedition, despite its obvious advantages,
advantages that even met with the approval of Colbert, was
therefore postponed.

When Lord Willoughby had sufficiently recovered from his illness to take an active part in the proceedings, he prepared to lead
an expedition in person for the recovery of St. Christopher. Help,
the help for which he had written the King when he heard of
Reymes's surrender, had just arrived. In his letter he had pointed
out the desperateness of the situation, for with St. Christopher
gone, Nevis might fall, then nothing could save Barbados; "and
if it come to run in a blood," he wrote, "God bless [he meant save]
Barbados that fair jewel in Your Majesty's crown." [15] But the help
which Charles sent, in the shape of two frigates of twenty-six and
forty guns, respectively, was not enough; so Willoughby, perforce
decided to stretch his authority and seize the merchant fleet which,
chanced to be riding at anchor in the harbor and press it into service. It consisted of fourteen large vessels, three barks, a fireship,
and a ketch. Placing aboard these ships a force of about one thous-
and men, he set out on the twenty-eighth of July. He arrived off
Martinique two days later.

When within two leagues of Fort St. Pierre, the ships broke out

[15] *Ibid.*, No. 1204.

the white flag of France. It was Willoughby's plan to capture as many boats as possible while passing Martinique and Guadeloupe, boats he could use as transports for the soldiers he expected to obtain at Nevis, Montserrat, and Antigua, and for this reason he wished to avoid a general engagement. The trick of sailing under false colors was all the more easily carried out since the French were daily expecting a fleet which, they had been told, M. de La Barre was to bring from France. For awhile he succeeded, then when he made off with a bark from Fond Capot, between Carbet and Case Pilote, the French suddenly realized what was afoot. The alarm was sounded calling the militia to arms. Governor de Clodoré ordered the warships lying in the roadstead to anchor "inshore," between the batteries of St. Robert and St. Sebastien, and to land six guns to arm the latter redoubt. He also sent a dispatch boat to carry the news to Du Lion, but it was driven ashore by the English.

The following day Willoughby set out for Guadeloupe, after making a half-hearted attempt to destroy the ships anchored under the batteries. A twenty-four hour sail brought him to his destination. For two days, that is, during the second and the third of August, the fleet glided to and fro along the coast, every now and then making a pretense of landing when they came to an unguarded spot. Du Lion kept pace with them, maneuvering a troop of cavalry in such a manner as to be always ready for a surprise attack. On the fourth, Willoughby held a council of war, at which it was decided to strike a blow at the little archipelago of the Saints just south of Guadeloupe. The main island was too well patrolled to permit him to land unmolested at this time, but he had noticed in passing the Saints two flutes of the West India Company anchored in the harbor, just the proper size for his purpose. He therefore detached from his fleet his vice-admiral, Captain William Hill in the "Coventry," the twenty-six-gun frigate he had just received from England, accompanied by a bark and a ketch, with orders to capture the two vessels. Running before a favorable wind, Hill entered the harbor, where he found the "Marianne" (Captain Baron) with the "Bergère" (Captain Reauville) riding peacefully at anchor. Action began at once. Attracted by the sound of firing, Governor du Lion and his cavalry hastened to Grand Anse in the southern part of

Guadeloupe, where they arrived in time to see across the channel separating them from the Saints the "Marianne" burning at her mooring, Captain Baron having fired her just before taking refuge with his crew in a small redoubt near the shore commanded by M. des Meuriers. Reauville chose to fight it out and was captured. Now the English troops landed to deliver the final blow. Baron, in the little fort, managed to withstand the assault; but when the supply of fresh water gave out, the two commanders led their men to a stronghold in the hills, entrenching themselves in a position from which the enemy found it impossible to dislodge them.[16]

During the day the sea had been calm, ruffled only by a light breeze just strong enough to allow the ships to make headway. Toward evening the weather changed, thanks, so Du Tertre tells us, to the concerted prayers of the inhabitants, who implored the Almighty for a storm to destroy the British fleet. The wind suddenly shifted to the north and blew with ever-increasing violence until midnight, when it stopped for a quarter of an hour; then it veered to east-southeast and came down on the devoted armada with hurricane force. Willoughby's ships were caught off the coast of Guadeloupe and in the roadstead of the Saints and piled up along the shore. Of the entire number, only two escaped: a flute, which made for Montserrat and arrived there with only the stump of her mizzenmast standing, and the fireship, which reached Antigua. Lord Willoughby perished in the catastrophe.

The devastation caused by the storm was enormous. The wind blew for twenty-four hours, uprooting trees, felling sugar cane, and wrecking houses, killing at the same time a few persons and a large number of animals. Du Lion himself nearly perished, for a house was overthrown shortly after he had left it, and he was forced to spend the night under the shelter of a wall in the drenching rain. Batteries and fortifications along the shore were dismantled by mountainous waves, which tore the guns from their emplacements and scattered the ammunition far and wide. The total damage was estimated at 1,500,000 francs. The effects of the storm were also felt in Martinique, but fortunately the damage there was light; the ships along the coast contrived to creep into the Cul de Sac Royal, where they were safe. Only one commander, stubborn

[16]Du Tertre, *Histoire générale des Antilles*, IV, 96–99.

Captain Bourdet, refused to take advantage of the shelter, and he lost his vessel, the "St. Sebastien,"[17] finest of the company's fleet. Later Captain Hill's badly damaged "Coventry" was salvaged by the French, renamed "Armes d'Angleterre," and given to Bourdet, who despite his bad judgment in this particular case was really an excellent seaman. Five days after the storm had passed the "St. Christophe" arrived in Martinique, bringing François de Loubière, who had been in France on a mission and now returned with 120 men and the welcome news that La Barre was on the way with a fleet.

In the aftermath of the storm Governor du Lion found himself in a peculiar position. The crews of the "Coventry" and her consort had managed to land on the same island of the Saints as the one where Captain Baron had sought refuge and were busy laying in such supplies as they could salvage from the wrecked ships, while fortifying themselves against possible attacks by the French. To Governor du Lion this made a dangerous situation. Should the English be able to hold the Saints, they might form the nucleus of a stronghold that would have French commerce between Martinique and Guadeloupe at its mercy, as well as the coastal trade between the Capesterre and Basseterre sections of the latter island. It was therefore necessary to dislodge the English from their position at all costs. While discussing with his subordinates the ways and means for accomplishing this end, two sailors painfully rowed across the channel, bearing a letter from Captain Baron in which he begged the Governor to help him bring his men to Guadeloupe, for the English, who far outnumbered his forces, had given him two days to surrender. Du Lion rushed a small supply of ammunition and promised immediate assistance. To relieve the Saints was a difficult task, for the hurricane had played havoc with the shipping. In order to obtain every craft available, Du Lion sent out a general call. He went in person from Three Rivers near Grande Anse over roads rendered nearly impassable by the recent storm to Capesterre, where he managed to pick up sixty men and three boats which he sent at once to reinforce Des Meuriers. Here he received an offer of assistance from Téméricourt, governor of nearby

[17]There were two ships named "St. Sebastien." The second, as we shall see, arrived in the West Indies later.

Mariegalante, which he accepted with thanks. Returning to Three Rivers, rendezvous for his proposed expedition, he found a large number of men already assembled there, with seven boats gathered at random from various parts of the island, to carry them to the Saints.

Leading the expedition in person, Du Lion left Three Rivers in a canoe on the fourteenth of August, followed by the motley collection of boats bearing his army. He made the crossing in two hours and landed in a little harbor, where he was met by the detachment from Mariegalante, consisting of fifty men and two cannon. The Governor had under him some four hundred men, made up of the various groups sent over: Téméricourt's detachment, those he had sent ahead of him and those he had just brought. With this respectable force he proceeded to pitch camp at a spot not far from where the enemy was entrenched. The English had taken advantage of the last few days to fortify themselves behind a double palisade of stakes, erected in the form of a rectangle, thirty feet wide and one hundred feet long, the rear backed up against a steep cliff. At ten o'clock that night Du Lion began his attack. The moon was at its full, making the fort a fair target for the little French battery. Apparently the English made little resistance. Save for a half-hearted sortie, quickly repulsed by the French, they did nothing spectacular, but returned the fire for a few hours and then quietly abandoned the redoubt and took refuge in a nearby fortified position, which Du Tertre calls the second fort. Here they put up a far more stubborn resistance. When Du Lion attacked the following evening, they were ready for him and defended themselves pike in hand. The battle lasted all night. At daybreak the Governor drew off his troops for a breathing spell and also to survey the extent of the damage he had inflicted. Casualties proved light, considering the heavy firing; the English suffered but thirty-three killed and eighty wounded, while the French losses were much less. Du Lion was therefore somewhat surprised, when he again opened fire, to see the foe run up a flag of truce and to have them ask for terms of surrender. The terms requested by the English were modest enough; all they asked was permission to retire from the island with their property; but Du Lion realized that he had them trapped, since the fleet had been de-

stroyed and there was no way to escape, and he would agree only
to unconditional surrender. In the end Du Lion's treatment of his
conquered foe was not harsh, for, though he permitted his soldiers
to loot the camp as a reward for their services, he took care to
prevent any unnecessary disorders during the proceedings. This
done, he returned with his captives to Guadeloupe, where he was
received as one who had conquered a mighty army.[18]

During the fortnight Hill had been master of the Saints he had
sent a messenger to Henry Willoughby (the Governor's nephew)
at Antigua requesting help. The younger Willoughby had already
begun preparations to send relief to the Saints by collecting all
manner of stray barks, ketches, and boats from Montserrat, Nevis,
and Antigua, together with a suitable number of soldiers, for he
realized that the death of his uncle had put him in supreme command, at least for the time being. It so happened, however, that
before Governor du Lion made his attack on the Saints he had
requested from Clodoré two men-of-war to blockade these islands,
as there were no ships left at Guadeloupe capable of doing such
work. The Governor of Martinique did not at this time know of
the complete destruction of the British fleet, and wishing to do a
thorough job, he sent four vessels completely equipped, preceded
by two barks as advance guard. Nearly four hundred men were
placed on board them, under the command of M. de Loubière.
The flotilla left Martinique in the evening and arrived off the
Saints the following morning, just when Du Lion was returning to
Guadeloupe with his prisoners. Mistaking him at first for an
enemy, Loubière's ships gave chase, but they soon realized their
mistake and falling in line behind him accompanied the returning
hero to Basseterre in time to witness his triumph.

When Loubière's armada arrived off Basseterre, Henry Willoughby's fleet of eight sail was seen coming from Montserrat. It
advanced slowly, bound for the Saints, and the French stood ready
to receive it. When it was off Basseterre, the four ships of Loubière weighed and attacked. Though the English had the greater
number of vessels, they were hopelessly outclassed; their largest
ship mounted only twelve guns, while the smallest French vessel
had fourteen. Seeing the hopelessness of the situation, Willoughby

[18]*Ibid.*, IV, 102–10.

abandoned his fleet, jumped into a fast sailing bark, and made off for Nevis. A few volleys settled the battle. The three largest English ships and two hundred men were captured, while the smaller ones, being speedy sailers, made good their escape. The prisoners were taken ashore and, together with those captured at the Saints, were put to work on the various plantations, while Captain Hill and his officers were entertained as guests at the Governor's residence.

❧ III ❧

THE BRITISH GET THE DECISION

THE READER will recall the good ship "Oranger" which sailed from Basseterre with the wives and children of certain wealthy planters on the eve of the battle of Cayonne. The "Oranger" in due course of time arrived at La Rochelle, bringing a graphic account of what had happened at St. Christopher, and thus the directors of the West India Company heard for the first time that hostilities between the two colonies on this island had actually begun.

For some time past the directors had known, and so had the government, of the trouble brewing in the islands, and had taken steps to deal with it. When M. de Loubière was in France he had carefully explained to them the economic difficulties in the French Caribbees, difficulties which had caused outbreaks in Martinique and reduced the company's profits to a minimum. They were busy devising ways and means of coping with this problem when the King's declaration of war against England on January 26, 1666, brought them face to face with the possibility of losing their possessions. To meet this situation they immediately summoned to a conference Le Febvre de la Barre, who at this moment happened to be in Holland. On his arrival they informed him of the signing of the treaty at St. Christopher on the twentieth of January, and said that, confident of Lord Willoughby's prompt ratification of the document, they had felt it sufficient to send out but two or three ships to patrol the islands against occasional freebooters. La Barre, however, knew better. He understood Willoughby thoroughly, and took no stock in the negotiations Du Blanc was then carrying on in Barbados. On the contrary, he urged the immediate dispatch of enough reinforcements to put the French islands in a condition to resist attack. Impressed by his forceful opinions, the directors ordered eight ships, fully equipped with guns, munitions, and supplies, to transport the much-needed military help. While they were thus engaged, they received word from Clodoré and Chambré telling of the collapse of Du Blanc's efforts. Realizing now the inevitability of war, they turned to the King for assistance. Louis replied at once. He sent commissions to four officers at La Rochelle authorizing them each to raise a company of men in the vicinity, and he placed the entire detachment under the command of the Chevalier de Saint-Léon, a captain in his own regiment of Navarre. Le Febvre de la Barre was put in command of the fleet. As soon as the recruits were signed up, Saint-Léon embarked them on the ships supplied by the company. He himself established his quarters on the "St. Christophe," while La Barre hoisted his flag on the "St. George"—both vessels of twenty-six guns each. These two ships, accompanied by six others, set sail from La Rochelle on the twenty-sixth of May. As they were leaving the harbor, the "Oranger" sailed in.

If the directors had had any doubts as to the possibility of hostilities breaking out in the West Indies, they were set at rest by the news which the passengers of the "Oranger" brought them. Too late they saw the disastrous effects of their procrastination. Yet, perhaps, it was not too late. By redoubling their efforts they might be able to get enough men across the ocean in time to save their possessions from Lord Willoughby. The fleet had sailed; but by chance the "St. George" was wrecked on leaving the harbor, and La Barre was obliged to put back into port bringing his entire squadron with him. While this unfortunate accident delayed the sailing of the troops it at any rate gave the directors time to make new arrangements. La Barre had been instructed to stop at Cayenne, but now this order was replaced by instructions telling him to proceed directly to the Caribbees. Thus the slight delay caused by the wreck of the "St. George" would, it was hoped, be more than compensated for by the elimination of the side trip to Cayenne. A messenger was at once sent to the King asking for additional assistance and requesting further orders, while a new ship, the "Florissant," was chartered for the commander in place of the

"St. George." On the eighth of June La Barre again gave the order to weigh anchor, and the fleet consisting of "Florissant," "St. Christophe," "Mercier," "Hirondelle," "Lion d'Or," "Dorothée," "Pucelle," and two small vessels set out from La Rochelle.[1]

Scarcely had the little armada got under way, when, as on the previous occasion, an accident occurred. This time the "St. Christophe," bearing M. de Saint-Léon, collided with one of her fellows and limped back into port, where she was at once laid up for repairs. La Barre, with the rest of the fleet, continued on his way.

When the courier sent by the directors at La Rochelle returned from Fontainebleau, he brought the encouraging news of the government's purpose to do something on a more impressive scale. The King, realizing the gravity of the situation from the reports brought him by the passengers of the "Oranger," was determined to send a sufficient force to protect the French possessions against all eventualities. A fleet of five ships, "St. Sebastian," "Aigle d'Or," "Aurore," "Cher Ami," and "Eglise," was brought together. Eight companies of soldiers, four from the regiment of Navarre and four from the regiment of Normandy, comprising about four hundred effectives, were put aboard the vessels under the command of Saint-Léon. Among the officers was Jean Blondel of the engineering corps, who was charged with the construction of whatever fortifications he might deem necessary. He did draw up plans for all the islands, but most of them, due to a lack of funds, remained on paper. The men were well provided for, the cost of the supplies and equipment amounting to more than fifty thousand francs. The fleet sailed on the twenty-seventh of July and arrived at Martinique two months later. Here Saint-Léon left the fleet and proceeded to St. Christopher.

When La Barre left La Rochelle he evidently had no intention of obeying the company's instructions to sail directly to the Caribbees, for, as it turned out, he was more interested in the colony at Cayenne than in fighting the company's battles in the West Indies. It was perhaps for this reason that he sailed before the return of the courier sent to ascertain the King's wishes, for though he might disobey the directors at La Rochelle, he did not care to take such liberties with His Majesty's orders should the head of the state

[1]Du Tertre mentions another ship, the "Cher. Ami," but she appears to have sailed later.

decide to back the company. To justify his conduct, so at variance with the assurances he had given the directors, he gave the specious excuse that the hurricane season was approaching, which would make it dangerous for him to take his fleet into Caribbean waters. He sailed first to the Madeiras, where he was advised by the French consul that an English fleet of a dozen sail had stopped there *en route* for the West Indies and had recently departed, having waited twelve days in the hope of meeting his squadron. Despite this threat to French security in the Caribbees, he decided to carry out his plan of going to Cayenne. He took on additional provisions and some cattle at Madeira, then set forth, hoping to carry these supplies to his colony. Here his good fortune seems to have deserted him, for he met with contrary winds that held him back until, buffeted by heavy seas, he ran out of fresh water and was obliged to make the most of what he could get from passing showers. At last, realizing he could never reach Guiana, he steered for Martinique, leaving his fleet to make its way as best it could to Cayenne. On the first day of October the "Florissant" anchored off St. Pierre.

When La Barre landed at Martinique he brought with him credentials giving him extensive powers. He had a commission from the directors making him superintendent over the commerce and revenues of the company and giving him authority to supervise the police and the administration of justice in order to guarantee the planters a modicum of fair treatment. The powers he received from the King, however, were somewhat limited. His Majesty, for some reason which Du Tertre declines to explain, did not fully trust M. de la Barre and confined his authority to naval affairs. The Lieutenant-General (he was then lieutenant-general of Guiana only) was to have supreme command of the vessels composing the fleets in West Indian waters. This authority also covered the troops on board the ships; but when the troops landed, they were to come under the jurisdiction of the various governors in whose districts they might be stationed. Even in case of an attack on English possessions, La Barre was to be deprived of his authority over them, once they left the ships. All landing parties were to be commanded by M. de Saint-Léon. To prevent any misunderstanding about this, the King sent letters to the various ship's captains and the governors explaining the powers he had given La Barre.[2]

No sooner had La Barre stepped ashore at Martinique, than he found himself involved in a controversy with the planters over the same economic problems that had vexed the authorities since the West India Company had taken over the islands. A petition was presented him by the leading colonists embodying their grievances and suggesting remedies. In the main it was a question of free trade, free in the sense of entire liberty to deal with merchants of other nations instead of being limited to transactions with the company. That the company had failed to supply the needs of its people was openly admitted by the local officials themselves, and La Barre, Clodoré, and Chambré felt the time had come to make concessions. The war, if nothing else, offered an excuse for a change in policy. Accordingly they signed an edict on the eighteenth of October granting the inhabitants of Martinique—this did not apply to the other islands—permission to trade freely with independent French merchants and with merchants of countries allied to France, with the understanding that they pay the company a tax of 2½ percent on both incoming and outgoing merchandise, while foreign traders were obliged to pay double this amount. Before the directors received notice of this arrangement, it so happened that they too had decided to admit the Dutch to their colonial trade, but they had fixed the tax rate on such transactions at 5 percent for Frenchmen and 10 percent for foreigners. When news of this decision reached the island, Clodoré and his colleagues were obliged to abide by it, despite their previous agreement with the inhabitants. The planters grumbled, but having gained their main point, they placed no further obstacles in the way of details.

Domestic matters having thus been settled, our gentlemen turned their attention to the war, which, to tell the truth, had been uppermost in their minds all the time. Clodoré, now that he had La Barre's ships and Saint-Léon's troops to back him up, eagerly revived his plan for the capture of Nevis. La Barre listened with hearty approval; in fact the Lieutenant-General had been expecting action from the start, for he had summoned Chambré from St.

---

[2]Du Tertre, *Histoire générale des Antilles*, IV, 126–32.

Christopher with all the ships he could collect. Objections to the plan were expected from St. Christopher, for Saint-Laurent had already expressed a dissenting opinion, and Saint-Léon, who was then with him, had taken the stand that he had been ordered to the West Indies to protect St. Christopher, not to engage in any schemes of conquest. La Barre, as we have pointed out, had no power to compel obedience once the troops were ashore; he could only get his way by persuasion. As they were discussing the situation, there was ushered into their presence a young surgeon named Urbain Frecine de Grandmaison, a former valet of M. de la Barre, and his companion, a man called Baston, who had just escaped from Antigua. These two men belonged to a group of Frenchmen who before the war had migrated to this island, where they settled down to work for the English planters. Here they had lived peacefully enough until the arrival of Henry Willoughby, who, enraged by the loss of St. Christopher, attempted to bully the French settlers into taking an oath of allegiance to the English king. Grandmaison and Baston, being young men of spirit, declined to conform. They managed to secure a boat and after many vicissitudes reached the northern section of St. Christopher, where they were kindly received by M. de Sanois. After listening to their story Sanois sent them to Saint-Laurent, who in turn dispatched them to Martinique. Grandmaison told an interesting tale. During his sojourn in Antigua he had made a careful survey of the place, noting all the weak spots of its system of defense, the number of available fighting men stationed there, the ships in its harbors, its fortifications, and the best places for making a landing. The information brought by him was a gift from the gods to Clodoré and Chambré. The latter had already suggested going to St. Christopher to interview Saint-Laurent, whom he believed amenable to reason, and he likewise thought Saint-Léon and his fellow-officers could be brought around. So he now suggested that the governor of St. Christopher would be more impressed if they should make a successful landing on some island and carry off a few prisoners. If they could only show up the vulnerability of the English islands, surely Saint-Laurent could not resist the temptation of attacking Nevis, stronghold of the British, which he feared because of its proximity to St. Christopher. Antigua seemed made to order for this scheme. Chambré therefore invited Clodoré and La Barre to join him in the enterprise; they would stop on the way at Guadeloupe to secure the coöperation of Du Lion. The invitation was accepted with alacrity, and on the twenty-fifth the triumvirate, taking with them every available ship in the roadstead, set sail for Guadeloupe. Governor du Lion was impressed with the idea. Despite his dislike for Clodoré, a dislike due to some dispute over the distribution of booty recently captured from the English at the Saints, he allowed himself to be convinced. On the second of November a fleet of eight well-armed vessels, led by La Barre's flagship, "Florissant," set out from Basseterre carrying the four leaders of the expedition.[3] There were on board three companies of infantry, one of which was commanded by the Sieur d'Orvilliers, La Barre's son-in-law. A frigate, "Armes d'Angleterre," and a smaller craft were left behind to convey M. de Téméricourt, as soon as he arrived, to the council to be held presently at St. Christopher.

Two days later the fleet approached Antigua, beating against a head wind. The ships flew the English flag at their mastheads to prevent being recognized as enemy vessels, and thus disguised they entered Five Islands Harbor. The "St. Christophe" and the "Vierge," in the van, were the first to exchange shots with two batteries set up on the shore. These redoubts were wretched affairs of six and eight guns each, mounted on platforms without protection of any sort. At the same time the flagship and the "Justice" engaged the fort, driving out its defenders at the first volley. Everything was now ready for a landing. The boats were swung out, the troops leaped into them, and soon a party of two hundred men led by Orvilliers landed on the beach. It took but a moment to destroy the few houses in the neighborhood, and then the French were masters of the situation.

La Barre now came ashore. His purpose was to induce Orvilliers to return on board with his troops, since he feared this small detachment might get into trouble; but he succumbed to the suggestion that they capture the governor's residence, a well-built

[3]The other ships were: "Le Lys Couronne," "Justice," "St. Sebastien," "Vierge," "Bergère," "Africaine," and "St. Christophe," Saint-Léon's former flagship recently repaired and sent to Martinique.

stone house situated about half a league inland. Taking with him his two hundred men, Orvilliers started during the night, led by Baston, who had accompanied the expedition in the capacity of guide; they reached their destination at dawn. The house was located on a little hill, and Orvilliers, placing his men in battle formation, rushed up the incline to attack it. The English soldiers on guard fired on the advancing column, but the marksmanship was poor, the casualties negligible, and the French quickly cleared the hill of its defenders. The commander, Colonel Robert Carden,[4] retreated into the house with thirty officers, where he surrendered after making a show of resistance. The building was quickly pillaged and burned, while Carden and his staff were carried off as prisoners.

Inspired by this victory, the French decided to continue their hostilities. Du Lion, wishing to try his hand, suggested that he and Clodoré should lead the next expedition. To this scheme La Barre willingly agreed, and the following day the little army was assembled on the shore ready for action. As the two governors had no troops of their own, Orvilliers was persuaded to humor them by surrendering his command temporarily. Lots were drawn as to who should command the right wing, and luck favored the Governor of Guadeloupe. On the morning of the sixth the detachments got under way, and upon reaching the site of Colonel Carden's house they perceived another of like construction situated some distance away. The French advanced upon it in two parallel columns, led by their guide, Baston, who was to play a distinguished part in the action. Each division, fearful of not being the first on the scene of action, eyed the other jealously; but Du Lion's men gradually drew ahead, and when they reached the level ground in front of the building they received the full blast of the volley fired by the four hundred defenders from behind the surrounding palisade. The effect was devastating. Du Lion fell, badly wounded, while his men fled to the protective shelter of a near-by wood, despite Orvilliers's gallant efforts to rally them. Clodoré rushed up with his troops and attempted to stem the tide. He

---

[4] Several authorities, including Du Tertre, apparently regard Carden as the governor of Antigua. A list of governors of the West Indies published in 1663, however, specifically mentions John Bunckley as governor. *Acts of the Privy Council, Colonial*, I, 365.

rallied those capable of being rallied, infused into them something of his own spirit, led them back to the palisade, and finally broke through it, driving the enemy before him with the able assistance of Orvilliers. Once within the stockade, the two men separated— Clodoré to finish the enemy, while Orvilliers broke into the house. Here he found the commander, Colonel Charles Ghest, seated in an armchair, pistol in hand, surrounded by his officers. Ghest asked for quarter and was answered by a pistol shot. The French then fired, killing all the staff and leaving the colonel himself badly wounded.

When Orvilliers informed Clodoré of this cowardly slaughter, the generous governor showed his indignation by rushing to the house and rescuing some sixty soldiers who had barricaded themselves in various rooms, resolved to sell their lives as dearly as possible. This done, he hastened to restore order among the troops, who, flushed with victory, had started to destroy the place. He knocked in several whiskey barrels, spilling their precious contents on the ground, then turned his attention to the removal of the wounded, both French and English, to a place of safety. To the suggestion, made by a practical soul, that Colonel Ghest might as well be finished off, since he was fatally wounded, he replied by ordering the Colonel to be carried on board a ship and given all possible care. Casualties had been rather heavy; the number of French wounded ran between fifty and sixty, including some officers who had played a prominent part in the engagement. Before leaving the scene of battle the invaders destroyed all houses in the vicinity, many of which were well-built affairs, made of stone with tile roofs, while the same treatment was also meted out to the mills and storehouses in order to teach the enemy, so it was said, not to hold out in the future against the French, but to surrender more readily.

The next day La Barre held a council of war and sent an ultimatum to the English to surrender within twenty-four hours under penalty of the total destruction of their property. The British asked for a day to consider the matter, and La Barre, after some hesitation, finally agreed to meet them in St. John's Harbor. Thither Clodoré and Chambré repaired at the appointed time, with a guard of eighty men escorted by the "Armes d'Angleterre."

When the plenipotentiaries met, they spent an entire day going over the terms of capitulation without reaching an agreement; on the following day, after further discussion, a decision was finally reached, and the treaty was signed on board the "Armes" by the two officers, acting as representatives of La Barre, and by Governor John Bunckley for the British. The treaty was an elaborate document of twenty-one articles, and we can pause only long enough to outline its salient points. Like the treaty made a few months earlier at St. Christopher, which it resembles in many respects, the present document provided for the continued residence in the island of any English people who chose to remain, on condition that they swear allegiance to the King of France and recognize the suzerainty of the West India Company. In return for this they would be allowed to keep their property and could also retain half the island of Barbuda (a dependency of Antigua), the other half being confiscated by the French. Somewhat greater religious liberty was granted them than to the inhabitants of conquered St. Christopher, for they were permitted to maintain Protestant churches in certain parts of the island. Those who wished to leave would be allowed to do so, and they might go anywhere except to Nevis (the French dreaded any increase in the armed forces so near St. Christopher) and might carry with them the proceeds of the sale of their property, six months being allowed for the consummation of such transactions. An indemnity of two hundred thousand pounds of sugar was levied on the inhabitants, Governor Bunckley being held as hostage for its payment. All forts, batteries, fortified houses, and munitions were to be surrendered within two days. Colonel Carden was liberated, with the understanding that he would take the oath of allegiance to France. The treaty signed, Bunckley and Carden went ashore to warn the colonists that if they did not comply with the terms of capitulation within ten days, they could expect no quarter. This done, the fleet set sail for St. Christopher.[5]

On the fifteenth La Barre and his colleagues anchored off Basseterre. Governor de Saint-Laurent at once came aboard the flagship with Saint-Léon to pay his respects. To do honor to such distinguished guests, he invited them to take up their residence on

[5]Du Tertre, *Histoire générales des Antilles*, IV, 141–64; Le Febvre de la Barre, *Relation de ce qui s'est passé dans les isles et terre-ferme de l'Amérique*, I, 282–321.

shore, and as they were rowed to the landing every gun in the harbor boomed a welcoming salute. The Governor gave an elaborate banquet, to which the leading persons of the island were invited, and after the customary wining and dining he led his guests to the quarters reserved for them in the mansion erected years before by Governor de Poincy in the hills back of Basseterre. Then La Barre learned of the recent taking of Tobago from the English by Governor Vincent, of Granada, and of a Franco-Dutch expedition which had just left St. Christopher for the conquest of St. Eustatius, which was then in the hands of Morgan's buccaneers. To aid this latter undertaking the Lieutenant-General sent Orvilliers and a detachment of men to help add this island to the colonies the French were rapidly acquiring; this was quickly accomplished.

The following day there was held the council for which all the officials had come to St. Christopher. Since Du Lion's wounds kept him confined to his cabin, the meeting took place on board his ship. La Barre, Saint-Léon, Clodoré, Chambré, Saint-Laurent, and Téméricourt were all present, and they seated themselves according to their rank. La Barre, as chief representative of the King, opened the discussion. He came out flatly for an immediate attack on Nevis, a feat he believed could be easily performed if his reception at Antigua was to be taken as a sample of English valor. The French now had enough ships and enough men; it was indeed the golden opportunity. Perhaps if they waited too long a fleet would come from England and the opportunity would be lost. From Martinique he could get six hundred men, from Guadeloupe, five hundred, while Mariegalante could furnish two hundred; then there were seven hundred of the King's troops and one hundred of the company's militia, all of which would bring the total to about 2,100 men. To transport them he could count on some thirty vessels of assorted sizes and a like number of boats. Du Lion opposed the scheme. For one thing, he thought Nevis was too well fortified; then, the French might be defeated, and if they were their hold on the other islands would be seriously weakened. As an alternative to La Barre's proposition, he thought it would be better first to return to Antigua and enforce the treaty and then to proceed to capture little Montserrat. After this they could attack Nevis, for by that time they would probably have received reinforcements from France. Saint-Léon upheld this view, reiterating his opinion that his troops had been sent over solely to preserve the conquest of St. Christopher. Clodoré sided with La Barre, and so did Chambré, while Saint-Laurent and Téméricourt saw eye to eye with Du Lion. Thus they were at loggerheads, four to three against the attack on Nevis. Tempers rose, and only the tactfulness and authority of La Barre prevented the conference from degenerating into a brawl. When quiet was finally restored, the question of the divided command, that peculiar arrangement by which La Barre controlled the troops only when they were on shipboard, was brought up for discussion. The governors decided to yield their authority over the soldiers to La Barre, who was thus entrusted with the supreme command on land as well as at sea, Saint-Léon commanding the troops of the King and each governor the militia of his own island, all under the Lieutenant-Governor as generalissimo of the entire naval and military forces.

Miffed by his defeat in the council, La Barre decided to wash his hands of the Antigua business. He left at once for Martinique, after turning the expedition over to Clodoré, who had warmly supported him in his wish to attack Nevis. On arriving at Martinique he took up the work of strengthening the French forces in the islands. More farsighted than the other officials in the Caribbees, and than those at home for that matter, he foresaw the coming storm and urged the company to send over immediately a plentiful supply of munitions, masts, spars, lumber, and all things necessary for keeping the ships well armed and in good repair. He also requested reinforcements to the number of five hundred men. When all this personnel and material arrived he would be in a position to resist any fleet the King of England might care to send over, and if no fleet came he would be strong enough to drive the English from all the Caribbees, including Barbados.

Acting according to a plan for reducing Antigua, as outlined by La Barre, Clodoré proceeded to Guadeloupe to pick up a little army recruited from the several colonies, which was to gather there by order of the Lieutenant-General. On reaching Basseterre he was astounded to learn from Loubière that a great fleet of forty-eight ships (doubtless an exaggeration), including six huge frigates of from fifty to sixty guns each, had assembled at Barbados for the recapture of St. Christopher. This report, when it spread throughout the archipelago, was naturally a source of grave anxiety to the governors. They refused to leave their islands unprotected and sent to the rendezvous at Guadeloupe only part of the troops requested by La Barre. Thus Clodoré was forced to content himself with about half as many men as he had been led to expect. His own contingent was there in full, having been brought thither by Loubière, and of these he retained 350, sending back the rest for the defense of Martinique. Du Lion would part with only 250, whom he placed under the command of Pierre Hencelin, while Téméricourt would not contribute a single man. Clodoré placed his troops—all local militia, not royal troops—on eleven ships and set sail for Antigua, arriving there the last day of November. Saint-Léon, who was to have led a contingent from St. Christopher, failed to come when he heard the news about the English fleet, but he sent his quota to join the expedition.

When Clodoré cast anchor in St. John's Harbor, he found a situation not at all to his liking. Reinforcements from Barbados had raised the number of effectives to nine hundred men, and Henry Willoughby, at Nevis, had sent Colonel Daniel Fitch, with the powers of acting governor, to command them. Clodoré was somewhat nonplussed. He had orders from La Barre to crush the inhabitants if they did not at once submit to the terms of capitulation; but this order was given him when he expected to have back of him twice the number of men he now commanded. In despair he consulted his two lieutenants, Pierre Hencelin and Jean Blondel, the engineer, and following their advice he decided to attack rather than to beat a shameful retreat. Colonel Carden came on board to inform him that all the English had taken an oath of allegiance to Colonel Fitch, who had gathered his army in the northern part of the island, in the district known as Pope's Head, where they were prepared to put up a resistance. Before beginning hostilities, Clodoré summoned them to surrender; but they refused even when Governor Bunckley, who was held as a hostage on the French commander's ship, ordered them to do so; they now, so they said, owed allegiance only to Colonel Fitch, representative of Henry Willoughby. Clodoré saw he must act quickly. Fear of the English fleet at Barbados made it necessary for him to subdue

Antigua with all possible haste in order to get his men back to Guadeloupe and Martinique in time to meet the coming danger. Without a moment's delay he landed his troops and marched on the enemy. Ignoring their last-minute offer of surrender, he charged them and put the entire band to rout without the loss of a man. When Fitch heard the French were marching on him, he hurriedly boarded his ship and set sail for Nevis, with scarcely a word of farewell to his men.

After the English commander's hasty departure, Clodoré called the inhabitants together, rebuked them for their bad faith, and offered terms which on the surface appeared fairly easy. Those who would swear allegiance to France would be pardoned and their goods would be restored; those who refused would have their property confiscated. In addition to this, an indemnity was levied on the colonists to be paid by the surrender of eight hundred slaves. While Clodoré had no intention of being too harsh, some of his subordinates took advantage of the situation to get what plunder they could. In the end the island was fairly well gutted. The planters had but five hundred slaves in all, and these were taken, while the soldiers were held as prisoners of war. All arms were removed, as well as the cattle and the sugar-making machinery belonging to persons whose property was adjudged confiscated. Several officers charged with the business of removing the property allowed their men to pillage. The looters even invaded the premises of Colonel Carden, which had been specifically exempted from seizure by Clodoré.

While La Barre, as we have said, did not himself take part in the expedition, he nevertheless sent troops as his contribution. When they arrived—they came too late to take part in the action, such as it was—their officers, seeing that the job had already been done, clamored for an attack on Montserrat. Clodoré, of course, had no intention of leading such an enterprise on his own responsibility, and he wisely put the suggestion aside until he could consult the Lieutenant-General. He set sail, therefore, for Martinique, while the others went to St. Christopher. On reaching St. Pierre he found his superior awaiting him. As soon as the two men had disposed of the usual amenities a violent quarrel broke out. La Barre, jealous, no doubt, of the other's success, took him to task for the treaty he had signed at Antigua promising protection to the English inhabitants under certain specified conditions. This arrangement, he said, showed an assumption of authority on the part of Clodoré that was unwarranted, so much so that it had already caused a feeling of resentment among the other officials, notably Du Lion, who now wanted to show his independence of the treaty by plundering the island himself. La Barre then hinted that he, as the King's lieutenant-general, was in supreme command, an assertion vigorously denied by Clodoré, who pointed out, with considerable justice, that La Barre's authority did not extend to the Caribbee Islands. An altercation took place which nearly led to blows, the quarrel raging for several days, until it was patched up by the good offices of the Jesuit Fathers. A formal reconciliation then took place, and the two men, their differences settled, put their heads together to lay out a plan of action for the good of the service. As the result of their deliberations cruisers were dispatched to watch the fleet at Barbados, arrangements were made for an attack on Montserrat, and the scheme for capturing Nevis was revived.

The expedition against Montserrat appealed particularly to La Barre, for before leaving St. Christopher he had discussed the project with the officers of the royal troops, who resented having been excluded from the Antigua affair and suggested that they alone take part in the new venture, without any assistance from the governors and their militia. The Lieutenant-Governor therefore returned to St. Christopher, where the bulk of the army was gathered. Sailing by Montserrat he gave orders to hug the shore closely, and he stood for several hours on the quarterdeck scanning the defenses along the coastline. On reaching Basseterre he promptly called Saint-Léon and Saint-Laurent into a conference at which he outlined his scheme. It met with an enthusiastic reception, and for ten days the colonists worked like beavers making the necessary preparations. According to the plan agreed upon by those in charge of the enterprise, La Barre was to be in supreme command both on land and at sea, while Saint-Léon was to have command under him of all the troops. A fleet of twenty-five good-size ships and a sprinkling of lesser craft were collected to transport the royal forces and five hundred men from the local militia, for it was realized that the royal troops alone were not enough. When all was ready, they weighed anchor and sailed for Guadeloupe, where the fleet was to rendezvous preparatory to launching the attack. But the winds were against them, and after beating about for four days La Barre was compelled to anchor his flagship off the westernmost point of Montserrat with six vessels, where he was presently joined by six others. The same day (February 4, 1667) he decided to go into action. The "Justice" and "Florissant" drew near the shore and began to exchange blows with the fort. Little damage was done until four others came alongside them; the combined force of all six quickly silenced the auxilliary batteries. Yet the fort, a solid affair of masonry, was not demolished. Anxious to put it out of commission before risking a landing, La Barre ordered a concentrated fire on its walls. It was a clear moonlight night, and the structure offered a fair target; but though the guns of the fleet kept up incessant firing—twelve hundred rounds were used in all—they could make no impression on its rocklike palisades.

Undaunted by the seeming impregnability of this fortification, La Barre was all for continuing the bombardment the following day; but his lieutenants, discouraged by the small progress made during the night, urged him to postpone further action until the arrival of the rest of the fleet. They did not have long to wait. In a few days the entire expedition was assembled off the island, and the commander, placing his ships in a little bay just out of range of the fort, prepared to make a landing. Before doing so, however, he sent ashore an officer under a flag of truce, bearing a summons to surrender. The English replied with spirit, saying they felt themselves strong enough to hold out. Meantime there had come aboard the flagship an Irish planter with a bit of information that did much to encourage the French. He told La Barre that the English forces consisted of nine hundred men, most of whom were his fellow-countrymen—the original settlers, who had come there some thirty years ago—men who because of their Roman Catholic faith had more in common with the French than with the English. These colonists, he said, were compelled to serve in the army against their will. La Barre no longer hesitated;

considering his own large force, he felt that if the enemy were divided there could be but one outcome.

The attack was planned in three waves. The first or right wing comprised three hundred men under Sieur Sanson, a captain in the regiment of Navarre; the second or left was made up of two hundred under Sieur de l'Ecossais of the regiment of Normandy; while the third or middle division consisted of five hundred (the militia of St. Christopher) headed by Pierre Giraud du Poyet. All were under the direction of Saint-Léon in his capacity of *maréchal de bataille*. When the red signal flag was unfurled at the flagship's mizzen truck, the troops were loaded into the boats. To protect them a brigantine was anchored a stone's throw from the beach, where it kept up such a hot fire with its main battery and small arms that it dislodged the enemy from a communication trench dug along the shore at this point. The other ships were unfortunately anchored too far out to support the landing party; thus the defenders were able to reform their lines just out of range and let loose a volley on the leading boats, effective enough to check them for a few moments. When at last the boats grounded, the French leaped ashore and rushed the main trench, led by their officers, sword in hand. The fighting was hand-to-hand and bitter. The men of Navarre, who were in the lead, lost two of their officers in the first rush; then, charging the trench, they drove the defenders from it. At the same time a small detachment under Sieur de Praille made a feint attack at a spot two leagues away, where they succeeded in routing the enemy with trifling losses.

Victorious in the first clash, the French reformed their lines to follow up the retreating foe. The troops of Normandy marched directly to the fort, those of Navarre took possession of a hill where they could prevent the colonists from marching inland to join Governor Osborne, who had sought refuge there, while the men from St. Christopher under their governor pressed hard upon the enemy while they fled from the scene of battle. La Barre had come ashore with the last men to land, and he set out at once to rejoin Saint-Laurent. He overtook him at a place well suited for a camp and there resolved to spend the night. All troops were sent for, and the entire army laid down their arms to enjoy a well-earned rest. Before the sun had set, three ships La Barre had sent out some time before to cruise off Barbados arrived with two prizes they had taken and also landed 150 men from the regiment of Poitou, who joined the main army at the camp, bringing the total forces up to twelve hundred. While at Bridgetown these ships had managed to intercept letters saying that the Barbadians were awaiting the arrival of a powerful fleet.

The following day scouts reported the presence of the enemy six or seven hundred strong in a nearby valley, called "The Gardens." La Barre gave an order, a bugle rang out, and the entire column was soon under way, led by the Lieutenant-General assisted by Saint-Léon and the governor of St. Christopher. A league's march brought them to a thick forest in the shadow of a hill on which sixty men had gathered to watch the army's progress. Here camp was pitched, and the French remained two days. During this time scouts were sent to ferret out the enemy, but they returned empty handed, save for a few Irishmen who came to volunteer the information that Governor Osborne was in the Capesterre district ready to surrender on reasonable terms. A flag of truce was immediately sent to sound him out. At the same time Orvilliers was dispatched with a detachment to ravage the interior and crush the enemy, accompanied by a band of Caribs who at this opportune moment had arrived in their canoes. He was successful, far beyond La Barre's wildest hopes, for in a few days he brought back as prisoners the Governor's wife and eighty persons, a blow which compelled Osborne to surrender with two hundred men.

The island was now given over to pillage. All houses, save those of the Irish colonists, were destroyed. More than forty sugar refineries were set on fire, as well as several storehouses, and more than three hundred English colonists, in addition to those who had already given themselves up, were taken prisoners. The loot yielded sixteen cannon and a large number of slaves, horses, and cattle. When La Barre withdrew from the island he left five hundred Irishmen who had taken the oath of allegiance to France. These men with their families accounted for two thousand souls. To supervise them for the time being La Barre detailed Sieur de Praille with eighty men, and he left two frigates to provide transportation for De Praille's detachment when he should be ready to leave.

With this victory to his credit, the Lieutenant-General proceeded to St. Christopher on the nineteenth of February, bringing with him forty barrels of gunpowder, five hundred muskets, and three thousand bullets. He was given an enthusiastic reception by the planters, who foresaw an early end of the war, with the British Caribbees in the possession of France. His first act was to load his prisoners on a ship, recently captured by him, and send them all to Jamaica, with the notable exception of Governor Osborne, his wife, and several officers. Five days later De Praille appeared with the two frigates, his little army, and sixty prisoners. [6]

News of the fall of St. Christopher and the capture of Antigua had, of course, reached England. From Nevis, Henry Willoughby had written his brother William[7] at Barbados asking his immediate help, and he, unable to furnish it, had applied to the King. West Indian affairs at this time were receiving the serious attention of the English government, for when the news of Francis Willoughby's death arrived in London the Barbadian merchants residing there at once called a meeting to select his succeor. The choice fell on Francis's younger brother, William, and at their request the Crown granted a commission to this gentleman early in January, 1667.[8] William Willoughby was also ordered to go to Barbados with Sir Tobias Bridge's regiment; but as arrangements for the transportation of these men would take some time and the need for help was pressing, an advance guard of four men-of-war (the "Colchester," the "Coronation," the "East India Merchant," and the "Quaker") was sent out under Captain John Berry. Accompanied by a squadron or merchantmen, Berry left in January and arrived at Bridgetown on the twenty-second of February. Willoughby did not go with him.

The arrival of the fleet was timely, for the Barbadian planters had reached a state bordering on panic. French privateers were

[6]Du Tertre, *Histoire générale des Antilles*, IV, 199–206; Le Febvre de la Barre, *Relation de ce qui s'est passé dans les isles et terre-ferme de l'Amérique*, II, 11–37.

[7]As will presently appear, there were four Willoughbys concerned in West Indian affairs: Francis, now deceased, William his younger brother, who was to succeed him, and William's two sons, Henry and William, Jr.   [8]*C.S.P.*, *America & West Indies*, *1661–68*, No. 1372.

ranging their coasts and threatening the island itself. Henry Willoughby was by this time back in Bridgetown, ready to lead any project for the defense of the colony that the authorities might care to organize. Having these reinforcements, the inhabitants took heart and decided to carry the war into the enemy's territory and recover the lost islands. The Assembly quickly voted an appropriation of one million pounds of sugar for the undertaking, and they authorized Berry to impress for His Majesty's service six ships lying in Carlisle Bay. The instructions given him by the Assembly authorized him "to use his utmost to take or sink vessels belonging to the enemies of England, destroy ships or fortifications, and with the Governor of Nevis attempt the destruction of St. Christopher or any other islands of the enemy, which he is directed to visit, and do his best to free English prisoners and kill and destroy enemies and their settlements."[9] The Captain set sail on the last day of March with his fleet, now augmented to ten vessels.[10] A month later William Willoughby, the new governor, landed at Bridgetown, bringing with him Sir Tobias Bridge and eight hundred men, plentifully supplied with artillery, powder, and munitions. Despite the loss of Francis Willoughby's squadron the previous year, the tide was now beginning to turn in favor of the British.

News of the preparations to recapture the lost island possessions did not fail to reach the ear of King Louis, who at once issued orders to send additional ships for their protection. He proposed to collect a fleet of eight vessels on which he would embark twenty companies of picked troops, drawn from the various garrisons in and about La Rochelle; the expedition was to be ready to sail in three weeks. To command this large force he selected Jean-Charles de Baas-Castlemore, an experienced veteran and, strange to say, a Protestant, who was given complete authority over all naval and military affairs in the West Indies, both on the mainland and among the islands, thus superseding M. de la Barre. He was named lieutenant-general for the King. La Barre also retained this title, but he was to hold it under the new commander. To compensate him for the loss of prestige he would thus suffer, he was appointed,

[9]*Ibid.*, No. 1446.   [10]The additional ships were: "Pearl," "Constant Katherine," "William," "Companion," "Phoenix," "John and Thomas." *Ibid.*, No. 1437.

as a reward for the excellent services he had rendered, commander-in-chief of all the forces in the West Indies and in Guiana until De Baas's arrival. In forwarding the new commission, the King expressed himself as well pleased 'with the actions at Antigua and St. Eustatius and warmly approved the plan for capturing Nevis, since he realized that this island would be a threat to French St. Christopher as long as it was in the hands of the English. Not only did he approve the plan, but he also ordered it carried out.

Meanwhile, in Guadeloupe Governor du Lion received some startling news. A Dutch captain who had overhauled a British merchantman amused himself by perusing the letters found aboard her and happened to run across accounts of the armada Captain Berry was organizing at Barbados.[11] In St. Christopher, La Barre also heard that a fleet of six ships—probably Willoughby's squadron—had recently sailed from England, and he decided to intercept it before it could join the flotilla at Bridgetown. For this purpose he selected seven vessels[12] belonging to the company, on one of which he placed two hundred men from the regiment of Poitou and sent them forth on their errand. He also called upon Clodoré to furnish five hundred men, who were to be paid by a share of the booty if they were successful. But Clodoré's call for volunteers met with no response, for his men still smarted under what they considered an unfair distribution of the loot taken at Antigua.

News of this powerful armada composed of Willoughby's and Berry's squadrons struck terror into the hearts of the French commanders, especially those assembled at St. Christopher. Here a council of war was called, at which it was decided to recall the seven vessels as well as all ships in the neighborhood and have them take refuge in the roadstead of Basseterre. For this purpose a brigantine was dispatched to follow the squadron. The council also ordered the batteries along the shore to be put into condition to meet the attack which every one believed to be imminent.

[11]Du Tertre says it consisted of six warships and seventy merchantmen. La Barre's figure of eleven vessels and a fire ship is probably more nearly correct. It may be well to state here that authorities giving the names of vessels and the numbers composing the various fleets are apt to disagree. We cannot therefore guarantee absolute accuracy.

[12]"Lys Couronne," "Justice," "Florissant," "St. Christophe," "Armes," "Vierge," and "Hirondelle."

After the conference La Barre received a letter from Clodoré point-ing out how much safer the fleet would be in the Cul-de-Sac Royal than in an open roadstead. The reasonableness of this was so ob-vious that the Lieutenant-General had no difficulty in persuading the officials to countermand their orders and send the fleet to Martinique. Then to protect St. Christopher he would have the "Armes d'Angleterre," which carried the soldiers of the Poitou regiment, return at once. To this sensible suggestion all agreed. Every ship in the harbor, save two, sailed for Martinique, and presently the "Armes" returned to Basseterre, to the great relief of the inhabitants. As for the fleet, it presently reached Martinique, where Clodoré and the captains, after lengthy deliberations, de-cided to lodge it in a pocket of the Cul-de-Sac Royal, known as the Carenage, where the enemy would find it difficult to attack.[13]

Early in April a Dutch ship arrived at St. Christopher and re-ported the presence of an English frigate not far from Martinique, headed evidently for Nevis. On hearing this La Barre decided to go at once to Martinique, where he would combine the French and the Dutch vessels and make ready for action. As he prepared to sail, a lookout on the mountain back of Basseterre reported a fleet of ten sail making for Nevis. It proved to be Berry's squadron coming from Barbados. Little credence was given this report at first, but when the Lieutenant-General boarded the "Armes" the following day to start on his journey, a frigate was seen off Nevis, which put an end to all doubts as to the presence of a hostile armada. Chambré and Saint-Laurent crowded about La Barre, begging him to give up his plans or at least to leave under cover of darkness, for the "Armes" was a small craft of only twenty-four guns, whereas the Englishman was a big fellow of twice that number. La Barre, however, felt that a change of plan would indicate fear and would have a bad effect on the morale of the island; besides, he must get to Martinique at once. He accord-ingly thanked his colleagues for their thoughtfulness, ordered them ashore, and was soon on his way southward, escorted by a small brigantine. No sooner had he reached a point opposite Charlestown, capital of Nevis, than the frigate—it was the "Col-chester"—gave chase. La Barre saw his predicament and ordered

[13]Du Tertre, *Histoire générale des Antilles*, IV, 218-20.

his crew to battle quarters. Urged to seek flight in the brigantine, as Henry Willoughby had once done, he scornfully refused and sent his little consort back to St. Christopher. As the day wore on, the Englishman gained on the "Armes," until at nightfall he was within hailing distance. To the enemy's "Ship ahoy" La Barre answered with his stern guns, but the "Colchester," instead of replying in kind, altered her course and bore down on him. Only a quick maneuver saved the "Armes" from being rammed; the frigate's bowsprit tore through her maincourse, while a volley of musketry swept her decks. La Barre fired his lower tier guns, double shotted, at the enemy's waterline and kept on firing them with telling effect during the entire action. The battle lasted until after dark, for the moon in its first quarter gave sufficient light; then, at last, after the "Colchester's" crew had been repulsed several times in a desperate attempt to board the "Armes," the "Colchester" drew off, leaking badly from the pounding she had received between wind and water, and presently sank beneath the surface of the sea.

The "Armes," though victorious, was severly damaged, and La Barre ordered her back to Basseterre. In her battered state it was no easy matter to sail her through the rough waters; progress was slow, especially as the course lay against the wind. At sunrise the French saw the English fleet far to windward of them entering the roadstead of Basseterre. It was too late now to get there and lie under the protection of the fort, so La Barre gave orders to head for St. Croix, where he could lay up the ship for repairs and nurse the wounds he had received in battle.

When Captain Berry reached Nevis he proceeded to throw a blockade around St. Christopher, using the former island as his base. To do this successfully he must first destroy whatever French shipping he could find at St. Christopher, and it was this object he had in mind when La Barre saw him heading into Basseterre. When the British fleet approached, Saint-Laurent sounded the alarm. Two vessels in the roadstead at once weighed anchor and sought to escape to Pointe de Sable. One, the better sailer of the two, got away, but the other was forced to seek refuge under the fort of Palmetto Point, where it was promptly attacked by seven ships. For some time the plucky Frenchman defended himself against a terrific bombardment, ably supported by the batteries of the fort, then the captain, despairing of ever getting away, set fire to his ship and escaped with his crew. Two Dutch ships now arrived just in time to share in the trouble. One anchored under the fort of Basseterre and managed to hold off three English frigates until her skipper could land his valuable cargo, then a fireship set her in flames. The other, seeking safety under the guns of Fort St. Louis at Pointe de Sable, gave two attackers such a warm reception that they were glad to withdraw. After that the English returned to the roadstead of Charlestown, leaving three or four frigates before Basseterre to maintain the blockade.

Cut off in this manner from normal communication with the other islands, Governor de Saint-Laurent nevertheless managed to get a message through to Du Lion and Clodoré imploring help, and these two men immediately pooled their resources to dispatch a small armada. These ships, by keeping to windward of Nevis, escaped the blockading vessels and landed some two hundred and fifty men on the eastern side of Christopher. Shortly after this Clodoré received word from La Barre, who was lying impatiently at St. Croix anxious to get back into the fray, telling him of his whereabouts and requesting the means of transportation back to the scene of action. The Governor sent him a speedy little frigate, the "Notre-Dame de Bon-Port." She had just arrived from France with La Barre's new commission and the joyful news concerning the great armada of De Baas then preparing to sail from La Rochelle with reinforcements sufficient to guarantee French supremacy in the Caribbees. Within a few days the Lieutenant-General was back in Martinique ready to organize an expedition to destroy the English fleet.

When La Barre reached St. Pierre he found that a certain amount of preliminary work had already been done. Three large Dutch ships had arrived, under the command of Abraham Crynssen, an able officer who had just recaptured the Dutch colony of Surinam from the English and was in fine fettle for another go at his country's foes. To these was added another Dutch vessel already in the harbor. When Clodoré invited Crynssen to join him in an undertaking against the British, the Dutchman promptly accepted; but, strange to say, it was the French captains who demurred, for they felt that success was not altogether certain, and furthermore they disliked the idea of stripping Martinique of its men and munitions. It would be far better, they thought, to await the coming of De Baas and his large reinforcements. The arrival of La Barre, however, inspired Clodoré to reopen the subject, and a council was called for this purpose. On hearing the arguments against the expedition, the Lieutenant-General expressed himself as being in agreement with them; but when the meeting was about to adjourn, four of the company's largest ships dropped anchor off the shore, bringing enough munitions to supply the entire French armada. Unfortunately they brought from La Rochelle some disquieting news. De Baas's fleet had not yet sailed and could not possibly reach the West Indies for at least six weeks. Furthermore, William Willoughby's squadron was about to sail from England (this had been heard before) and was to be followed a month later by still another flotilla under Sir John Harman. There was no time to lose. La Barre and Clodoré must strike promptly if they would strike at all. A plan of campaign was accordingly drawn up to attack the English fleet at once and break the blockade of St. Christopher, whose inhabitants were already beginning to feel the pinch of hunger.

The fleet, comprising both Dutch and French vessels, was divided into two squadrons. La Barre, with his commission of lieutenant-general safe in his pocket, took supreme command, hoisting his flag on Captain d'Elbée's "Lys Couronné," largest of the entire armada. He led the first squadron, with Clodoré as vice-admiral in the "Justice" and Du Lion as rear-admiral in the "Concorde." Thus all the leading officials were provided with high naval ranks. The second division was under Captain Crynssen, in the "Zelandia." As the Dutch commander had but few ships under his command, some of the French vessels were placed in his squadron to make the strength of both divisions fairly even. There were nineteen ships in all, mounting 452 guns. [14] Six hundred men were furnished by Martinique as soldiers; five hundred by

[14]Under La Barre were: "Florissant," "Armes," "St. Christophe," "Harmonie," "Notre-Dame," "Marsouin," "Cher Ami." Under Crynssen were: "Levrier," "Hercule," "Hirondelle," "Mercier," "St. Jean," "Soucy," and two Dutch vessels, names unknown. For lists see Du Tertre, *Histoire générale des Antilles*, IV, 242–43, and La Roncière, *Histoire de la marine française*, V, 465.

Guadeloupe. Elaborate and detailed instructions were drawn up for the coming campaign. After leaving St. Pierre the fleet was to go to Guadeloupe to pick up that island's quota of men; then it was to alter its course so as to pass to windward (eastward) of Monserrat, regulating its speed to arrive at the southeastern point of Nevis at daybreak. If the English vessels were found at anchor, the French were to close in to prevent their setting sail, but if the British should succeed in getting under way before the French had rounded the point, each ship was to head for the shore as quickly as possible in order to get between the English and the land, a maneuver which would give them the windward position, thus putting the enemy to leeward of the fireships.

On the fourteenth of May, from the deck of La Barre's flagship there was run up the signal to weigh anchor, and the entire fleet was soon headed for Guadeloupe. They arrived there two days later, to find Du Lion ready with his men. He came on board the "Concorde" with the lieutenant-governor of the island, M. Hencelin, whom he had permitted to accompany him, in contrast to Clodoré, who had compelled his second-in-command, Loubière, to remain behind in charge of Martinique. All was ready on the eighteenth, and the fleet set sail for Nevis. Everything turned out as planned. At daybreak on the twentieth the fleet found itself off the southeastern point of Nevis between that island and the islet or rock of Rodonda. Here they saw an English scout ship, placed there for the purpose of spotting the French when they came in sight. La Barre gave chase, his van firing as he advanced; but the Englishman proved a good sailer and managed to gain safety under the guns of the island's southernmost battery. This preliminary skirmish proved to be a mistake, for the English, roused by the cannonading promptly weighed anchor and came forward to meet their foes.

When the English came within range, the French saw a sight not at all to their liking. They were huge ships, these British vessels, huge and powerful. Captain Berry's flagship, "Coronation," mounted fifty-two guns, while the others ranged from twenty-eight to thirty-eight. Though their number, thirteen in all, was somewhat inferior to the French, the individual ships made up

for this deficiency by weight of metal.[15] Since his chief purpose
was to break the blockade and bring supplies to St. Christopher,
La Barre had brought with him several vessels loaded with provisions. These he ordered shoreward out of harm's way, then he
brought his ships together in order to concentrate his attack on
a certain sector of the line which Berry had thrown across his
path, a line which extended from the southwestern tip of Nevis
directly westward. To break through this he led the van in person,
followed by the "Justice," the "Florissant," the "Armes," and
a fireship, giving Du Lion orders to back him up with the "Harmonie," the "Marsouin," and the "Notre-Dame." At this moment Berry broke out his battle signal, ordering part of his fleet to
head in toward the shore so as to obtain a windward position; but
La Barre quickly saw the Englishman's purpose and, to forestall
him, changed his formation. He placed his ships in column instead
of sailing against the enemy in line of battle, keeping in toward
Nevis to gain that position himself. In veering from line to column,
the "St. Christophe" found itself in the lead followed by Clodoré
in the "Justice." Closing in on the enemy's leading ship, the "St.
Christophe" fired a broadside, then veered about on the other
tack, while the "Justice" bore down on the British vice-admiral,
her captain urging Clodoré to have his men ready to board. But
the governor of Martinique refused, for he found himself followed
only by La Barre in the flagship and he considered it too risky
to engage so large a craft without proper support. He bore off to
the southwest, leaving the "Lys Couronné" engaged with Berry's
"Coronation" and surrounded by a large part of the English
squadron. La Barre and Elbée fought their ship well. The "Lys,"
with only thirty-eight guns, was no match for the larger English
vessels, and despite the gallant manner in which her crew served
their pieces, she was soon badly shattered and in desperate need of
help. Du Lion, who commanded the rear division, saw his superior's predicament and gave orders to close in, but an explosion
set fire to his main-topsail and caused him to heave to until it
could be extinguished.

[15]Both La Barre and Du Tertre say there were seventeen ships in the British fleet, but the
latter goes on to say that four immediately withdrew.

Meanwhile from the quarterdeck of the "Zelandia" Abraham Crynssen had been viewing with a seadog's contempt this exhibition of lubberly ineptitude in the management of naval tactics. In disgust he gave orders for his squadron to advance and attack. Bearing down full sail on the "Coronation," he would have boarded her at once if a fireship had not got itself in the way at this moment and caused him to veer off. His maneuver, however, changed the tide of battle. The English broke and scurried for the protection of the fort at Charlestown, pursued by Crynssen and also by Du Lion, who by this time had repaired his damage and was following close on the Dutchman's heels. La Barre's division now rallied to him, and all ships joined in the pursuit, firing as they went, until one of them dropped a shell in the magazine of an English frigate and blew her up. The English fled to the shore batteries, chased by the French, who kept up an incessant firing. The fort, it so happened, did not prove such a protection as the British had hoped, and on reaching the roadstead they tacked and headed southward, intent on keeping a windward position well out of range of La Barre's guns. They were better sailers than the French, and it soon became evident to La Barre and Crynssen, as the day wore on, that the battle was over and that nothing could be gained by keeping up the pursuit. Orders were accordingly given to come about, and the French headed for Basseterre. The losses in this battle were not heavy. The English lost two ships— some authorities say three—and about eighty men, while the French admitted the loss of no vessel and only about a score of men. The British fleet remained intact, still able to defend Nevis; yet the French had accomplished part of what they had set out to do when they landed their supplies at Basseterre.[16]

The following day a council of war was held. Captain Crynssen informed his allies that he must leave for New England, which he was to visit before returning home. At the same time, the French, who had accomplished their purpose, were ready to return to Guadeloupe and Martinique. As Crynssen's departure would weaken the fleet considerably, La Barre persuaded him to accompany them as far as St. Eustatius, that is, as long as they

[16]Le Febvre de la Barre, *Relation de ce qui s'est passé dans les isles et terre-ferme de l'Amérique*, II, 149–69; Du Tertre, *Histoire générale des Antilles*, IV, 244–55.

could be seen by the English ships now cruising off Nevis and along the western coast of St. Christopher; for the French commander, in order to escape the British fleet, had decided to swing northward around the island to Capesterre, then set his course for Guadeloupe, keeping to the east of Nevis and Montserrat. This plan was acceptable to Crynssen and the entire fleet set out. They rounded Point de Sable and separated only when off the island of St. Bartholomew. La Barre then turned southward, steering for Mariegalante. When off Rodonda, he was sighted by the English cruisers and barely made his escape. The following day he was becalmed off Guadeloupe, with the enemy headed toward him; but a friendly breeze sprang up, driving him out of harm's way. In due course he reached Martinique, where he anchored off St. Pierre and sent three of his ships to carry the Guadeloupians back to their island home.

In Nevis, Governor Russell began his preparations for recapturing St. Christopher. Thanks to Captain Berry's fleet, he now felt not only secure at home but also able to carry the war into the enemy's territory. Berry had brought much-needed help to Nevis in the shape of supplies and had also sent ships to Montserrat and Antigua to remove as many English colonists as possible. The Governor added these refugees to the forces under his command, thus raising the number of his troops to about two thousand. These were enough, so he thought, to enable him to attack his neighbor successfully. Both he and Berry had written to Barbados asking for men and munitions as well as for the return of Henry Willoughby, saying they regarded him as equal to five hundred men.[17] Flattered by this compliment, Willoughby lost no time in coming to Nevis. On the fifth of June he appeared with the "Jersey," the "East India Merchant," and a supply ship. He was received with the wildest enthusiasm, for with these added reinforcements and the French expeditionary force in far-off Martinique, where La Barre was patiently awaiting the coming of of De Baas, they could easily attack St. Christopher. Hastily mustering the soldiers and sailors, Captain Berry found they numbered 3,200, while he had a fleet of fourteen ships and as many boats. It was enough; they could start immediately.

[17]C.S.P., *America & West Indies, 1661–68*, No. 1477.

In St. Christopher, Governor de Saint-Laurent, sensing that something was in the wind when he saw Willoughby's ships dropping anchor off Charlestown, made ready for the coming attack. He realized he would have to rely on his own resources for defense, as no help would be forthcoming from the outside. The alarm was sounded. Saint-Léon took command of both royal troops and militia, which amounted to about two thousand and included companies of the regiments of Navarre, Normandy, and Poitou which had been brought there after the campaign of Montserrat and left by La Barre when he returned to Martinique. Besides these, there were many planters capable of bearing arms.[18]

On the sixteenth, Saint-Laurent received word from observers in the southern part of the island that there were suspicious movements in the roadstead of Charlestown. Boats filled with men were seen scurrying between ships and shore, evidence that something was afoot. The Governor sent out orders to be ready; that night all slept under arms.

At dawn of the following day the English fleet, under the supreme command of Henry Willoughby, appeared in the offing. The vessels quickly split into two squadrons—one of which headed for Old Road Town, while the other sailed into Basseterre. All morning they moved to and fro, until the commander brought them to anchor in the roadstead of the capital, just out of range of the fort. Here they remained for the night, closely watched by the French. Just before daybreak lights appeared on the flagship, a signal, evidently, and soon the entire fleet was moving toward Palmetto Point. Saint-Laurent at once ordered the cavalry to follow them along shore. He himself set forth post haste, and on reaching the old fort situated at Palmetto Point he saw the English troops preparing to land just north of it, near the Pelham River. He hurried on, but before he had come abreast of the landing place the enemy had already placed three hundred men ashore ready to give him a warm reception. Unfortunately for them, they had not chosen a particularly favorable spot. The shore at this point offered good landing facilities, but it was flanked by steep bluffs that rendered any attempt to work inland extremely difficult. A narrow path, where men could walk only in single file, was the sole means

[10]*Ibid.*, No. 1531; *ibid.*, No. 1488, says there were 3,000 men.

of reaching the top. To make matters worse, the path was flanked by thick bushes that formed an impenetrable hedge. Saint-Laurent grasped the situation immediately. He had but ten men with him, among whom were our old acquaintances Giraud du Poyet and Des Vergers de Sanois; these he placed at the edge of the cliff overlooking the landing place and where they taunted the English and dared them to come on. A small detachment accepted the challenge and clambered up the face of the palisade. It was a gallant attempt, for the French had the advantage of position and without difficulty held them off until twenty French horsemen came galloping up, in the nick of time. When this help arrived, the invaders were quickly driven back.

Unable to take the bluff by assault, the English sought to make their way up the ravine just north of it, the ravine formed by the Pelham in cutting its way through the height of land. They might have succeeded in surrounding Saint-Laurent's men if Orvilliers had not arrived with a detachment from the Poitou regiment, 120 strong, and driven them back to the shore. At the same time, a second column of English attacked Saint-Laurent on his left flank, making their way up the height by a more gentle slope that rose beside an indigo factory. To meet this assault, the Governor was supported by a body of horsemen who had just arrived on the scene and by four companies of the regiment of Navarre. Not only did he repulse the enemy on all sides, but by now he had enough men to spare and was able to send a detachment of fifty to the support of Orvilliers. As the fight progressed, the French brought up still more troops drawn from the militia of Martinique, Guadeloupe, and St. Christopher, until at last they were no longer obliged to fight a defensive action but could bring a hot fire to bear on the enemy as they landed and even on those coming ashore in small boats. Within a short time the English were getting the worst of the encounter. Huddled together under the cliff, they were out of range of musket-fire, though the French succeeded in inflicting considerable damage by rolling huge rocks onto them from above. When they stepped from this shelter into the open, they were at once exposed to volleys from both sides.

In the rear and somewhat to the south stood M. de Saint-Léon, the *maréchal de bataille*, with four companies of the Normandy regiment, two of Poitou, and two of the St. Christopher militia. From there he could see the ships landing their men and the attack on the bluff. He was cautious, however, for he believed that all this might be but a feint and that the main attack might be somewhere else, and he wished to be ready to move at once to the point of danger. But when he saw the English troops landing in ever-increasing numbers, he soon realized that the battle would be decided here. Anxious not to lose the opportunity of taking part in such an important engagement, he gave the order to march and was soon standing beside Saint-Laurent, ready to put the finishing touches on the victory. As he was bringing his men into position, three large boats loaded to the gunwales with troops left the English fleet and made for the shore to attempt a landing at a spot somewhat removed from the field of battle. As they neared the beach, a number of French soldiers, without waiting for the word of command, rushed to meet them, fired a volley, then throwing down their guns waded into the water sword in hand and killed every member of the attacking party.

When he had reached Saint-Laurent, M. de Saint-Léon, somewhat disgruntled at not having had a hand in the business, begged his superior to let him dislodge the enemy under the cliff. Saint-Laurent gave his consent with considerable reluctance. It was a dangerous maneuver, and to succeed the French must leave the summit of the cliff, where they enjoyed a certain measure of protection, and march down the ravine onto the open shore, where they would face the direct fire of the enemy. Saint-Léon sent a detachment of his men down to the bottom of the ravine, where they had no difficulty in driving the English back to the shore. Here, however, the soldiers crouching under the bluff joined their comrades and succeeded in turning the tide against the French. Only the prompt action of a captain named Giraudière saved the situation. Rallying the French troops, he drove back the English to the protection of the cliff. Giraudière was anxious to follow up his success by a second attack, but Saint-Laurent, who had no desire to sacrifice his men uselessly in order to slaughter an enemy who would presently fall into his hand, ordered all soldiers to keep well under cover and to fire only on those who came out from the shelter of the palisade.

The resistance of the English now began to crack. The French had gained the upper hand and were gathered on the heights in such numbers that they could repel any attempt on the part of the fleet to rescue their comrades marooned on shore. It was a curious situation; the English at the foot of the cliff were sheltered from the fire of the French, yet the French could prevent their escaping to the ships. It was, in short, a sort of deadlock. After six hours of ineffectual fighting the landing party sent a messenger to the flagship to request assistance; he returned with the disquieting answer that there was nothing the fleet could do. Up to that time they had not dared to ask for quarter, fearing Saint-Laurent was bent on destroying them; but now, having nothing to lose, they determined to risk an appeal to his clemency, and tying handkerchiefs to the muzzles of their guns they clambered up the face of the cliff. No sooner were the signals recognized, than the French ceased firing. The English threw down their arms in token of surrender and gave themselves up to the number of 550, most of whom were severely wounded. They were received in a kindly manner by the victors. Once the battle was over, Saint-Laurent had no desire to mistreat a gallant enemy, and he gave orders to his men to treat their prisoners as humanely as circumstances permitted.

Wild with rage at his defeat, Henry Willoughby (that valiant commander, worth five hundred men, had lain all morning, so De Tertre tells us, in a drunken stupor) now vented his spleen on the troops he had left to their fate by opening a galling fire, contrary to all the rules of warfare, on the French and English as they mingled together. Toward noon, when he saw beyond a doubt that he was beaten, he gave the order to retreat, despite the presence on board his ships of 1,500 men who could at least have made a showing and might, perhaps, have turned defeat into victory. Willoughby returned to Nevis, leaving on the field of battle and in the hands of the enemy more than seven hundred killed and wounded and six hundred prisoners,[19] including a large number of officers.

Two days after Henry Willoughby's return to Nevis, a formid-

[19]So says Du Tertre. John Scott gives the figures as 506 killed, 284 wounded, and 140 prisoners; *ibid*., No. 1531.

able fleet under Sir John Harman anchored off Charlestown with men and supplies. Harman had arrived at Barbados on the eighteenth of June and was sent immediately to the scene of action by Governor Willoughby. His fleet consisted of the "Lion," a powerful ship of sixty-eight guns, the largest in the West Indies, which carried his flag. She was followed by the "Crown," the "Newcastle," the "Dover," the "Bonaventure," the "Assistance," the "Assurance," two fireships, and two ketches.[20] Harman at once began a survey of the situation in the fond hope of finding some way to repair the damage inflicted on British prestige. He cruised along the coast of St. Christopher, looking for a weak spot, but was soon obliged to admit that the island was too well defended to permit a successful attack. At this point, however, one of his ships captured a French vessel, and from the prisoners he was able to get a line on the general situation in the French islands. He was informed that De Baas's expedition had not arrived and that the ships at Martinique were in sad need of gunpowder. With the consent of Willoughby he therefore decided to make an attack on the Martinican squadron. On the twenty-fourth of June he set forth with the ships he had brought from England, to which he added the "Jersey" and the "Norwich," leaving Captain Berry at Nevis in charge of the rest.

On the twenty-ninth, Harman's fleet was sighted off Dominica, and news of its presence was quickly brought to St. Pierre by fishing boats. M. de Loubière, who was in command during the temporary absence of La Barre and Clodoré, who had gone to the Capesterre section on an exploratory mission, sent word to them at once, while he busied himself with making the preliminary arrangements for defense.

The fortifications protecting St. Pierre at this time were fairly adequate, though they had been used only to protect the settlement against local uprisings, never against a foreign invasion. Just north of the town, near the mouth of the Rivière des Pères, was a battery covering this part of the harbor; while to the south Fort St. Pierre itself stood close to the shore, its southern rampart washed by the Roxelane River.[21] This fort, recently built by Clodoré, was constructed in the shape of a rectangle; one of its

____

[20]*Ibid.*, No. 1524.   [21]Now called the St. Pierre River.

longer sides faced the sea and protected the roadstead with its guns. The opposite or inland side was flanked by two towers and faced the parade ground. On the northern side was a courtyard containing a chapel, and this yard was surrounded by a high wall pierced by a gateway which gave access to the fort. Farther down the coast, in the southern section of St. Pierre, known as the Quartier du Mouillage, were the batteries of St. Sebastian and St. Robert, situated near the mouth of the Rivière de la Touche. Thus the roadstead of St. Pierre was protected by a fort and three redoubts.[22]

Toward evening Harman entered the roadstead, where he found the French armada anchored within musket shot of the shore, nineteen ships and fourteen smaller craft, strung out in a line under the protection of the fort and batteries. To add to the firing power of the ships, the guns on the side facing the shore had been dragged across the decks to the side facing the enemy. At four thirty in the afternoon the British came within range and were greeted with a broadside from the entire fleet; but they declined action and stood out to sea. All this was part of Harman's plan: knowing the shortage of powder in the French magazines, he would tempt them to waste their supply, while conserving his own.

Early next morning La Barre and Clodoré appeared at St. Pierre, worn and travel stained after an all-night forced march across the mountains. The Lieutenant-General took charge of operations. He dispatched Clodoré to the Mouillage to check the arrangements Loubière had been making in that quarter. Since La Barre was anxious to reinforce the crews who were to bear the brunt of the attack, Clodoré sent on board the various ships some five hundred men he felt he could spare from the land forces, at the same time ordering the captains to concentrate their fire, when the battle began, on the British flagship. He then whipped up the fighting spirit of his men, encouraging the fainthearted, assuring all of ample support from the land forces, arranging for boats to ply between ship and shore with all necessary supplies. This done he took his station at the battery of St. Sebastien. In the afternoon La Barre arrived at the Mouillage, gave a hurried glance of approval at the Governor's work, then posted himself on a neigh-

[22]Labat, *Nouveau voyage aux isles de l'Amérique*, I, 25.

boring eminence, three hundred paces from the shore, ready to rush down on any party bold enough to attempt a landing.

When the British sailed in, action began at once. The vanguard of the fleet, three frigates led by the formidable "Lion," at once closed in to try conclusions with the French. Having waited for the "Lion" to come within close range, La Barre's captains let fly their broadsides. The flagship stopped dead in her tracks, badly shattered, and presently withdrew to a safe distance for temporary repairs. The frigates, unhurt by the discharge, now took up the tale, taking and giving volley after volley, until the rest of the fleet closed in and the action became general. Whenever the British seamen attempted to board the French ships they were met with hot musketry fire from the defenders that prevented them from getting near enough to throw their grappling irons. After four hours of desperate fighting the flagship rejoined the fleet. Then the wind fell, and the entire British squadron found itself trapped within range of the shore batteries. The boats were immediately dropped overboard and the crews struggled manfully at the oars to tow their ships out of danger. This maneuver exposed them to such a concentrated fire from ships, batteries, and soldiers lined up along the shore that not more than a third escaped alive and unwounded. At last, after tremendous exertion, they succeeded in getting clear of the land and withdrew to a safe distance to recuperate. Though the British had got the worse of the duel, so far as injuries were concerned, the tremendous bombardment let loose by the French—some six or seven thousand shots had been fired—took heavy toll on their supply of powder. To remedy this La Barre sent a boat through the blockade to request from Du Lion a fresh supply, as well as a couple of boats to cruise the waters to the east in search of De Baas's fleet.

On the second of July the English again entered the roadstead. La Barre had established his headquarters in Fort St. Pierre, behind which the cavalry stood ready; Clodoré remained at St. Sebastien; Loubière, with three hundred men, took his stand on a hill situated a short distance south of the Mouillage where he could watch the battle and be ready to rush his men to any spot where the enemy might attempt a landing; the company's chief factor, Picquet de la Calle, was placed in command of St. Robert.

Harman led the attack in the "Lion," preceded by four ships, which opened up a terrific fire on the French fleet and the buildings along the shore. The French made a spirited reply, the guns in the batteries backing up those of the vessels, until after three hours of incessant cannonading the enemy drew off for repairs.

After a lapse of two days the English were ready for another attempt. During the interval Clodoré had sent a detachment of men under Valmenière, with some English prisoners and Negroes, to build two redoubts at the Carénage down at the Cul-de-Sac, for word had been received that the English intended to force the place. This was the southernmost of a series of defenses Clodoré had constructed over a distance of eight leagues along the coast. At ten o'clock on the morning of the fourth of July, the English approached St. Pierre for the third attempt. It lasted only a couple of hours and was a drawn battle, but it served the useful purpose of diminishing the French supply of powder.

The fourth attack was far more formidable than the previous three and resulted in serious losses to the defenders. When on the sixth, La Barre saw the British fleet advancing under full sail, he felt certain his ships would be annihilated. He placed himself in readiness to repel an assault should the enemy land and ordered Clodoré and Loubière to the posts previously assigned to them. After a prolonged cannonade a British fireship, superbly handled, bore down on the "St. Jean," barely missed it, and came alongside the "Lys Couronné." With little difficulty her crew threw their grappling hooks on the "Lys" and made fast. There was something amusing about this, for M. d'Elbée, captain of the "Lys," had boasted that he could take care of any fireship that tried to tackle him, and now he was its first victim, for the English skipper quickly touched off his ship and made off in the boats without the loss of a man. The "Lys" was soon ablaze, and the conflagration spread to the "St. Jean," the "Mercier," and the "Lion d'Or." These vessels, which bore in their holds 1,200,000 pounds of sugar ready to be carried to France, burned to the waterline, a total loss. Panic now spread through the other craft. Terrified at the possibility of being burned alive, the crews leaped overboard and swam ashore. Lined up as they were, cheek by jowl, a large portion of the fleet might have been destroyed in the general conflagration had not the wind shifted providentially, carrying the sparks and flames away from the shore. To add to the confusion a French fireship, the "Pucelle," was attacked with such fury that her captain set her on fire himself and then escaped with his crew.

The galling fire from the English fleet and the havoc it created among the French so terrified those escaping from the ships that it was impossible to stop them. Clodoré received these wretched men kindly, calmed their fears as best he could, gave them clothes and weapons—for they had lost everything in the general *sauve qui peut*—and sent them to a nearby post, where they would be able to rest and get a fresh grip on themselves. Since he felt there was worse to come, the Governor determined to hold his position and let the fleet perish rather than weaken the land forces by sending a single man to reinforce the doomed vessels. He sent word to all the captains of the land forces to be ready to concentrate their men at whatever spot the enemy might attempt to land. The battery of St. Robert had been demolished by the enemy's fire and was perforce abandoned. St. Sebastien, however, fared better. Here Guillaume d'Orange, one of Martinique's most distinguished colonists, was stationed with his sons, gallantly serving the guns and exchanging blow for blow with the English fleet. When his gunners fell, his daughter, Madeleine Valence, took up the burden of serving the artillery, courageously bringing cartridges, bullets, and supplies from the magazines, without showing the slightest concern for the slaughter that was taking place about her.

After five hours of continuous fighting the enemy withdrew, well content with what they had accomplished. An inventory taken by the French after the battle showed a serious condition. The entire fleet had but five or six hundred rounds of ammunition, while the batteries on shore had but one thousand. It was therefore impossible to withstand another attack like the one they had just experienced. With great reluctance La Barre gave orders to strip the vessels of all but their guns and make ready to sink them when their ammunition had been exhausted. He worked out a plan whereby the gunners were not to open fire on the enemy's ships, but were to wait until the boats sent to capture them came within range and then fire at the crews in the hope of wiping them out. Fortunately the situation was improved by the arrival of one thousand pounds of powder from Du Lion and half that amount from Saint-Laurent. With this the French could accept battle with a certain degree of confidence.

On the seventh, the British fleet advanced for what was to be the deciding conflict. Closing in, they opened up a bombardment that struck terror into the hearts of the defenders. Never before had the crews been called upon to bear such gunfire. All plans for defense so carefully worked out were forgotten in the confusion that ensued; the little ammunition on board the ships was quickly used up, the colors were struck, and the vessels scuttled as they stood. In the general panic Clodoré saw that one ship had escaped destruction; it was the "Soucy," a fireship which, if properly handled, could still inflict considerable damage on the enemy. Her captain, however, refused to budge, saying that his men were in a state of panic and could not be trusted. Clodoré therefore caused her ammunition to be removed to St. Sebastien, where he dug himself in, hoping to be able to beat off the attack. Short of powder, he held his fire until the British fleet came within point blank range, then he opened up with such telling effect that after an hour and a half the English were glad enough to call it quits and sail away. Such, at any rate, is the story told by Du Tertre; but perhaps the British were satisfied with what they had done, for they left behind them twenty-three enemy ships sunk, burned, or otherwise destroyed. They had annihilated the French armada.[23]

The victory was an expensive one. Though the English lost only eighty[24] men killed, besides the wounded, their ships were badly shaken, so badly, in fact, as to be unseaworthy without extensive repairs. It was probably for this reason that Harman did not follow up his success by destroying what little remained of the French fleet, a failure for which he was later severely censured. The following day he ran in toward the shore and sent a messenger to La Barre under a flag of truce, bearing a letter in which the British commander complained of the cruel treatment meted out to English prisoners in Martinique and threatened to destroy the entire colony if they were not surrendered. La Barre, however, was not to be

[23]Du Tertre, Histoire générale des Antilles, IV, 278-91; Le Febvre de la Barre, Relation de ce qui s'est passé dans les isles et terre-ferme de l'Amérique, II. 238-71.
[24]C.S.P., America & West Indies, 1661-68, No. 1517. Du Tertre, Histoire générale des Antilles, IV, 291, says six hundred.

intimidated. He courteously received the messenger, an Irish officer named Captain James Barrett, showed him the prisoners, who were being treated as well as possible, offered to fight the English whenever they wished, and sent him back with a letter suggesting an exchange of prisoners. Since Harman had no Frenchmen in his fleet to offer, he felt that his bluff had been called and presently sailed back to Nevis, where he discussed with Governor Russell and Henry Willoughby the possibilities of recapturing St. Christopher.[25]

When leaving Martinique, Captain Harman had sent a frigate to Barbados with news of his victory. Immensely pleased at an English victory after so many reverses, Lord Willoughby anticipated his nephew's plan for attacking St. Christopher by sending him at once two ships with three hundred men and the necessary supplies. As soon as they reached Nevis, Henry Willoughby held a review of all his forces, now consisting of twenty-two ships and three thousand troops—quite enough, he believed, to insure the success of the undertaking. In St. Christopher, Governor de Saint-Laurent got wind of what was going on and spared no effort to put the island in condition to meet the emergency. To an envoy sent from Nevis to reclaim English prisoners, a man who demanded in an insolent manner the surrender of the former English territory, he replied with spirit, threatening to toss him into the sea if he did not mend his manners.

On the twenty-sixth of July, Harman led a squadron of twelve ships to Basseterre and proceeded to sail along the coast to Pointe de Sable, firing away at the various batteries and troops that lined the shore. The French returned the fire with telling effect. Saint-Laurent kept five hundred men along the shore following the progress of the fleet, ready to pounce on any party that might attempt a landing. The sight of these men discouraged Harman, who realized at last that the French were fully prepared to cope with any situation, more fully in fact than he had expected. He returned, therefore, to Nevis where, with Willoughby, he presently organized an expedition for the capture of Cayenne.

The islands were now beginning to feel the effects of the long-

[25]Le Febvre de la Barre, *Relation de ce qui s'est passé dans les isles et terre-ferme de l'Amérique*, II, 273–80.

drawn-out hostilities. Since so many men were constantly under arms, plantations had suffered from neglect and there had resulted a loss in such staples as sugar, tobacco, and indigo, which had served as a medium of exchange for supplies brought in from abroad. Moreover, the danger of becoming involved in hostilities had kept merchantmen away, especially from blockaded St. Christopher, so that despite their early victories the French on this island suffered quite as much as the English at Nevis. Le Febvre de la Barre worked heroically in Martinique to repair the damage done there by the English and to salvage what he could of his fleet. Ships which had been sunk but not burned were floated and sent to the Carénage for repairs. While this work was going on, six well-laden vessels arrived from France, to the great joy of the colonists, for they brought the lumber and the material so badly needed for repairs, as well as provisions and ammunition. They also brought two important bits of news: first, that negotiations for a treaty of peace were under way; second, which followed from this, that orders had been issued countermanding De Baas's expedition.

For reasons which had nothing to do with the West Indian situation representatives of the three nations concerned, France, England, and the Netherlands had met at Breda to discuss terms of peace. After two months of parleying their efforts were crowned with success, and on July 31, 1667, there was signed the famous trilateral agreement known as the Treaty of Breda. So far as the Anglo-French struggle in the West Indies was concerned, the treaty reverted to the *status quo ante bellum*. It provided for the return of all colonies captured during the war by the French. The King of France promised to surrender to Charles of England the portion of St. Christopher he had taken, as well as Antigua, Montserrat, and all other islands, countries, lands, and fortresses belonging to his British Majesty before the war. Six months after the date of the treaty was the date set for the cession of St. Christopher. As the return of this island involved some complications, due to the purchase of English plantations by French individuals, it was expressly stipulated that the original owners could not recover their property unless they paid back the sum they had received for it; this applied also to slaves sold by their original owners. English subjects who had joined the French armies or had bound themselves to work for a French planter were released from their oaths of allegiance and permitted to resume their English citizenship. These clauses in the treaty were sure to cause disputes and did, indeed, lead to a long series of legal quibbles, misunderstandings, delays, and bargaining that lasted for about four years.[26] We shall take up the story of these negotiations in the following chapter.

In this manner did the first clash in the long-drawn-out struggle between the French and the English in the West Indies come to an end. The French had taken the aggressive and maintained it during the entire campaign, capturing English territory and holding it against recapture by their foes. Only toward the end, at the battle of St. Pierre, did they encounter defeat; but it was the plenipotentiaries at Breda who robbed them of the fruits of victory by compelling them to surrender what they had won by force of arms. Thus, thanks to Breda and St. Pierre, the English recovered what they had lost and were now masters of the sea.

[26]Articles of the Treaty of Breda covering West Indian affairs may be found in Du Tertre, *Histoire générale des Antilles*, IV, 318–25.

⟡ IV ⟡

THE FRENCH TRIUMPH OVER THE DUTCH

Nᴇᴡs of the Treaty of Breda spread rapidly through the islands, and its terms were known to everyone a month before La Barre received official notification from the directors of the West India Company. Yet, since neither he nor the English governors had been ordered to suspend hostilities a state of war still existed, and he found it difficult, if not impossible, to run enough provisions through the blockade to feed the inhabitants of St. Christopher in a proper manner. To solve this problem he decided to offer a specific inducement to the British authorities to get them to sign an armistice. On October 20, 1667, he dispatched a messenger to Governor Russell, of Nevis, and Captain William Poole, commander of the naval contingent during Harman's absence on the Cayenne venture, with a copy of the treaty, expressing at the same time his willingness to supply Nevis with provisions if they would agree to end hostilities. Somewhat embarrassed by the suggestion, for they had received no instructions from home, these men finally struck a bargain by which Nevis should be provisioned by the French, who, in turn, should be permitted to run the blockade, provided they did so at night, since Russell and Poole did not wish to be accused of connivance in helping the enemy. Pleased with this arrangement La Barre sent a bark loaded with foodstuffs to the half-famished British colonists, at the same time dispatching a small squadron of merchantmen with the necessary supplies to St. Christopher. Though this arrangement was of obvious advantage to the French, La Barre's critics did not fail to suggest that he was making a good profit by illicit dealings with the enemy, all at the expense of the West India Company, which had a legal monopoly of West Indian trade.

As the principal struggle over the enforcement of the treaty promised to take place at St. Christopher, where the French would be obliged to surrender the middle section of the island, La Barre betook himself thither with every vessel he could find in the roadstead of St. Pierre, bringing at the same time a six month's supply of food for the inhabitants. If there was to be any trouble, he was ready for it. Orders from the company now arrived, and on the twenty-sixth of December the Lieutenant-General proclaimed the peace to the colonists assembled at Basseterre, while at the same time the various governors, acting under his instructions, announced the ratification of the treaty in their respective colonies.

On the twenty-eighth, Governor Willoughby arrived at Nevis with three great ships on a tour of inspection. Learning of La Barre's presence on St. Christopher, he proceeded there immediately to open negotiations for carrying out the terms of the treaty. In doing so he realized, as did La Barre, that the situation in this island was bound to cause serious difficulties when it came to applying those clauses which ordered the restoration of the plantations captured during the war to their original owners. When the English, on the arrival of Berry's fleet had regained command of the seas, Antigua and Montserrat had fallen into their hands as a matter of course; but it was quite another thing to secure the restoration of St. Christopher, though the treaty gave them a rightful title to it. The French planters thought the terms harsh, too harsh in fact, if it meant that they must give up what they had captured by force of arms, especially since the disorders of the past eighteen months had brought about complications difficult to unravel when it came to returning the plantations to their rightful owners. Property, real as well as personal, had passed from hand to hand during this time, making it well-nigh impossible to decide, when the English claimants appeared, whose property should be surrendered to whom. Moreover, there was the question of the price to be paid. Many French planters had spent time and money enhancing the value of their estates by erecting new buildings or repairing old ones. In some cases these structures had been entirely destroyed by a recent hurricane; in others, the French had been unable to cultivate the fields because their slaves had been drafted to work on the fortifications for long periods of time.

How, then, could one compute the just value which the English planters should pay the French when they came to reclaim their land? Then, too, colonists from St. Martin and St. Bartholomew, some eight hundred in number, had come to St. Christopher at De Sales's urgent request to help in the defense of the island and had received plots of ground in the English section to recompense them for the sacrifices they had made. To make matters worse their own farms on these little islands had been ravaged by the English during the war, leaving no homes for them to return to should they leave their present plantations. What would become of these people if they should be obliged to surrender their newly acquired property in accordance with the terms of the treaty?

The English colonists were equally determined to secure the return of their erstwhile possessions. In fact, a group of influential planters presented a petition to the Crown in behalf of several thousand dispossessed people, saying "that St. Christopher's was one of the flourishing colonies, the first and best on earth that ever was inhabited by Englishmen amongst the heathen cannibals in America," and pleaded that it might not fall into the hands of another nation; and to enlist the royal sympathy for their cause they pointed out for the special benefit of King Charles that the island had received during Cromwell's usurpation many persons devoted to His Majesty's service, including brave and able divines who had kept their parishes free from Independents, Anabaptists, Quakers, and rigid Presbyterians.[1] This purely colonial enthusiasm, however, was not fully shared by Lord Willoughby, who, seeing the intense desire of the French to retain the island, thought it would be no ill bargain to let them have it in exchange for Grenada.[2] Whether such a suggestion was seriously considered at home is doubtful, for the French ambassador who was sent to London to work out the details of the treaty obtained no concessions on this point, and the treaty stood as written.

In his present dealings with La Barre, Willoughby did not bring up the subject of restitution, for he had not yet received definite orders from home to do so; instead he sent a representative to request of the Lieutenant-Governor the surrender of the prisoners he was holding at Basseterre, asking at the same time that the

[1]C.S.P., *America & West Indies, 1661–68*, No. 1629.   [2]*Ibid.*, No. 1692.

question of their upkeep be left open until his government had signified its wishes on this subject. Approached in this courteous manner, the French commander replied in kind. He at once turned over to the envoy some three hundred prisoners captured at Pelham River, and he accepted an invitation to dine on board Willoughby's flagship, where he was royally entertained. This civility he repaid by turning over to his host the famous half-breed, Thomas Warner, former governor of Dominica, who had been in some manner or other captured by the French, with the request that he be made to live like an Englishman, not like a savage. Willoughby, however, reinstated him as ruler of Dominica. When these amenities were over, La Barre proceeded to Martinique for a brief stay, while Willoughby returned to Barbados.

Willoughby's stay in Barbados was a short one. Early in February, 1668, he decided to return to Nevis. With a number of prospective colonists on board, his fleet set sail, crossing to St. Vincent, then proceeding northward through the archipelago. At Martinique he learned that La Barre had just departed; continuing on his way, he reached Nevis on the fourteenth. Here he remained until the fourth of May, busying himself with restoring order out of the chaos caused by the war, then he sailed for Montserrat to land his colonists. Scarcely had he weighed anchor, when he met a ship bringing from England a formal order instructing him to proceed at once to St. Christopher and demand the restitution of the island in accordance with the terms of the treaty. There was no mistaking the urgency of these commands. Putting his ship about, he returned to Nevis, and after a consultation with his officers dispatched Colonel Henry Drax and Colonel William Stapleton to explain his mission to Governor Saint-Laurent. This was the first move in that long series of diplomatic duels that put off the final settlement of the St. Christopher question for three more long, weary years.

Saint-Laurent received the envoys with a great display of civility and at once began to spar for time. He explained carefully that the settlement of such an important affair was in the hands of his superior, M. de la Barre, who at this time was unfortunately absent, but that since he would presently return, no one need be discouraged. The matter would not suffer because of a short delay.

Willoughby was unruffled by this rebuff; he held all the cards and had no cause to worry, for the ship which brought him his instructions also brought him letters written by the King of France to Saint-Laurent, La Barre, and the directors of the company advising them to make immediate restitution.[3] And in addition to right, Willoughby also had might, for when news of the peace was received at St. Christopher, La Barre hastily returned the King's troops to France and sent back to Martinique and Guadeloupe the militia Clodoré and Du Lion had loaned for the occasion, thus seriously weakening his defenses. To make matters worse for the French, there were still many English colonists on the island ready to rise against them at the slightest provocation. Armed with these two weapons, Willoughby now decided to proceed to Basseterre and demand the immediate surrender of the portion rightfully belonging to England without waiting for the return of La Barre. He felt he could bring sufficient pressure to bear on the Governor and also on Chambré, who happened to be there, to accomplish his purpose. Thus it happened that early one morning the French awoke to see four large English frigates riding peacefully at anchor in the roadstead, their bulwarks crowded with soldiers and volunteers.

Saint-Laurent and Chambré were equal to the occasion. When they saw their distinguished visitor was about to come ashore, they rushed down to the landing to meet him. They received him affably and led him to a large pavilion, where they urged him to make himself at home. Willoughby came to the point with little formality. He tossed on the table a packet containing the letters of King Louis, as well as his own credentials from King Charles authorizing him to take over the English portion of the island. He also presented the French King's letter to La Barre expressing at the same time his own disappointment that the Lieutenant-General was not present to receive it. Saint-Laurent and Chambré gazed at the letters with pursed lips. They were in order, of course; but after all it was La Barre who was in charge; he alone could make the legal transfer. Willoughby, however, demanded an immediate answer. The Frenchmen, somewhat at their wits' end, countered by inviting him to dinner. During the repast they had time

[3]Duplicates, no doubt. The original letters were probably sent directly by the King to his officials.

to consider the situation, and no sooner had they risen from the table than they drafted a reply consisting of two letters: in one Saint-Laurent pointed out that as far as his end of the business was concerned it was all in the hands of his superior, La Barre; while the Intendant, in his communication, said that the letter given him was addressed to the directors of the company and he could only act on receipt of orders from them. They both closed by saying that they had sent word to La Barre urging him to hasten to Basseterre, and they further promised that if the dispatch boat returned without having located him, they would surrender the disputed territory without more ado. With this answer Willoughby returned to his flagship to spend the night.

The following day produced the same result. This time the scene was laid at Old Road Town, whither Willoughby had moved in order to be on the land he had come to reclaim. Again he expressed his desire for an immediate cession, and again the French put him off until the return of La Barre or the boat. For a day or so this ruse succeeded, but the Governor of Barbados finally became impatient, and to pacify him Saint-Laurent, in a letter dated May 9, definitely promised to surrender five days later if neither La Barre nor the boat had returned by that time. Willoughby toyed with this offer for a while, then decided to submit to no further delay. He sent for Chambré and presented him with an ultimatum demanding immediate surrender; he asked Chambré to sign it and have the Governor affix his signature also. But Saint-Laurent held his ground; he had made all the concessions he felt he could make and would go no further. Two days later Willoughby sent his aide, Colonel Stapleton, ashore to reopen the discussion. Saint-Laurent, now thoroughly exasperated by the whole business—one cannot understand exactly why, since Willoughby was clearly in the right—gave the Colonel the following blunt message: "Let us say in one word to my Lord Willoughby, Captain-General for the King of England in America, that we have nothing further to say to him concerning his demands than what I said in my letter of the ninth instant of which I hold a copy on which is signed his receipt of the original."[4] Enraged at this communication, the Lord of Barbados set sail in high dudgeon, his only word

[4] Du Tertre, *Histoire générale des Antilles*, IV, 348.

of farewell to his hosts being a long-winded document, couched in legal phraseology, by which he entered a formal protest against their high-handed action in refusing to surrender the colony.

On leaving Old Road Town, Willoughby sailed directly to Bridgetown, where word was presently brought to him that the French, fearing they would soon have to surrender the middle section of St. Christopher, were carrying off what portable property they could.[5] He promptly sent Colonel Drax to Martinique with a protest to La Barre, and he received from the Lieutenant-General the following reply. The English part of St. Christopher, so the French commander said, could not be surrendered by Saint-Laurent and Chambré, since the orders to yield the district were addressed to their superior, that is, to himself, who alone could legally turn the territory over to the British representatives. Moreover, according to the terms agreed upon at Breda, the English must first buy back from the French their former properties as well as pay them for the improvements they had made and reimburse them for the food they had furnished for the English prisoners. With regard to the damage done to property, La Barre pointed out that the houses built by the French in the British section since the recent hurricane belonged by right to them, not to the English, and that the French were under no obligation to pay for any of these they might have dismantled; nor should they pay for the movable property they had carried off, since this belonged to them by right of war. La Barre raised no objections to making a formal surrender of the territory to duly authorized representatives of the British Crown, but private individuals must not take possession of their former plantations without paying the French for them. Political jurisdiction might be ceded; not private property.[6]

A month later La Barre was in Guadeloupe. Here he received a visit from Colonel Simon Lambert, one of a quartet appointed by the King to receive the surrender of St. Christopher. To Lambert's request for compliance with the terms of the treaty La Barre gave a refusal. He now appears to have been more exacting in the terms upon which he would surrender than upon previous occasions. He

---

[5] An excellent account of the transactions leading up to the surrender of St. Christopher may be found in Higham, *The Development of the Leeward Islands*, chap. iii.

[6] *C.S.P., America & West Indies, 1661–68*, No. 1764.

demanded that the French be reimbursed for expenses incurred in the care of English prisoners and be paid for certain things the British had taken since the end of hostilities, to wit: thirty-nine Negroes, three thousand florins in plate, movable property taken by Henry Willoughby from Cayenne, and some odds and ends. All this, he said, must be paid for before he would yield anything, even jurisdiction over the territory. To much of this Lambert was willing to agree. He was willing to allow the French to remain in possession of their property until their claims could be settled by the governments at home. Yet, having gained these concessions, La Barre still remained obdurate; he would not yield an inch until the English had paid his fellow countrymen in full for whatever they might claim.[7] Two or three days later, when the Lieutenant-General had moved to St. Christopher, Lambert again approached him, but the Frenchman refused to recede from his position. When this impasse was reached, both parties decided to refer the dispute to their respective governments for further instructions. We can thus leave the question of the surrender of St. Christopher for a moment to glance at the situation into which the war had plunged the West India Company.

The end of hostilities found the company in a precarious condition; indeed, it was on the verge of bankruptcy, and it would have gone under had not the King and Colbert come to the rescue. The report had run like wild fire through the colonies that the corporation was totally ruined and that Governor Houël would soon be reëstablished in Guadeloupe and the Du Parquets in Martinique; then, the company's monopoly broken, Dutch traders would resume their traffic with the islands unrestricted, all to the great advantage of the colonists. Joy at this prospect, however, was short-lived; Colbert would not concede defeat. He had no intention of giving up the fight he had waged against the Dutch and allowing the precious colonies to become appendages of the United Netherlands in all but name.[8]

In the autumn of 1667 the directors wrote Colbert giving him a summary of their financial position, showing a deficit due entirely

[7]*Ibid.*, No. 1775.   [8]Several authorities on the West Indies have stated that Colbert was at this time ready to give up the company, but S. L. Mims quotes several documents to show that such was not the case (*Colbert's West India Policy*, p. 151).

to the war. From trading operations they would have made 500,000 livres during the past four years, but the cost of the war and the losses sustained because of it had more than offset this gain. The statement shows these losses summarized under such heads as "expenses of the war," "sundry losses caused by the war," "destruction by fire of five vessels and their cargoes at Martinique," all of which made a staggering total of 2,222,000 livres and brought the actual deficit of the company to 1,639,860 livres. Obviously help was needed at once if the concern was to be kept going. To meet these losses Colbert immediately advanced 713,000 livres from the royal treasury, which brought the total received that year from various sources up to 1,601,040 livres, of which the King contributed 1,134,000. The number of ships in the company's service had shrunk, after the battle of St. Pierre, from forty to thirty-two, many of which were still unseaworthy after the beating they had received.

Colbert threw himself into the business of reorganization with his accustomed energy. A squadron was dispatched under La Rabesnières de Treillebois to remain in the islands for three months and to break up the trade which the Dutch were carrying on with the colonies. The corporation's policy of keeping all trade in the hands of its own members—a policy held in abeyance during the war—was now broadened to permit all French, as distinguished from foreign, merchants to share in this trade if they would secure a license from the company. An edict to this effect was issued on September 10, 1668. After the return of Treillebois's fleet the King dispatched another under Comte Jean d'Estrées et de Tourpes to see that the ordinance was enforced. Since neither of these men took his duties very seriously, Colbert in desperation at last sent out three vessels under Louis Gabaret with orders "to sink or take or capture all foreign ships sailing in the waters about the islands or attempting to anchor in the roads or harbors of the islands." Gabaret interpreted his instructions in the spirit in which they were written, cruising about the archipelago, seizing everything he could get his hands on, until his rough-and-ready methods drew protests. But in the long run this policy accomplished little; treat them kindly or treat them roughly, the Dutch continued to come.

Changes were also made in the administrative personnel. Jean-Charles de Baas, whose coming had been awaited for so long, at last got under way and arrived at Martinique on February 4, 1669, as a passenger on D'Estrée's flagship. Since he selected St. Pierre for his residence, his presence there made Martinique the capital of the archipelago. During his long incumbency Governor de Poincy had chosen Basseterre, St. Christopher, as the seat of government, while La Barre apparently moved about from place to place without what might be called a fixed home. Martinique as the capital was an improvement over St. Christopher, for the latter was uncomfortably near Nevis and might be captured should another war break out. Moreover, the former island was by far the larger of the two, possessed much greater potential wealth, boasted of a real harbor, and was more centrally located, being nearly midway between the two extremities of the French group. In addition to the title lieutenant-general for the King, De Baas had been given the status of governor-general of the French West Indies; that is, he was to be the ruler of the entire archipelago, the various governors being under his jurisdiction, whereas during La Barre's administration they had been independent, responsible only to the home government. La Barre's authority was purely military and did not extend over the civil administration.

M. de Baas brought with him elaborate instructions for the carrying out of an ambitious program of reorganization. By sending over the Marquis de Tracy and establishing the West India Company the King hoped to rescue the colonies from the chaotic condition into which they had fallen and unite them under that company's authority. This program had been rudely interrupted by the war, and now that peace was restored De Baas was to pick up the loose threads and continue the work begun by De Tracy. The new governor-general was admonished to work in harmony with the officials and councils of the several islands; to maintain the police system where it was already established and introduce it into new territory as fast as it was needed; and to make a careful study of prevalent diseases with a view to improving the health of the colonists. Steps were to be taken to increase the number of settlers by attracting immigrants from France and by encouraging the marriage of young persons. A survey of the plantations was to be made for the purpose of ascertaining what particular crops were yielding a profit and which ones it would be wise to replace with something else. Thus, if agriculture were improved, new acreage would be opened up and the islands could accommodate more colonists. In order to assist those who felt they could make a better living by trade than by farming it was suggested that a reciprocal arrangement might be made with Canada whereby the West Indians could exchange their produce for wood wherewith to build the much-needed ships, for lumber was one important thing in which the Caribbees were lacking. De Baas was to make a careful examination of the plans for defense drawn up by the engineer, Jean Blondel, for the King wished to have at least one good fort on each island—a fort able to protect the French fleet, repel an enemy, and keep the colonists in subjection. He was also to visit each island two or three times a year in order to keep himself posted and to assure the planters that the King wanted only peace and prosperity for them; thus their loyalty to the Crown would be strengthened. The Governor-General was particularly ordered to study the Treaty of Breda with a view to yielding the disputed section to the English and at the same time to impress these neighbors with the power of the French fleet, which was soon to be strengthened in such a manner as to present a serious threat to their commerce, should hostilities break out again. Military drill was to be given close attention, the inhabitants being divided for this purpose into militia companies. A complete census was to be compiled, classified according to localities, race, and sex—this for the benefit of Colbert. Lefebvre de la Barre was to return to his old colonial venture in Guiana, and with him De Baas was to maintain a correspondence, as well as with Governor d'Ogeron of San Domingo, with a view to military coöperation. [9]

Shortly before De Baas's arrival Martinique lost the services of her able governor, M. de Clodoré. For sometime past there had been friction between him and La Barre, and this now came to a head. Clodoré was popular, and during his administration had shown himself to be a capable governor indeed. He had incurred the respect of the Martinicans by his energetic suppression of disorders which had troubled the peace of the island and had served

[9]Clément, *Lettres . . . de Colbert*, III (Part 2), 406–14.

with distinction at the battle of St. Pierre. This may have excited the jealously of La Barre, as some have suggested,[10] but it is just possible that Clodoré was glad to relinquish a post he held under a man he disliked. At any rate, he resigned the governorship and returned to France.

While awaiting the appointment of a new governor, M. de Loubière, lieutenant for the southern part of Martinique, filled the gubernatorial position. The King took his time in selecting Clodoré's successor, and the year 1670 was drawing to a close when Antoine-André de Sainte-Marthe landed at St. Pierre with his commission, his wife, and his six children. M. de Sainte-Marthe was a military man who had served his country with distinction. At the time of his appointment he was nearing sixty years of age, rather old, one would say, to begin a new career; but since he had the confidence of many influential persons, Colbert included, the King did not hesitate to give him a commission. De Baas eyed the new governor with no great enthusiasm. He had had an easy time of it with Loubière as his subordinate, but a stranger coming directly from the King might not be so easy to handle. Fortunately no friction arose, and six months later, in writing to Colbert, the Governor-General gave the new ruler of Martinique due credit for his abilities. In the general shake-up M. de Chambré was replaced by M. Cartier who for some time past had been the company's agent at Bordeaux. Since the company had now decided to conduct its trade as a wholesale business, a large number of clerks and agents were dismissed and the colonists were supplied by two warehouses on each island, situated at strategic points.[11]

If the new governor-general had ever believed his position as ruler of the Caribees would be an easy one, he was soon undeceived. The representative of the company, M. Cartier, proved to be dishonest, intent only upon his own enrichment. He took over some of his employers' property for his own use and accepted bribes paid him by Dutch traders who wished to do business in the islands, contrary to the King's ordinances. Thus the Dutch prospered, while the corporation's vessels lay idle at their anchors. Disgusted with their representative, the directors soon replaced him with a more reliable man. Bertrand Pallu du Ruau, a former official of Tours,

[10]Guët, *Le Colonel François de Collart*, p. 136.   [11]Mims, *Colbert's West India Policy*, p. 156.

was selected for the post. He arrived in 1670 and remained until the dissolution of the company. As a check on him, though he appears to have discharged his duties honestly, the directors sent out one of their own number, a man named Pélissier, with instructions to make a complete survey of the situation. Though M. Pélissier was to occupy himself principally with trade, he had other duties besides. He and Du Ruau were to see what could be done to bolster up the Church, the courts of justice, and the police. In this matter of general reform he had been preceded by De Baas, who had already given some impetus to the moral uplift of the community by publishing an edict regulating the conduct of Protestants, Jews, saloonkeepers, harlots, and other undesirables, whose activities were giving the respectable element some concern.[12] Colbert's fine hand was shown by his suggestion that the French should be discouraged from making any improvements in the disputed section of St. Christopher so that the English would not be so anxious to have it restored to them. Pélissier was also urged to see what could be done to gain control of the islands still the exclusive property of the savages, to wit: Dominica and St. Vincent. Evidently Colbert hoped to steal a march on the English in some manner.

Yet despite the ordinances of the King, the administration of Colbert, and the coöperation of Pélissier, it seemed impossible to exclude the Dutch. Ways were found to circumvent the royal orders and hoodwink the minister. A year after the arrival of De Baas, Louis issued an edict forbidding foreign ships from even lying in French ports or sailing in the vicinity of the islands under pain of seizure and confiscation while French colonists who abetted the Dutch were subject to severe penalties. A year later, when the King learned that French merchants had formed a secret understanding with foreigners whereby the colonists built ships in the islands in which to carry their produce to foreign ports, thereby defrauding the company's vessels of the freight charges, he issued an order by which he hoped to plug this leak.[13] It was all in vain; the company simply could not compete with the Dutch under any system of trade, whether free or restricted, for the planters were

[12]Moreau de Saint-Méry, *Lois et constitutions des colonies françoises*, I, 180–82.
[13]*Ibid.*, pp. 227–228.

determined by hook or by crook to take advantage of the best bargain. It was like defying the law of gravitation. The company system was doomed to failure, and all the schemes to bolster it up which the clever mind of Colbert was able to concoct could not save it from destruction.

When De Baas landed, the problem of the surrender of St. Christopher was nowhere near its final solution. In the spring of 1668 news of the failure of Willoughby to secure the territory reached England, and King Charles promptly wrote the French monarch, requesting that he immediately give orders to his officials in the West Indies to comply with the terms of Breda without further delay. This Louis agreed to do, excusing himself for the delay by saying that it was presumably occasioned by the temporary absence of La Barre. At any rate, he promised to at once issue orders to his Lieutenant-General commanding him to make immediate surrender. In short, His Majesty was most apologetic about the whole business. Scarcely, however, had he dispatched his instructions, when La Barre's account of the affair came to hand. In his letter the Lieutenant-General assured the King of his readiness to yield the island as soon as the planters had been paid for their property. But since this payment, as Colbert could readily see, would call for complicated calculations, the idea occurred to him that he might be able to persuade the English government to relinquish its claims in exchange for some other island or for a sum of money. With this purpose in mind, he sent his brother to London to seek a revision of the treaty. The idea was not entirely new to the English, nor did it appear to them very drastic. Even the British ambassador to the French Court, the Earl of St. Albans, seems to have approved the suggestion, for he wrote Secretary Arlington, pointing out the excessive cost as well as the difficulty of reëstablishing the original owners, now widely scattered, and the great length of time it would take for new colonists to develop the plantations to their former productive capacity. When Charles heard of these negotiations, he decided to strengthen his position by holding up the surrender of Acadia, promised to the French by the treaty, until the affair of St. Christopher was settled one way or another.

In September, Colbert was ready with his proposition. He offered two solutions: one, that the treaty should be carried out as written, the English government to receive the territory, with the understanding that the planters would take possession of their property only when they had reimbursed the French owners; two, that the British should leave the French in possession, being compensated by the cession of some other island or the payment of a sum of money.[14] After mature deliberation King Charles decided to reject any compromise and to insist upon the fulfillment of the treaty. Unable to obtain concessions, Louis accordingly ordered La Barre to make restitution without further ado, under penalty of rebellion. Copies of this order were also sent to MM. de Baas and Saint-Laurent, followed presently by instructions modifying it, for meanwhile Colbert had worked out with the English King a more detailed method of procedure for the transfer. The new plan provided for the appointment by both parties of commissioners with full power to adjust all difficulties and ambiguities arising out of the transfer of and payment for the plantations. The British colonists who had not sold their property to the French, but had left the island, should return immediately and recover their estates, while those who had sold their land should be given a year and a day in which to buy it back. If payment was not made within this time, the French owners could retain the property and continue to live in the English section enjoying the same rights and protection as the English themselves.[15] Such was the state of affairs when De Baas took over the command.

The new governor-general, however, was not as yet called upon to trouble himself greatly about the matter, for a change had taken place in the attitude of the English colonists which delayed still further the final settlement. Lord Willoughby had returned to England without leaving any instructions with his deputy-governor, Christopher Codrington, at Barbados, or with Henry Willoughby, at Antigua. On receiving the King's orders to surrender St. Christopher, De Baas sent a ship to Bridgetown to notify the authorities of his readiness to carry out his master's commands; but there was no one there with the proper authority to accept the transfer. He then requested Henry Willoughby to act during his father's absence, "for," he said, "I intend perfectly

[14]*C.S.P., America & West Indies, 1661–68*, No. 1840.   [15]*Ibid.*, Nos. 1886, 1888.

to repossess you, and reëstablish a firm peace, and [one] of long duration.'' At the same time, he threatened to keep the island until further orders from home if no one came forward within a month to take it over. Like Codrington at Barbados, Willoughby pleaded lack of proper authority, saying he was expecting orders from his father, who was then in England discussing the matter with the King.

This strange *volte-face* on the part of the English was due to the rising influence of a strong faction which had good business reasons for wishing to see the last of St. Christopher. These men were sugar planters with extensive holdings in Barbados, who for some time had regarded the colonists in the northern islands as rivals whom they would like to see eliminated. Why not, then, leave St. Christopher in French hands? Its sugar would then be removed from the British market. The Barbadian agriculturists were therefore opposed to Lord Willoughby's efforts to expand his dominions, fearing they would result in increased sugar acreage and the transfer of some of the labor from Barbados to the new fields. When the commission to settle the vexed question of St. Christopher was appointed in accordance with Colbert's plan, only one of the five members, Philip Payne, of Nevis, was not a resident of Barbados. The commissioners consequently adopted Fabian tactics; for one thing, they could find no ship to take them to St. Christopher, and they refused to budge. The Leeward Islanders, anxious to regain possession of their erstwhile colony, took sides against them and complained to the Council of Foreign Plantations at home. The council took prompt action, dissolved the commission, and appointed a new one, composed this time of men from the northern islands, with only one from Barbados. The rift caused by divergent interests, which had long been growing between the men of Barbados and the men of the north, now resulted in open rupture. The governorship of the Leeward Islands was taken from Lord Willoughby and placed in the hands of Sir Charles Wheler, thus making these islands a group of independent colonies, free from the influence of Barbados which for years had acted as a brake on their economic development. Wheler's commission was signed on January 25 (O.S.), 1671.

In May, Sir Charles set sail, with instructions to settle once for all the St. Christopher affair by taking over the disputed district from the French. After stopping at Barbados, he continued on his way to St. Christopher, whither M. de Baas had preceded him. The French governor arrived on the eighth of July, but he gave no inkling of his presence until five days later, when he sent Pallu du Ruau and several gentlemen to Wheler with the pleasing news that he was ready to surrender the territory to him at any time with appropriate ceremonies. Meanwhile, would the English governor and his staff be his guests at dinner? Wheler, it must be admitted, did not respond in a particularly gracious manner. He refused to set foot on the island for any purpose save to take possession of it, and he dismissed the deputation, saying that he would wait on De Baas the following day. Next morning he sent ashore three high-ranking officers, who made arrangements with De Baas for a meeting at Old Road Town, where a formal restitution of the territory would take place. The Governor-General was as good as his word. On the morning of the fifteenth Governor Wheler landed with his officers and was presented with a document duly signed and sealed by which the middle section of St. Christopher was restored to its original owners. The business of the day thus happily concluded, all proceeded to the Governor's mansion, where a sumptuous banquet was spread. Hosts and guests spent the afternoon drinking each other's health and pledging undying friendship.[16] Thus, after four years of negotiation, seemingly without end, did the English regain possession of their first colony in the Caribbee Islands.

Colbert was now beginning to realize the impossibility of keeping the West India Company afloat. The unseaworthy craft, patched and leaking in a dozen places, was about to founder. The war, the inroads of the Dutch merchants, which no royal edict, no matter how severe, had been able to prevent entirely, the general unpopularity of the corporation, its semi-bankrupt condition—all these things pointed to the handwriting on the wall. As a last attempt to save the wreck, Colbert issued an order forbidding it to engage in any commerce save carrying slaves from the Guinea Coast and livestock and salt meat from France, articles which private traders could not supply. Vessels sent to Africa managed

[16] C.S.P., America & West Indies, 1669–74, No. 586.

to pick up a supply of blacks, which were sold in the Caribbees for a profit, and for a while it seemed as though the minister had hit upon a good idea, for in addition to the French West Indian market there was always a demand for slaves in the Spanish colonies. Yet in the end the business proved but a flash in the pan. Do what he would, the Dutch always underbid him. Nor was the plan to ship meat any more successful. He offered to pay the company four thousand *écus* if it would ship a like number of barrels of meat during the year 1671; but the cost of French beef was too high, and even an edict forbidding the importation of foreign meat into the West Indies, an edict providing corporal punishment for a second offense, could not stem the natural flow of commerce. It was the same also with livestock. A few trifling shipments were made, which served only to raise a cry of protest at the exorbitant prices demanded by the company—nine or ten thousand pounds of sugar for a horse.

At last, early in 1673, a commission was appointed to audit the company's books with a view to winding up its affairs. The work went forward slowly, and it was not until February 21, 1674, that the committee was ready with its report. On that day it handed in a balance sheet showing a deficit of 3,328,553 livres. The King was the heaviest loser, the indebtedness of the company to him being 5,382,628 livres. Liquidation now proceeded apace. The assets brought in a little more than one million livres, just enough, with what the King presently advanced, to reimburse all the subscribers. In this manner, the creditors and owners having been paid off, the colonies reverted to the Crown. This was by no means a bad bargain for the King, for the Dutch offered twenty-four million livres for the property, whereas it had cost the French monarch all told somewhat less the six million. In December, 1674, the company was officially dissolved, and the King became owner as well as ruler of his West Indian domain. [17]

While the directors were attending the last solemn rites for their defunct corporation war broke out in the West Indies. Early in 1672 the Dutch found themselves involved in a struggle against two formidable adversaries: in March, King Charles of England

[17] An account of the dissolution of the company is found in Mims, *Colbert's West India Policy*, chap. vii.

had declared war against them; in April, Louis of France followed suit. This was further complicated by the outbreak of hostilities between France and Spain eighteen months later. In the general confusion engendered by this state of affairs Governor de Baas conceived the idea of attacking the Dutch settlement at Curaçao, which he had been informed was insufficiently protected. It would be wrong to charge him with lack of compunction in attacking a nation whose merchants had so long supplied the French colonists with goods which they had found difficult to obtain even from the company, for he was merely anticipating what the men of Holland presently attempted to do to him, and, moreover, he probably had his orders. Hastily collecting a fleet, consisting of a ship-of-the-line, two frigates, and three transports, he set sail in March, 1673, for St. Croix, where he had ordered Bertrand d'Ogeron, Governor of Tortuga, to meet him with a contingent of his own.[18] En route De Baas stopped at Guadeloupe and St. Christopher to add to his force, which finally reached the total of six hundred men. Ogeron, it so happened, met with misfortune on his voyage to the rendez-vous. His own ship the "Ecueil," carrying three hundred buc-caneers gathered from the more-or-less disreputable elements of his colonies, had foundered off Puerto Rico. The men apparently man-aged to get safely ashore, where they were cruelly treated by the Spanish governor, who allowed many to starve; Ogeron escaped to Tortuga and raised a force of seven hundred men, with which he took his revenge on the Spaniards of Puerto Rico. His consort, however, arrived on time at St. Croix with one hundred men. With his motley collection of colonists and freebooters De Baas set sail for Curaçao. He arrived there on the fourteenth and landed on the northern shore of the Bay of St. Barbara. From the top of a neighboring hill he surveyed the scene of his expected conquest. To his dismay he saw a large fleet in the harbor while he listened to the mournful tale poured into his ears by his engineer, Louis de Gémosat, who explained that the place was impregnable to the limited forces and equipment he had with him. So M. de Baas, like the King of France, having marched up the hill, was obliged to march down again and sail home.

[18]Ogeron was at this time governor of Tortuga and of western, or French, San Domingo which today is called Haiti. We shall discuss his interesting career in the following chapter.

It was not long before the Dutch struck back. From the beginning of the war the States General had realized the serious loss
of trade that would result from their rupture with France and the
enormous gain that would eventually be theirs if they could only
capture the French West Indies. Busy at first with the British fleet
in the Channel, they could do nothing until they had disposed of it.
At the Battle of the Texel in August, 1673, a smashing victory gave
them command of the narrow seas. The following May, peace
having been signed with England, a gigantic armada of sixty-six
ships-of-the-line, eighteen fire ships, and fifty-four assorted vessels
sailed westward by Calais under Admirals Cornelius van Tromp
and Michel de Ruyter. Once in the open sea, the fleet divided; one
squadron, under Van Tromp, headed for La Rochelle; the other,
commanded by De Ruyter, stood out into the Atlantic, bound for
Martinique, which the Dutch commander had visited several
years before while recuperating after his battle off Bridgetown.
Fortunately for Governor de Baas, the French authorities guessed
the Dutchman's intentions and dispatched a fast-sailing frigate to
warn him of the coming danger.

De Ruyter, when he arrived at Martinique, found the French
ready to receive him. He steered for the Cul-de-Sac Royal, in the
southern part of the island, not for Fort St. Pierre, for he believed
from what he had been able to learn on his previous visit that the
former place was the more vulnerable of the two. The Cul-de-Sac
was one of the best harbors in the French possessions, a shelter so
well protected from the seas that vessels found it a Heaven-sent
place of refuge in the most violent storms. At the entrance a promontory, connected to the mainland by a narrow isthmus and rising
about one hundred feet above sea level, juts out from the shore.
On the crest of this hill a modest redoubt, Fort Royal, had been
erected by the late Governor du Parquet. It was an enclosure surrounded by a palisade consisting of a single row of pickets eighteen
feet high, protected from a land attack by a double palisade running
across the isthmus. There were also two batteries; one at the
water's edge faced the bay called the Carénage, which was formed
by the southern side of the promontory; the other faced the main
harbor. The entire armament consisted of forty guns mounted on
rough wooden carriages. The ground just back of it, where the

modern town of Fort de France stands, was at this time a marsh covered with reeds on which a few mean houses stood, buildings which served as warehouses for merchandise. Yet despite its fairly good supply of ordnance, the fort lacked an adequate garrison. It was to remedy this defect that De Baas applied himself as soon as the enemy hove in sight.

When news was brought to St. Pierre that De Ruyter's fleet had arrived off the southern coast and was headed for Fort Royal, De Baas acted with great energy. Though ill, he directed operations from his bed. He sent his nephew De Baas de l'Herpinière with orders to collect what men he could for the defense of Fort Royal. In truth De Ruyter's maneuver had caught the French commander off guard, for he expected the attack would be aimed at the stronghold of the island—St. Pierre. There was little time to lose, and L'Herpinière hastened to the fort. He found in the Carénage four merchantmen under the protection of a thirty-four-gun ship, the "Jeux," commanded by the Marquis d'Amblimont,[19] who immediately offered him his valuable assistance. L'Herpinière was accompanied by Valmenière, the engineer, Gémosat, and last, but not least, old Guillaume d'Orange. The first of these brought with him twenty-two cavalrymen, who were presently joined by eighteen militiamen from Case Pilote and seventy-six from the Cul-de-Sac region. M. d'Amblimont added some of his sailors, the merchantmen contributed a small quota, others came from various places, until the French commander was able to scrape together 161 men capable of giving an account of themselves. He would have had more, if some had not deserted on the way. Fearing some friction might arise between L'Herpinière and Amblimont concerning who was to be in supreme command, De Baas wisely sent Governor de Saint-Marthe to take charge of the assembled forces. The Governor left St. Pierre by boat at five o'clock in the evening and reached Fort Royal early the next morning.

De Ruyter arrived with his squadron on July 19, 1674, at about three o'clock in the afternoon, at least that was when he was first sighted off Anse d'Arlet. Compared to the French forces, his fleet presented a mighty host. It consisted of forty-eight vessels, of which twenty were ships-of-the-line, mounting all told 1,142

[19]Thomas-Claude Renard de Fuchsemberg, Marquis d'Amblimont.

guns and having on board 4,336 sailors and 3,386 soldiers. The flagship carried the Comte de Stirum, who was sent out to act as governor of the West Indies when the Dutch had conquered them. If there were any doubts as to where De Ruyter was to attack— though apparently there were no doubts—they were quickly dispelled the following morning, when he headed boldly into the Cul-de-Sac with the evident purpose of sinking the vessels in the Carénage. The entrance to the Carénage was narrow, too narrow, in fact, for a number of ships to enter at once, so De Ruyter detached three frigates to explore the channel and to feel out the resistance he would have to encounter. A chain of booms had been thrown across the entrance, leaving only a small space through which ships could pass. It was for this opening that the Dutch frigates steered. M. de Sainte-Marthe at once guessed the maneuver. With great presence of mind he ordered two of the merchantmen to be sunk across the channel thus blocking access to the Carénage. At the same time, in order to impress the enemy with the size of his forces, he resorted to the timeworn device of parading a detachment of fifty men with shining muskets up a path leading to the fort, then when out of sight behind a clump of bushes having them wheel back and again march up the path, giving the impression that a large force was joining the garrison.

Foiled in his attempt to force the Carénage, De Ruyter recalled his frigates and decided to sail boldly toward the fort with his entire fleet and put a landing party on shore. For this purpose he swept the ground beneath the redoubt with gunfire, then lowered his boats and sent them away. As they neared the shore, French sharpshooters hidden behind a clusters of reeds opened a galling fire, but despite their excellent marksmanship there were too few of them to prevail against the Dutch, who kept piling in on them in ever-increasing numbers. Sainte-Marthe now called in all his men to hold the place against the coming attack. On landing, the enemy formed two columns: one to make an assault on the palisade running across the isthmus; the other, led by the Comte de Stirum, to capture the fort proper. At this point De Ruyter was guilty of a grievous error. Confident of success, he failed to land his artillery, and he also kept his vessels out of range instead of using his broad-

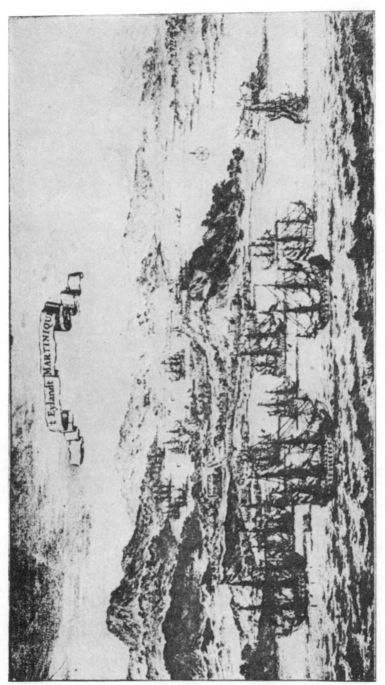

't Eylandt MARTINIQU

DE RUYTER'S ATTACK ON FORT ROYAL, 1674

sides to cover the advancing troops. Nor did he provide scaling ladders for the men detailed to attack the palisade.

Comte de Stirum advanced against the fort with his detachment. He had landed at the foot of the rocky elevation on which the structure was located and sent his men to scramble up the declivity, hoping to take the place by storm. This form of attack, unsupported by artillery, was a difficult one; the defense was comparatively simple. Valmenière and D'Orange, who had charge of the redoubt, knew exactly what to do. As the troops advanced to the foot of the cliff, they let loose volley after volley of musket fire supplemented by an avalanche of rocks that broke the assaulting columns and drove them back to the shore. Here the assailants formed their ranks anew and again attempted to scale the declivity, only to be again repulsed with heavy losses after a half-hour's continuous fighting. By this time the Dutch had had enough, and from the parapet Valmenière could see them gathered on the shore in small groups, inspecting their dead and carrying off their wounded.

A heavier attack was now launched at the palisade where Sainte-Marthe, Gémosat, and L'Herpinière were in command. The militia received the enemy with a rolling fire that quickly drove them to take refuge in a sugar-cane plantation behind the warehouses. It was a safe place, beyond the reach of French muskets; but the Dutch soon engaged in a maneuver that proved their undoing. The warehouses were filled with barrels of rum, which the thirsty troops quickly stove in. The fiery liquor gave them fresh courage, and they poured out into the clearing in front of the buildings, where they made an easy target for the men behind the palisade supported by the guns of the "Jeux" and the "Saint-Eustache," anchored near the shore by Amblimont for this very purpose. There was no withstanding the withering fire of the French, and the Dutch rushed to the shelter of a neighboring cliff to reform their ranks. At the suggestion of L'Herpinière, Amblimont now landed six small guns, which he placed on a mound overlooking the enemy's position. It was indeed high time for such help, for the French militia, impatient because of the non-appearance of reinforcements, said to be on the way from St. Pierre, were becoming discouraged at the sight of such overwhelming odds. Fortunately the guns brought ashore by Amblimont had the desired effect, and by eleven o'clock the danger of a further assault by the drunken troops was over.

At two in the afternoon fresh contingents arrived from the fleet under the command of Rear-Admiral Engel de Ruyter. They made a gallant attempt to capture the fort, but it was hopeless from the very outset. With no artillery to batter a breach in the wall, and the French able to catch them between the fire of their ships on the flank and their own musketry fire in front, the Dutch found it impossible to make any impression on an enemy safely ensconced behind a thick palisade. After having sustained a terrific punishment for two hours, they at last retreated with heavy losses. Not only were the losses heavy but they also included some prominent men, Comte de Stirum and Engel de Ruyter among them. On the French side casualties were amazingly light, only five killed and ten wounded; but among the dead was found the gallant Guillaume d'Orange, one of the oldest habitans of the French colonies, the friend and confidant of D'Esnambuc and Du Parquet, who had seen some forty years of service in the principal islands ruled by France. He was the last of the great pioneers who from the embryo colony of St. Christopher had spread out over the archipelago to build up the French West Indian empire.

When darkness came on, the signal to cease firing was broken out at the masthead of the flagship, and De Ruyter proceeded to reëmbark his troops. It had been a frightful defeat for the Dutch armada, a bitter humiliation for the sea captain whose career had been marked by so many victories. Scarcely a year had elapsed since he had shared Van Tromp's brilliant victory over the British fleet at the Texel, and now he was defeated by a handful of colonial militiamen entrenched behind a third-rate fort. His losses had been enormous, 574 killed and wounded; and to make matters worse dysentery and scurvy took as many more on the voyage home.[20]

During the night many curious things happened. Governor-

---

[20]Quoting the *Mercure hollandois*, 1677, La Roncière gives De Ruyter's losses as 35 officers killed and wounded, 159 men killed, 380 wounded. G. Brandt, *Vie de Ruiter*, gives 143 killed, 378 wounded. La Roncière, *Histoire de la marine française*, V, 595n.

General de Baas heard the sound of firing and could no longer re-main inactive. Though still weak with fever, he gathered a small force and sent it ahead, while he followed with a larger detach-ment. On reaching Fort Royal a strange sight met the eyes of the advance guard. The entire place seemed deserted save for the corpses lying about the field of battle. There was no one to be seen along the shore in the sector occupied by the Dutch, nor did there seem to be any life in the fort, except a sentinel, who was snoring loudly at his post. Gazing out to sea as the dawn broke, they perceived De Ruyter's fleet disappearing in the distance; then, glancing up at the fort, they saw to their dismay the Dutch flag floating high over the ramparts. At the same time a valet of M. de l'Herpinière also happened to see the strange colors and rushed forth to warn De Baas, who was following his advance guard with the main body of troops. Meeting him at Case Pilote, he informed him that Fort Royal was in the hands of the enemy. De Baas did not stop to hear more. Turning about, he rushed his men back to Fort St. Pierre, routed out the garrison, and proceeded with preparations to repel the expected attack.

This is what had happened. When the Dutch retreated from the last assault, Sainte-Marthe called his officers together to make arrange-ments for repelling an attack the following day. There were loud murmurs at this suggestion. No one wished to hold out any longer. Ammunition was lacking, they said; De Baas had sent no rein-forcement; De Ruyter, it was believed, had landed his artillery; it was therefore impossible to hold out any longer. By a strange coincidence, both besiegers and besieged were ready to give up the contest. Sainte-Marthe's men began to desert; the sailors re-turned to their ships, the militia to their homes. As a precaution the guns were spiked, and everything movable was taken from the fort, especially munitions that might be useful to the enemy. The noise made by all this work reached the ears of the Dutch encamped along the shore, and they, fearing a sortie was about to be made, proceeded to put themselves in a state of defense. They broke open the warehouses, rolled out the now empty barrels and hogsheads, and erected a barricade. The pounding, yelling, and general uproar incident to such work was quickly heard by the French, who, thinking the Dutch were preparing an assault, hastened their preparations for departure. By midnight the fort was deserted save for Sainte-Marthe. Seeing the folly of remaining there in solitary grandeur, the Governor detailed a militiaman to stay behind as watchman and to notify him in case of an attack. Then he joined Amblimont on board the "Jeux," where he spent the night in the company of his fellow officers. But before leaving the fort he had, as evidence of the day's victory, planted a captured Dutch flag above the rampart. As the fort became quiet, the Dutch took heart, abandoned their engineering work, and hurried aboard their ships. At dawn Sainte-Marthe and his officers stealthily returned. As they peered over the parapet they saw in the distance De Ruyter's fleet making tracks for the open sea. Then, making their way through the gate in the palisade, they proceeded somewhat shamefacedly to survey the field of battle. The victory was complete; not an enemy remained in sight save a few who, overcome by liquor, were dozing comfortably amid the piles of dead where the struggle had raged the day before.[21]

Humiliated by the defeat of their great fleet, there was nothing more the Dutch could do, and they were obliged to content themselves with minor attacks on the lesser possessions of the French. Two Dutch buccaneers attempted to seize the little fort at Grenada. They put ashore a landing party of one hundred men, armed to the teeth with guns, pistols, cutlasses, grenades, and similar implements, and were proceeding to capture the tiny garrison of eight men, when a French man-of-war slipped unnoticed into the harbor, opened up on the two ships of the freebooters, and soon landed a force of marines that took them into camp. The following year (1676) the Hollanders were more dangerous. A fleet of ten sail under Vice-admiral Jacob Binckes captured Cayenne, landed on Mariegalante, and made an attack on St. Martin, which the French managed to repel. In retaliation the French admiral, Rouxel de Médavy, Marquis de Grancey d'Argentan, though equipped with only a small fleet, caused some damage to the Dutch off Guadeloupe and again off Nevis and rescued the French at Mariegalante. Pieter Constant, one of Binckes's captains, mindful of his success

[21]Labat, *Nouveau voyage aux isles de l'Amérique*, I, 67; La Roncière, *Histoire de la marine française*, V, 587–96; Guët, *Le Colonel François de Collart*, pp. 149–61.

several years earlier,[22] steered with five ships for San Domingo, where he attempted to rouse the unruly inhabitants to "throw off the unbearable yoke of the King." His efforts to assist them in this "laudable" purpose met with no response from the loyal colonists save a volley of musketry. Swarming on board the few armed merchantmen that chanced to be in the bay, they rushed to attack the Dutch in their own element. The gallant effort was in vain, for the Dutchmen outnumbered them, and after twenty-four hours of continual fighting lack of powder compelled the Frenchmen to abandon their ships. On the following day Governor de Cussy arrived from Tortuga with a detachment and managed to rally the inhabitants in time to prevent the Dutch from landing.

During this time the French were not idle. King Louis realized the seriousness of the situation and introduced vigorous measures to defend his islands. He forbade captains of his men-of-war to recruit soldiers and sailors for their crews from the inhabitants of the colonies, for this practice tended to depopulate them. While this may not have been a strictly military measure, it was helpful in the present emergency, when the colonies might need all their man power for defense. When informed of the sailing of Jacob Binckes's fleet from the Netherlands, Louis took steps to check this commander's activities by sending out Comte d'Estrées with a squadron of ten ships, two frigates, and three barks to recapture Cayenne and attack Surinam, Tobago, and Curaçao. Orders were at the same time issued to De Baas commanding him to embark in this armada the eight companies recently sent over and urge colonists to enlist in the coming naval campaign against the Dutch.[23] Since this was to be a temporary undertaking it was not considered that the enlistment of colonists conflicted with the orders previously issued to prevent the depopulation of the colonies. M. de Baas received the news of D'Estrée's appointment with joy, for the Marquis de Grancey had proved insubordinate, trying to play the admiral, as the Governor-General put it, until De Baas had felt obliged to dismiss him. All was therefore in order for complete cooperation between D'Estrées and the Governor-General when the former made his appearance.

[22]For account of this see the following chapter.

[23]Moreau de Saint-Méry, *Lois et constitutions des colonies françoises de l'Amérique sous le vent,* I, 300.

Admiral D'Estrées first made for Cayenne. Arriving there on December 17, 1676, he landed eight hundred men, formed them into two columns, one of which he commanded personally, then attacked the fort. The spirited resistance which the defendants offered lasted but a brief half hour; then, hopelessly outnumbered, they offered to surrender. Leaving a small garrison there under the Chevalier Lefebvre de Lézy, D'Estrées proceeded to Martinique, where he assembled the volunteers from Guadeloupe, St. Christopher, and Tortuga for the annihilation of Jacob Binckes, who was then at Tobago making arrangements with the Caribs of St. Vincent and Dominica for a joint attack on the French possessions.

The island of Tobago is a small island situated some forty miles northeast of Trinidad. Thanks to Daniel Defoe, who placed his famous Robinson Crusoe on its shores, it has enjoyed a renown far out of proportion to its importance. Though included in the Pembroke Patent,[24] it had nevertheless been previously obtained by the Duke of Courland in the reign of James I, and during his proprietorship it was settled by the Dutch. Later these colonists revolted and proclaimed themselves free from the Duke's overlordship. From that time the island had a rather hectic history, its ownership changing hands on several occasions; now it was safely in the hands of the Dutch.

When Admiral d'Estrées set sail from Martinique, his departure was saddened by the death of Governor-General de Baas, who expired on January 24, 1677, at the residence recently given him by the King at Fond Capot, just south of Le Carbet.[25] Governor de Baas's administration had been on the whole a creditable one, distinguished among other things by the construction of public highways, particularly in Martinique. He was, it is true, accused of permitting illicit trade with foreign merchantmen, and there is little doubt that the accusation was a valid one. But there were extenuating circumstances. Neither the West India Company nor the French merchants could keep the colonists properly supplied, and De Baas was unquestionably driven at times to admit Dutch traders out of sheer pity for his own people. At any rate, Colbert,

---

[24]This patent, issued in 1628 by Charles I, granted to the Earl of Pembroke "Trinidado, Tobago, Barbudos, and Fonseca."
[25]This is the date given by Mims; other authorities differ as to the exact day.

who believed the charges against him, was content to keep him in office until his death. Perhaps the minister saw that there were occasions when one must be realistic.

D'Estrées arrived at Tobago on February 20, 1677. During his sojourn in Martinique he had not been idle, for he had obtained from the principal islands a contingent of some three or four hundred men, which more than replaced his casualties at Cayenne. His fleet consisted of ten warships and six lesser craft of various styles and shapes, which mounted in the aggregate 446 guns and carried all told 2,660 men.[26] The Admiral flew his flag from the maintruck of the sixty-gun "Glorieux." Among the prominent captains of the French fleet were Louis Gabaret of the "Intrepide" and Comte Charles de la Roche-Courbon-Blénac, presently to be appointed governor-general of the French islands, who commanded the "Fendant." Binckes's fleet was somewhat smaller in number than the French, and with only 356 guns it had decidedly inferior firing power.[27] The "Bescherming" was the flagship. The number of men comprising the crews was a trifle more than seven hundred, but this must not be compared with the 2,660 of D'Estrées, for the French contingent included land forces to be used ashore, while Binckes also had his land troops amounting to six or seven hundred.

The French admiral had hoped to meet the Dutch fleet in the open sea, where it would not enjoy the protection of land batteries; but on reaching Tobago he learned that it had been in Rockly Harbor for a fortnight. This harbor is situated on the southern shore of the island, near its western extremity, and shelters the modern capital of Scarborough. It is more of a bight than a protected harbor, but it is closed by a reef of submerged rocks through which there is only a narrow channel, requiring the most delicate navigation for those unfamiliar with it. The fort defending the settlement at this time was only partially completed, its rampart surmounted by a row of hogsheads to serve as a temporary palisade.

[26]The warships were: "Intrepide," "Fendant," "Marquis," "Gallant," "Soliel d'Afrique," "Brillant" (some say "Jeux"), "Glorieux," "Precieux," "Emerillon," and "Laurier." Others were: "Fanfaron," "Coche," "Bayonnais," "Entreprenant," "Adroite," and "Assurée."

[27]They were: "Zaager," "Zeelandia," "Alcyon," "Bescherming," "Duke of York," "'t Huis te Kruiningen," "Gouden Monnik," "Middleburg," "Gouden Star," "Popkesburg," "Leyden," and "Sphoera Mundi," and a few others.

It was manned by a garrison of seven hundred men. The Dutch fleet was anchored in the form of a crescent in front of the fort, and back of this line lay two or three merchantmen containing a number of settlers, with their families and slaves, who had sought refuge there from any fighting that might take place on shore. The narrow channel covered by the guns of the fort led to that part of the harbor where the fleet was anchored. D'Estrées, on arriving at Tobago, sailed for the entrance of Rockly Bay, intent on making a surprise attack. Leading the van was Gabaret in the "Intrepide." When entering the channel, this vessel had the misfortune to strike a sunken rock. It was only a glancing blow to be sure, which fortunately did no damage, but the incident cooled the ardor of the captains, who drew off their ships to formulate a less risky plan of attack. As a result of their deliberations they decided, with the Admiral's approval, of course, to land a sufficient force to capture the fort, then to turn its guns on the Dutch ships, while the fleet, which it was hoped could be conned through the channel in some way or other, would attack them from the sea, thus catching them between two fires.

A formidable landing party of seven infantry companies and two hundred marines, commanded by D'Andigny de Grandfontaine, was therefore disembarked under the protecting fire of two vessels to open a path from the shore to an eminence seven hundred paces from the fort, where the little army could survey the enemy from a point of vantage. A brief glance at the situation showed Grandfontaine that the capture of the fort would be a more difficult undertaking than he had imagined, particularly since recent rains had swollen the little river that ran between him and the redoubt. He sent word of this to D'Estrées, who dispatched a hundred men, under Hérouard de la Piogerie, to his assistance with orders to lay a regular siege to the place rather than attempt to capture it by assault. Two days were spent digging trenches. Then La Piogerie reported to his superior that this regular procedure would take at least a week, whereas results could be obtained more quickly if the fleet would attack by sea. An attack by sea, however, presented certain difficulties, for the channel was difficult to navigate. Vice-admiral D'Estrées himself was not a trained seaman, despite his title, and though he was well versed in operations by land he lacked the technical knowledge necessary for carrying out the details of a naval engagement. Fortunately he realized this and, being a wise man, bowed to the opinions of his captains when they pointed out the folly of risking the fleet amid the rocks and shoals of the harbor. In desperation he ordered his barge alongside and started for the shore, hoping to direct a successful attack on the fort. But scarcely had he landed, when a messenger from Louis Gabaret reached him informing him that a pilot had been captured who offered, in consideration for his subsequent freedom, to lead the squadron through the channel. This settled the problem. All now agreed upon the plan for a simultaneous attack by land and by sea.

On the third of March the battle began. Thanks to an onshore wind that permitted the ships to sail directly up the channel, D'Estrées was able, despite its narrowness, to advance in two columns. He himself in the "Glorieux" led the left division, while Gabaret in the "Intrepide" led the right. The gunners held their fire until they had come within pistol shot, for it was D'Estrée's plan to fight at close quarters, grappling and boarding the enemy whenever possible. Whether this was wise or not made little difference, for the harbor was small and there was no opportunity to fight even at a moderate range. The French entered under a fair wind, which drove them toward the Dutch fleet and made it almost impossible for them to retreat. Thus willy nilly they found themselves engaged in a fight to the finish. As each ship approached the battle line it selected an enemy vessel and bore down upon it, dropping anchor within a biscuit's toss to prevent drifting aground in the heat of battle. D'Estrées, on board the "Glorieux," ordered his pilot to steer for the "'t Huis te Kruiningen," largest of the fleet and flagship of the Dutch rear-admiral, Roemer Vlacq. Admiral Binckes's vessel was attacked by the "Precieux." The "Marquis" grappled with the "Leyden," boarded her, drove her sailors down into the hold, and nailed down the hatches. At this moment a red-hot cannon ball set fire to the top hamper, and in a few moments the entire ship was a mass of flames, despite the efforts of the French to extinguish them. Moored to her prize, the "Marquis" caught fire herself before she could escape and blew up, killing the greater part of her crew.

During this time the batteries on the shore supported the fleet by a continuous fire on the French vessels, for the detachments led by Grandfontaine and La Piogerie had failed dismally in their attempts to capture the place. La Piogerie had led his troops in three waves against "a double palisade without rampart or moat." Three separate times did he attack, and on each occasion he was beaten back. In the last assault he was killed outright, leaving the wounded Grandfontaine to lead back what was left of the broken columns. It was this failure that made matters so difficult for the French, for the shore batteries neutralized the superior gunfire which they held over the Dutch.

In the struggle between the "Precieux" and the "Bescherming," flagship of Jacob Binckes, the French vessel was dismasted, and her cable was cut by a stray cannon ball, causing her to drift slowly toward the shore, where she ran aground. Seeing the helpless condition of the ship, her commander, Captain Mascarany, attempted to save the crew in his boats. Two vessels, seeing his predicament, each sent one of their boats, but these could only land the ship's company by making several trips, and once they had got away they failed for some reason or other to return. A third boat arrived and offered to take off a load, but refused to make more than one trip. Frantic at his inability to save the men (mostly wounded) who still remained with him, Mascarany went in a boat to the "Glorieux" to beg D'Estrées to use his authority to secure some means of assistance. The Vice-admiral was sympathetic, but his own position was too critical to permit him to help. He urged Mascarany to do his best to save his men and to burn his ship rather than let her fall into the enemy's hands. The unfortunate captain, after rowing from ship to ship imploring a spare boat or two, was obliged to return to his command empty-handed. Unable to secure the necessary means of transportation, he decided to carry out the second part of D'Estrée's orders. Torch in hand, he called his mutilated crew together, urged those still able to do so to swim for shore, and started to fire his vessel, unmindful of the lives of those who could not escape. A roar of disapproval greeted his decision. The wretched men swarmed about him, wild at the thought of being abandoned on a burning ship, seized his torch, and forced the unfortunate officer over the side while they struck the colors, glad to escape certain death by surrender.

Meanwhile D'Estrées was waging a terrific battle with the "Kruiningen." At first the capture of the Rear-Admiral's flagship seemed easy enough. Running up alongside, the crew of the "Glorieux" had thrown out their grappling hooks and boarded her, driven her men below, and hauled down her flag. Then, as in the case of the "Leyden," a blazing cannon ball embedded itself in the wood and touched off a fire near the powder magazine. The French clambered back on the "Glorieux" and were frantically trying to get her clear of the doomed vessel, when the "Duke of York" in a mass of flames bore down on their other side. Caught between the two ships, they were vainly trying to fend them off, when the "Kruiningen" exploded, blowing out her sides and wrecking the "Glorieux's" stern. D'Estrées, badly wounded, his boats completely wrecked, stood on his quarterdeck waiting for the final explosion that would finish off the "Glorieux." At this moment two sailors succeeded in swimming to one of the enemy's ships and cutting away a boat moored under her stern while she was pouring her broadsides into the French flagship. D'Estrées quickly boarded the little craft with his officers, promising to bring back help for the crew he was abandoning; but scarcely had he cleared the ship when a shot pierced the side of his boat and compelled him to head for shore. Here he landed within musket shot of the fort and managed to reach a little eminence where he could survey the scene of carnage spread out over the bay. The sight before him, however, was more cheering than he had expected, for now the Dutch vessels were catching fire one by one and burning to the waterline or being blown apart by the explosions of their magazines. Before nightfall the entire fleet was destroyed in a general conflagration, all save three, now no more than battered hulks, that sank in the shallow waters of the bay. The number of killed and wounded among the Dutch was estimated at 344 men, besides a large number of colonists and slaves who had taken refuge on board the merchantmen. They lost ten ships, practically the entire fleet.[28]

[28]For descriptions of this battle see Guérin, *Histoire maritime de France*, III, 307–13; La Roncière, *Histoire de la marine française*, V, 652–59; Saint-Yves, "Les Campagnes de Jean d'Estrées," *Bulletin de géographie historique et descriptive*, 1899, No. 2, pp. 217–46.

As D'Estrées stood on the shore watching the outcome of the struggle, he realized that his victory was not complete. The Dutch had fought with all the stubbornness of the Beggars of the Sea, allowing their ships to be sunk or burned rather than surrender them; and when night closed in and their fleet lay beneath the waters of the harbor they still held the fort, thanks to the gallant resistance of the garrison. It had been a costly victory, or partial victory, if one prefers, for the French. They had lost the "Glorieux," the "Precieux," the "Intrepide," and the "Marquis." Eight hundred men, land troops as well as sailors, were killed or wounded, Louis Gabaret among the former. It was a terrible price to pay for the sinking of the Dutch fleet, especially since the French found it impossible to take the fort. Unable to do any more at this time, D'Estrées decided to rest on his laurels for the present, so he gathered together the remnant of his squadron and set sail for Brest, determined to return at a later day and finish the job. During his absence Tobago continued to be the headquarters of Dutch buccaneers who preyed upon French shipping.

Early in October, D'Estrées was in Brest with another fleet ready to sail for the West Indies to complete the work he had begun. It consisted of eleven ships-of-the-line and six flutes. D'Estrées chose the "Terrible" as his flagship, while his second-in-command, the Marquis de Grancey, who replaced Louis Gabaret, selected the "Tonnant." The Comte de Blénac boarded the "Belliqueux," with a commission from the King appointing him Governor-General of the West Indies to succeed M. de Baas. Setting sail on the third, the fleet proceeded to Tobago, stopping on the way at Goree, Cape Verde, to destroy the Dutch post established there. On the sixth of December the Admiral reached his destination, where he was joined by what was left of his former fleet, four ships all told. He was not altogether ignorant of the situation before him, for he had stopped a few days at Barbados, where he picked up some useful information regarding changes which had been made at Tobago since his previous campaign. The fleet anchored in a little harbor called by the French Anse des Palmistes, situated two leagues distant from the fort. Here a detachment of 550 men under Blénac's command was put ashore to make a surprise attack. On landing, D'Estrées learned that Binckes had taken complete charge of the entire establishment, though his navy now consisted of only two ships, salvaged from the wreck of battle, and three small vessels. In order to prevent quarreling over precedence Grancey and Blénac alternated between command of the land forces, which were to do the actual fighting, and command of the fleet, now anchored in battle formation in case a squadron, reported to have sailed recently from Holland, should appear unexpectedly. D'Estrées, of course, retained supreme command over all. Two days later the rest of the troops were landed, bringing the total up to 950 men, not counting officers. They brought with them the necessary artillery and siege machinery. With great difficulty the heavy apparatus was moved a distance of four miles to a hill a hundred paces from the fort, where the guns were set up within easy range. Fearing the Dutch might force their French prisoners to serve against their own countrymen, D'Estrées sent word to Binckes that he held four hundred Dutchmen he had taken at Cape Verde and would regard them as hostages against any such action.

The weather was not propitious for an attack. Torrential rains were pouring down, dampening the spirits of the men and making transportation well-nigh impossible. Yet despite these obstacles a battery was constructed, and the bombardment began. The chief gunner offered odds that he would blow up the fort at the third shot and proved as good as his word. The first bomb cleared the fort by a wide margin; the second fell short; then, having got his range, he dropped the third into the powder magazine, which exploded with tremendous effect killing Admiral Binckes and some two hundred and fifty men. Before the Dutch could rally from the blow the French advanced and swarmed over the place, capturing ships as well as the fort. The prisoners taken numbered six hundred, and in addition there were those captured at Goree. D'Estrées computed the enemy's losses in both this and in the former battle at fifteen hundred persons who perished by fire and sword as well as six or seven hundred who died from disease after the first engagement. Captured or destroyed were sixteen ships of various sizes, while the fort yielded forty-five guns and, together with what could be salvaged from the wrecks, about thirty thousand bullets. Dutch power in the West Indies was well-nigh broken.[29]

[29]Account of D'Estrées in Dessalles, *Histoire générale des Antilles*, II, 6–9.

Vice-admiral D'Estrées was now riding on the crest of the wave; one more blow, the destruction of Curaçao, and the Dutch trader would be swept from the Caribbean Sea. After leaving Tobago, he visited Grenada and St. Christopher; then in April, 1678, he put into Martinique, where he organized his expedition against Curaçao. From St. Pierre he forwarded a message to the Governor of San Domingo, asking him to send a detachment of buccaneers to St. Christopher, the rendezvous for the coming undertaking. It was here, on the seventh of May, that he found himself at the head of eighteen of the King's ships, supported by a thousand buccaneers in twelve of their own vessels. The arrival of this imposing fleet caused consternation among the English colonists. Rumors had reached them of an impending rupture between the Crowns of England and France, and they felt themselves too far outnumbered for comfort. The situation was indeed serious; the French King had even gone so far as to warn Blénac to be ready to seize the English portion of the island should war be declared. Fortunately for them, Blénac chose to disregard the warning and offered Governor William Stapleton of St. Christopher a treaty stipulating that both colonies should remain at peace despite hostilities in Europe. Stapleton signed without argument, and England later ratified the agreement; but the French King was in no mood for peaceful arrangements, and the entire matter was dropped. The treaty of peace, signed three months later between the two governments, fortunately put an end to any possibility of attack.

Four days after leaving St. Christopher, D'Estrées was off the coast of Venezuela, headed for Curaçao. Perhaps his recent successes had gone to his head and made him forget that he was, after all, no seaman and led him to spurn the advice of men better qualified than he to navigate a fleet. On the evening of the eleventh of May he replied to the observation of his flag captain that there was no one on board familiar with these waters by giving abrupt orders to head directly for the island of Orchilla. He believed himself to be twenty leagues north of this island and refused to heed his pilot's warning that they were well to the west of it. At nine o'clock, while the fleet was proceeding slowly, a signal gun was fired from a buccaneer vessel ahead of the flagship. The signal was unmistakable; the buccaneer had struck a reef. The "Terrible" veered off, but too late; she too was soon fast on the rocks. When day broke a desolate scene presented itself. Of the powerful armada that had sailed so confidently from St. Christopher a few days before one could see seven ships-of-the-line, three transports, and three buccaneers fast on the jagged rocks of the Isle of Aves. The great French fleet was destroyed.[30]

Fortunately for the French, the Dutch could not take advantage of the catastrophe to regain their possessions, for negotiations for peace had already begun. In the preceding November, William of Orange had married the niece of Charles II, and the Dutch prince had at once approached his uncle-in-law with a view to detaching him from his alliance with France. Under pressure of public opinion Charles at last signed an agreement with the Netherlands, and Louis XIV, finding himself isolated, placed his signature to the Treaty of Nymwegen on August 10, 1678. The treaty signed on this day proclaimed the peace between France and the States General. It dealt primarily with European affairs, but under Article VII each party was to retain whatever territory it held at the time the treaty was signed, whether such territory was in its possession when the war broke out or had been captured during the conflict. This gave the French Tobago and Cayenne.[31] Had D'Estrées avoided the reefs of Aves, Curaçao might have fallen to him, thus giving the French complete control of the Dutch West Indies. Five weeks later, on the seventeenth of September, to be precise, a further treaty was signed between France and Spain, one in which no mention was made of the West Indian situation. Thus all belligerents in the recent struggle were now officially at peace. After the treaty of Nymwegen the Dutch merchantmen ceased to be serious factors in the Caribbean trade. Excluded from the British islands by the Treaty of Breda, they now found themselves cut off from the French: Colbert's anti-Dutch policy had triumphed at last. Thereafter the struggle in the Caribbees was confined to France and England.

[30]Account of the shipwreck is given in a letter of Sieur de Méricourt, June 2, 1678, reproduced in Dessalles, *Histoire générale des Antilles*, Vol. II.
[31]Vast, *Les Grands traités du règne de Louis XIV*, II, 56.

V

HAITIAN INTERLUDE

IT IS NOW TIME to leave the Caribbee Islands for a while and turn our attention to San Domingo, with its appendant, Tortuga, to which we have frequently had occasion to refer. San Domingo was a Spanish colony, the oldest in the Western Hemisphere. Its capital, a town of the same name, known today as the city of Trujillo, is located on its southern side. As the western and northern parts of the island received little attention from their owners, there gathered here a group of outcasts and castaways who had bound themselves together into a loose-knit brotherhood and managed to eke out a livelihood by hunting the wild cattle that roamed through the mountains. These men was called *boucaniers* by the French, from which we get our word "buccaneers." Off the coast of San Domingo lies the little island of Tortuga, first claimed by the Spaniards, then by the English, who attempted to settle it, then occupied by the French, who drove out the English.[1] In the year 1654 it was taken from the French by the Spaniards, who attempted to make it a permanent possession. But the following year, when Admiral Penn bore down on San Domingo to effect its capture, the Governor called in all the outlying colonists for the defense of his province, and the settlers of Tortuga, in responding to his call, abandoned the place, having destroyed the buildings and blown up the fort.

Two years after the departure of the Spanish garrison an Englishman named Elias Watts (Du Tertre called him Elyazoüard), filled with the laudable ambition to found a colony with himself as its ruler, sailed from Jamaica which Penn had captured in 1655 for the British Crown. Chancing to find Tortuga deserted, he

[1] For the early history of Tortuga see Crouse, *French Pioneers in the West Indies*, chap. v.

settled there with his family and ten or twelve colonists in the
year 1656. Prospects appeared good, and Watts soon returned to
Jamaica, where he obtained from Governor William Brayne[2] a
commission as governor of his island. Armed with this authority,
he brought back some one hundred and fifty men to form the
nucleus of his settlement.

The venture prospered; Frenchmen as well as Englishmen were
attracted to the island, and gradually the colony grew in numbers
until, three years after its founding, its members felt strong enough
to launch an attack on their Spanish neighbors. The *casus belli*
was a grievance that for some time had rankled in their bosoms. A
Spanish captain, it seems, had captured a handful of Frenchmen
who were proceeding peacefully from Tortuga to the Leeward Islands and put them to death after having promised upon oath to
keep them unharmed. When the time was ripe for a reprisal, the
Tortugans were able to muster a force of four hundred men. The
personnel of the expedition was drawn almost entirely from the
French element of the population and placed under a Frenchman,
a certain Captain de l'Isle. A commission was secured from Elias
Watts, who was not unwilling to share in the expected booty,
and a handsome frigate which happened to be in the harbor was
commandeered to transport the little army to San Domingo. The
specific objective was the town of Santiago, a prosperous community located in the northern part of the island. The venture was
in all probability little more than a marauding expedition with a
quasi-legal status, launched for the purpose of robbing a wealthy
neighbor; the outrage perpetrated on the French some years before was advanced merely to give it the appearance of being inspired by a lofty motive, if one can consider revenge more lofty
than gain.

The sea voyage was a short one, and the buccanners landed and
marched some twenty leagues through the Haitian jungle, only to
reach their objective on the eve of Good Friday. Undeterred by the
sacredness of the season, they attacked the town under cover of
darkness, killed some twenty-five or thirty persons who were
rash enough to oppose them, and captured the Governor in his

---

[2]*C.S.P., America & West Indies, 1661–68,* No. 817, gives the name as Bryant, but this is
probably an error.

house before he had time to rise from his bed. The wretched man expressed surprise at this attack, for he had just received word of the cessation of hostilities between Spain and France; but the French were ready with an answer, pointing out that they were acting under an English commission. Then they advised him to prepare for death. While the Governor was kneeling in prayer, it dawned on his tormentors that he might be worth more to them alive than dead. They suggested that he pay a ransom, and he agreed to give over everything he had. The amount was fixed at sixty thousand pieces-of-eight, part of which was immediately paid in leather and hides, while the balance was to be paid in silver as soon as the Governor could raise it. While awaiting final payment the French proceeded to loot the place. Bells, ornaments, and sacred vessels were taken from the churches, and private houses were robbed of whatever valuables they contained. After twenty-four hours spent in pillage the buccaneers started forth on their return journey.

Meanwhile news of the attack had spread throughout the neighborhood, and upwards of a thousand men had rallied from the various settlements to cut off the retreat. Throwing themselves across the road taken by the retreating French, they formed an ambuscade. Though taken by surprise, the buccaneers did not hesitate for a moment, for they well knew they could expect no quarter. They were excellent marksmen and, though outnumbered three to one, managed to keep up such a galling fire that their enemies after two hours of fighting were willing to draw off for a breathing spell, leaving a hundred or so of their men dead on the field. At this point the French decided to play their trump card. Bringing forth their prisoners, among whom was the unfortunate governor, they threatened to dispose of them at once if another shot was fired. This ended the battle at once. Anxious to save the lives of their countrymen, the Spaniards retreated, allowing the French to make their way unmolested to the sea. A few days later, after waiting somewhat naïvely for the money due them for the Governor's ransom, they released all their prisoners, satisfied with the loot they had already taken. The outcome of the expedition was rather curious. Pleased with their success, the buccaneers decided to reward their commander. Some presented him with rings,

others with plate, still others with various jewels, until he became wealthy enough to return to France to enjoy his fortune. He
embarked on an English ship; but during the crossing her captain,
anxious to secure his property, picked a quarrel with him and
threw him overboard. His fate was symbolical of what happened
to many others, for, strange to say, no member of this expedition,
so DuTertre tells us, ever prospered from his share of the booty,
and many died in misery.[3]

The success of Elias Watts as a colonizer did not fail to arouse
envy. Tortuga had once been French, and the French could not
allow it to pass quietly into the hands of another nation without
making some effort to regain it. There happened to be in France at
this time an adventurer named Jérémie du Rausset,[4] who had been
a member of the original band that settled on the island twenty
years earlier. Du Rausset, anxious to save the island from foreign
control and incidentally to carve out a province for himself, obtained from the King on November 26, 1656, a commission appointing him Governor of Tortuga. This, however, he feared would
not be enough, for Watts was popular with his people, and they
might not submit tamely to his being set aside by an outsider,
especially as he had the backing of the Governor of Jamaica and
consequently some standing with the English government. Du
Rausset therefore proceeded to London, where he managed in
some manner or other to persuade the Crown to give him an order
authorizing Jamaica to recognize him as the lawful ruler of Tortuga
on condition that he would grant the English colonists the same
privileges as the French. Returning then to La Rochelle, Du
Rausset raised a company of thirty men, with whom he took
passage (in 1659) for Jamaica. There he showed his credentials to
Governor Edward d'Oyley and obtained from him the commission
he sought. When Elias Watts heard of this, he became panic
stricken, seized a ship lying in the harbor, placed his family and
property on board, and set sail for New England, abandoning the
colony he had hoped to rule.

After the departure of his rival Du Rausset had no trouble in
taking over the government; in fact he moved in the day after

[3]Du Tertre, *Histoire générale des Antilles*, III, 130–34.
[4]Jérémie Deschamps de Moussac et du Rausset.

Watts had taken leave. Unfortunately he found it impossible to make a prolonged stay; his health forced him to seek a more secluded spot, and he selected a quiet place on San Domingo, probably near modern Port au Prince, where he could recuperate. He left the command in the hands of his nephew, Frédéric Deschamps de la Place. During his absence Colonel James Arundell, son-in-law of Elias Watts, declared Tortuga too valuable a colony to be abandoned without a struggle. Being a man of spirit, he applied to Governor d'Oyley for help and succeeded in persuading him to sponsor an expedition against the island on the ground that the French had torn down the English colors and run up those of France. This act of hostility came as something of a surprise to D'Oyley, for he had given Du Rausset an English commission with the understanding that the Frenchman would act as a representative of the English Crown, not knowing, perhaps, that he also had authority from the King of France. At any rate, Arundell had no difficulty in securing the Governor's blessing for his undertaking, though he could get no actual help. Early in the year 1662 he got together some thirty men on his own responsibility and started forth to try his luck. Landing on the island he marched his men to the commander's house in the dead of night, hoping to seize La Place and force him to surrender; but the Frenchman, by good fortune, was absent when they arrived. On hearing the uproar caused by the invaders, he collected his men, surrounded his own house, and captured the landing party without striking a blow. La Place did not deal severely with the intruders. Placing them on board their ship, he ordered them back to Jamaica, glad to be rid of them at so small a cost. On their way back they were taken by Spaniards, who carried them to Puerto Principe, Cuba. After a month's imprisonment there Colonel Arundell was murdered.

Undaunted by the failure of Arundell, the colonists of Jamaica made yet another attempt to recapture Tortuga. When their next governor, Thomas Windsor, received an order from the King commanding him to "use his utmost endeavors to reduce said Frenchmen and said island to obedience," the Council promptly concurred in this by passing a resolution to bring the place under its jurisdiction. In truth, Jamaicans were beginning to fear Tortuga as a rival, for it was a port where privateers could take their prizes and buy supplies instead of bringing their trade to Jamaica. The situation was further complicated by a recent order from the King forbidding the colonists from fitting out buccaneering expeditions against the Spaniards; because of this Tortuga would now become the headquarters of the lucrative privateer business.

There are twenty privateers of all nations under the protection of Jamaica, [runs a contemporary document] which being now debarred from taking in their prizes there, will from Tortudos [Tortuga] take French and Portugal commissions or none at all, and will hinder all trade to and from Jamaica and obstruct Spanish ships from going there to buy negroes. In fine, if Tortudos be not reduced to the obedience of the Governor of Jamaica, it will cause the ruin thereof and the harboring of rogues and pirates who make it [piracy] their living, by which means the inhabitants of Jamaica will desert the country. This may be prevented by demanding Tortudos with two of the King's ships from Jamaica, which may very easily be done, as there are but 150 Frenchmen and one fort with four guns, and it is certain if demanded the island will be delivered.[5]

Preparations for an expedition against Tortuga were therefore rushed to conclusion. The details concerning this undertaking are very meager, for Tortuga was of no particular importance to the home governments, and an elaborate report of the affair was not considered necessary. Furthermore, since King Charles had no desire to make an issue of the matter with the powerful King of France, the expedition was organized in a semiofficial sort of way by the Jamaican authorities. The Deputy-Governor started the ball rolling on December 26, 1662, by a proclamation which authorized Robert Munden, captain of the frigate "Charles," to transport Colonel Samuel Barry and Captain Abraham Langford to Tortuga. So far as the capture of Tortuga was concerned, the venture appears to have been a failure; but Langford eventually reached Petit-Goave, a French settlement located on the southern side of the huge Gulf of Leogane, which indents the western coastline of San Domingo, where he was elected governor by the buccaneers living there and unfurled for the first time the English flag on this island.[6] Langford stayed here for about two years, making occasional efforts to get control of Tortuga, with little, if any, support from Jamaica. He was not well regarded there, being described by one influential colonist in the following manner: "Captain Lang-

[5]*C.S.P., America & West Indies, 1661-68*, No. 817.   [6]*Ibid.*, No. 474.

ford speaks not French, nor does he understand it; he is a man of no wisdom, his interest in Jamaica and [his] person [are] despicable, his fortune forlorn, his honesty questionable." But while Langford was thus struggling with a hopeless situation, events were transpiring in France which led to the acquisition of Tortuga and San Domingo by the West India Company.

We left M. de Rausset sunning himself at Port au Prince in a valiant effort to regain his health. Apparently he had little success in this, for it was not long before we find him in France, where he was soon in trouble. When the West India Company was formed, it tried to acquire Tortuga as one of the French possessions; but for some reason or other, perhaps it was a question of price, Du Rausset was unwilling to sell his interest and offered the colony to England for £6,000. For this lack of patriotism he was placed in the Bastille. A year in this institution evidently brought him to a more reasonable frame of mind, for he wrote a letter to Colbert, couched in the most respectful, if not humble, terms, requesting the minister to dispose of his person and his interest in Tortuga as he might see fit. This was all Colbert wanted. Du Rausset was immediately released from prison, and he lost no time in signing, on November 15, 1664, a bill of sale transferring his ownership of the island to the company for 10,000 livres.[7]

Having thus disposed of Jérémie du Rausset, the directors of the company proceeded to secure the appointment of a man highly recommended to them by M. de Clodoré as governor of their newly acquired property. This was Bertrand d'Ogeron de la Bouëre, a man destined to a brillant career as ruler of San Domingo. Bertrand d'Ogeron was a native of Anjou who had served in a regiment of the Marine. Some eight years before his appointment he had been asked by a group of adventurers to put some money into a scheme for maintaining a colony already founded in the Western Hemisphere and to take charge of the colony in person. He fell in with the plan and sailed to Martinique, where he learned to his chagrin of the failure of the colony. Having no place to go, he decided to settle here under the kindly rule of Governor du Parquet and acquire the Quartier du Cul-de-Sac. Though promised this dis-

[7]Ravaisson, *Archives de la Bastille*, pp. 435–37; F. Funck-Brentano, *Les Lettres de cachet à Paris*, p. 26.

trict by the Governor himself, the promise was presently with-
drawn, owing, so it was said, to some objections raised by Mme du
Parquet. In place of this Ogeron was offered another *quartier*.
Angered at the treatment he had received, he refused it, and falling in with some buccaneers, he moved with his people to San
Domingo. He was wrecked off Leogane, not far from Petit-Goave,
and lost all the expensive equipment in which he had invested his
money. He returned at once to France, bought a fresh load of supplies, and was soon back in San Domingo. Finding that during
his absence his colonists had been provided for by passing ships,
he took his cargo to Jamaica and placed it in the hands of an agent,
by whom he was roundly swindled. Nothing daunted, Ogeron
again returned to France and again raised a band of men which he
transported to San Domingo, where he presently established settlements at Leogane, Petit-Goave, and at Port-à-Margot on the
northern coastline near Tortuga. Financially this venture, like his
previous one, was not a success. He lost money; then by good
fortune the West India Company took over the colony and had
him appointed governor.

M. d'Ogeron received his commission in February, 1665. He was
then in San Domingo, probably at Port-à-Margot, busy with the
affairs of his unprofitable colony, and he must have been well
pleased to learn that a powerful company would now assume the
financial risks, at the same time naming him its representative.
Since the principal settlement was then at Tortuga, Ogeron sent a
messenger there in June armed with a *lettre de cachet* from the King
ordering La Place to surrender the settlement to the agent of the
new owners. Du Rausset's nephew complied, without the slightest
ill feeling at seeing himself thus deprived of his command. He
called the inhabitants together, introduced the new incumbent,
whom they greeted with enthusiastic cries of *Vive le Roi et Nosseigneurs de la Compagnie des Indes Occidentales*, and handed over the
command to him. In this manner was Bertrand d'Ogeron, called by
Du Tertre the true founder and father of the French colony of San
Domingo, inducted into office.

The problem which confronted Ogeron demanded the greatest
skill. Tortuga, the capital, had but 250 inhabitants, Port-à-
Margot about 150, and Leogane perhaps 120. They were men who

had settled in these places with the hope of developing a plantation or building up some sort of trade; in other words they were *habitans* as distinguished from the *boucaniers* of the hinterland. Shortly after Ogeron's arrival he thus describes the latter class, which it was now his duty to bring under the jurisdiction of the government and the company.

Seven or eight hundred Frenchmen [he explained to Colbert] are living along the shores of this Spanish island in inaccessible places surrounded by mountains, or huge rocks, or the sea and go abroad everywhere in little canoes. They live three or four or six or ten together, more or less separated one group from the other by distances of two or three or six or eight leagues wherever they find suitable places, and live like savages without recognizing any authority, without a leader of their own, and they commit a thousand robberies. They have stolen several Dutch and English ships which has caused us much trouble; they live on the meat of wild boars and cattle, and grow a little tobacco which they trade for arms, munitions and supplies. Thus it will be necessary for His Majesty to give an order which would compel these men to leave the Spanish island. They should be ordered under pain of death to settle in Tortuga which they would do without doubt if it were fortified.[8]

As an additional penalty, he went on to say, merchants should be forbidden to trade with these buccaneers while they remained in San Domingo.

Besides the *boucaniers* proper there was yet another class, called the *flibustiers*,[9] which gradually absorbed the *boucaniers*, until the term "buccaneer" can be safely applied to both. These *flibustiers* were a free-lance group of sea rovers—Charlevoix speaks of them as "corsairs"—who had drifted, no one knows how, to San Domingo, where they formed a sort of organization known as the "Brothers of the Coast," at least that was the name used in describing them. As a rule they were the type of men who chafe under the restrictions of civilized communities. They were bold, carefree, unscrupulous, poor colonists, but grand fellows for daring ventures. At first they carried on their marauding expeditions in boats accommodating twenty-five or thirty men, with which they were able to capture seagoing ships and enlarge the scope of their activities. South of San Domingo lay the Spanish Main, its

---

[8]Ogeron to Colbert, July 20, 1665; quoted in Vaissière, *Saint-Domingue*, pp. 18–19.
[9]According to some authorities the French transformed the word "freebooter" into "flibustier," then the English took "flibustier" and transformed it back into "filibuster."

opulent settlements and wealthy towns offering untold opportunities for the exercise of their talents. Being for the most part Englishmen and Frenchmen, they regarded their attacks on Spanish property as semiofficial warfare, and in truth it was so considered by the governments at home. With the signing of the Treaty of Madrid between England and Spain in 1670, the English, in compliance with the articles of that agreement, made serious attempts to put a stop to these piratical expeditions, and ten years later the French grudgingly strove, at least officially, to follow suit, though for various reasons it proved impossible to suppress the evil entirely. Gradually, as governments came more and more to frown upon these activities, the more substantial element among the buccaneers turned to legitimate enterprise, while those who remained in the business degenerated into mere pirates, outlaws who preyed on all commerce and were hunted in turn by the navies of all nations.

The buccaneers—we shall now use the term to describe both *boucaniers* and *flibustiers*—organized their expeditions according to an elaborately worked out system. When starting out on a venture, word to that effect was spread about the community and all who wished to go gathered on board the ship selected, each with his supply of ammunition. Food was then obtained by a forceful levy on the local stores and hog-pens. Articles of agreement were drawn up at a general meeting and were scrupulously obeyed by the members of the undertaking, who generally observed toward each other a loyal and generous attitude. These articles specified the share each man was to have in the expected booty, the share being governed by the position he held in the ship's company. In addition to this, a system of compensation insurance had been evolved which provided for the payment of certain sums in addition to his regular share to any man suffering loss of limb. Beginning with a right arm, valued generally at six hundred pieces-of-eight, the scale ran down to mere fingers, worth only one hundred. The articles were sworn to by all members of the company, who solemnly promised never to conceal anything they might take during the expedition or withhold it from the common fund. In the early days the crews elected their captain and deposed him at will; but by the time the English had established themselves at Jamaica and the French, beginning with Ogeron, at Tortuga, buccaneering ventures sailed under commissions issued by the governors of these places which gave them a certain legal standing, and in these cases the captain was appointed by the governor who reserved one-tenth of the profits for his office.

Since these lawless elements formed the backbone of his colony, it is easy to see that Governor d'Ogeron's task was no sinecure. It was his duty to call in the *boucaniers* from their roving existence and persuade them to adopt the more orderly life of planters and also, which was perhaps still more difficult, to control the wild impulses of the *flibustiers*, who held a nice balance between the threat they offered to the stability of the colony, the wealth they brought it in the shape of plunder, and the protection they afforded it in time of war. His task was made all the more difficult by his position as representative of the West India Company, for despite the enthusiastic cheers for *Nosseigneurs de la Compagnie* given when the news of his appointment was received at Tortuga, these men soon developed the same dislike for the corporation as had the colonists of the Leeward Islands. Moreover, they did not relish the King's prohibition of trade with the Dutch. As free spirits, they demanded the right to trade with whomsoever they wished. Fortunately Ogeron was blessed with qualities that won the confidence of these intractable natures. Not only did he attach them to his person but also in the long run succeeded in instilling them with a liking for the government and due respect for its laws, which for years they had not considered binding on their actions.

To wean these men away from their wanderlust and encourage them to adopt the life of habitans Ogeron, like other administrators similarly situated, appealed to the company for wive Thes. directors promptly showed their approval of the request by sending over some fifty eligible girls. The quality of these ladies is open to question and was seriously debated by historians for some time thereafter. Moreau de Saint-Méry, writing in the romantic vein of a Chateaubriand, says:

In order to tame the intrepid conquerors of San Domingo Ogeron called in the help of that powerful sex which always knows how to soften man and increase his yearnings for sociability . . . he obtained from France a supply of charming creatures, timid orphans, to bring to heel these arrogant men accustomed to rebellion and change them into sensible husbands and virtuous father of families.[10]

Baron Wimpffen, however, evidently under the influence of the school of realism, gives an entirely different impression. In writing to the Duke of Wurtemberg about the directors' selection of Ogeron as governor he says:

The choice of women was less diffcult to make. France, at that time, abounded with poor, industrious, and modest females, whose sweet and ingenuous dispositions would have softened, nay, purified the morals of men, rather improved than corrupted. What, Sir, did they do? They sent some prostitutes from the hospitals, abandoned wretches raked up from the mud of the capital, disgusting compounds of filth and impurity of the grossest kind. And it is astonishing to me, that their manners, as dissolute as their language, are not perpetuated in their posterity to a greater degree than they appear to be.[11]

With such extremes of opinion, the true character of these ladies can never be discovered. The buccaneers themselves were probably not greatly concerned over the matter, important as it may appear to posterity; they took what was offered and asked no questions. On the whole the women seem to have had a steadying influence on the men they married, while they themselves acquired some of the virtues of the frontier. They developed, or at least many of them did, into amazons who could shoot, ride, and hunt with their husbands. Unfortunately the company did not follow up its first shipment with others, so that when a lull came in the marauding expeditions a number of young men drifted away to colonies where women were more plentiful.

Governor d'Ogeron's activities in behalf of his people took many forms. He noticed that some buccaneers continued to live their wandering lives because of inability to obtain the necessary means for settling down. To meet this condition he urged the company to advance funds, and in some cases he even financed prospective settlers out of his own pocket. When he became governor there were about four hundred men at Tortuga and San Domingo; four years later there were fifteen hundred, thanks to the three hundred persons he brought in each year at his own expense, and this he did while the war between England and France was raging.

[10]Quoted in Vaissière, *Saint-Domingue*, pp. 21–22.
[11]Wimpffen, *A Voyage to Saint Domingo*, pp. 81–82.

On one occasion he purchased two ships, into which the colonists loaded their produce; and when the vessels returned with a supply of merchandise, he distributed it among the settlers, exacting only a verbal promise of payment to be made whenever the buyer could raise the money. He did everything in his power to increase the number of the inhabitants. Certain colonists who were in his debt were allowed to discharge their obligations to him by returning to France for the purpose of securing indentured servants and merchandise which they could afterward sell in the colony. A regulation was issued at his suggestion forbidding any planter from employing more slaves than Frenchmen, for the practice of giving preference to the cheaper black labor had discouraged the importation of white servants, thus diminishing the fighting strength of the colony in the face of Spanish San Domingo and weakening the white population against a possible slave revolt. Ogeron also made many excellent suggestions to the company, which were approved in principle, though little was done to carry them out. The fort at Tortuga, he said, should be put into first-class condition; a road should be built between the various settlements on San Domingo; prices on goods coming from France should be materially reduced if they hoped to persuade the buccaneers to become habitans; one thousand to twelve hundred persons should be sent to the island each year; duties on tobacco shipped to France should be halved; Dutch merchantmen should be permitted to trade on the island. In the end Ogeron's methods proved eminently successful, for six years after his appointment as governor it was asserted that the shores of the great Gulf of Leogane held twelve hundred habitans and only one hundred *boucaniers* who still clung to the old mode of life. Ogeron estimated two thousand inhabitants for the French section of the island.

The absorption of the *flibustiers* into the settled element of the colony was accomplished more gradually. When Ogeron was succeeded by his nephew, Jacques Nepveu de Pouançay, the latter reported that more than a thousand of these men roamed about the settlements, a figure confirmed a few years later in a report made by the council of the colony to Colbert. This was qualified shortly afterward by Governor de Cussy, who stated that about half of them had become habitans. But though they worked to transform the buccaneers into settlers, the governors had no desire to wipe them out completely. No one knew better than they the value of these lawless men as defenders of the colony in time of war and purveyors of wealth in the shape of booty in time of peace. To give an idea of their depredations, it has been estimated that between 1655 and 1671 the buccaneers of all the West Indies sacked eighteen cities, four towns, and more than thirty-five villages along the Spanish Main.[12] Yet in the end the wishes of the home government had to be obeyed, and the French governors, like the English, had to destroy the buccaneers. Writing at a later period, Governor de Cussy said: "I destroyed the *flibustiers* because the Court wished it, and I only succeeded after a great deal of trouble. I wish at present I had not succeeded, for there would then be along the coast ten or twelve good ships manned by a goodly number of brave fellows." Despite all this there were always some freebooters to be found in San Domingo ready for adventure.

San Domingo was not affected by the Anglo-French war of 1666. The Council of Jamaica, after toying with the idea of launching an attack on the colony, decided not to do so. The French, they had heard, were leaving Tortuga because of its unhealthy climate, and besides the place, so it was said, was not worth holding. Moreover, should they fail in the attempt, they would stir up a hornet's nest, for the desperate characters who inhabited San Domingo would at once seek revenge by destroying the plantations of Jamaica. Whether this decision was a mistake or not will, of course, never be known. Had the Jamaicans destroyed Ogeron's colony, they would have removed a threat that lay across their route to the Caribbee Islands and cut them off from other British colonies. In fact, during the war the Governor on one occasion excused himself from sending aid to Nevis on the ground that this might bring the buccaneers down on him, for he knew that Ogeron had five hundred trained fighters ready to pounce on him, though he did not know that they were short of powder and shot. So great was his respect for these hardy freebooters that he hastened to put his fortifications in order as soon as war broke out, and he even offered Ogeron an arrangement assuring perpetual neutrality between the colonies, an arrangement similar to the famous treaties at St.

[12]Haring, *The Buccaneers in the West Indies in the XVII Century*, p. 267.

Christopher. In the same way San Domingo was a source of strength to the French islands, protecting them from attacks by the semibuccaneering colonists of Jamaica. As it grew in population, it gradually became the greatest of the French West Indian possessions, a force to be reckoned with in the series of Anglo-French wars that mark the eighteenth century. By failing to destroy it at its inception the Jamaicans lost the opportunity to rid themselves of a formidable enemy.

The signing of the Treaty of the Pyrenees in 1659, which brought to an end the war between France and Spain, did little to promote peace in San Domingo. Ogeron had received orders to remain on the defensive; but the Spanish officials received no such instructions—or if they did, they chose to disregard them—and they kept harassing the French colonists by sudden raids, keeping them continually on the *qui vive*. The buccaneers finally retaliated by an unofficial war of their own. When news came that war had been declared against Spain, in May, 1667—the short-lived conflict known as the War of Devolution—there was great rejoicing in French San Domingo, for it gave official standing to an expedition then being organized to sack the Spanish town of Maracaibo.

Among the ruffians who frequented the piratical resorts of San Domingo at this time was a French seaman named Jean-David Nau,[13] a native of the district in France known as Les Sables d'Ollone, whence he derived his *nom de guerre* L'Olonnais, sometimes lengthened to L'Olonnais the Cruel because of its owners, ferocity. This man had already made his mark in the colony by his recklessness, resourcefulness, and brutality. After several encounters with the Spaniards he determined to attack them in the grand manner, and it was for this purpose that he organized the expedition against Maracaibo. L'Olonnais brought together a fleet of eight vessels, manned by a force of 660 men, and set sail toward the end of April from Tortuga with another buccaneer, named Michel le Basque, whose tastes were similar to his own. They anchored first in a port of northern San Domingo, where they spent three months victualing the fleet in a leisurely manner and securing additional recruits from among the buccaneers in this part of the island. Late in July they set forth. Scarcely had they

[13]Esquemeling calls him François Nau.

doubled the eastern end of the island, when they sighted a Spanish ship bound for New Spain. Signaling his fleet to meet him at the neighboring island of Saona, L'Olonnais started off to take care of the stranger himself. It proved to be an easy task, and after an engagement of three hours the French found themselves in possession of a cargo consisting of 120,000 pounds of cocoa, 40,000 pieces-of-eight in cash, and 10,000 more in jewelry. This rich prize was sent to Tortuga, there to unload her cargo, then she was to come to the rendezvous at Saona. By this time the fleet had already reached Saona, where it found and captured a Spanish ship of eight guns, carrying a vast supply of muskets and ammunition besides 12,000 pieces-of-eight, a valuable addition indeed to the enterprise. Shortly after this, the first prize joined them, bringing from Tortuga provisions and a supply of fresh recruits to replace those fallen in the recent engagement. All was now ready for the attack on Maracaibo.

West of the city of Caracas in Venezuela there is a peculiar geographical formation known as Lake Maracaibo. This is a body of fresh water, some sixty leagues in length by thirty in width, which empties into the Gulf of Venezuela through a comparatively narrow passage. The passage itself is blocked by two good-size islands, Isla de las Vigilas to the east and Isla de las Palmas to the west, forming a narrow channel between them by which ships can enter the lake beyond. A fort on the latter island had been erected to cover the approach. On the western shore of the lake stood the town of Maracaibo, a prosperous place of some three or four thousand inhabitants comprising eight hundred men capable of bearing arms. It was a fairly rich community with a handsome church, well worth the looting, four monasteries, and a hospital. Hides and tobacco were the principal articles offered by the local merchants, while well-to-do planters gathered coconuts and miscellaneous fruit from their extensive plantations. On the eastern shore and farther to the south lay the town of Gibraltar, a place of fifteen hundred inhabitants with which Maracaibo carried on a brisk trade, supplying its less fortunate neighbor with large quantities of meat.

When L'Olonnais arrived with his fleet, he cast anchor in the Gulf of Venezuela, just out of sight of Las Vigilas, and the following day he sailed boldly into Maracaibo and anchored before a fort situated some six leagues from the town. No time was lost in getting down to business. The buccaneers hurried ashore and at once launched an attack on the fort. This redoubt does not seem to have been a particularly formidable affair. It consisted merely of "several baskets of earth, placed upon a rising ground, upon which were planted sixteen great guns, with several other heaps of earth round about, for covering the men within." L'Olonnais landed his men about a league from the fort, but its commander saw the maneuver and at once sent a detachment to throw an ambuscade across the path in such a manner as to cut the French off. It proved a vain attempt. The buccaneers quickly discovered the ambush and as quickly cleared it from their path, leaving the road to the fort open. The Spaniards, however, put up a brave defense and held the foe at bay for three hours, giving the inhabitants of the city time enough to escape to Gibraltar with a large quantity of their valuables. These wretched people had suffered the horrors of a buccaneer sack before, and the memory of what they had endured still lingered with them.

The fort captured, the pirates brought their fleet closer inshore and spent the rest of the day demolishing the fortifications, spiking the guns and wrecking everything they could not carry off. Two days later they entered Maracaibo. A heavy barrage was laid down on the shore to clear away any defense that might lie hidden among the trees and shrubs, then the men landed and marched into the town, which they found practically deserted. Enough food was found in the shape of flour, bread, pork, brandy, wines, and poultry to satisfy the hungry free-booters, who sat down to a sumptuous banquet, "for in four weeks before they had no opportunity of filling their stomachs with such plenty." The best houses were requisitioned for sleeping quarters, while the church was used as a *corps de garde*. The following day a detachment was spread over the countryside to ferret out any inhabitants who might have sought refuge in neighboring places. They returned toward night with several mule loads of pieces-of-eight and about twenty prisoners. L'Olonnais now proceeded to gather in additional booty by using the methods that had gained him his sobriquet. The prisoners were put to the rack to extort information as to where they had hidden their wealth, and the buccaneer, to show that he meant business, hacked one of them to pieces with his cutlass, saying: "If you do not confess and declare where you have hidden the rest of your goods, I will do the like to all your companions." At last he succeeded in getting one man who was willing to disclose the place where a number of his fellows had taken refuge. Fortunately word got to them in time. They buried their possessions and fled to the friendly forest, where by keeping constantly on the move they managed to elude their pursuers.

After a fortnight in Maracaibo the buccaneers set out for Gibraltar, intending to continue to nearby Merida when they had thoroughly gutted the former place. The citizens of Gibraltar had, of course, anticipated such a move and had sent word to the Governor of Merida, who at once responded with a force of four hundred men. These, together with a like number raised by the inhabitants, formed an army strong enough to put up a stout resistance. Two redoubts, one of twenty, the other of eight guns, were quickly constructed, a barricade was thrown across the highway leading to the town, a road was built over swampy ground in order to lead the enemy into a trap, and everything was made ready to give the French a warm reception.

When L'Olonnais arrived with his fleet before Gibraltar, he saw that the inhabitants were determined to resist to the last ditch. He guessed also from the elaborateness of the preparations that much of the booty which had escaped him at Maracaibo had been transported to Gibraltar for safekeeping. All this made the capture of the place an exceedingly hazardous undertaking, but the desperate crew were ready to take the chance. Landing on the shore, the buccaneer led his men up the highway leading to the city. On reaching the barricade they found themselves blocked, and unable to get through they turned up the side road as the Spaniards had expected they would. This path had been so laid out as to bring them within range of the larger fort, and as they advanced the defenders opened up on them with their guns. Nothing daunted, the French cut down branches to form a better footing across the swampy soil and finally managed to scramble through to more solid ground. Here they were met with volley after volley from the smaller redoubt, until they found it impossible to make any further headway. L'Olonnais now resorted to a strategem. Giving the order to retreat, he started back over the road, drawing the Spaniards after him. It was an unfortunate move for the Spaniards, for once they left the protection of their forts, they were no match for the pirates. When these ruthless fighters had their foes in the open, they turned on them with their swords and pikes and soon cut their way through them to take possession of the main fort.

Seeing themselves defeated, the Spaniards took to flight, and those in the smaller fort surrendered. The buccaneer victory was complete. Five hundred Spaniards were left dead on the field, while only forty Frenchmen were killed, though many soon died of wounds. The number of prisoners taken amounted to one hundred and fifty whites and five hundred slaves. The booty was enormous. Much was found in the houses, and many prisoners were forced to disgorge by means of torture. The amount of food, however, was insufficient for the needs of the entire population, and it was not long before many Spaniards died of hunger after the French had generously helped themselves.

At last, after four weeks of rapine and bloodshed, the buccaneers decided to withdraw. As a farewell gesture they sent a messenger to the colonists who had fled to the woods, threatening to burn the city if ten thousand pieces-of-eight were not paid over to them in two days. This demand was not at first taken seriously, but at the end of the allotted time the buccaneers started to make good their promise. As the fire spread, the unfortunate inhabitants managed to scrape together the exorbitant sum, and they turned it over to their tormenters on condition that they would help them to extinguish the flames. The pirates did their best to repair the damage they had caused, yet despite the combined efforts of both French and Spaniards a large part of the town was reduced to ashes.

L'Olonnais and his cutthroats now returned to Maracaibo, flushed with success, and proceeded to make the same offer to its inhabitants as they had to the burghers of Gibraltar, only in this case the amount demanded was placed at thirty thousand pieces-of-eight. After much negotiation this enormous sum was reduced to twenty thousand pieces and five hundred cows, a ransom which was promptly, if not cheerfully, paid. Then the pirates, true to

their promise, took their departure, to the great relief of all concerned. Returning to San Domingo, L'Olonnais unloaded his
ships and proceeded to an accounting. An inventory of the loot
showed the staggering total of 260,000 pieces-of-eight in cash
alone, which was divided among the crews, each man receiving
his allotted share. The plate was then weighed and valued at ten
pieces the pound, while jewelry, the value of which they did not
understand, was appraised by a hit-or-miss plan. Everyone took
an oath that he had withheld nothing from the general plunder,
then a dividend was declared to all who had taken part in the
expedition, while shares were set aside for the heirs of those who
had died or had been killed in battle. This done, all returned to
Tortuga, where they proceeded to spend their gains with such
rapidity that at the end of three weeks most of them had little
left. [14]

Three years after his appointment M. d'Ogeron decided to
return to France for the purpose of placing his views on administrative policy before the directors and obtaining fresh recruits for
the colony. During his absence Pounçay acted as governor. Ogeron
was able to obtain additional colonists without much trouble,
but his plans for the expansion of the French system fell on deaf
ears. He suggested founding a station somewhere on the Florida
coast or in the Bahama islands where the French could control
Spanish commerce as it came northward through the Straits of
Florida on its way to Spain. Here, he felt, supplies could be obtained for less money than in San Domingo, where excessive prices
were driving the buccaneers to the better markets of Jamaica.
Such a settlement, he pointed out, would also tend to curb British
power, already a source of annoyance to the French. Ogeron,
although unsuccessful in selling this plan to the company, was
able to dissuade Colbert from erecting a powerful and expensive
fortress in San Domingo by persuading him that the buccaneers
could put up a far better defense by luring the enemy into the jungle
and there dispatching them than by shutting themselves up behind
a barricade. The worst an enemy fleet could do along this coast
was to burn a few wretched houses which could be rebuilt in a few
days.

[14]Esquemeling, *The Buccaneers of America*, Part II, chap. ii.

Governor d'Ogeron returned to Tortuga in September, 1669, armed with a new commission. Early the following May he found himself faced with a revolt against the company. It was the old struggle for freedom to trade with all comers. Ogeron had succeeded for awhile in reconciling his unruly colonists to the demands exacted by the government and had managed gradually to divert their trade to French ships exclusively; but now they were determined to submit no longer to any restrictions. Two Dutch merchants, Pieter Constant and Pieter Marc, were in the Gulf of Leogane inciting the inhabitants to break the chains that bound them to the company. Since they offered goods at lower prices, their suggestion was received with enthusiasm. This incident took place at the town of Leogane, where the rebels celebrated what they believed was their declaration of independence by the discharge of cannon. When M. Renou, commander of the district, heard the salutes from his nearby residence at Petit-Goave, he came at once to investigate the meaning of the disturbance. Learning what had taken place, he issued an order forbidding the French from trading with the interlopers; he then seized two of their boats and carried them back to Petit-Goave. The Dutchmen, feeling that they had the colonists with them, followed him along the coast, recaptured their property, laid hands on the commander and brought him on board their ship, where they held him prisoner. Such was the situation when Ogeron, who had been advised of pending trouble, arrived from Tortuga.

Ogeron began operations in his usual energetic manner. He boarded the Dutch vessel where Renou was held in durance and quickly bullied the captain into surrendering him. He next tried to reinstate the commander at Petit-Goave, but when he arrived there the mutineers—for the mutiny had now reached this settlement—opened fire on his ship with such telling effect that he was glad to slip out of the harbor and return to Tortuga. Here he learned of a plot hatched by the men of the Leogane district to march northward, enlist the buccaneers and habitans of the coastal settlements, seize all shipping, and attack Tortuga itself. Realizing the gravity of the situation, he dispatched Renou to Governor de Baas with an urgent request for an armed vessel to aid him in suppressing the revolt. Renou reached St. Christopher on the twenty-fifth of September and was immediately sent by De Baas to Grenada, where Louis Gabaret was stationed. He gave Renou a letter ordering Gabaret to sail at once for San Domingo, there to coöperate with Ogeron in putting down the uprising. Despite the orders of the Governor-General, Gabaret refused to leave his post, for he had been sent to these waters for the sole purpose of suppressing foreign commerce in the Caribbee Islands, and he had no intention of being drawn so far from his station even in such an emergency.

Meanwhile Ogeron was growing apprehensive. The mutineers were becoming more and more insolent. They had anchored in the harbor of Tortuga, where they were levying a sort of tribute on all whom they could intimidate. In desperation he wrote Colbert requesting permission to transport a few of his faithful followers to Florida or some other place where he could found a colony and live peacefully. Fortunately for the future of the French colonial empire, the King and Colbert realized that the removal of the more reliable element from San Domingo would leave the colony in the hands of semilawless buccaneers who might well go over to the English or the Spaniards, whichever offered the higher bid for their services. To forestall this calamity Louis sent orders to Gabaret commanding him to stop at San Domingo on his way back to France and remain there long enough to destroy any Dutch shipping he might find and do whatever Ogeron thought necessary for the suppression of the mutiny. Gabaret obeyed at once. He set sail in the frigate "Aurore" and proceeded to Tortuga. No sooner had he anchored, than Ogeron was on board bringing with him some leaders of the mutiny as samples of what he had captured. These men were clapped into irons with little ceremony. As Tortuga had been fairly quiet, Gabaret contented himself with administering an oath of loyalty to the inhabitants; then he set out with Ogeron for the seat of trouble at the Gulf of Leogane. Here at Leogane an officer was sent ashore to summon the rebels to obedience. They replied that they were loyal subjects of the King, but that they would have nothing to do with M. d'Ogeron and would not take any orders from the company. On hearing this Ogeron sent Gabaret to see what he could accomplish by his eloquence. The captain found a body of three or four hundred men drawn up ready to receive him and another two hundred a short distance away. He addressed the former group and received the same answer which his subordinates had received. Even threats had no effect, and he was told that it was lucky for M. Ogeron that he had not come ashore. Seeing the uselessness of further parley, Gabaret returned on board to make his report. The advisability of attempting to land was discussed, but it was quickly dismissed for the terrain along the shore was too marshy to permit troops to disembark. Proceeding thence to Petit-Goave, Ogeron found the inhabitants of this place also drawn up under arms, equally determined to have no dealings with him and ready to defend themselves should he try to land. Ogeron accepted the challenge. Rushing a detachment ashore, he made short work of the opposition, driving them back to the woods and burning their houses. Notwithstanding this easy victory, he realized he could accomplish nothing permanent in the Gulf at this time, so weighing anchor he returned to Tortuga. From here he was able to reach the settlements on the northern shore, notably Port de Paix and Port François, where he was more successful; for the colonists, though somewhat fearful of the reprisals the buccaneers of the Gulf might visit on them, proved more tractable and in the end were induced to subscribe to a new oath of allegiance to the King.

This business concluded, Gabaret took his leave, assuring Ogeron that help would presently arrive from France. After his departure the Governor, conscience-smitten over his failure to suppress the rebellion, returned to the Gulf with Renou. He was cheered by the change that had taken place during his absence. On thinking the matter over, the mutineers realized that as long as the French government sent men-of-war to patrol the coast foreign merchantmen could not land their cargoes. They therefore entered into an agreement with Ogeron, promising to submit to his authority on condition that all French vessels be permitted to trade at San Domingo on payment to the company of a 5 percent tax on all the goods they bought and sold, foreigners being altogether ex-excluded from the business. And so toward the end of April (1671) the revolt ended, and all was quiet in the Gulf of Leogane.

Once he had suppressed the revolt, Ogeron again became the magnanimous ruler. He sent M. de Renou to France with a letter for Colbert requesting a general amnesty for all who had taken part in the recent disturbance. Colbert raised no objections to this request, and the following year sent the pardon restoring all rebels to their former status, without singling out any leaders for exemplary punishment. In thanking the minister for his clemency Ogeron asked for troops to assist the colonists in resisting the temptation to revolt and to furnish garrisons at Tortuga and Petit-Goave, for news had just reached him of the outbreak of war between France and the Netherlands. For his part in the defense of the colony he offered two thousand buccaneers.[15]

In the year 1675 Governor d'Ogeron, whose health had been gradually failing, returned to France, where he presently died. The governorship of San Domingo then fell into other hands. Before he left his post Ogeron placed Pouançay in command of the settlements in the Gulf of Leogane and named Jean-Paul Tarin de Cussy temporary governor of Tortuga. When news of the leader's death reached them, a feeling of rivalry sprang up between the two men as to which should be his successor. Pouançay's relationship to Ogeron gave him the edge, as might be expected in those days, when family connections counted for so much, and on March 16, 1676, the King issued a commission appointing him Governor of Tortuga and San Domingo.

At the time of the passing of Bertrand d'Ogeron the colony of San Domingo may be said to be securely established. Thanks to his skill and enterprise, the *boucaniers* and *flibustiers* had been welded together into a fairly homogeneous group, willing to accept the rule of France and ready—for the sake of booty, to be sure—to fight her battles in the West Indies. It had been a difficult task to make colonists out of the unpromising material that wandered through the jungles of San Domingo and used its ports as headquarters for piratical forays, and it cannot be said that Ogeron had tamed these lawless spirits entirely and transformed them into reliable settlers, but he had done a great service for France by laying the foundations of what was destined to become during the eighteenth century her greatest West Indian colony.

[15]For account of this revolt see Charlevoix, *Histoire de l'isle de . . . S. Domingue*, III, 112–29.

VI

THE BEGINNING OF THE GREAT
ANGLO-FRENCH STRUGGLE

THE DECADE following the Treaty of Nymwegen may be regarded as one of peace in the West Indies. The peace, of course,
was official, that is, England, France, Spain, and the Netherlands were not at war. Hence the various nations in the Caribbees
merely looked at each other with suspicion; but the buccaneers of
San Domingo carried on their depredations against the Spanish
settlements with all their old-time vigor. Louis of France adopted
a twofold policy of refusing royal commissions to freebooters and
at the same time permitting Governor de Pouançay to issue them,
thus benefiting by the injury done to his powerful neighbor, while
allowing the privateers to enrich his colony. Yet the day of the
buccaneers was passing, and the sack of San Juan de Ulua (Vera
Cruz) in 1683 by the Dutchman Van Horn and the Frenchman De
Grammont, acting with the blessing of Pouançay, brought matters
to a head. Wild with rage at the terrible destruction visited upon
his wealthy colony, as well as at the recent actions of Louis in
the Spanish Netherlands, Charles II of Spain declared war. It was,
however, a vain gesture, for his government could get no assistance
from the English or the Dutch, and six months after the beginning
of hostilities he was obliged to sign the Truce of Ratisbon (August,
1684). Fortunately for King Charles, the French monarch was
commencing to sense the antagonism of the European nations
toward his ambitions and was willing to make some concessions
to his southern neighbor, in the hope, no doubt, of securing his
good will in the conflict he knew must break out sooner or later.
The terms of the treaty therefore provided for peace between the
contracting parties, not only in Europe but also in the West

Indies. To show his good intentions Louis replaced Governor de Pouançay by Tarin de Cussy, to whom he gave explicit orders to suppress the buccaneers.

Efforts were also made at this time by the French and English sovereigns to insure peace between their subjects in the Leeward Islands. Acting on the precedent established years before by Warner and D'Esnambuc in settling their differences at St. Christopher, the two kings proceeded to extend the same principle throughout the West Indies. On November 16, 1686, they signed an agreement pledging themselves to refrain from encouraging buccaneering expeditions against each other's colonies. They also agreed that should differences arise between the various colonies the governors should refer the matter to their home governments without interrupting the peaceful relations between the disputants; what was more to the point, they added an article providing for peace between the colonials when the mother countries were at war. Why this article was inserted in the treaty it is difficulty to say, for when war broke out two years later it was quickly tossed out of the window.

The situation in Europe was now rapidly coming to a head, and events were shaping themselves for the outbreak of the war known as the War of the League of Augsburg (King William's War in North America), which began the long struggle between France and England for world supremacy. Louis was all powerful on the continent. His old rival, Spain, was already weak and tottering, and his new rival, England, was just emerging from a second-rate position. The success of French arms had made him an object of distrust to his neighbors, who saw the necessity of forming some sort of union for mutual protection in case he should strike again. For this purpose the Empire, Sweden, Spain, Bavaria, Saxony, and the Palatinate organized on July 6, 1686, the League of Augsburg. Faced by such powerful opposition, Louis felt it advisable, particularly since the victories of the Emperor over the Turks were increasing the League's prestige, to take some sort of action. Casting about for a *casus belli*, he decided to advance claims to certain districts in the Palatinate, claims that were mere lawyers' quibbles, and on the strength of them he began the invasion of these districts in September, 1688. In doing so he relied upon the friendly attitude of England, for this nation, if it did not help him, would, he felt, at least remain neutral.

So long as the Roman Catholic James II ruled England, Louis had reason to feel confident. But now a reaction against the Stuart monarch, which had been simmering for a long time, came to a head. The Anglicans had become alarmed at the favoritism shown members of the Roman Church by their sovereign and had decided to replace him by a prince who could be trusted to protect and preserve the Protestant religion. Their choice fell upon William, Prince of Orange, husband of Mary, the daughter of James; and to this couple they offered the throne. When the French armies entered the Palatinate, William and his wife set sail from Holland. Events now followed rapidly. Louis declared war on Holland in December, and the following April on Spain. On the twelfth of May, England and the Netherlands joined with the members of the League of Augsburg to form the Grand Alliance against France, and within six weeks France and England had declared war on each other. The stage was now set for the beginning of the great struggle.

Numerous changes had taken place in both French and English officialdom since the Treaty of Nymwegen. The Comte de Blénac still represented his sovereign as governor-general, but his authority had been restricted by the creation of the important post of intendant, held at this time by Dumaitz de Goimpy. The powers of the Intendant were great. He ranked below the governor-general and had jurisdiction over public works, the judicial system, and the police, all of which gave him authority to name notaries, bailiffs, registrars, post captains, and surveyors. This naturally encroached on the prerogatives of the governor-general, and friction occasionally arose; but the King made it clear that he would not tolerate any interference with the authority of his intendant, and the governor was obliged to content himself with command of the military establishment, which involved the most important business of defending His Majesty's possessions and the regulation (or suppression) of trade with foreign merchants. Under the Comte de Blénac the following incumbents now ruled the various islands: Tarin de Cussy, San Domingo; Pierre Hencelin, Guadeloupe; Jean Gabaret, elder brother of Louis, Martinique; Comminge de Guitaud,[1] St. Christopher (including St. Martin

[1]Charles de Peychpeyrou-Comminge de Guitaud.

and St. Bartholomew); Charles Auger, Mariegalante. For the British possessions Sir Nathaniel Johnson acted as governor-general, with headquarters at Antigua. He was replaced in September by Sir Christopher Codrington. Richard Dutton was governor of Barbados and was succeeded in July by James Kendall, with Edwin Stede as his lieutenant. Thomas Hill ruled at St. Christopher, William Burt at Nevis, Nathaniel Blakiston at Montserrat, and Abraham Howell at Anguilla.

No sooner had King Louis declared war on Holland than he issued an order for the capture of St. Eustatius. On this island the Dutch had established a valuable trading post, well stocked with slaves, sugar, and European merchandise to be sold to all comers, particularly to French colonists, this in the face of all efforts to suppress them. The place had long been a sore spot to the King, and he now seized the opportunity to destroy it. With his letter to Blénac announcing the declaration of war he enclosed another giving him formal instructions to proceed at once with ships and men to the destruction of St. Eustatius. On receipt of these, Blénac, who was then residing at Fort Royal, sent at once for the Intendant, and the two sat down together to work out the details.

For some reason or other, probably for the sake of striking unexpectedly, the King had ordered the utmost secrecy concerning the destination of the proposed expedition. Even De Goimpy was not enlightened on this point, but told to go full speed ahead with his part of the work of securing ships and seeing that they were suitably provisioned. When the declaration of war was promulgated, on March 7, 1689, it was received with enthusiasm by the French colonists. Letters of marque were issued to those who wished to enroll their ships in Blénac's expedition, and a force was raised, partly from the local militia, partly from volunteers, and to these was added a number of distinguished persons, such as Colonel François de Collart, who, when he found that his company was not among those selected, promptly raised a detachment of volunteers.

On the twenty-eighth of March the fleet, consisting of vessels of various ratings—three ships, a brigantine, a bark, and three half-barks—set sail under sealed orders. The very uncertainty of the ultimate destination added a flavor of excitement to the enterprise. The first stop was at Guadeloupe, where Hencelin had a detachment ready to embark, for it was considered ill-advised to deplete the forces of Martinqiue by enlisting too many men there. Blénac, finding his vessels somewhat crowded, picked up another ship at Guadeloupe for the reinforcements awaiting him at St. Christopher. There, however, he found such a large number that he was obliged to commandeer three barks and a like number of brigantines, thus augmenting his fleet to seventeen sail and his army to 1,200 men.

Blénac reached St. Eustatius on the third of April. Thanks to the policy of secrecy, the attack was a complete surprise to the Dutch. As soon as the governor of the island, Mynheer Schorer, saw the French fleet he sought to save his most valuable possessions by placing them in a couple of ships, on which he also thoughtfully embarked some French Protestants who had sought refuge with him after the revolution of the Edict of Nantes. Blénac let these vessels escape, for he had his hands full with the capture of the island. There were two places where a landing could be made, one at Interlopers Cove, on the side facing St. Christopher, the other at a little bay called Pointe Blanche, on the windward side. Blénac planned to strike from both places at once. The larger portion of his forces he placed under our old friend François le Vassor, and he sent them to Pointe Blanche, where they were quickly landed after the shore had been carefully swept by artillery fire. He himself directed the operations at Interlopers Cove. It was his intention to effect a landing here in the same way as at the Pointe, that is, after thorough artillery preparation from the larger vessels and rifle fire from the smaller ones. But a swift current unexpectedly swept the fleet past the Cove to the foot of a cliff, where it managed to come to anchor. The narrowness of the shoreline at this point made landing very difficult. Collart and his men, however, proved equal to the occasion. They led the way, and presently the entire detachment was safely ashore and ready for action. While these maneuvers were taking place the Dutch had managed to ensconce themselves on the cliff, a vantage point from which they were able to open a galling fire on the French, which the latter found difficult to return. Collart again found a solution. Leading his men up the cliff by a winding path, he slipped behind a barrier of rocks which commanded the Dutch position and was thus able to fire on the enemy without being seen. On the other flank a band of men led by Pierre du Buc climbed up over the rocks and duplicated Collart's performance, while the ships at last managed to bring their guns into play. Caught thus between three fires, the Dutch saw the impossibility of holding out. Rushing out from their trenches, they hurled themselves into a steep, narrow ravine, where they hoped the French would not follow them. But Collart and his lieutenant, Pierre du Buc, did not hesitate; they were ready to follow wherever the enemy led. Over rocks and through heavy undergrowth pursued and pursuers exchanged shots, the Hollanders making a valiant effort to cover up their retreat by some excellent marksmanship, which wounded the two French leaders. At last, after a desperate resistance, they succeeded in reaching their fort, leaving twenty of their number dead or wounded in the ravine.

At this point Blénac called a halt. He feared a sortie and ordered the Martinican detachment to fall back for a rest while the wounded were given first-aid treatment. Since the day was now far spent, no further action took place, but early next morning Le Vassor's troops from Pointe Blanche joined Blénac's army and pitched camp close to the fort. The Governor had evidently decided not to take the place by assault, for at Goimpy's suggestion he landed several guns and set them up within easy firing distance. In order to save any further bloodshed he sent a flag of truce to Governor Schorer with a summons to surrender. The Dutch commander, when he saw the French forces deployed before him, realized the futility of further resistance and agreed to the harsh terms Blénac saw fit to impose in order to fulfill his royal master's orders. According to these terms the Dutch, colonists as well as soldiers, agreed to transport themselves to Nevis, the officers alone being permitted to take with them their personal belongings and a few slaves. The entire settlement was then destroyed with the exception of the fort, where Blénac left a garrison under the command of Donon de Gallifet. This done, all the booty (horses, slaves, furniture, and merchandise) was transported to Martinique, where it was presently sold. The expedition, when an audit was made, showed a profit of 345,656 livres over and above expenses.[2]

At the outbreak of war between France and England apparently the French were better prepared than the English. Louis had kept a watchful eye on the troops in the West Indies, both royal and local militia, issuing orders for their proper equipment and discipline. Inspections were to be held at regular intervals and reports of their condition were to be sent to the Governor-General and the Intendant. To supply these troops French vessels had been compelled for some time to bring over guns free of charge and sell them at cost. As to the number of fighting men, the French had a decided edge over their foes. Taking rough figures, they claimed for Martinique 2,100 armed men besides 850 not armed; for Guadeloupe 1,200 armed, 950 not armed; St. Christopher, scene of the first encounter, 900 armed, 700 not armed; for San Domingo the figures equaled those of Martinique.[3] In contrast to this, the outlook for the British was not encouraging. At St. Christopher, most vulnerable of all the colonies, the troops were in a sad state of disorganization. Numbering but 600 all told, against a French host of nearly three times that figure, they lacked both spirit and equipment. With their pay six years in arrears, they had no credit with the local traders and were obliged to live on the scantiest budget, while their French neighbors were well treated and well fed. True, there were reinforcements to be had from the neighboring islands —1,000 men at Antigua, 1,400 at Nevis, 900 at Montserrat—but there was not even a frigate to protect a rescue party should it attempt to cross the intervening waters. As for Montserrat and Nevis, Governor Johnson felt little apprehension, since they were "so well fortified by nature as to be easily defensible against invasion"; Antigua was put in condition to resist capture by the construction of a fort, situated well inland, to be used as a refuge for women, children, and slaves, while the shore was protected from landing parties by a series of ambuscades. St. Christopher, then, was the only colony that caused the Governor-General any serious worry, and frantic last-minute attempts were made by Thomas Hill to make up for what he lacked in men by hastily

[2]Guët, *Le Colonel François de Collart*, pp. 181–95. Labat, *Nouveau voyage aux isles de l'Amérique*, II, 98.
[3]Census of 1687 as given in Dessalles, *Histoire générale des Antilles*, II, 454.

repairing Fort Charles at Old Road Town. "Even then," as he himself said, "we shall want guns of all sizes, carriages, ammunition, and a gunner and gunsmith or two."[4]

To complicate matters there was also the religious situation, now made more acute by the change of sovereignty in England. The expulsion of Catholic James and the enthronement of Protestant William naturally caused as much resentment among the Catholic colonists as it did among their coreligionists at home. The island of Montserrat had been orginally settled by the Irish, and many of them were also to be found in the other islands, particularly St. Christopher. For religious reasons these people had always tended to lean toward the French—as we saw when La Barre captured Montserrat—and in time of war their loyalty to the British Crown was always questionable. On this occasion they did not wait for a declaration of war to show their hostility. At St. Christopher the trouble came to a head as soon as the news of William's succession had been received. The Irish settlers, numbering 130 armed men, deserted to the French, thus reinforcing an already powerful enemy. Governor Hill, seeing the impossibility of guarding himself against such an overwhelming force, took refuge with his people in the fort, sending out urgent requests to the neighboring colonies for help. The French governor *pro tempore*, M. de Salnave, received these deserters with joy, and they, confident of his protection, vented their spite on the English by predatory raids into their territory. Thus, while Hill stayed cooped up in his fort French and Irish marauders invaded British territory to burn, ravage, plunder, and steal all they could lay their hands on under the specious pretext that the English were rebels against King James, whose faithful subjects the Irish claimed to be. The Frenchmen who took part in these expeditions were for the most part mulattoes and slaves. Salnave did nothing to restrain them; and as for the Irish, he frankly declared to the indignant Governor Hill that he would grant them protection in the name of religion as the English had done with the Huguenots. On one occasion, when in order to forestall trouble Hill had ordered the Irish to surrender their arms, they deserted to the French, who gave them asylum and aided them in driving the English from Pointe de Sable

[4]*C.S.P., America & West Indies, 1689–92,* Nos. 65, 83.

to the safety of Fort Charles, leaving the district free to the Irish rebels, who promptly settled there. As for Salnave, he disowned all responsibility for these disorders. He said he had not received any notice of a declaration of war from his sovereign, thus implying that the raids were undertaken without his knowledge or consent; but doubtless he foresaw the eventual outbreak of war, and for this reason did nothing to restrain his people.

William III declared war on France on May 17, 1689. No sooner did this news reach Versailles than Louis began his preparations; but before making a formal declaration of hostilities himself he wished to place his colonies in a position to strike first. He had already dispatched the Chevalier d'Arbouville in the "Perle," and he now sent out a squadron of five armed vessels[5] to assist the colonials in their attacks on the enemy. In contrast to this encouraging help for the French colonials, was the sad plight of the English.

We are dreading every day [writes Joseph Crispe, of St. Christopher] to hear news of war with France, which will mean ruin to our estates if not a total loss; for at the first alarm we must betake ourselves to a fort, which of late we have worked hard to build, in the hope of maintaining ourselves till we are helped from home, or from the neighboring islands. It is vain for us to think of meeting the French in the field; they are twice our numbers, better disciplined, better officered, armed and ammunitioned, and so jealous of us since the proclamation of King William that they are all hands upon their guard every night. We are obliged to do the like, which tires our men out, so they will be unfit for service when they do come to it. I hoped, when I saw the petition which you in England presented to the Prince of Orange in reference to the scarcity of these naked islands, that before now we should have been encouraged by the sight of a squadron, but we see no sign of one yet, and fear none is intended. If so, and if there be a war, all is lost.[6]

Edwin Stede, of Barbados, however, held out a ray of hope to the discouraged Kittefonians, as the inhabitants of St. Christopher are called. At the request of Governor Hill he raised a contingent of three hundred men, placed it under the command of Sir Timothy Thornhill, and agreed to send more if necessary. He seemed confident of his power, for he boasted that he could readily reduce the whole of the French islands to the British King's obedience—an

---

[5]"Hazardeux," "Emérillon," "Loire," "Dauphine," "(Cheval?) Marin."
[6]*C.S.P.*, *America & West Indies, 1689–92*, No. 193.

idle boast, of course, but one which may have acted as a stimulus to his despondent fellow countrymen

No sooner had Blénac received notice of King William's declaration of war than he proceeded to carry out his master's wishes. Setting sail from Fort Royal with his six men-of-war, accompanied by fourteen merchantmen and twenty-three sloops, he arrived off Basseterre, St. Christopher, on the twenty-seventh of July. Here the troops were landed, and word was sent to the militia of the Basseterre and Capesterre sections to advance during the night on the English quarter. Meanwhile the British troops, numbering five hundred men, had for the most part ensconced themselves in Fort Charles at Old Road Town, there to await whatever fate had in store for them. Around this stronghold Blénac placed his little army, reinforced by 120 men from a privateer under the command of Jean du Casse, a man destined to play a leading role in San Domingo, who had just joined the expedition. The fort itself was apparently not very formidable or particularly well equipped. It was a fairly old structure, built of stone, on a cliff overlooking the sea. It presented to attacking fleets a long curtain connecting two bastions set on a rampart of considerable height, but of such a gentle slope that it could be easily scaled. There was no moat on the land side, and to make matters worse the walls were topped by a neighboring hill, from whose summit the interior of the fort could be swept by artillery fire.

Blénac decided to begin operations by the classical method of opening a trench and bringing it as near the fort as possible. He then placed his artillery, consisting of ten large pieces, at a spot where he could batter away at the gate. To create a diversion while this work was going on, the fleet opened a tremendous fire, which spent itself on the walls of the cliff without doing any serious damage, though it prevented any communication between the defenders and the outside. According to one report the French fired 1,138 shots and 22 bombs, killing "only a dog or two, one Christian man, three children and a negro." Other accounts differ in detail, but the score remains approximately the same. The defenders, it must be admitted, put up a gallant resistance, returning the French fire with their collection of rusty guns as long as the powder held out. After a siege of two weeks Du Casse became im-

patient at the Governor's cautious methods, for Blénac, fearful
of losing men, hesitated to batter down the gate with his guns and
give the order for an assault. Du Casse suggested placing a battery
on the hill overlooking the fort and volunteered to do the work
himself. Blénac at last consented. During the night Du Casse
caused his men to drag six heavy pieces to the top of the hill, and
the following morning the English awoke to find themselves at
the mercy of the enemy. At first they tried to dislodge the French
by their fire; but their wretched guns could not reach the enemy's
battery, and Du Casse replied with such telling effect that they
soon hauled down their flag and surrendered. This was on the
fifteenth of August. The terms of surrender were simple. The
English were sent to Nevis, while the Irish, in compliance with
their own request, were permitted to remain among the French.
The storehouses were stripped of their contents and then burned—
as had been done at St. Eustatius. The net profit of the expedition
was computed at 39,895 livres. Ten days afterward Blénac returned
to Martinique, leaving Goimpy to wind up the business together
with Comminge de Guitaud, whom he now officially installed as
governor of St. Christopher.[7]

The fall of St. Christopher spread consternation throughout the
English islands. While the siege was in progress Sir Christopher
Codrington, who had just arrived at Antigua to be the governor-
general, disarmed the Catholics on this island and confined them
to their plantations. Nevis he believed in good enough condition
to withstand an attack, having sixteen hundred trained men to
defend its fortifications; but Montserrat, with its large Irish population, he considered hopeless, for though he had these people
disarmed, there were hardly enough loyal Englishmen there to
put up a stout fight. The great weakness in the British line of defense was the lack of an adequate fleet, for to protect the islands
effectively it was estimated that a squadron of ten ships would be
needed together with an additional force of about one thousand
men. Little could be done while the French were masters of the
seas.

Yet despite these handicaps Codrington managed to hold his

[7]Guët, *Le Colonel François de Collart*, pp. 201–5; *C.S.P., America & West Indies, 1689–92*,
Nos. 280, 345, 348.

own. Setting out from Antigua in two small vessels, he reached the little island of Barbuda, another Irish colony, and disarmed the inhabitants. On his way back he was met by two sloops manned by French and Irish sailors who had come to sack the place. Codrington turned on them, put them to flight, and would have captured them, so he tells us, had not his ammunition given out.

With this pathetic naval victory the British colonists were obliged to rest content for the time being. Despite their desperate need of a fleet, the colonists could expect nothing from the home authorities this year, for they were occupied with James's invasion of Ireland and hostilities in the Channel. Sir Timothy Thornhill did at last reach Antigua with reinforcements to the tune of eight hundred men, considerably more than the number originally promised, but he did not arrive until the twenty-fourth of August, too late to be of assistance at St. Christopher. At this low point in English fortunes Sir Christopher showed himself to be the man of the hour. On hearing of grave disturbances in Nevis, caused by certain seditious spirits, he sent Thornhill with his troops to handle the situation. He followed this up by a tour of inspection, bolstering up the spirit of the inhabitants, examining fortifications, reviewing the militia, and helping to put the islands in a condition to resist attack. At Montserrat he tackled the troublesome Irish question with great tact, finally persuading these unruly subjects of King William that they would be better off under English than under French rule. At Nevis he readily consented to the Council's request to use Thornhill's regiment for a raid on the French controlled islands of St. Martin and St. Bartholomew, where a supply of cattle might be procured to relieve the shortage of meat that was fast becoming acute. Thornhill, eager for some sort of action, was only too glad to comply. He sailed on the twenty-sixth of December for St. Martin, but finding the inhabitants under arms he steered for St. Bartholomew, which he seized without too much difficulty, the governor of the place surrendering after a slight resistance. Six or seven hundred prisoners fell into Thornhill's hands. The Governor with the men, slaves, and cattle was sent to Nevis, while the women and children were sent to St. Christopher.

Encouraged by his success, Thornhill, after a three weeks' stay at St. Bartholomew, returned to St. Martin. This time he proposed to take the place by stratagem similar to that used at St. Eustatius by Blénac. Detaching a portion of his men under Captain Walter Hamilton to make a landing on the windward side and thus draw off the defenders, he put the main body ashore on the leeward side and proceeded to march across the island. About two miles inland the French had erected a breastwork, protected by two guns, and here they were gathered to make a stand. It proved a difficult matter to dislodge them. For two days the defenders kept the English at bay, and then they retreated only after the English had brought up enough artillery from the ships to demolish the slender fortifications. Once the breastwork was taken, Thornhill's men started out in pursuit of the enemy, driving them into a little fort mounting six guns and as quickly driving them out again. For two or three days a desultory warfare continued, then as he was about to deliver the final blow Thornhill saw in·the offing three great ships, a brigantine, and a sloop standing in toward the island. It was the squadron of Du Casse bringing seven hundred men to the rescue of the defenders.

Thornhill saw that he was caught in a trap. He immediately gave orders to cease firing and rushed his men to the various landing places to make ready for an attack. He also sent a sloop to Nevis with an urgent request for help. Du Casse, however, showed no disposition to land; on the contrary, he contented himself with pursuing such English vessels as tried to break through his blockade and actually managed to capture one. During the night he stood on and off, and at noon the following day he came to anchor close enough to land men and guns, while the French, encouraged by his appearance, came down from their fastnesses, recaptured their little fort, and prepared to join in an attack against the invaders. Despite these reinforcements the English were powerful enough to hold their own. For three days they stood on guard, the French not yet daring to take the initiative, then to their consternation they saw heading toward them on the sea three ships. It was a little fleet sent out by the Governor of St. Christopher to join forces with Du Casse.

Meanwhile the sloop sent out by Thornhill had reached its destination, and Codrington, realizing the seriousness of the situation, had immediately dispatched a squadron to rescue the expedition. Fortunately he happened to have at hand just the right man for the job. Captain Thomas Hewetson, a brutal scoundrel whose cruelties to his own men had caused much scandal at Barbados, had just distinguished himself by a successful raid on Mariegalante —not very startling, it is true, just an attack on a few wretched planters, but at least it was something in contrast to the disaster at St. Christopher.

It was to this hero, then, that Codrington entrusted the business of rescuing Thornhill and his men. Hewetson set sail on January 24, 1690, a few days after his victorious return from Mariegalante with three ships and four hundred men. On the way he had the good fortune to recapture one of Thornhill's sloops from the French and thus to learn in detail the true situation at St. Martin. Thornhill was now, so it appeared, surrounded by a formidable host. To the three hundred men already living on the island Du Casse had added half as many more, while St. Christopher had sent a contingent of five hundred with promise of more if needed. On hearing this, Hewetson crowded on all sail, hoping to make a surprise attack on the French fleet as it lay at anchor off the island. It was daybreak when he neared the island, and as the sun was rising the French slipped their cables and bore down upon his fleet. The French outnumbered the English five to three, so Hewetson had to make up in seamanship what he lacked in strength. Du Casse, leading his squadron, was the first to open fire, having selected the English flagship as his target. Hewetson returned the compliment as soon as he was within musket shot, then, sailing down the line, he exchanged broadsides with the rest of the fleet one after the other. After coming about he repeated this maneuver, apparently with little result, for he now decided to come to actual grips with his foe—that is, he would board ship. To gain a windward position he bore away for some distance. Now the French, strange to say, declined action, and set out in the direction of St. Christopher, leaving the English free to land on the island and rescue Thornhill and his men. Hewetson quickly came to anchor and sent a message to Thornhill, urging him to embark without loss of time. But before this could be done Du Casse was back again, ready to take up where he had left off. The English at once weighed anchor and set forth to meet the French on the open sea. Here they were outmaneuvered by Du Casse, who slipped between them and the place on the shore where Thornhill had collected his men. Since it was now near sunset, Hewetson decided to stand off during the night, ready to pounce upon the enemy when daylight came. But when the sun rose the French got under way and instead of joining battle-headed for Anguilla. Now that the coast was clear the English commander worked his way toward the shore and managed without much difficulty to embark Thornhill, his men, and his artillery. The following day they were again at Nevis. [8]

Despite these moderate successes Sir Christopher Codrington did not regard the situation as particularly encouraging. A deputation sent by him to St. Christopher to negotiate for an exchange of prisoners brought back news of a fleet of thirty merchantmen recently arrived at Martinique with four ships of war and a quota of soldiers. One wonders then why the French did not take advantage of the situation to attack Nevis as they had threatened to do. If we are to believe Guitaud, the fault lay entirely with Blénac. In the first place he had shipped the prisoners taken at St. Christopher to Nevis, where they were in a position to attempt to regain their colony, instead of sending them to far-off Jamaica as his officers had suggested. Then he had set off for Martinique with his army, leaving St. Christopher too badly equipped to withstand a counterattack. There were not enough supplies, munitions, arms, and artillery, and only one thousand men to protect the island from invasion. Guitaud and Goimpy, thrown on their own resources, could do little about it; but at least they could, and did, make a desperate attempt to interest the King in their plight. They wrote his minister, the Marquis Jean-Baptiste de Seignelay, son and successor of the great Colbert, requesting a huge consignment of supplies and at least six companies of soldiers well armed with guns of the type used by the buccaneers. Thus, when Goimpy returned to Martinique in October he had no reason to think well of Blénac's abilities as a leader. He managed to ally himself with Jean du Casse and Louis de Gemosat, who were already causing the Governor-General considerable trouble, and thus found himself involved in a faction opposed to his superior.

[8]C.S.P., America & West Indies, 1689-92, No. 789. Thomas Spencer's narrative in Harleian Miscellany, II, 565-70.

Guitaud, too, was antagonistic, expressing his feelings by criticisms of Blénac, in which he compared him unfavorably to the Intendant. Stung by these repeated attacks, coming as they did from the men who should have been his closest collaborators, Blénac tendered his resignation as governor-general. He was succeeded by the Marquis d'Alesso d'Eragny, who received his appointment on May 1, 1690, though he did not arrive at Martinique until the following February.

The British now determined to stike a blow for the recovery of St. Christopher. On the last day of the year 1689 the Admiralty issued instructions to Captain Lawrence Wright putting him in charge of a squadron of thirteen ships[9] with orders to proceed at once to the West Indies, taking with him the Duke of Bolton's regiment. He was to stop first at Barbados for a consultation with the Governor and the Council and then proceed to the Caribbees, where he was to place himself under the orders of Governor Codrington. He was, however, to retain considerable independence of action, since he was permitted to use his own judgment about attacking the French if he found them in possession of the British islands, though he was forbidden to send his ships cruising at a distance if they were needed to protect the English possessions. It was an unfortunate choice. Wright proved himself a poor collaborator. He regarded the Caribbees as colonies little worth preserving—an impression he may have picked up from certain persons at Barbados—and was a constant source of annoyance to Codrington, going so far as to refuse to attack the French fleet when he had it bottled up in the cul-de-sac of Guadeloupe.[10]

When Captain Wright's fleet arrived at Antigua on June 10, 1690, Codrington had some comforting news for its commander. He had sent a deputation to Martinique to arrange for an exchange of prisoners and had learned that Arbouville's squadron was about to return to France, thus clearing the waters of French warships. Codrington now called a council of war to decide on the next step. He began by complaining of the quality of the munitions sent him, particularly the muskets, which he denounced as the worst he

[9]"Mary," "Foresight," "Tiger," "Bristol," "Hampshire," "Assistance," "Antelope," "Jersey," "Guernsey," "Swan," "St. Paul," "Richard & John," "Quaker Knight."

[10]C.S.P., Domestic, 1689-90, pp. 363-64; C.S.P., America & West Indies, 1689-92, No. 625.

had ever seen. Neither was he enthusiastic about the number of men at his disposal—no more than two thousand, he said—hardly enough for a grandiose plan he had evolved for complete conquest of the French islands. Nevertheless the situation was so greatly improved that he decided to send the fleet first to Montserrat for water, as well as men, then to Nevis for additional recruits, after which he would see what he could do.

As Codrington ordered, so it was done, and on the twenty-third of June all the troops landed at Nevis for a final review. The entire force now consisted of three thousand men divided for purposes of flexibility into seven regiments, one of which was commanded by Thornhill and another by Governor Blakiston of Montserrat.[11] A council of war decided to attempt the recovery of St. Christopher as the first blow in the coming campaign. To accomplish this, Codrington acted cautiously, for he considered his force not sufficiently large to attack the fifteen hundred Frenchmen protected by forts and breastworks. A small contingent of armed vessels was sent out to harass the enemy; then on the twenty-ninth the entire armada, consisting of ten men-of-war, two fire ships, and about twenty brigantines and sloops, set sail for St. Christopher and in a few hours hove to in Frigate Bay to make a surprise landing.

Frigate Bay is situated a short distance south of the town of Basseterre on the narrowest part of the island. Here Governor de Guitaud, who had been forewarned by two refugees recently escaped from Nevis, had made preparations to withstand an attack. Trenches had been dug and breastworks erected, all well manned by about a thousand men. It was in the face of this opposition that the English were obliged to land, a difficult if not impossible maneuver, since the ships' boats would not hold more than six hundred men in all at one time, too small a number to carry the trenches. Codrington was quick to realize the folly of making such an attempt and ordered his men to remain on board while the guns of the entire fleet were turned on the fortifications to prepare the terrain for a landing. Toward evening he decided to alter the general plan of attack, for the trenches proved stronger than he had

[11]These regiments were: Duke of Bolton's, 700 men; Thornhill's, 500; Antigua, 400; Montserrat, 300; two of Nevis, 600; Marine, 400; Captain-General's guard, 100. Spencer in Harleian Miscellany, II, 570.

expected. South of Frigate Bay was another landing place at a little salt pond, called by the French Petite Saline, which was separated from Frigate Bay by a steep hill. Since scouts had reported this hill to be passable he decided upon a strategem to outflank the enemy. Selecting a detachment of six hundred men under Thornhill and Blakiston, he landed them in the dead of night at the salt pond, whence they were to make their way over the hill to the French encampment; then in order to create a diversion Wright was sent with his frigates to Basseterre, a clever maneuver which caused the French to draw three hundred men from Frigate Bay for the protection of the town.

At daybreak the landing party reached the summit of the hill, after an arduous climb up its steep slopes. Here in the light of the early morning sun they were seen by the French sentinels outlined against the brightening sky. The sound of firing awoke the men in the trenches, who sprang to arms just in time to meet the English charging down the hill at them. At this moment Codrington, who had been watching the outcome from the deck of his flagship, landed another detachment of six hundred, which he hurled directly at the trenches while Thornhill caught the enemy on the flank. Taken by surprise, the French fired a few volleys, then fled precipitately, leaving their foes in full possession of the fortifications. It was a victory cheaply bought, for the invaders lost but ten killed and thirty wounded, Captain Thornhill being among the latter.

Codrington now landed all his men and began his march on the capital. The Duke of Bolton's regiment took the van, moving along the shore; Thornhill followed a parallel route somewhat inland; the men of Antigua brought up the rear; while the other four regiments kept their posts at the French encampment, awaiting further orders. They had gone but a short distance when they were stopped by the French, who had been rallied by reinforcements coming up from Basseterre; now, numbering eleven hundred men, they turned upon their assailants. The two lines clashed about a mile from Frigate Bay. During the first half-hour the British were driven back and nearly surrounded, then the Antigua regiment joined battle and in a desperate effort routed the French forces and drove them into Basseterre. On reaching the capital the English found it deserted, for the French did not attempt to hold it, and the inhabitants had already retreated into the interior. Here the victors would have halted for the night had not their commanders found the warehouses well stocked with liquor; they wisely marched their men to the Jesuit compound just outside the town, where they could rest soberly until the morning.

Next day the English continued their march, reinforced by some artillery landed during the night from the ships, until at last they entered their own territory and pitched their tents at Old Road Town. The following morning they advanced to Cleverley Point, where Guitaud had halted to make a stand. Cleverley Point is a promontory just north of Brimstone Hill. This hill is a curious formation that appears to any one approaching the island like a giant bastion set on the slope of Mt. Misery, though in reality it is a hill entirely separate from the mountain. The fort itself was a pretentious affair, recently constructed at the urgent suggestion of the Lords of Trade. It was rectangular in shape: four bastions connected by curtains or walls rising to a height of twenty feet. The entire structure was of stone. Each bastion boasted five guns, while two mounds within the enclosure supported other batteries. The name of this fortification was Fort Charles, the same as the redoubt at Old Road Town, or at least such is the conclusion we must draw from contemporary documents. It is possible that the older structure was abandoned at this time, perhaps after its capture by the French the previous year, and the name now transferred to the new and stronger fort for the sake of sentiment.[12] It was here Governor Guitaud had taken refuge with 150 soldiers and 250 planters, leaving the rest of his people to shift for themselves. To capture the place, which would make his victory complete, Codrington evolved the bold plan of placing his artillery on Brimstone Hill, from which point of vantage he would command

[12]There are numerous documents to show that the Charles Fort (or Fort Charles) of the campaign of 1666 was at Old Road Town some three and one-half miles south of Brimstone Hill. This must have been the Charles Fort captured by the French in 1689 (C.S.P., America & West Indies, 1689-92, No. 280), since its description is totally different from that of the one at Cleverly Point, as can be seen by comparing the two. In the present campaign the fort held by the French was the one at Cleverly as the narrative clearly indicates. When Codrington captured the place he listed the supplies he found therein as the inventory of Charles Fort. Ibid., No. 1004, Section III. A map of the island by Anthony Ravell published in 1794 shows Charles Fort near Brimstone Hill.

Cleverley Point. A path was accordingly constructed up the side of the hill, and with tremendous labor two guns of 2,400 pounds each were dragged up the slope and wheeled into position.

On the morning of the tenth of July the assault began. When the guns opened fire from Brimstone Hill the frigates assisted by pouring their broadsides into the fort. The soldiers took up their position in a trench between Brimstone and the fort, within musket-shot of the latter, and from this protection proceeded to run out another trench capable of accommodating four hundred men. So great was the damage done by the two guns on Brimstone that Codrington prepared another platform lower down the hill, some two hundred yards nearer the fort, and placed three guns on it. Still another trench was dug, additional batteries were prepared, and sixteen nine-pounders were brought ashore to equip them. So rapidly did the work progress and so fearful was the havoc wrought by the big guns that on the twenty-second the French commander sent out a flag of truce to secure an armistice for three days for the purpose of discussing terms of capitulation. Codrington consented to a two-day truce, reserving the right, however, to continue work on his fortifications. Indeed, he had the French at his mercy, for opposite the gate of the fort he had already completed a half-moon connected with one of the trenches, and at its left was a battery capable of mounting six great guns, two eighteen-pounders and four twelve-pounders.

On the sixteenth Guitaud surrendered amid the cheers of the English army. "After the enemy marched out," says an eye witness, "the English flag was put up, the King's and Queen's health was drunk, and the great guns three times fired, three volleys being also made by the whole army." On entering the fort Codrington found the houses terribly battered by the guns on Brimstone Hill. Of the 480 men comprising the garrison, about 80 had been killed. An inventory of the matériel captured showed 29 cannon, 275 small arms, and 145 barrels of powder. The terms of surrender were harsh. Codrington was determined to break the French power in St. Christopher forever, and for this reason he refused to permit the colonists to seek refuge in the strongholds of nearby Martinique and Guadeloupe. With the exception of the Governor and a favored few who were sent to the capital and six hundred refugees from St. Martin who were returned to their homes, the greater part were to be transported to San Domingo, where they would not be tempted, so it was hoped, to meddle with the affairs of the Leeward Islands.

After the surrender of St. Christopher, Codrington turned his attention to gathering up a few loose ends left by the French. Sir Timothy, having recovered from his wound, was sent with his own regiment, reinforced by the marine regiment, to effect the capture of St. Eustatius. To a summons of surrender the French commander replied that he would defend his post to the last. Under cover of his guns Thornhill therefore landed his men and was proceeding toward the fort when he perceived some Dutch flags in a nearby wood. It was Governor Schorer, with a hundred Dutchmen at his back, who had come from Saba to recapture his former colony. Not being strong enough to oust the French garrison, he had decided to take what plunder he could and make off with it. For some reason or other he refused to collaborate with Thornhill, possibly because he felt that an English victory would be of no advantage to his nation. At any rate he departed from the island leaving Thornhill to carry on the siege by himself. The siege was a brief one. There were only sixty men in the fort, and the enemy could not hold out against the English army. After a brief defense of five days the French commander yielded his post and suffered himself and his garrison to be transported to San Domingo.[13]

Flushed with confidence, Governor Codrington now advocated the capture of Guadeloupe. Martinique, farther away and better defended, would have to wait, so he said, for he would seize the easier prize first. But when Thornhill returned, his men were too exhausted for any further campaign that year and the Governor was obliged to postpone his plans. Furthermore, there appears to have been considerable sickness in the army and a dearth of supplies of all kinds; then, to make matters worse, Wright sailed with his fleet to Barbados to avoid the hurricane season. Codrington therefore remained at St. Christopher, where he spent the next three months superintending the expulsion of the French colonists. It was not until the middle of October that he felt he had the situa-

[13]For accounts of the St. Christopher campaign see C.S.P., America & West Indies, 1689–92, Nos. 977, 988, 1004, 1034, and Harleian Miscellany, II, 507–75.

tion well enough in hand to return to Antigua. On the way he stopped at Nevis and Montserrat.

Early in February, 1691, the Marquis d'Eragny arrived at Fort Royal with a fleet of fourteen men-of-war to take the position recently occupied by the Comte de Blénac. He found Martinique in a dilapidated state, and fearing the war might be of long duration he set himself to the task of reorganization, with the able assistance of M. de Goimpy. To replace the scarcity of food supplies he arranged for the cultivation of enough acreage to insure a sufficient amount for the colonists. Batteries were erected along the shore at points where an enemy might land, while the more important fortifications were stocked with munitions, and arms were distributed to the militia. Steps were even taken to enroll a few slaves in military companies. Under his direction Governor Hencelin, though now greatly enfeebled by illness, took similar measures at Guadeloupe. There was little doubt among the French officials that the English would strike, and strike soon.

Codrington now began his preparations for capturing Guadeloupe. On the twenty-second of March, Wright was back at Antigua with a powerful squadron of sixteen men-of-war, mounting 570 guns and carrying 2,570 men.[14] To this were presently added three Brandenburg vessels recently arrived in the West Indies with four hundred men. Encouraged by this powerful showing, the Governor now put forth a bolder plan, that is, the capture of Martinique, capital and heart of the French West Indian possessions. With this prize in his grasp it would be a simple matter to take over Guadeloupe and Mariegalante, and French power in the Caribbees would be broken. He put forth this scheme with great cogency and eloquence to the council of war summoned to discuss the coming campaign, but the majority could not be brought to share his enthusiasm, and after a long debate it was decided to adhere to the original plan. This plan, adopted in its final form, was to seize Mariegalante with the Duke of Bolton's regiment, carried there in some merchantmen hired for the purpose, and then,

[14]This was the total number under Wright's command. Perhaps all may not have come to Antigua at this time, but may have joined the main fleet later. They were: "Mary," "Bristol," "Antelope," "Assistance," "Jersey," "Tiger," "Success," "Princess Ann," "Hampshire," "Swan," "Guernsey," "Quaker (Knight?)," "St. Paul," "Wolf," "Experiment," "Dumbarton." *Ibid.*, Nos. 1343, 1357.

leaving this contingent to garrison the island, proceed with Wright's squadron to Guadeloupe. This island captured, the next move was to be against Martinique with the help of additional reinforcements now promised by Barbados.

On the sixth of April the British fleet arrived off Mariegalante, and the following day Bolton's regiment, under Major Edward Nott, was put ashore, while Captain Wright sailed off to make a preliminary survey of Guadeloupe. The French governor Charles Auger does not seem to have put up a serious defense. He was frightened, no doubt, by the superior force that had come to attack him. The French fled incontinently to the woods, leaving their fortified places to the enemy, thus forcing the English troops to engage in a sort of hunting expedition before the French could be subdued. After a week of skirmishing Nott had the situation well in hand and was able to send Auger a summons to surrender. Hopelessly outnumbered, for he had but 240 men in all, the French commander saw the folly of further resistance and yielded at discretion. Codrington stripped the island of its entire population, sending the wretched inhabitants to Martinique and Guadeloupe, while he kept the able-bodied men prisoners in his ships.

The entire British fleet now steered northward along the western coast of Guadeloupe within half a cannon shot of the shore, stopping at Wright's suggestion before the town of Le Baillif, four miles north of Basseterre, to exchange shots with the local batteries, a bit of exercise that cost him a few lives and did no harm to the French. Then the squadron proceeded on its way toward Anse à la Barque, where Codrington proposed to make a landing. On seeing the fleet sail past Basseterre, Governor Hencelin promptly went into action. He was at this time suffering from a lingering illness that prevented him from taking the field in person, yet he managed to direct the campaign in a fairly efficient manner. Sizing up the situation, he concluded—erroneously, as it turned out —that Codrington had no intention of landing so far from Basseterre, but was making a feint in the direction of Anse à la Barque in order to draw the French troops away from the logical objective of the expedition. He therefore was content to send his aide, Sieur de Bordenave, with a platoon of twenty-five men, to the Anse, supported by a detachment of one hundred under Major Le Cler, who stationed himself just south of the Rivière Beaugendre, while Hencelin remained with the bulk of his forces at Fort de la Madeleine, a rather dilapidated structure protecting Le Baillif. Hémon de la Malmaison, lieutenant of the King, was ordered to remain with his command at Fort St. Charles, Basseterre, and not to stir without positive orders.

On the first of May, Codrington landed his men. The squadron was then some two or three miles south of Anse à la Barque. The wind had dropped, and the Governor, feeling that further delay might be dangerous, decided to put his men ashore at a little bay near by rather than waste any more time in getting to the Anse.[15] The signal was broken out at the masthead, and the troops were quickly landed, Codrington being the first to set foot on shore. Facing the landing place was a steep cliff, whose summit could be reached only by following a narrow path strewn with loose stones, up which the men were obliged to walk, or rather climb, in single file. To accomplish the difficult task of gaining the top required a good half-hour's time, and when five or six hundred of his little army had succeeded in reaching it, Codrington placed Nott in charge of them with orders to take the road to Basseterre.

Meanwhile Bordenave, from his point of vantage, had seen the English army disembarking in the distance. Quick to realize what it would mean for the capital if this force were not checked, he swung his men into the saddle and galloped southward to head them off; at the same time he sent a message to Hencelin. The place he selected to make his stand was the southern slope of a ravine some two and a half miles south of the landing place. He deployed his men along its summit, across a path just wide enough to allow three men to walk abreast. It was the only path leading up from the ravine and the one the English troops would be obliged to take. The terrain along this path was covered by a dense forest growth to within fifty paces of the top, and there Bordenave had thrown up a breastwork to stop further progress. When Nott's men appeared, the French were ready for them. When they started up the path, Bordenave gave the order to fire, and from behind

[15]The account given by Archibald Hutcheson (*C.S.P.*, *America & West Indies, 1689–92*, No. 1557) says they landed south of the Anse while Father Labat places the landing in the Anse itself. Since Hutcheson was present during the campaign and Labat wrote from hearsay years later, Hutcheson is more likely to be correct.

the barricade came volley after volley which the English found difficult to return, for those in the rear ranks dared not use their guns for fear of hitting those in front of them. Bordenave had shown sound judgment in selecting this position, for he was able to hold the enemy at bay for three hours; but at last, thanks to his immensely superior numbers, Nott was able to reach the top, where he could deploy his men and catch the defenders on the flank. There was nothing for the French to do now but beat an orderly retreat and hope to make another stand later on, for the help they had sent for did not come, their ammunition was running low, and on top of all this Bordenave had been killed. Hurrying southward, they reached the Rivière des Habitans, where they joined forces with Major Le Cler and dug themselves in for further resistance.

The following day Codrington continued his triumphant march as far as the Rivière des Habitans, where he found the French, now five hundred strong, ready to receive him. The spot where Codrington halted his troops was high above the river bank, and there was an easy descent to a small hill near the river's edge, whence a steep, narrow path led to the river and then up the opposite side to a barricade erected by Le Cler. In order to feel out the enemy, Codrington told off a detachment of 250 men to take up a protected position lower down on the escarpment and open fire. When the action was well under way, another contingent was sent to reinforce them, and the exchange of shots continued without interruption for a couple of hours. Thanks to the protected positions taken by both parties, neither side suffered much damage, and the action might have continued indefinitely if Codrington had not hit upon a scheme to carry the place by assault. He detached Colonel Rowland Williams and sent him with a body of men to cross the river at a point some distance upstream and thus catch the French on the flank while the troops lower down on the slope kept up their fire and the main body on the summit remained in full sight of the enemy. Williams was thus able to cross the river undetected, climb up the hill, and launch an attack from the other side. Caught in this trap, the French were driven from their fortifications, and they fled along the road to Le Baillif. In abandoning their post, it must be admitted, they were also influenced by the fear that the

English would embark in their ships and move down the coast during the night to Anse Val de Lorge, where they could land and attack them in the rear. By the time Codrington had crossed the river with the main army it was dusk, so he camped his men for the night on the spot vacated by the French.[16]

In retreating, the French had gone southward to the Rivière du Plessis, crossed it, and taken a position behind a stout barricade. When Codrington arrived with his forces at ten o'clock the following morning, he immediately went into action, expecting to carry the position as easily as he had taken the previous ones. But here at last he apparently met with serious resistance, for the French were able to hold him at bay for four hours, inflicting the heaviest losses he had suffered thus far. So desperate was the situation, so Labat tells us, that Codrington was on the point of abandoning the enterprise and recalling his men to the ships, when a rumor spread through the French lines—no one knew who started it—that the English had forced a passage some distance up the river. Thinking their defense had crumbled, the French were seized with a panic, and before the officers could restore order, the men had abandoned their positions and were rushing headlong to safety at Le Baillif. Here, owing to the confusion that still reigned in their ranks, they failed to make a stand at Fort La Madeleine, where they could at least have given their foe considerable trouble; abandoning the place to them, they fled across the Rivière St. Louis and did not stop until they had reached the confines of Basseterre. The English pursued them as far as Le Baillif, where they spent the night. Codrington now sent out Nathaniel Blakiston with four hundred men to look over the situation at Basseterre, and he followed with the entire force when he received the false news that his lieutenant had gone into action. On arriving at the capital he found that the French, far from giving battle, had retreated across the Rivière des Gallions, leaving the English in full possession of the town. Codrington established himself in the Capuchin convent situated in the village of St. François, a northerly

[16]Hutcheson's narrative of these events (*ibid.*, No. 1557) says that Codrington and a detachment pressed on to Le Baillif, one mile distant. The distance is actually five miles. Furthermore, Hutcheson omits all reference to the events of the following day, when the French made a stand at Rivière du Plessis. For this we must turn to Labat, *Nouveau voyage aux isles de l'Amérique* I (Part II), 89–91.

extension of Basseterre, separated from it by the Rivière des Herbes.

On the southern side of Des Gallions the French had deployed themselves along the bank for a distance of three thousand paces, from the sea to a ford called the Passage de Madame. Besides this, the main army, there remained on the northern side a contingent safely ensconced in the fort, while the inhabitants had fled to the hills behind. This fort had been built around the old Fort St. Charles, erected years before by Governor Houël. It was originally little more than a stone house that offered protection against the incursions of the savages, then gradually walls were added. When the King took over the colony, the structure was enlarged. A parapet was thrown up around the existing fortifications and extended inland up the side of the hill for some two hundred paces, where it was made to enclose a cavalier, or covered battery built of stone and irregular in shape, on which were mounted eight guns. A smaller battery of three pieces was located near the donjon, as the first building, the one erected by Houël, was now called. The fort proved quite adequate for the task imposed on it, for it held out until after the English had left. It was commanded by La Malmaison. Codrington, on finding the town stripped of all its movables save wine and brandy wisely encamped his men on a hillside above the cavalier, well out of temptation's way, and gave orders to fire the town. So carefully were these orders carried out that the villages of Basseterre and St. François were wiped out, with the exception of the convent where Codrington had taken up his residence.

When the English first landed on Guadeloupe, Governor Hencelin sent a message to the Marquis d'Eragny at Martinique requesting immediate aid. There were then at Fort Royal four warships: the "Mignon," commanded by Arbouville; the "Hazardeux," under Du Casse; the "Emerillon," and the "Cheval Marin," besides three merchantmen of twenty guns each. At a council of war held on receipt of Hencelin's letter it was decided to use this little fleet to transport reinforcements to Guadeloupe, the captains overruling D'Eragny's suggestion that they attack the English by sea, as the French vessels were insufficient in numbers and in guns to oppose the British squadron. These officers accordingly embarked in their ships, under the Marquis's personal leadership, with two

companies of infantry reinforced by six hundred volunteers and
freebooters, and set sail for Guadeloupe. In order to avoid contact
with the British fleet, they passed to windward of Dominica,
stopping en route at Mariegalante to drive out the English forces
left there, and landed at Gosier in the Grande-Terre section of
Guadeloupe, whence they proposed to march overland to Basseterre and treat the English to something in the nature of a surprise.

While Hencelin was waiting patiently for reinforcements, Codrington was seeking aid from Barbados. On the sixteenth of May
his messenger, Archibald Hutcheson, handed Governor Kendall a
letter describing the situation in a brief, graphic manner. The size
of Guadeloupe, it said, the mountainous topography of its western
section made its complete subjugation a very difficult task, certainly an impossible one with the number of men at hand, particularly when the French were daily expecting reinforcements.
He therefore requested the immediate dispatch of some troops.

This [he said] will assure us victory, and dispatch our business here at
half the cost of men and time; indeed the arrival of such a reinforcement
may so damp the courage of the enemy as to drive them to surrender. As
to Martinique we shall be ready enough to take it in hand when this
affair is ended; and doubt not of your help. It would be a pity to let the matter
grow cool just now, when the French star was on the decline in America.
The squadron's provisions are beginning to fail. Pray make up the
proportion that is lacking and send them down by this frigate. Also
could you lend us a hundred barrels of powder? It shall be repaid from the
next stores sent us by the King.[17]

While awaiting results from Hutcheson's mission, Governor
Codrington redoubled his efforts to capture Ft. St. Charles. The
French troops which had crossed the Gallions seem to have disappeared from the scene, perhaps they fled inland to the mountains,
for the English gave all their attention to the garrison holding the
fort. Batteries were raised and armed with guns captured from the
enemy. Their fire, however, proved ineffective, for the ramparts
of St. Charles were stout affairs built of solid masonry, and presently the attackers were forced to erect another battery, this time
within pistol-shot of the cavalier. On this rocklike structure they
wasted their fire for many days. On the twenty-third Codrington
received from the "Antelope," on patrol duty in the neighboring

---

[17]C.S.P., *America & West Indies, 1689–92*, No. 1557, sec. i.

waters, the alarming news that eleven enemy vessels had been sighted in the distance. Captain Wright, anxious not to be caught short-handed, sent for the sailors who had been taking part in the siege, while the Governor dispatched two sloops during the night to gather further information. Next morning Wright sent word that he had decided to go in pursuit of the French fleet, now located in the gulf, or cul-de-sac, between the two halves of the island, and asked Codrington if he wished to embark the army. Angered at this, the Governor called a council of war, hoping to shame his officers into refusing to relinquish their conquest; but despite all his eloquence it was decided to abandon the island and sail with the fleet. The officers had become discouraged. Violent rains had made operations difficult, sickness was decimating the ranks, provisions were running low, the French were receiving help, and no word had come from Barbados. Outvoted, Codrington determined to make still one more attempt to save what had been won by such great effort. When the council broke up, he sent a message to Wright, offering to remain and hold the island if the latter would give him five merchantmen to protect his small vessels and cover a retreat in case he should be obliged to withdraw. To this reasonable request Wright gave an emphatic "no." He would not leave a single ship or venture into action, even against the very inferior French, without every vessel under his command, for so far as he was concerned he would rather see all the Leeward Islands destroyed than lose his precious flagship, and he wound up his insolent answer by informing the Governor-General that if he did not embark at once his entire army would be left behind.

Faced with this choice, which was really no choice at all, Codrington embarked his men, and all set sail on the twenty-fifth, while the captain paced his quarterdeck foaming with rage at the entire Leeward group which for some reason or other he held responsible for his troubles. The fleet, now consisting of seven frigates,[18] a fire ship, and a number of merchantmen headed southward to round the tip of Guadeloupe and reach the French fleet in the cul-de-sac. Despite his immense superiority—the French had only four undersized warships besides merchant vessels—Wright showed no eagerness to close with the enemy. After beating

[18]"Mary," "Assistance," "Jersey," "Antelope," "Hampshire," "St. Paul," "Tiger."

about the Saints for two days, held back by contrary winds and Wright's fatuous insistence on sending the entire fleet to help a partially disabled merchantman, Codrington at last found himself at the entrance of the cul-de-sac facing the French squadron. When he urged the captain to close in, the latter raised objections too trivial and tedious, said the Governor, to be recorded. When night came, the two fleets met, and during the darkness the French managed to seep through the blockade, so that when dawn broke the English saw their foe scattered "across the sea heading in various directions." To meet the situation, Wright, instead of sending his ships to pursue them individually, signalled his command to form in line of battle. This strange, unseamanlike maneuver eventually led to the escape of the entire fleet save one vessel, which sought refuge among the Saints in a slightly damaged condition.

Next day the bickering between the Governor and the captain continued. Wright insisted on returning to Barbados, pleading shortage of provisions, though Codrington offered him an ample supply from his merchantmen. Unable to detain the stubborn captain, Codrington then pointed to the Admiralty's orders forbidding him (Wright) to leave the station without the Governor-General's permission; but the commander waxed obdurate and finally showed his true colors by shouting out that if the Leeward Islands were lost it was no great matter, since Barbados and Jamaica would supply England with enough sugar for her needs. Being unable to agree on anything, the two men decided to part company. Wright returned to Barbados in time to head off the reinforcements Kendall was preparing to send out at Hutcheson's request, while Codrington carried his troops back to Antigua in the "Antelope" and the "Jersey," grudgingly loaned him by the irascible captain.

Such was the situation at the end of this phase of the war. British St. Christopher, captured by the French, had been retaken by its original masters, while the French had repulsed the English attacks on Guadeloupe. For the better part of a year these Caribbee Islands now enjoyed a period of comparative peace.

VII

FRENCH AND BRITISH EXCHANGE BLOWS

W HILE THE FRENCH were successfully defending Guadeloupe from English attacks, they were at the same time meeting with reverses at the hands of the Spaniards in San Domingo. The first clash, however, did result in a measure of victory. In the year 1690 Governor de Cussy began operations against his neighbors by launching an expedition to capture St. Iago, a venture which had for its ultimate purpose the destruction of the Spanish army and the subjugation of the entire island to French rule. With an army of 400 cavaliers, 450 foot soldiers, and 150 Negroes he set out in June from Port de Paix, going first by sea to Cap François, then overland through the plains of Artibonite to St. Iago, where he easily disposed of the resistance offered him. Here a sudden unaccountable illness seized the men, an illness which they attributed to poisoned food left for them by the defenders, and in revenge for this they set fire to the entire city, sparing only the chapels and churches. After a stay of twenty-four hours De Cussy gave the order to leave the place, for he feared the approach of the rainy season. Slowly the buccaneer army retreated until they reached Artibonite, where they disbanded, while the Governor returned to Cap François, satisfied with having done a good day's work. In this case virtue was its own reward, for apparently he took no booty.[1]

At this time the population of the San Domingo colonies was increased by the advent of a large number of people from St. Christopher, expelled from that island, as we have said, when the British captured it. Most of these people landed at Port de Paix, where the Governor allotted them land for plantations.

[1]Charlevoix, *Histoire de l'isle espagnole*, III, 284–91.

There were upward of one thousand, mostly men capable of bearing arms. Lord Inchiquin,[2] Governor of Jamaica, did not relish the proximity of such a powerful force. He voiced his disapproval of Codrington's policy by complaining that these men had been sent into his own government—for so he was pleased to designate San Domingo—to which Codrington tartly replied that he wished Inchiquin would make the island his government, for then he could dispose of the prisoners as he wished. But if the English were alarmed, so too were the Spaniards, who viewed this strengthening of their hereditary enemies with grave apprehension. In the year 1691, still smarting under the defeat at St. Iago, they determined to get their revenge by launching an expedition against the French colony.

When De Cussy heard of the coming attack, he returned from Petit-Goave, whither he had gone after the victory of the previous year, to Port de Paix, where he would be nearer the scene of action. It was early in January when he arrived, and there he was informed of the presence off Cap François of a Spanish fleet of six vessels, carrying 2,600 men, who were to be joined by a small army of 700 coming overland. On learning this De Cussy hurried to the Cap. Here he found that the Spaniards had landed twelve hundred men at Limonade, a short distance east of the Cap and then, sailing westward to a spot not far distant, had landed five hundred more. These two detachments had no difficulty in forming a junction with the expedition coming by land. The failure of the French to take advantage of the enemy when they were divided was due to a difference of opinion between De Cussy and his lieutenant, Franquenay, as to the proper strategem of defense. The Governor wished to make an ambuscade with some forty men at a place called Bayaha to harry the oncoming troops, while Franquenay, on the other hand, wanted to make a stand with all his forces on the plain of Limonade, through which the invaders would be obliged to pass on their way to the Cap. This latter scheme was a foolish one, for the French could produce but a thousand men to oppose the Spanish force of more than three times that number. De Cussy's plan was, however, cried down by the buccaneers, who clamored to be led to Limonade, confident that they were more than a match

[2]William O'Brien, Earl of Inchiquin.

for the Spaniards. Unable to withstand such insistance, for discipline was slack among the freebooters, De Cussy was obliged to yield and lead his men to the plain where they wished to give battle. The Spaniards did not keep them waiting long. On the morning of the twenty-first of January they appeared and at once went into action. The struggle was a brief one: it lasted only an hour and a half. At first the Spanish infantry seemed unable to hold up against the furious and accurate fire of the buccaneers; then their commander, seeing them waver, waved his hat as a signal, and at once three hundred lancers who had been lying prone in the grass sprang to their feet and charged, breaking the French center. The battle line thus broken, the army folded up. The men took to flight, all save a small group around De Cussy and Franquenay. The Governor proved himself a gallant fighter, holding off single-handed a half-dozen Spaniards, until, completely surrounded, he fell with Franquenay beside him. The leaders dead, the battle soon became a rout; and when the French at last succeeded in escaping, they found they had left from four to five hundred dead on the field.[3] Flushed with victory, the Spaniards proceeded to abuse it, in retaliation, no doubt, for what they had suffered the previous year at St. Iago. They burned Cap François, massacred whatever men they could find, and carried off the women, children, and slaves. On this occasion, it is recorded, the slaves showed a surprising loyalty to their masters—convincing proof, Charlevoix observes, of the kindness with which they had been treated and the care taken by their owners to rear them in the Christian faith.

News of this disaster caused great consternation in France. This feeling was shared by Jean du Casse, who had returned home after his activities at St. Christopher; for the retention of San Domingo, a colony he had studied and helped for many years, was to him essential if France was to hold her West Indian empire. Jean du Casse[4] was one of the most celebrated buccaneers of his

[3] *Ibid.*, pp. 294–97. In reading Charlevoix's account one is apt to gain the impression that an English fleet from St. Christopher took part in this campaign as an ally of the Spaniards. Adrien Dessalles, *Histoire générale des Antilles*, (II, 115) says so specifically. Southey, *Chronological History of the West Indies*, on the other hand, makes no mention of a British fleet (II, 159), and this is borne out by the complete absence of any reference to such a naval engagement in the *Calendar of State Papers*. The British attack on San Domingo did not take place until 1695.

[4] Many authorities give the name as "Jean-Baptiste," but his biographer, Robert du Casse, speaks of him as "Jean."

day, an able sea captain, very popular in naval circles because of his modesty and liberality. His talents were soon recognized at court. He was made a captain in the Royal Navy and given the governorship of San Domingo, where for many years he ruled wisely and well, an antagonist greatly dreaded by the English. When he heard of De Cussy's death, he wrote the minister of marine, Louis Phelypeaux, Comte de Pontchartrain, expressing his opinions and suggesting various methods for recapturing Cap François. He offered to lead an expedition for that purpose and was taken at his word. On the twenty-fifth of March he was given a letter to the Marquis d'Eragny, containing orders to give him all possible assistance. Du Casse set sail a few days later and reached Fort Royal early enough in May to join Arbouville's fleet when it sailed to relieve Guadeloupe. Returning from this successful venture, he held several conferences with Governor d'Eragny to devise some means of protecting the French colonies from the continual attacks of the Englishmen and Spaniards, and it was while thus engaged that a virulent epidemic of yellow fever (called by the French *mal de Siam*) broke out, which carried off the Marquis. His place was taken temporarily by Comminge de Guitaud. To escape this plague Du Casse betook himself with his ships to the island of St. Croix. A week later he left that island for Port de Paix, where he heard that an English fleet was threatening Leogane. Hastening thither, he found awaiting him a commission from the King naming him Governor of San Domingo. We must now leave San Domingo for a moment and return to the Leeward Islands to examine the efforts of the English to recoup the losses they had suffered during the first years of the war.

Though they had been compelled to withdraw from Guadeloupe when victory was seemingly close at hand, the British never lost heart. The plans of the aggressive Governor-General had evidently found favor in London, for William Blathwayt of the Privy Council drew up a proposal for destroying the French plantations which had for its first objective the capture of Martinique. This taken, he believed, it would be comparatively easy to launch successful attacks on Guadeloupe and San Domingo. The project, however, was doomed to lie in abeyance for nearly two years, for the French were too strongly entrenched in Martinique to be dislodged by anything short of an expedition of considerable magnitude, carefully planned, and generously reinforced from England. Moreover, the French were now superior at sea.

At the beginning of the year 1692 the English made an attempt to regain their customary supremacy. Captain Ralph Wrenn had replaced the incompetent Wright as commander in the West Indies, and he was then at Barbados with five warships, the "Norwich," the "Diamond," the "Mordaunt," the "Mary," and the "Antelope." While lying at anchor off Bridgetown, he received word of a French fleet of seven sail sighted some eight leagues to the northeast which, so French prisoners said, had been sent out to bombard the town. A council of war was called, and its startled members ordered all merchant ships and sloops in the harbor to join Wrenn's squadron and sent the Captain forth to attack the enemy, if he felt himself strong enough to do so. The arrival of an English officer from Martinique bringing the news that ten men-of-war and several frigates were leaving Fort Royal to intercept the fleet expected from England gave further alarm and caused a slight change of plans. Wrenn had by this time returned from his cruise to the northeast without having found any trace of the French fleet—its presence in that locality was purely imaginary—and he was now told to proceed to the Leeward Islands, taking under his protection the merchantmen bound for these parts and for Jamaica, and there to join, if possible, the "Assistance," the "Hampshire," and the "St. Paul," which were stationed somewhere among the islands. This done, he was to attack the enemy.

Wrenn obeyed his orders carefully. On the second of March he found the French squadron of eighteen vessels in the channel between Desirade and Guadeloupe.[5] They were commanded by the Comte de Blénac, who had recently returned to Martinique to resume his former post of governor-general and had hoisted his flag on the "Vermandois," a ship of sixty guns. Outnumbered, the English did not rush to the attack, their business being to protect the convoy first and keep it from falling into the enemy's hands. All through the night the two fleets remained near each other,

---

[5]The fleet consisted of the "Vaillant," "Léger," "François," "Emerillon," "Faucon," "Droite," "Vermandois," "Basque," "Chasseur," "Solide," "Bouffonne," "Jersey" (recently captured from the English), "Neptune," and five others.

barely moving through the water. At daybreak the French commander signaled his captains to form into a line of battle, and at
eight o'clock a strong wind sprang up, giving him a windward
position. With the "Vermandois" in the lead, he bore down on the
English, attacking first the "Mary," then engaging the entire
squadron. For four hours the battle raged, neither side inflicting
much damage on the other; then the British commander managed
to shake off his foes and bring the convoy out of danger. It was
indeed a moral if not an actual victory, for by superior seamanship
Wrenn had managed in the face of greater numbers to save from
capture the ships intrusted to him. A few days later he returned to
Bridgetown to report his success to Governor Kendall. [6]

When the French government dispatched Blénac to Martinique,
it had no illusions as to its immunity from attack. The officials
knew well enough that an all-out effort would soon be made by
England to capture the island, and it proposed to have the place
ready when the time came. With Blénac the King had sent the
engineer De Caylus with instructions to see to it that Fort Royal
was well fortified. The protection of this town was stressed because Louis had finally decided to make it the official capital of the
West Indian colonies and concentrate the government there. For
some fifteen years the Governor-General had made it his residence,
while his official family had for the most part remained at St.
Pierre; now the Intendant and the Council received positive orders
to remove themselves to the southern settlement. The chief reason
for this change was that the Cul-de-Sac Royal offered immensely
superior harbor facilities compared to the open roadstead of St.
Pierre. Furthermore, the repulse of De Ruyter's great armada had
shown how easily the place might be defended. The colonists
rallied behind Blénac in his work of organizing the defense. They
gave freely the services of their slaves to repair the fortifications
under the able direction of De Caylus. In organizing the military
establishment the militia, numbering fourteen hundred men,
were divided for purposes of flexibility into four batallions of three
companies each. The battalion of St. Pierre was under command of
Governor Jean de Gabaret, that of Fort Royal under Comminge
de Guitaud, that of the Marine under Charles Auger, of Marie-

[6] *C.S.P., America & West Indies, 1689–92,* No. 2110.

galante (this little island having been temporarily abandoned), that of the Trinity under Jean du Buc. Pending the organization of cavalry units, soldiers who owned horses rode at the head of each company. The road between St. Pierre and Fort Royal was enlarged and repaired, thus making it easy to rush troops from one town to the other as occasion might require. In this way did the Martinicans spend the rest of the year, making ready for the attack they knew might come at any time.

While the French were thus preparing to ward off the blow, the English were preparing to deliver it. Captain Wright had returned to England in disgrace, and the Admiralty selected Sir Francis Wheler, a captain just promoted to the rank of rear-admiral of the blue, to command the coming expedition. The agents of the Leeward Islands had suggested a fairly sound plan for the undertaking. They requested two thousand soldiers from England, one thousand from Barbados, and a fleet of ten or twelve men-of-war, to which force they would add twelve hundred men recruited in the Caribbees. The fleet should go first to Barbados, and upon its arrival the governor of the Leeward Islands should be notified at once to hold himself in readiness to coöperate. This plan formed the basis of what was eventually done. Orders were sent to Governor Kendall to muster all the forces in Barbados and to summon a council of war as often as Wheler and the commander of the land forces, John Foulke, should desire it. Wheler was ordered to capture Martinique first, then to proceed to Jamaica, where he was to launch an expedition against the French at San Domingo, and for this purpose he was given a fleet of thirteen warships and three fire ships, to which twenty-eight transports were added, capable of carrying nearly two thousand men. Before they left, the plan was altered, or rather expanded, by orders telling Wheler to proceed to New England when he had finished the West Indian business, where he was to join with William Phipps for an attack on Canada.

Admiral Wheler set sail early in January, 1693, and arrived off Bridgetown on the tenth of March, where he was enthusiastically received. His flagship was the "Resolution," and he had among the other vessels the "Dragon," the "Experiment," the "Mermaid," the "Cygnet," the "Falcon," the "Chester," and the "Norwich"; the last of which presently blew up at her anchor. Governor Kendall had done his best to fulfill his duty toward the expedition and had collected some nine hundred men, the colony's finest, fully equipped, and he had provided transports to carry them to Martinique. On the arrival of Wheler he called a council of war, at which it was decided to send a sloop to Governor Codrington apprizing him of the situation. At Antigua Codrington had been doing his best. Ever since the previous autumn he had been rushing from one island to another enacting laws for raising forces and issuing commissions and press warrants for commandeering transports, hoping the fleet from England might come at any time. When the fleet did put in an appearance, everything was ready for the Leeward Islanders to do their share. Only at St. Christopher does Codrington seem to have met with opposition, and this quickly vanished when he offered to lead the expedition in person.[7]

When Kendall sent Codrington the news of Wheler's arrival, the message also contained an outline of the plan of campaign. It was pointed out to him that it would be impractical for the fleet to beat up to Antigua and that much more could be accomplished by the Barbadian and Leeward forces meeting off Martinique. The council sent two frigates, the "Chester" and the "Mermaid," to convoy Codrington's forces, at the same time requesting the Governor-General to inform them at once when he would have his men at Martinique. He was also cautioned to bring artillery and two months' provisions, for Fort Royal was admittedly a hard nut to crack. A sloop was also sent to Martinique to report on the situation there. The question of the division of plunder, always a source of dispute, was settled in the council by the simple expedient of appointing an officer for each of the five Barbadian regiments to whom all loot should be brought and who should be responsible for its equitable distribution.[8] To satisfy a possible feeling of unrest, it was agreed that the Barbadians should be sent home after the capture of Martinique. Ten sloops were pressed into service to transport the troops. On the twenty-sixth a letter was received from Codrington suggesting Mariegalante as a rendezvous; but the council held to its original decision to meet at Martinique, where there was a better supply of fresh water. Wheler ordered a frigate to carry the final plans of the council to Codrington, together with

[7]*C.S.P., America & West Indies, 1693–96*, No. 336.   [8]*Ibid.*, No. 200.

two hundred muskets. He was also asked to advise at once when he intended to sail.

On the ninth of April the fleet left Barbados. The thoroughness with which the expedition was made ready in so short a time was due largely to the energy of Francis Wheler who acted in all capacities from admiral to purser in his eagerness to expedite the business. Governor Kendall was especially impressed, and prophesied the speedy reduction of Martinique. He was distressed, however, by the orders Wheler had received to be back in England by the end of the year, as he foresaw the necessity of keeping a squadron in the West Indies for the duration of the war if the enemy was to be defeated and the security of British commerce made permanent. This was particularly important in October, when the French King was bound to send relief to "the miserable remainders of his subjects in these islands"; for there were bound to be "remainders" on the islands, since the English had no means of removing them as prisoners of war after the conquest. [9]

The run to Martinique was rapid, thanks to the favorable trade winds, and on the eleventh Wheler dropped anchor in the Cul-de-Sac Marin, a bay just south of the Cul-de-Sac Royal. It was a huge squadron that greeted the astonished French, a squadron consisting of thirty-two ships of various sizes, nine barks, three brigantines, two ketches, and a galiot, making forty-seven sail in all, in short a fleet that reminded them of De Ruyter's armada of twenty years earlier. For some reason or other Codrington had not yet arrived, nor did the Admiral receive any word as to when he would come. The French were ready for Wheler. In approaching Martinique he had sailed around the northern end and had been sighted at Fort St. Pierre, where the alarm was given by Governor Gabaret, who at once sent François de Collart with his cavalry to follow the progress of the fleet along the shore, thinking, of course, that Fort Royal was the objective. Then, to the surprise of the onlookers, the British fleet sailed past Pointe d'Arlet, doubled Pointe du Diamant, and headed for the Cul-de-Sac Marin.

Wheler's move was a wise one. He knew the strength of Fort Royal and guessed the warm reception awaiting him at St. Pierre, so he decided to land on the southern extremity of the island, where

[9] *Ibid.*, No. 259.

there were no defenses. The maneuver was similar to the one employed three years before by Codrington at St. Christopher, when
he made his surprise landing at Frigate Bay. By landing at Marin,
Wheler believed he could march northward along the coast and
attack the forts from the land side by surrounding them and cutting
them off from all sources of supply, thus ensuring their eventual
surrender. He anchored his ships along the southern shore of the
cul-de-sac, near its entrance at a bight, or roadstead, known today
as Anse de Ste. Anne. The plan was well thought out and began
well. The French governor, believing the blow would fall first
on Fort Royal, had drawn off all the troops from the southern part
of the island, including the few at the Cul-de-Sac Marin, to bolster
up the defense of the capital, leaving only the local commander
Charles Auger with his guard. Even when he saw the fleet sail
past the Pointe d'Arlet, Gabaret felt it was a feint and contented
himself with reinforcing Auger by sending him a detachment of
sixty men under Henri de Saint-Amour. A strong breeze blowing
offshore prevented the English from landing when they sailed into
the harbor; but the following morning the weather was more
propitious, and Foulke was sent ashore with a thousand men,
whom he spread out over a front half a league in length. Later in
the day these men were reinforced by the rest of the landing force,
so that by nightfall twenty-five hundred were ashore ready for
action. In the face of such gigantic numbers Auger, with his handful, could do nothing. He placed them in ambush and let them
fire away from a safe distance, which they did, occasionally killing
or wounding a man. On the thirteenth the Admiral dispatched a
small flotilla of thirty boats, supported by the galiot and two
barks, to attack the settlement at the head of the bay. The barks
first swept the landing place with their guns, while Auger and his
people, ensconced safely out of range, watched the operation. The
English troops, once they had landed, did, of course, as they
pleased. They burned the local church, destroyed the sugar plantations and mills, and damaged as much as they could; only at the
mouth of the Rivière Pilote on the western side of the cul-de-sac,
where the reinforcements under Saint-Amour had been stationed,
were the English repulsed. But even this triumph was short-lived,
for the invaders speedily sent by land a strong detachment which

proceeded to clean up the little village of the Rivière Pilote. Toward noon on the fifteenth a squadron of five barks, three brigantines, and twenty-eight boats landed nine hundred men at the Pilote; they speedily routed the feeble defense of the French and proceeded to set fire to whatever was left from the previous raids. From here they spread out westward, overrunning the Quartier de Ste. Luce and destroying everything that stood in their way.

On the nineteenth Codrington arrived. Four ships, four brigantines, and two barks bore his army of thirteen hundred men, divided into three regiments, one under Rowland Williams, one under Nathaniel Blakiston, and the third under Godfrey Lloyd. For a day or two the new detachments joined in the marauding, then on the twenty-second Wheler embarked his men and set forth to strike a direct blow at Fort Royal. The plan to march overland was abandoned, for it was now realized that it would be easier to transport the army by sea to the vicinity of the fort than to march across the intervening peninsula.

As soon as the fleet had disappeared around Pointe du Diamant, Auger gathered his men together and hurried northward across the peninsula and at four in the afternoon reached the shore of Cul-de-Sac à Vaches, at the entrance of the main harbor and directly opposite the fort. He placed his men in ambush along the shore, while the British fleet anchored not far off. It was evidently Wheler's idea not to make a frontal attack on the fort, but to adhere to his general plan and land some distance away, then approach the fort from the rear. To carry this out, the boats were lowered and sent to look for a suitable landing. As they were approaching the shore Auger's men, from their concealed position, greeted them with volley after volley, and they were unable to return the fire. Driven away, the boats rowed farther in toward the fort, where they were driven off by salvos from the big guns. Orders now reached Auger to hold himself ready to join Blénac at Fort Royal in case it was attacked, or in case the fleet set sail for St. Pierre. For two or three days the English sent their boats along the shore looking for an opening, only to be repulsed when they came in close enough to try a landing; then Wheler called a council on board the "Resolution," at which his officers decided to abandon the attempt to reduce Fort Royal and try their luck at St. Pierre.

On the twenty-seventh the fleet left the Cul-de-Sac, and Auger proceeded to rejoin his commander at the fort. On arriving there he learned that Blénac had gone on to St. Pierre, leaving Guitaud in charge of the capital, and that he (Auger) was to follow him there. Auger did not stop, but hurried on at once to carry out his orders, arriving at St. Pierre the following morning after an all night's march. During the afternoon startling news reached the Governor-General: the British fleet, so it was reported, had stopped some three miles south of St. Pierre at the Carbet, where the Admiral would land his men. Governor Gabaret forestalled this move by sending a detachment to the point of danger. This was wise, for he could not afford to take chances under the circumstances; but it is doubtful if Wheler intended to land here, for the following morning he weighed anchor when a breeze sprang up and continued on his way to St. Pierre, where he came to anchor at a point somewhat north of it, near Canouville, well out of range of the guns of a battery recently erected to protect this locality. Here he landed his men without much opposition. There were only a few militiamen at the place, for all the available men had been sent to St. Pierre to man the fortifications. Gabaret hurried up to take command, but he could accomplish nothing, for the colonists had fled inland as soon as they saw the fleet, leaving him alone with a lieutenant to hold the place. At this moment Blénac arrived with the men he had brought from Fort Royal, and his appearance brought hope to the panicky inhabitants, who quickly ranged themselves under his standard and began to annoy the invaders by a few feeble attacks. But the men from Fort Royal were too tired by their forced march to give any assistance other than moral support, and the colonists were obliged to await the arrival of reinforcements from St. Pierre and the return of the detachment which had been told off to guard the Carbet.

Once ashore, the English commander quickly sized up the situation and hurried a company of marines southward to cut off the Blénac-Gabaret contingent. Fortunately for the French, the maneuver did not succeed. At this moment Collart arrived with his cavalry, closely followed by the militia of St. Pierre under François le Vassor and Giraud du Poyet, who hurled themselves on the English, drove them back, and forced them to seek refuge for the night in a building at the bottom of a ravine. Next morning the marines found themselves caught in a trap. To escape, they had to scale the sides of the ravine; but as soon as they made the attempt Blénac sent the companies of Saint-Amour, Christophe Renaudot, and Lefebvre de Méricourt, three hundred men in all, to seize the heights before them. As the French sprang forward, Blénac opened fire on the enemy, the guns of the battery driving them back down the slopes of the ravine as quickly as they could gain a footing. Blocked in this direction, Codrington's men decided to escape over the route they had taken the previous day, namely, the road leading southward along the shore to St. Pierre. Auger, who had been held in reserve, guessed their intention and now came forward, aided by Collart's cavalry, and drove them back to their camp. Once in their former position in the ravine, some seized a sugar mill near enough the French position to cause Blénac considerable trouble, and protected by the surrounding hedges they managed to keep up an annoying fire. To capture the place, or at any rate to silence it, Blénac sent out his men to fight Indian fashion; they took advantage of every bit of cover as they advanced, keeping up an incessant fire on the garrison. The English commander quickly perceived that the loss of this place meant a general retreat and brought up half his entire force to save it. But when they began their advance, the French succeeded in opening a breach in the hedge, through which Collart rushed his cavalry, closely followed by a company of militia, which drove the reinforcements back to the landing place. It was the end of the attack on Martinique. Seeing themselves deserted, the garrison in the sugar mill surrendered without further ado.

That night a council was held on board the "Resolution," at which Wheler listened gravely to the opinions of his subordinates. Of the various officers who ventured an opinion, a strong majority expressed themselves in favor of abandoning the enterprise. They were impressed by the strength of the fort, the number and fighting quality of the French, and most of all by their own losses, which amounted to eight hundred killed, wounded, or incapacitated by illness, leaving only some three thousand capable of service, including a large number of Irishmen whose loyalty was open to question.[10] Such being the case, Wheler had no choice but to

[10]*Ibid.*, No. 281.

reëmbark his troops and sail northward to the conquest of Guadeloupe, in the hope that it might prove easier. But off the coast of
Dominica their hearts failed them, and at a council called to consider the matter it was decided to abandon the enterprise entirely
and send the troops back to their homes in Barbados and the
Leeward Islands.[11]

News of this *volte-face* caused great consternation in Barbados,
as it put an entirely new face on the situation. Instead of asking
for ships to attack the French possessions, Kendall wrote home for
vessels and a regiment of infantry to protect his own colony from
French aggression. Codrington, too, shared this fear for the islands
under his rule. He was disappointed in the expedition. It had not
been sent soon enough, for one thing, and since the King had
given positive orders for the fleet to leave the West Indies by the
last of May, this meant that they had only two months to capture
the two French islands, a job that would take at least four. He also
complained of the paucity of the forces sent by the island governors;
two more regiments of seasoned men were needed if the French
colonies were to be destroyed. Yet despite all this, despite his con-
viction that if all the forces under his jurisdiction were assembled
on one of his islands they would not be sufficient to defend it, the
doughty governor was willing to risk all to conquer his ancient
enemies, and he felt sure his colonists shared his enthusiasm. When
writing to the Lords of Trade for a fleet, he closed his letter by
saying: "Should he [the King] favor us with a land force also,
strong enough to attempt the French islands, he will find the inhabitants [will] express their loyalty zealously and cheerfully by
venturing their lives and fortunes in his service."[12]

The arrival of Wheler's fleet in the West Indies had caused considerable apprehension in San Domingo, especially as the buccaneers were at that time away on marauding expeditions, leaving
the island open to possible capture. The fleet, according to the
original plan, was to have sailed against San Domingo, after taking
Martinique and Guadeloupe, in order to complete the conquest of
the French islands. This campaign was to be carried out with the

---

[11]The French account of the attack on Martinique is in the relation of Blénac used by Guët,
Le Colonel François de Collart, pp. 217–19. On the English side there is the journal kept by
Francis Wheler, to be found in the manuscripts of the Duke of Portland. The documents in
the *Calendar of State Papers, America & West Indies, 1693–96*, are brief and rather unsatisfactory.
They are: Nos. 281, 334, 336.   [12]*Ibid.*, No. 336.

assistance of the Spaniards, for there had just arrived from Spain a powerful squadron of ten vessels and six thousand men. The failure of Wheler at Martinique therefore saved San Domingo, since the Spanish admiral showed no disposition to attack the French single-handed.

During this trying time Governor du Casse kept the few buccaneers he could muster in training by sending them on a freebooting expedition against Jamaica, in which he succeeded in carrying off 350 slaves. Encouraged by this moderate success, he got together some four or five hundred and sent them under the command of Sieur de Beauregard [13] in a fleet of six ships to plunder the parishes of St. Thomas and St. David at the eastern end of Jamaica. Fortunately for the planters, Governor William Beeston had sent out the "Falcon" to patrol the coast. As soon as Beauregard saw her, he called a council of war and spoke loudly in favor of attacking this lone ship, the only thing that stood between them and their prey. Strange to say, the buccaneers, who were usually ready for any sort of fight, feared to tackle the Englishman, saying that "at best they would get only broken bones and spoil their men for any further design." In defiance to the traditions of the coast, the little fleet of six ships turned tail and ran, closely pursued by the "Falcon," which succeeded in capturing one of their number and bringing her safely to Jamaica. Within forty-eight hours the "Falcon" was back on her beat. But now there arrived another French squadron of an entirely different caliber. Governor du Casse had set out from Petit-Goave with the "Temeraire," the "Envieux," and the "Solide," and when he sighted the "Falcon" he at once closed in; he captured her after she had put up a spirited resistance. [14]

Sir William Beeston was not inclined to take these attacks lying down. Long before the capture of the "Falcon" he had boldly suggested to the Assembly to stop the trouble at its source by a counterattack on San Domingo. At a meeting held in October he had, to quote his own words, "moved them to consider the state of the country, the necessity of preventing the daily depredations of French privateers on our coasts, as the means for better collection of quit-rents." To all this the members turned a deaf ear.

[13]Charles-François le Vassor de Beauregard.   [14]*Ibid.*, No. 1236.

They complained of the expense of fitting out the necessary sloops, of the "recent calamities and discouragements," and refused to appropriate any more money. Governor Beeston, however, persevered, for he realized better than they did the danger in which the island stood, and in due course he was able to bring them to a more reasonable frame of mind, until at last they were willing to join with him in his plans for defense.[15]

In addition to his other problems, Governor Beeston had had considerable trouble with his Irish-Catholic population, who like their coreligionists in the Leeward Islands were still loyal to King James and felt more closely bound to the French by religious ties than to the subjects of King William. Since privateering had been discouraged in Jamaica while it was encouraged in San Domingo, many English colonists who liked this kind of life had gone to the French settlements, thus strengthening the French at the expense of the English. Thanks to the knowledge these deserters had of Jamaican topography, the French gained an excellent picture of the state of affairs in the island, the condition of the fortifications, the number of defenders, the resistance they might expect to encounter, and the best places at which to launch an attack. This information led to a number of minor raids; but at last, early in June, 1694, a Captain Stephen Eliot appeared before the Governor with the startling news that the French were on the way with a powerful armada. Eliot had been a prisoner in San Domingo and had just escaped in a canoe with two companions. After a perilous journey in this little craft he had managed to reach Jamaica; he gave warning that the French would soon be upon the island with twenty ships and three thousand men. The French, he went on to say, were well posted on conditions in Jamaica, for deserters had told them that the fortifications were in a state of disrepair and that they might expect five hundred followers of King James to join them when they landed. The news was indeed correct, for Governor du Casse had finally managed to collect a fleet of twenty-two ships mounting 278 guns and carrying 3,164 fighting men.[16] Hoisting his flag on the "Temeraire," commanded by Captain du Rollon, he had sailed on ahead with the naval vessels "Hazardeux" and "Envieux," having named Cap Tiburon at the western ex-

[15]*Ibid.*, No. 635.   [16]*Ibid.*, No. 1113.

tremity of the southern peninsula of San Domingo as the rendezvous. On the twenty-seventh of June the major part of the fleet
anchored in Cow Bay, fifteen miles east of the entrance to Port
Royal (modern Kingston harbor), ready to attack the colonists of
Jamaica.

On hearing the news from Captain Eliot, Governor Beeston
quickly called his council together, adjourned the assembly, and
proclaimed martial law. This done, he rushed forward the work
of defense. Fort Charles, at the entrance to Port Royal, mounted
thirty-eight guns. Though it had been shaken by a recent earth-
quake, it was still in good condition save for one of its bastions
which was not yet completed. An energetic officer, Colonel Peter
Beckford, was put in charge of the work, and within a remarkably
short time he had finished the bastion, had laid the platform,
mounted the guns, and put the fort in excellent order. He then
placed nineteen culverins to the east of the fort and five to the west.
A vessel was fitted out as a fire ship, the merchantmen lying in the
harbor were formed into line, the streets leading to the fort were
barricaded, and guns were mounted behind the barricades. Beeston
sent the Colonel a reinforcement of two hundred men, whites and
slaves. The slaves were placed on board the "Advice," which had
been anchored in such a position as to protect the fort with her
fire. Led by Colonel Nicholas Lawes, the citizens of nearby St.
Andrew's constructed lines of defense and secured a pass at the
eastern end of Port Royal where they feared the enemy might
break in. Breastworks were also thrown up to protect Old Harbor
west of the town. Since the island was too large to be defended on
all fronts, Beeston wisely concentrated his forces for the protection of the capital and its vicinity. He accordingly withdrew the
colonists from the easternmost parishes, where the enemy would
probably strike first, that is, from St. Thomas's and St. David's,
and transported them to St. Dorothy's, St. Catherine's, and St.
Andrew's. Only a few were left to defend Carlisle Bay, thirty
miles to the westward. At Port Morant, at the eastern extremity,
the guns of Fort William were spiked, the shot buried, the ammunition carried away, and the buildings burned.

It was the twenty-seventh of June, then, early on a Sunday
morning, when the French fleet hove in sight, scudding before a

fresh breeze. Du Casse had sent eight ships into Port Morant, and now he anchored the rest of his fleet, as we have said, in Cow Bay. He was anxious to attack Port Royal at once, to force the entrance to the harbor under the guns of Fort Charles, and to carry the town by assault. But as naval commander of the expedition Du Rollon promptly vetoed the plan as being too risky, for a slave who had just boarded his ship brought him a detailed account of the preparations made by Governor Beeston for the protection of the capital. Balked in this direction, Du Casse landed eight hundred men under Beauregard, who led them eastward along the coast, plundering, burning, and destroying all that lay before them, killing cattle and the fowl, driving sheep into houses, which were then set on fire, damaging fruit trees and standing crops. The inhabitants they encountered were murdered or tortured, and the women were turned over to the Negroes. In this manner they made a clean sweep of the coast as far as Port Morant. Now the entire fleet was moved to Port Morant, which was used as headquarters, while numerous expeditions were sent along the northern shore, where they landed at various points and did considerable damage. Before they left Cow Bay, however, a sudden blow from offshore carried away the "Temeraire" and landed her in Bluefield Bay in the western part of the island. Du Casse, fortunately, was not on board. Returning after the storm, Du Rollon missed the fleet and poked about in various places in search of it, on one occasion landing and engaging in a skirmish with the enemy, until he heard from a prisoner that his squadron had been sighted on the northern side of the island. He attempted to get there, but, caught by contrary winds, he ran short of provisions and was obliged to make for Petit-Goave in order to replenish his stores. Here he learned that the expedition had gone to Port Morant. He made a gallant attempt to rejoin his command there, but an epidemic broke out among the crew which forced him into Leogane, there to await the return of the armada.

After a month spent at Port Morant, Du Casse decided to return to Cow Bay and prepare to attack Port Royal by land. Before leaving he put Fort William out of commission, battering down its walls and destroying its gun carriages. On the twenty-seventh of July the entire fleet was back in Cow Bay. A landing party was now put ashore and marched ostentatiously toward Port Royal.

Beeston, fearing the invaders intended to force the pass at St. Andrew's, rushed a hundred men to bar the way. Even as he did so, he suspected that the entire maneuver might be a feint. And so it proved to be, for when night fell the French quickly reëmbarked and sailed westward, leaving but three vessels in the bay. Du Casse, it seems, had called a council of war at which it was decided to launch the main attack at Carlisle Bay, some thirty-five miles west of Kingston, since he believed the capital itself was too well fortified on all sides to permit its being taken by assault. The execution of this plan had been assigned to a lieutenant of Du Casse's named Baldran de Graff,[17] who was to have full command and responsibility, while the Governor himself was to remain at Cow Bay. On seeing the vessels depart Beeston guessed their destination, and he immediately dispatched to Carlisle Bay two troops of horse and one of foot. These men all got away in the evening, the cavalry arriving during the night, the foot soldiers early the next morning, after a long march, all of them in time to take part in the battle.

Carlisle Bay was defended by Colonel Thomas Sutton with a force of 250 men, besides a large number of slaves, who had fortified themselves by throwing up a breastwork of rather poor quality. It faced the sea, flanked on the west by a small river, on the east by a grove of standing timber. On the twenty-ninth the French started the battle. A formidable detachment, fifteen hundred strong, had been put ashore during the previous night, and when the French opened the attack, Beauregard led the van with the buccaneers, while De Graff followed with the colonists, who formed the main body. When they came through the woods on the eastern flank of the breastwork, they were met by the fire of twelve pieces of artillery backed up by the musketry of the defenders. The attackers held their fire until within pointblank range, then opened up with deadly effect; and as the enemy fell back before the storm, they rushed in, sword in hand, to carry the place by assault. Retreating pell-mell across the river, the English garrison was about to break into flight when the reinforcements arriving on foot from Port Royal thrust themselves into the breach and, despite their all-night march, managed to hold off the buccaneers until

[17]Laurens-Cornille Baldran de Graff.

the defenders could get safely across the river. In the end all the English forces succeeded in escaping, but not until they had suffered severe losses in matériel, as well as in personnel. According to the French accounts they lost 360 men and left behind 150 horses all saddled and bridled, to say nothing of flags and equipment. As for the English, they modestly put their casualties at twenty-two.

The following day De Graff told off five hundred men to round up the stray cattle, bring in the prisoners, and ravage the neighborhood. In carrying out this order the French found themselves badly hampered, and in the end they were completely checked by the methods which the planters used for the protection of their property. Each house was strongly fortified, and into it the owner moved his valuables and as many of his men as were needed for its defense. From this point of vantage, protected by stout walls, he could give as good as he got. The buccaneers, foiled on several occasions in their attempts to capture these strongholds, seriously considered bringing ashore the heavy guns from the fleet; and they would have done so had the scheme been practicable. As an example of the difficulties encountered in storming these places, a group of buccaneers came upon the house of a certain planter who had locked himself in it with a band of twenty-five, plentifully supplied with provisions and determined to defend his property at all cost. As the attackers opened upon the house, Major Richard Lloyd heard the firing in the distance and rushed up to help beat off the attack. He succeeded in doing so; but later during the night, he heard from scouts that the French planned to bring up the artillery. To be ready for them, he threw sixty men into the house and placed the rest of his command in ambush around the place. So well did he have the plantation covered, that the French made no attempt to take it. They saw at once that its capture, even if it could be effected, would be accompanied by too great a loss of life to make it worth while. As it was in this instance, so it was in many others, and the plan to ravage the countryside was perforce reluctantly abandoned. Instead, the buccaneers contented themselves with plundering the little town of Carlisle.

A few days later Du Casse arrived with the ships he had kept at Cow Bay, and he went ashore to supervise the general destruction of the place. To his intense disappointment his men had managed to collect very little booty, thanks to the resistance put up by the English at their fortified farmhouses, and he was obliged to rest content with sixteen hundred slaves (three thousand according to Charlevoix), some indigo, and a few pieces of sugar-making machinery to carry back to San Domingo with him. On the third of August he gave the order to sail. When the fleet left the harbor, Major Lloyd also took his departure, after placing a small detachment to guard what remained of Carlisle, and marched to St. Dorothy's parish to protect Old Harbor should the French attempt to land there. Du Casse was satisfied with his efforts, however, and continued on his way to Port Morant, where he landed his prisoners and presently set sail for Petit-Goave, which he reached on the fourteenth of August.[18]

The British were not slow to seek revenge. Beeston was quick to write for assistance, not only financial but also military, to help him destroy the buccaneer menace hanging over his colony. The Lords promised aid, for they realized fully the gravity of the situation, and set about the laborious task of raising an army and collecting a fleet. While awaiting reinforcements, Beeston determined to strike at San Domingo with the meager forces at his disposal. Late in September he dispatched his entire fleet, consisting of three men-of-war, a fire ship, and two barks to inflict what damage they could on the French colony. The squadron arrived off Leogane on the eleventh of October, and from eight in the morning until three in the afternoon they bombarded the nearby village of Esterre; then, having done all the harm they could, they set sail in the direction of Petit-Goave, where Beauregard, warned of their coming, was ready to receive them. But the English veered off and made for the Isle Avache, on the southern side of the peninsula, where they satisfied their craving for destruction by burning a few huts.

Meanwhile, in England the work of supplying aid was not running at all smoothly. The Admiralty had its hands full with plans for an expedition to the Mediterranean, an expedition which to them was far more important than protecting a colony in the West

[18]For the best account of this campaign see Beeston's report in *C.S.P., America & West Indies, 1693–96*, No. 1236. A modified version of this is found in Bridges, *The Annals of Jamaica*, I, 312–22. See also Charlevoix, *Histoire de l'isle espagnole*, IV, 35–43.

Indies from buccaneers. They had already collected sixty-three ships for European service during the coming winter and could spare only three or four vessels and two fire ships. Shortly afterward the commissioner of transportation managed, after considerable haggling, to secure five ships, capable of carrying a little more than one thousand men. This, at any rate, was a start, and the work of organization began to move along, albeit in a cumbersome manner. There was considerable discussion as to the proper number of men for the expedition. The first suggestion was to send two regiments, each of ten companies of sixty men each, making a total of twelve hundred. But this was not enough; the Privy Council wanted to raise the number to sixteen hundred, the Lords of Trade held out for one hundred more. In the end the figure agreed upon was eighteen hundred. To command the expedition, the government selected Colonel Luke Lillingston, who had served his apprenticeship in the West Indies under Sir Francis Wheler and had recently been raised to the rank of general. The naval officer chosen as commander of the fleet was Commodore Robert Wilmot, while John Murrey was placed in charge of the commissary department. The fifteenth of October, was set as a tentative date for the fleet to proceed from Gravesend to the place where the troops were to be embarked.[19]

The instructions given Wilmot for handling the expedition were secret. They were presented to him in a sealed envelope which was not to be opened until he reached the fortieth parallel. He was given considerable latitude in what he was expected to do, a wise decision under the circumstances, and a great deal of responsibility was thrown upon councils of war which were to be held "as often as there should be occasion." The fleet was to proceed to Jamaica, where at a council held with the Governor a plan of action was to be outlined. From there Wilmot was to go to San Domingo, preferably to Petit-Goave, and begin his operations. Before doing this, however, he was to get into touch with the President of Spanish San Domingo and work out a scheme of concerted action with him. At the end of two or three months he was to return to England, unless a council judged it wise for him to remain longer.[20]

[19]C.S.P., *America & West Indies*, *1693–96*, Nos. 1239, 1259, 1262, 1302, 1360, 1377.
[20]These instructions are given in Burchett, *Memoirs of Transactions at Sea*, pp. 306–9.

Orders were also sent Governor Beeston telling him to summon a council of war when the expedition arrived and instructing him to advise this body that if Petit-Goave were taken it must be kept as a permanent English possession; on no account were the Spaniards to be informed of this plan, since they might refuse to collaborate in a venture that might bring yet another foreign nation to Hispaniola.

The fleet sailed February 1, 1695: fourteen transport ships, one store ship, one hospital ship, and three private merchantmen. The following day they met off Falmouth the warships, led by the flagship "Dunkirk," that were to convoy them to their destination.[21]

On the twenty-second of February the fleet anchored at Funchal, Madeira, all save the "Swan," which was sent on ahead to San Domingo with letters for the Spanish president apprizing him of the purpose of the expedition and requesting a meeting with him to discuss the possibilities of coöperating in a joint campaign against the common enemy. By the first of April the ship bearing Commissary Murrey reached St. Christopher, the rendezvous agreed upon, and in the course of a few days the entire squadron came to anchor in the roadstead; not a single ship was missing; 400 men were ill, and 130 had died, leaving some 700 fit for service. Here at St. Christopher a feud between the two branches of the service broke out with a violence that had been increased by the hardships of the voyage. If we are to believe Captain John Lilly, who was present at these scenes of discord, it reached a degree "that upbraidings of cowardice and several unbecoming words passed between them in the presence of General Codrington and others, where it seemed to me that the Commodore was the aggressor." At last, having wasted several days in this manner and having exhausted themselves by abuse, they set sail for the little island of Saona, off San Domingo, where Wilmot had instructed the "Swan" to meet him with the President's reply.

Wilmot arrived at Saona in due course of time and he met not only the "Swan" but the "Hampshire" also, which arrived from Jamaica bearing Colonel Beckford, recently sent out by Governor

[21]These ships were: the "Winchester," "Ruby," "Swan," "Reserve," and the fire ships "Terrible," and "Firebrand."

Beeston to sound out the Spaniard. The news brought to Lillingston by these ships was an invitation to a conference at the Spanish
capital. Thither he went with three men-of-war and a fire ship,
having sent the rest of his fleet to the Gulf of Samana on the northern coast of San Domingo. On arriving in the harbor he was
greeted by the fort with a salute of eleven guns, a courtesy he
promptly returned. Going ashore, he was received by the Lieutenant-General, the Council, and a guard of honor of five hundred
men, who escorted him to the outer gate of the palace. The President was cordiality itself, anxious to do honor to the distinguished
Englishman who was to act as his ally. But here the enthusiasm
seemed to stop. At the conference held to determine a plan of campaign the deliberations were carried on with eagerness by the guest
and considerable hesitation on the part of his host; and it was only
after a twelve days' discussion that they agreed upon a plan which
provided for a Spanish army of fifteen hundred men to march overland to Manzanillo Bay on the north side of the island, at the line
of demarcation between modern Haiti and San Domingo proper,
where they were to be met by the British fleet. The reason behind
the Spaniard's hesitation was that he had been instructed by his
government to coöperate with the British land forces only. He
even refused at first to admit Wilmot, as naval commander, to his
conferences and was prevailed upon to do so only when Lillingston
pointed out the necessity of both branches acting in concert if the
venture was to be a success. The strategy of the campaign, as it was
eventually worked out, was to catch the French between the
English forces attacking by sea and the Spanish forces coming
overland and falling upon their rear. The date set for the meeting
at Manzanillo Bay was the twelfth of May.

News of the coming of Wilmot's armada had, of course, preceded it, for an expedition of such magnitude could not be kept a
secret, and Du Casse well knew he might expect an attack at any
time. Blénac had been advised of it by the government at home and
had quickly sent all the men-of-war and privateers at Martinique
to San Domingo. He had also turned down overtures from Barbados to exchange prisoners, on the ground that those he released
might be sent to Jamaica to take part in the war. Forewarned Du
Casse did his best to prepare himself. Unfortunately most of his

buccaneers had gone off on cruises and could not be recalled. He sent a ship to the town of San Domingo to see what the Spaniards were doing, but her captain returned, to report that he had seen no suspicious activities in the harbor. On the first of May a Danish vessel arrived from St. Thomas with news that a Spanish squadron of five ships filled with soldiers had anchored there and that a powerful fleet (Wilmot's) had been seen sailing from St. Christopher. What bothered Du Casse was not the size of these forces, but whether or not they planned a joint attack on one place, and, if so, where the blow would fall. In this uncertain frame of mind, he decided to remain at Leogane and send Major Bernanos, with one hundred men, to reinforce the garrison at Port de Paix commanded by Le Clerc de la Boulaye, while he retained but a meager five hundred wherewith to defend the southern country. Baldran de Graff was in command of Cap François. It was understood that if it were attacked Bernanos would move to its support, and that if the enemy came down upon it both by land and by sea Sieur Girardin would command the force opposing the landing party, the Chevalier du Lion[22] would have charge of the batteries, and De Graff would take care of the Spaniards. Since De Graff did not have a sufficient number of men to meet the Spaniards in the open field, he was to hold them off as much as possible, disputing every foot of territory, and if the worse came to the worst to spike the guns of the batteries, burn the ammunition, and retreat to Port de Paix.

On the tenth of May, Wilmot gave the word to leave Samana and sail to Manzanillo. The "Swan" was sent on ahead to take soundings and keep a sharp lookout for any Spanish vessels that might be there, for they, too, might be pressed into service. Two days later the "Swan" rejoined the fleet, having captured three Frenchmen in a canoe, who gave Wilmot the news of the presence of a French squadron at Cap François. The commander at once despatched the "Terrible," the "Hampshire," and the "Reserve" to block these ships, while he anchored his fleet for the time being off Monte Christe, just north of Manzanillo. A day or so later contact was made with the Spanish command, and Bayaha (later known as Baie du Fort Dauphin), a place west of Manzanillo, was

[22]Probably a relative of Governor du Lion, of Guadeloupe.

selected as the meeting place where the British troops should de-
bark. Sailing now into Manzanillo, Wilmot found and took over a
wretched Spanish squadron of three indifferent ships, carrying
about one hundred guns, which was called the Barlovento Fleet.
Passing on to Bayaha, the British officers went ashore to hold a
conference with the Spanish generals. It was agreed to send 150
men from the English forces to join the Spaniards on the plain of
Limonade, scene of Tarin de Cussy's defeat. On the twenty-fourth
the campaign against the French began in earnest. Lillington landed
the promised number of men, accompanied by one hundred from
the Barlovento Fleet for good measure, while two frigates and the
two fire ships sailed for Cap François, and the remainder of the
land forces were put upon four transports to follow the warships.

As soon as the French learned of the Anglo-Spanish expedition's
arrival at Manzanillo they took steps to repel the coming attack.
De Graff appealed to La Boulaye for help, and the latter sent him
Bernanos with 130 men. When De Graff's scouts reported the
enemy deployed on the plain of Limonade, the main French army
was already intrenched near by in a ravine. For some reason or
other De Graff failed to take advantage of the opportunity to attack, but retreated to a second position nearer Cap François on the
bank of the Rivière du Haut du Cap, which lay across the only
road leading from Limonade to the town of Cap François. His
action was undoubtedly due to the paucity of the forces under him,
only three hundred men in addition to the reinforcements of
Bernanos, too small a number to cope with the Spanish army. On
the bank of the stream he proceeded to fortify himself with the
four small pieces of artillery at his disposal, while the Spaniards
occupied the trenches he had just abandoned. At this time, so
Charlevoix tells us, the French began to lose heart. They had lost
confidence in their leader who had shown no inclination to do
anything in the way of an offensive, and was ready, so it seemed,
to abandon the struggle before it had begun. Thus, finding no one
to oppose them in the plains of Limonade, the allies advanced
boldly, setting fire to the houses as fast as they came upon them.
Arriving at the shore near the mouth of a small creek, they fired a
cabin, which was to be a signal to the fleet that the land forces
had arrived within striking distance of the Cap.

Whatever may have been De Graff's attitude about the situation, and it is quite possible that Charlevoix is too severe with him, his fellow officers were not so pessimistic. Everything had been done to make the Cap as strong as possible with the limited number of men at their command. The place was defended by 250 militia, one company of infantry and one colored unit. Their commander, Girardin, had placed them effectively along the shore to beat back any possible landing party, and De Graff, overconfident of the strength of his position on the bank of the Rivière du Haut du Cap, had added a company of men to Girardin's forces. On retreating from his first position De Graff had left a small detachment, which he deemed sufficient to check the enemy for a while at least; but these men did not share his enthusiasm and soon abandoned the place to join their commander at his second position, thus demoralizing the men defending it by their panic and allowing the Spaniards to overrun the locality known as the Quartier Morin without opposition.

Though unaware of the situation among the French, Wilmot decided to land a detachment and feel out the enemy's position. The place selected for this was the Haut du Cap, and thither he sent the "Swan" and two fire ships to sweep the ground with their guns and clear the way for the landing party. The boats were lowered, and the men climbed in and started for the shore; but Girardin was quick enough to guess what was afoot and sent a detachment to defend the place. After some desultory firing the attempt was abandoned, or rather put off until the next day. All this time the Spanish forces had been advancing, and when they approached the town, De Graff made ready to retire. He sent word to Girardin and Du Lion to abandon the batteries and the town and join him with all their forces, for he had now given up all hope of holding out and felt that there was nothing to do but to retreat to Port de Paix. Girardin obeyed, but Du Lion, being a man of spirit, answered that the King's batteries were not to be surrendered in this fashion. Far from being angered at this seeming defiance of his authority, De Graff allowed his stout lieutenant to remain, with the understanding that he would spike his guns and destroy his ammunition should he be obliged to evacuate the place.

On the morning of the twenty-ninth the English stood in toward the shore to begin a bombardment of the batteries, and at four in the afternoon, under cover of a storm, the boats were lowered to attempt once again to make a landing. This time there was no trouble. Du Lion had at last realized the folly of opposing an army and navy which outnumbered him ten to one, and when Wilmot's men advanced he spiked his guns, fired the storehouse, and, destroying all he could, marched out at ten in the evening to rejoin De Graff.

The day after this retreat Lillingston arrived with his detachment and his Spanish allies. The sight of the English flag floating high over the battlements of the demolished fort filled the Spanish general with rage, for he mistook the emblem of victory for a symbol of possession, and he had no intention of aiding one foreign power to supplant another in Hispaniola. So far as he was concerned, the English were as objectionable as the French, probably more so, since he regarded them as heretics. To placate him Lillingston lowered the flag and allowed the Spanish colors to be run up, for, as he pointed out to Wilmot when the latter objected, the Spaniard had ordered his men to shoot any English sailor found carrying off provisions, "swearing that all that was in Hispaniola was his." Now the English soldiers united with the Spaniards in voicing their anger at the situation which greeted them when they entered the ruined town. Wilmot's sailors had completely looted the place, leaving nothing for those who had made the dreary march overland. Lillingston's men were enraged at the perfidy of their fellow countrymen, and it was only with the greatest difficulty that he kept them from open mutiny. Anxious to get under way before serious trouble broke out, Wilmot suggested demolishing what remained of the fort, dividing the guns, thirty-three in number, between the two nationalities, and then sending a detachment of three hundred men to join the Spaniards on a march to Port de Paix, estimated as a five days' march of forty-two miles, for thither the French had retreated. Lillingston, however, was determined to manage the land part of the campaign in his own way Though not on particularly good terms with his Spanish allies, he disliked Wilmot still more, and the feelings of his men toward the sailors after the plunder of Cap François was extremely bitter, to say the least. He therefore obtained, without consulting Wil-

mot, a ten days' ration of biscuit from Murrey and started off for
Port de Paix with his entire force, now numbering eight hundred
men, leaving the Spanish commander to bring his army there by a
different route. Captain Lilly, who took part in the campaign and
later wrote a caustic criticism of its management, bitterly attacked
the Colonel's action, pointing out that the march overland involved tremendous hardships and caused a serious loss of men, all
to no purpose, since the journey could easily have been made by
sea. But he overlooks the difficulties that might have arisen during the voyage with all the plunder of the Cap in the hands of the
sailors. Wilmot's decks might well have become the scenes of
pitched battles.

On the tenth of June the fleet set sail for Port de Paix, reinforced
by two privateers and a galley from Jamaica. Stopping for five days
at Baie de la Cul, two leagues west of Cap François, in the vain
hope of meeting the land forces, the transports proceeded on their
way to an anchorage five leagues east of the Port, while the men-
of-war took their position two leagues west of that place near the
settlement of St. Louis. Here Wilmot called a council, which decided, since nothing could be learned of the whereabouts of
Lillingston's division, to put four hundred men ashore at once for
an attack on Port de Paix. The plan was carried out with some
difficulty, for a handful of men on guard here kept up a galling
fire from ambush on the landing party and drove them off. But the
disparity between the battling forces was too great, and the French
were soon obliged to give ground, leaving the field to the invaders.
Major Bernanos, meanwhile, had advanced from Port de Paix
with a detachment to assist the defenders, and the two units now
joined forces. To cut them off from the Port, Wilmot sent three
ships and two barks to attempt a landing farther up the coast; but
the shore was too well guarded, and landing parties met with a
musketry fire sufficiently hot to discourage them. Despite this
valiant defense, the number of seamen who gradually made their
way ashore in small groups at last became too great for any forces
De Graff could send to oppose them. In a few hours they had
sacked St. Louis and overrun the countryside as far as Port de
Paix.

On the twenty-fifth the overland expedition at last put in an appearance. The terrible march had taken its toll. There were two roads, or rather two routes, from Cap François to Port de Paix: one, the shorter of the two, lay along the shore across well-nigh impassable terrain; the other, though considerably longer, offered fewer obstacles. The English had chosen the former; the Spaniards the latter. Lillingston, then, had led his men along the coast, stopping at Port à Margot long enough to plunder it. Though the retreating French had offered no opposition to either party, the natural impediments had been enough to work havoc with the English soldiers, unaccustomed as they were to heavy marching in torrid climates. For fifteen long, weary days they had toiled along, "forced to wade over vast rivers, crossing one in particular forty or fifty times and generally up to their necks, and there were neither roads nor paths but such as were made by floods." Captain Lilly, who saw the miserable remnant arrive, says:

I counted his numbers as he [Lillingston] advanced to the place appointed to him near the fortress, and there were not above thirty-seven files, four deep. I know of none that were on duty except a sergeant and twelve men; which in all could not make up above 160 private men. Now this sudden and great loss of men could have been due only to the needless fatigues of this march, for so far they had yet been in no engagement. This regiment left England with twelve hundred men besides officers, and all this happened before the enemy offered to defend themselves.

The Spaniards, who had taken the easier route, had suffered less; moreover, they were better inured to the climate and the fatigues of a long match.

Emboldened by the presence of these forces, though their appearance was not particularly encouraging, Wilmot sent a summons of surrender to Port de Paix on the very day of their arrival. It was promptly refused, and the commander, seeing that he must begin a siege, proceeded to land his artillery. Since he did not care to trust his sailors under the command of Lillingston, he arranged to have them operate as a separate unit, leaving the colonel to make whatever arrangements he saw fit with the Spanish forces. This feeling of distrust was, of course, heartily reciprocated, for Lillingston had as little use for Wilmot as Wilmot had for him. It also proved a sort of bond between the colonel and the Spanish commander, for the latter cordially disliked the commodore and his officers who had beaten him to the plunder of Cap François and were destined in the coming siege to show the same grasping spirit, carrying off the loot to their ships without allowing the land forces to get their hands on even one boatload. During the campaign, therefore, Lillingston and Wilmot gave each other as little assistance as possible, and what little they were forced to give was granted in a grudging manner. Yet in spite of this lack of coöperation between the sea and the land forces, preparations were begun for the siege of the fort of Port de Paix. With the aid of the Spaniards, Lillingston mounted two guns on the west side of the fort and two more with a mortar to the south, while Wilmot had ten guns in all, mounted in batteries on the Morne de St. Ouën.

M. de la Boulaye, the local commander, had shown no ability in organizing the defense. When Major Bernanos and a handful of men were attempting to prevent a junction between the English and the Spanish armies La Boulaye had had them recalled. As in the case of De Graff at Cap François, he seemed willing to abandon the field with only the semblance of a struggle. Save on one occasion, when the fleet passed by the fort, the guns were not used at all, and the English commanders were able to erect batteries without molestation. He did not even attempt a sortie against the besiegers. Thus Englishmen and Spaniards roamed over the countryside at will, spreading desolation in their wake and carrying off slaves whenever they found them.

In far-off Leogane, Governor du Casse received the news from the front with many misgivings. His first impulse was to rush to Port de Paix with reinforcements and rally the colonists there, but a council of war quickly vetoed this plan, pointing out that with the small detachment he proposed to take with him he could easily be cut off and perhaps captured and that even if he did succeed in reaching Port de Paix he might find that all positions were being attacked simultaneously, and he might be unable to protect any one of them. Du Casse, of course, realized all this; yet, fearing he might be accused of indifference to the fate of his colony if he did nothing, he wished to make at least a gesture of defending it. Blocked in this direction by the council, he now felt himself relieved of responsibility and began to devote his efforts to protecting the settlements in the Gulf of Leogane. With two hundred buccaneers, a thousand miscellaneous Frenchmen, and a hundred slaves at his disposal, he sent half this force to Petit-Goave, half to the Petite Rivière, while he remained at Leogane midway between them.

On the tenth of July the siege of Port de Paix began. To carry the place by assault was out of the question, for the fortress was located on top of a hill, or cliff with precipitous sides, the side toward the sea rising sixty-five feet above the water's edge. On top of this cliff a wall had been constructed around a strong castle, and within the enclosure thus formed more than six hundred men and women were housed. When the storm of shells and bombs began to fall, these people lost all stomach for a fight. Terrified, they signed a petition asking La Boulaye's permission to retire from the place, adding that if this was refused they would sneak off during the night. The commander, of course, sympathized with them. He had said more than once that he was in favor of abandoning the place and letting each man shift for himself. He had even neglected to take any measures for the defense of the post, and it was only due to the energy of Bernanos and other subordinates that it was in condition to withstand a siege. Nevertheless, in a halting speech La Boulaye gave his consent to the departure of the garrison; then he distributed arms to those who wished to remain. No sooner was this done, than the deserters changed their minds and decided to stay in the fort; but the following day they again clamored to be released, while the soldiers, as distinct from the civilians, demanded a surrender, threatening to give up the place without the consent of their officers if the latter would not side with them. La Boulaye, nonplussed, said nothing. Two days later, after the garrison had sustained a bombardment that cost a few lives, the complaints were renewed. This time the officers joined with the malcontents, saying they had no intention of letting themselves be trapped in a position completely controlled by the enemy while the enemy carried off their wives and children. At this moment a flag of truce appeared in the hands of a messenger from the English camp, bringing a summons of surrender. The messenger concealed his knowledge of French so that officers might speak freely before him in their own tongue, and in this manner he managed to learn what was going on. La Boulaye made no direct reply, but said he would send his answer in a day or two. Having thus dismissed the flag, the French decided they must act promptly.

A council was called at once to determine what was to be done, for no one now paid any attention to La Boulaye, and it was decided to spike the guns, destroy the ammunition, and abandon the place; yet there were at this time only seven men killed and eleven wounded, while there remained 310 white men still capable of putting up some sort of fight, besides 200 armed Negroes and 150 unarmed persons. There were also 8,000 pounds of powder, shot in proportion, and a three week's supply of food. Several officers, blessed with more spirit than their chief, opposed this ignominious retreat and offered to lead a sortie against the besiegers; but the demoralization had spread so far that the troops mutinied when the suggestion was made to them. One of the officers, Jean-Joseph de Paty, in a rage at such cowardice, blew out the brains of his sergeant, while Du Lion slew one of his soldiers with his sword. To make matters worse, a man escaped during the fracas and had the baseness to carry the news of the mutiny and the proposed evacuation of the fort to the English camp. Wilmot needed no second hint; he hurried forward his men to lie in ambush alongside the road which the refugees must take.

At eight in the evening the garrison filed out, all save a few who had elected to remain. La Boulaye, Bernanos, and Girardin were in the lead, followed by a hundred female slaves who carried the baggage, while the rear was commanded by the Chevalier du Lion. They had gone but three hundred paces when Wilmot's men opened fire on the head of the column. A panic seized the French; some rushed back to the fort, while others fled, including La Boulaye, who hurried off to his mountain home with his slaves, glad to be rid of the whole business. Fortunately Bernanos kept his head, as did the officers in the rear, and a semblance of order was soon restored. The column resumed its march; but after a few steps the men found themselves caught by a second ambuscade, composed chiefly of Spanish lancers. These they drove back after a short scuffle in which they suffered the irreparable loss of their leader, Major Bernanos.

Chevalier du Lion and the remaining officers now placed themselves at the head of the column, which marched on, four abreast,

PORT DE PAIX

firing right and left, until they came to the edge of a river where the main body of the enemy, part lancers and part musketeers, to the number of seven hundred, awaited them, hidden in clumps of reeds along the bank. Here the French paused, and the English in some manner or other disclosed their presence prematurely. Thus the French, seeing that the passage across the river was blocked, skirted the bank until they came to a ford, where they could cross the stream waist high. Under cover of a heavy fire from the main body, the van made its way to the other side; then in turn it covered the rear while it followed them. In this way the entire army crossed the river without mishap. Thence they marched to the summit of a neighboring hill, arriving there just before dawn. Scarcely had they thrown down their arms to rest, when cries, punctuated by musketry fire, arose from the river's bank. At this sound panic seized the French, and all who could do so fled. It was again Du Lion who came to the fore. He rallied some fifty men and dispersed a detachment of the enemy which had attempted to plunder a band of slaves at the crossing; in fact the attackers fled quickly, for they were more interested in securing their plunder than in facing the French fire. After this last stand the resistance of the French broke down completely. Their forces scattered over the countryside, each man for himself, leaving the English masters of the field.

While the French were thus being routed in the field, the English were not neglecting the fort. The sailors were the first to reach it. Some entered and wandered about inside the walls, while others, with their officers, stood outside, afraid to enter lest it be blown up. Just before daylight Colonel Lillingston and a detachment of two or three hundred men marched in to take possession of the place; but they had hardly got down to the business of looting, when Wilmot appeared with a much larger force, tapped Lillingston on the shoulder, and said: "Major, I am now stronger than you." And with that his men fell to and plundered the fortress. This done, he caused the gates to be closed, barred them, and refused point blank to share the prize with his Spanish allies. The two armies did, however, divide the inhabitants between them, the French taking the men, the Spaniards the women and children. On the seventeenth the allies separated, for the expedition, despite the incessant bickering of the commanders, had been brought to a successful conclusion. If the extent of its success is to be measured by the amount of material captured, we can do no better than quote Colonel Lillingston's inventory.

There were taken at Cap François [he said] 33 cannon, of which we had 17 and the Spaniards 16, besides 1,000 shot to each of us. The cannon taken at Port de Paix were 107 great and small and 3,662 great shot, of which we and the Spaniards each took 53 guns and 1,831 shot; but we also took 8 guns of which the Spaniards had no share. I was informed by two French gentlemen that in the fort and castle the French abandoned 700 barrels of powder, naval stores to the value of £1,500, three months' provisions for six hundred men, and money, plate, etc., worth £14,000, all of which, with £3,000 worth of indigo at Cap François, was taken by the sea-officers, who searched all boats that came off to the fleet. The Spanish General's letter will show how the sea-officers behaved.²³

Though the allies had been successful, they parted with mutual recriminations. Wilmot wished to move on to Petit-Goave, supported by the Spanish troops, to complete the destruction of the French colony, while the Spanish commander pressed him to destroy the fort and divide the guns between them. The Spaniard also feared that Wilmot was using this expedition against Petit-Goave as a lure to get his allies away from Port de Paix so that the Jamaica privateers could loot the place to their hearts' content. Furthermore, there was trouble about the churches. A clause in the agreement drawn up at San Domingo by the two commanders provided that these buildings should be protected and their contents divided equally between the two parties. But religious as well as national antagonism had been too much for the English sailors and privateers, who destroyed what they could not carry off and abused the clergy. There had also been incipient riots, in which a few Spaniards had been killed. For these reasons the Spanish commander excused himself from going to Petit-Goave, saying that his troops were too ill for such an undertaking.²⁴

²³For data on the expedition to San Domingo see *C.S.P., America & West Indies, 1693–96.* There is an excellent summary of the expedition in the Preface to this volume, giving some information not found in the documents listed in the book itself. For important documents in this volume see: Narrative of Peter Beckford, No. 1946; Wilmot's report to Blathwayt, No. 1980; John Murrey's journal, No. 1983; Lillingston to the Marquis of Normanby, No. 2021; Sir William Beeston's narrative, to which is added a summary of much of his correspondence, No. 2022; the case of Colonel Lillingston, with numerous documents, No. 2324; and in volume 1696–97 Lillingston's memorandum, No. 50; and Captain Lilly's account, No. 384. For the French side of the affair see Charlevoix, *Histoire de l'isle espagnole*, IV, 47–75.

²⁴*C.S.P., America & West Indies, 1693–96*, No. 2021.

In Jamaica, Governor Beeston was anxious to have the fleet move on Leogane and Petit-Goave as the instructions to Wilmot had ordered. He felt that now was the opportunity to destroy the French colony completely and that this opportunity might not present itself again. If it were not done now, Jamaica would always be in danger of an attack. In his enthusiasm he even offered to raise five hundred men to send to Wilmot. In spite of all this, an expedition was out of the question at this time, for among other obstacles illness had begun to ravage the forces of Wilmot and Lillingston. The latter wrote that he had only forty men fit for service and that his own life was despaired of by his physician, while most of Wilmot's officers were similarly incapacitated. On placing his views before the Council of Jamaica, Beeston received a rebuff, for the members of that body realized that even a thousand men raised on the island to assist the fleet would be insufficient to cope with Du Casse's men secure behind their fortifications. Besides, there was the question of money. As for the French, they quickly recovered from their defeat, for the defeat did not entail serious losses. Some houses had been destroyed, and two little villages; cattle and poultry had been killed, and about six hundred slaves had been carried off. Only two hundred men had been slain or captured. Taking a long range view of the situation, we see that these losses were not severe when compared to the total wealth and population of the island. Du Casse was not slow in realizing this, and he soon proposed an expedition to seek revenge by attacking Spanish San Domingo. An expedition was indeed organized the following year, but by order of the King it was given another objective and ended by capturing Carthagena.

VIII

SIEGE OF CARTHAGENA

I F THE WILMOT-LILLINGSTON expedition against French San
Domingo failed to accomplish much because of the incessant
bickering between its two commanders, its success, such as it
was, may be credited to a certain extent to a similar condition in
the French ranks. Baldran de Graff and Le Clerc de la Boulaye had
certainly given a sad exhibition of the qualities requisite for leadership; because of this they soon incurred the wrath of Governor
du Casse. Scarcely had the enemy sailed away, when the Governor
started an investigation of their conduct; and the more he learned
about it, the angrier he became. When he had heard enough, he
wrote the home government demanding their recall and suggesting
that they be brought to trial. In the case of De Graff, he first hinted
that this officer might have had some secret understanding with the
enemy—a suspicion aggravated by the fact that De Graff was a
Dutchman by birth—then he changed this hint to a blunt accusation of cowardice. La Boulaye tried to defend his obvious incom-
petence by complaining that the Governor had not supported him;
but this line of defense only made him a laughingstock, and at
last public indignation against the two men became so strong
that Du Casse felt obliged to warn M. de Pontchartrain that if the
government would do nothing no self-respecting man in the colony
would be willing to serve under them. Finally an order came recalling them to France to stand trial, but for some reason or other
it was never enforced, and the colonists were obliged to be satisfied
that their erstwhile leaders were removed from their respective
commands and given other employment.

Apparently both San Domingo and Jamaica were this time exhausted by the recent expeditions against them. Neither could now

attack the other, yet each lived in deadly fear of a possible invasion by its neighbor. Urged by Pontchartrain to do something, Governor du Casse complained loudly of the paucity of his forces, saying he could put only six hundred men in the field to oppose sixteen hundred from the English colony. These men were all in the vicinity of Leogane and Petit-Goave. In the northern part of the island he had attempted to strengthen his position by evacuating Port de Paix and transferring its inhabitants to Cap François, to which he also transported the colonists from St. Croix, recently abandoned by order of the King.

In Jamaica, Governor Beeston was in despair. In addition to the losses sustained during Du Casse's attack there had been a general exodus of fighting men. From a total of 2,440 effectives, as shown by the muster roll of August, 1695, there were now but 1,390. The loss of man power was most seriously felt among the sailors, whose numbers were reduced from 1,200 to 300, a loss due to arbitrary actions on the part of captains of the Royal Navy who impressed seamen contrary to the Governor's orders. Many of these sailors had fled to Petit-Goave, where they enlisted with the French privateers.

Of the two governors, Beeston was the more apprehensive. And indeed this was not strange, for the British government, after its reluctant organization of the Wilmot expedition, seems to have shot its bolt for the time being; while the King of France, on the other hand, was preparing to act. In the month of April, 1696, Louis sent out a small fleet under Chevalier Petit-Renau,[1] which captured a Spanish ship off the coast of Cuba, an English prize or two, caused Governor Beeston many a sleepless night, then sailed back to France without having accomplished anything worth while. News of this squadron's arrival had, of course, been promptly reported to Beeston, with the usual exaggerations, and he as promptly wrote the Lords of Trade, telling them that some French prisoners recently captured by his men had brought word of a squadron at Petit-Goave, newly arrived from France, which had just sailed fourteen strong, presumably to capture Carthagena. When they return [he said] (unless they take and keep Carthagena) I expect them here, but have no apprehension of them in respect of the

[1]Bernard Renau d'Elisaçarai, known as Petit-Renau.

island [Jamaica], though I fear they may bomb and destroy Port Royal to avoid which I have given all the necessary orders that I can, and intend to lay the men-of-war so as, if possible, to prevent their bomb-ketches coming within reach of the town.[2]

Yet after Petit-Renau's departure Beeston continued to worry. Reports kept piling in which told of the gathering of French vessels for no good purpose. He had heard (and believed) a report that forty ships and men-of-war were cruising off Havana preparing to sail for Martinique, where they were to join a dozen more warships and as many victualers and then proceed to destroy Jamaica and Carthagena.[3]

Codrington also kept a watchful eye on the situation. In September he reported twelve men-of-war at Petit-Goave making ready to attack Jamaica, a number he later reduced to seven. Like Beeston, he had his worries, for the population of his islands had been greatly reduced by warfare. He did not so much fear an attack on his own possessions as the possibility of losing the French portion of St. Christopher, now in English hands, by a treaty of peace, as the French had been obliged to surrender their conquests at the settlement of Breda. To add to his troubles, the uncertainty of the situation was deterring English colonists from making permanent settlements on French territory, and for this reason he urged the Lords of Trade to call the matter to the King's attention before the end of the war in order to forestall any possibility of losing the territory at the peace table.

The fears of the English governors were by no means groundless. In October a French fleet of six vessels under Chevalier des Augiers arrived in the West Indies. The elaborate instructions given its commander were never carried out, but the presence of the squadron was enough to cause Beeston some anxiety. Augiers was ordered to get into touch with Du Casse at Leogane, then go to Puerto Rico, attack the Barlovento Fleet when it came there, and return to San Domingo to discuss with Du Casse the possibilities of an attack on Jamaica. If such a plan were feasible, he was to carry it out; but in any case his last move before coming home was to capture the richly laden Spanish ships to be found in the ports of Honduras. Augiers met with very mediocre success. He managed to capture a galleon loaded with cocoa, vanilla, and cochineal.

[2]C.S.P., America & West Indies, 1696–97, No. 72.   [3]Ibid., No. 224.

Off San Domingo he met the Spanish fleet, which fled before him and escaped with the loss of only one ship. With this modest victory to his credit, Augiers steered for Honduras, where he captured exactly nothing; he presently sailed back to France. In doing so he failed to put in at Leogane and thus missed taking part in the coming expedition against Carthagena, for orders were awaiting him there to remain and join the great armada then being organized in France for this purpose.

Toward the end of the year definite rumors got abroad in the West Indies of the coming of this great French expedition. Beeston and the Jamaica officials were, of course, among the first to hear of it, and they quickly relayed the information to England. "A fleet of fifteen sail with land-soldiers and several warlike instruments proper for the West Indies," they said, was in the making; the objective, Jamaica or Havana. Fortunately the Lords of Trade were fully awake to the seriousness of the situation. Long before they received Beeston's communication they had heard of the French King's project and had sent word to Beeston, to Codrington, and to Barbados that English men-of-war were being fitted out to act as convoys for the merchantmen going to the islands and that they would remain there to aid the colonists in repelling any attack that might be directed against them. They also placed an urgent request for a powerful fleet before King William.

The expedition now sponsored by Louis of France for the capture of Carthagena ranks among the great expeditions to the Spanish Main and is, perhaps, the most important naval campaign we shall have occasion to describe. It was undertaken at a time when the war was drawing to a close and peace feelers had already been sent out by the King to see on what basis he could arrange for an early cessation of hostilities. It was a grand opportunity to gather an enormous amount of plunder before a treaty put an end to such depredations; and if it was successful it would greatly weaken the King of Spain. In addition to the political importance of the expedition it was also a business venture, private individuals having invested their money in the hope of large returns from the booty captured in this rich city. A naval officer of some prominence, the Baron de Pointis,[4] had long entertained the hope of launching such a project, and when in the year 1696 the Toulon

[4]Jean-Bernard-Louis Desjean, Baron de Pointis.

fleet was sent to Brest to be laid up, he saw his opportunity, for this released a large number of ships from the service. When the news of Pointis's plan was released, the public came forward eagerly to underwrite the venture, and the treasurer was soon swamped with subscriptions. But at this moment news came that peace had been concluded with Savoy, and the public, fearing that a general peace might be declared at any time, lost interest. No more money was forthcoming, though the King offered to reimburse the investors in case the expedition did not come off. Thus M. de Pointis had to be content to organize his venture on a smaller scale than he had planned. He arrived at Brest early in October. His work was at first somewhat delayed by unfavorable weather, and it was January before he was ready to sail. When all preparations were complete, the squadron numbered seven ships-of-the-line and three frigates, mounting 538 guns, and in addition to these were a bomb-galliot, a corvette, two flutes, and five dispatch boats.[5] The commander-in-chief hoisted his flag on the eighty-four-gun "Sceptre." The exact number of men embarked in the expedition is not known for the various accounts are by no means unanimous. The estimate generally accepted is 110 officers, 2,100 seamen, 1,750 soldiers, and 55 marines. The land forces were organized in six battalions, with an additional battalion of 400 sailors to be used in landing parties.[6]

In San Domingo, Governor du Casse had been made privy to the plan long before it had reached its formative stage. Early in the previous March, M. de Pontchartrain had written him that De Pointis would go to the West Indies to attack the enemies of France, though he gave no specific details. In September the frigate "Marin," one of the fleet at Brest, was sent to San Domingo with the joyful news that the armada would presently sail, and she also brought orders for the Governor to collect about twelve hundred men if he could spare that many without weakening his own defense. At this time Carthagena had not been definitely selected

---

[5]The ships were "Sceptre," "Saint-Louis," "Fort," "Vermandois," "Apollon," "Furieux," "Saint-Michel;" the frigates were "Mutine," "Avenant," and "Marin." The bomb-galliot was "Eclatante," the corvette, "Providence," the flutes, "Dieppeoise" and "Ville d'Amsterdam." La Roncière, *Histoire de la marine française*, VI, 276n. Pointis, *Account of the Taking of Carthagena*, 1740, p. 19.

[6]*Ibid.*, p. 20.

as the object of attack—Jamaica was still under consideration—
and Du Casse, in replying to the instructions sent him, gave many
reasons for proceeding against Puerto Bello, for it was here the
Spanish fleet, laden with the treasures of Peru, would gather for
the journey home. Carthagena, he thought, was invincible. He
also expressed a keen desire to crush once for all the Spanish
colony of San Domingo; but since the expedition was a business
venture as well as a political venture the wealth of the place to
be attacked was of prime importance.[7]

De Pointis set sail from Brest with his powerful armada on
January 7, 1697, and managing to elude the British fleet of forty
sail that was attempting to blockade the harbor he arrived at
Cap François in fifty-five days. Here he was informed by the local
commander, Donon de Gallifet, that Du Casse had been able to
collect only four hundred men. The collection of even this number
had been something of a feat, for De Pointis was overdue, and the
buccaneers were not men to be kept waiting. Anxious to see what
could still be done, De Pointis proceeded as soon as possible to
Petit-Goave in his flagship, arriving there on the sixteenth of
March. Here he was disappointed, if not actually alarmed, at the
paucity of men furnished by the colony, as he had been led to expect
a far greater number. When Du Casse came on board to pay him
a visit, he berated him soundly for his negligence and vowed that
unless fifteen hundred men could be furnished he would have to
abandon his project. Du Casse was not upset by the commander's
attitude, for his own instructions gave him some latitude in deciding how many men he could supply without endangering the safety
of the colony. As the discussion waxed, Du Casse still refused to
be hurried, for he well knew that no buccaneers could be recruited
in San Domingo without his coöperation. This De Pointis learned
a few days later, when the following incident occurred. An officer
of the flagship doing guard duty at Petit-Goave placed an unruly
buccaneer under arrest in the fort. The fellow's friends quickly
gathered around the place clamoring for his release. Ordered to
disperse, they became more violent, and the officer finally commanded his men to fire on the crowd, which they did, stretching
two or three dead on the ground. Enraged at this, the mob threat-

[7]Charlevoix, *Histoire de l'isle espagnole*, IV, 94–99.

ened to storm the place, demanding the surrender of the officer who had given the order to fire. De Pointis, advised of the disorder, rushed up to take charge, but his presence served only to exasperate the crowd. At last Du Casse was sent for. Thanks to the influence he exerted over his unruly colonists, he was able to bring them to heel without the slightest difficulty, and he quickly suppressed the incipient riot.

In the end De Pointis was able to obtain a sufficient number of men. He did this by threatening to burn the buccaneers' ships, down to the smallest boat, a proceeding that would have deprived them of the means of carrying on their depredations for some years to come, if not forever. This threat they soon realized was no mere bluff, for the commander had taken a dislike to the freebooters, whom he regarded as a detriment to the orderly development of the colony. This dislike was intensified during the campaign, for in his memoirs he constantly accuses them of inefficiency, shiftlessness, and sometimes of downright cowardice. Much credit is also due Governor du Casse for the unselfish spirit he showed at this time, an unselfishness that did much to smooth over difficulties and get the expedition under way. Although De Pointis would not give him a rank in the undertaking suitable to his position as Governor of San Domingo—second-in-command, let us say—he offered to go as a mere ship's captain and as commander of the contingent from his colony. This broke the deadlock, and the buccaneers rushed in to enlist, happy to serve under a man they liked and trusted. As in the case of the expedition from France, the numbers of Du Casse's division are given differently by different authorities. There were probably between eleven and twelve hundred men, divided as follows: 170 soldiers, 110 colonists (under Donon de Gallifet), 180 Negroes (under Jean-Joseph de Paty), and 650 buccaneers. This would raise the grand total of the expedition to a little more than 5,000 men. [8] The fleet carrying Du Casse's men consisted of ten ships, mostly frigates, of which the "Pontchartrain" was the flagship. [9]

[8]Pointis, *A Genuine and Particular Account of the Taking of Carthagena*, p. 20.

[9]The others were: "Serpente," "Gracieuse," "Pembroke," "Cerf-Volant," "Mutine," "Jersey," "Françoise," "Anglais," and "Brigantin." To these was added the "Christ," a ship captured by Augiers. Southey, *History of the West Indies*, II, 171; La Roncière, *Histoire de la marine française*, VI, 277.

With the number of men now at his disposal De Pointis was, perforce, obliged to be content, although he would have liked to have more. They were sufficient, however, as events proved, to enable him to accomplish his purpose. He made ready to sail, but before embarking his buccaneers Du Casse insisted upon a written agreement covering the distribution of booty, for he well knew that it was doubtful if his people would leave unless this important matter was clearly undrestood in advance. To this De Pointis quickly agreed and signed on the spot, with suspicious alacrity, a brief statement declaring that the men of San Domingo would share in the profits of the enterprise in the same manner as the men of His Majesty's ships. What the commander had in mind was something far different from the interpretation placed on the document by Du Casse and his men. Perhaps De Pointis thought a too-detailed explanation of the situation at this time might discourage volunteers. At any rate, there arose a misunderstanding which, as we shall see, nearly caused a mutiny when the booty was divided.

On the eighteenth of March the rest of the fleet, which De Pointis had left at Cap François, rejoined him, and the following day he set out for Cape Tiburon. He was anxious to get away. His control of the buccaneers was tenuous, and the sooner he got them away from Petit-Goave, the better. A violent storm delayed the passage to the cape, and it was ten days before he anchored there. Here Du Casse renewed his arguments for making Puerto Bello their objective instead of Carthagena, for he considered the force too small to capture the latter place, protected as it was by forts and bastions. Moreover, he argued, the galleons had probably not yer arrived there, but were either on the way or still at anchor in the harbor of Puerto Bello. He suggested Vera Cruz as an alternative. His reasons did not seem good to De Pointis, who had his own orders as to what place to attack; so after weighing all the arguments of his subordinate, he gave the order to steer for Carthagena.

After an uneventful crossing of the Caribbean, the fleet arrived before the city on the thirteenth of April. Before leaving France, De Pointis had been given detailed instructions as to what strategy he should use in carrying on his operations. This was the work of bureaucrats, whose knowledge of the topography was necessarily limited; and though Du Casse offered him more accurate informa-

tion, recently gleaned by his own spies, the commander was determined to stick to his book. Fortunately he had with him an
English sea captain, long in the service of Spain, but now with
France, who was able to supply the data for drawing a remarkably
accurate map of the place. De Pointis's instructions, which he now
proceeded to carry out, ordered him first to seize the fortified convent of La Poupe,[10] a position which would enable him to cut
off the town from any reinforcements that might approach overland. The plan was a sensible one, and there were two ways of
carrying it out. De Pointis weighed both plans carefully: one was
to land east of Carthagena and take the shortest road to the fort;
the other was to enter the harbor through the fortified Boucachique
Passage and approach the place from the opposite direction. The
latter maneuver was a difficult one, for it involved running the batteries of the fort and warping the ships through an entrance so
narrow that it could be easily blocked by two vessels stationed
within the harbor at the head of the channel. De Pointis therefore
chose the former alternative and took his fleet to a spot east of the
city, where he believed a landing could be made. The plan was to
land the buccaneers and send them to La Poupe under cover of the
night. Du Casse, who was to lead them, could keep in touch with
the flagship by means of signal fires.

These arrangements made, the commander took his ships into
a large bay at Point Hicacos, four leagues east of the city, where
he found good anchorage. The buccaneers were ordered into the
boats, a maneuver they executed with great reluctance, so De
Pointis tells us, for they were terrified at the thought of marching
against a foe capable of putting up a stout defense. Before
giving the order to cast off, the commander decided to make a
reconnaisance of the shore to select the best place at which to land.
Embarking in a boat with Du Casse, he rowed to the shore and
there found to his surprise that a heavy surf was breaking over a
reef of sunken rocks. This barrier, he found, was not local but
extended along the shore for a considerable distance. While they
were exploring the possibilities of a landing, his boat was upset,
and the occupants barely managed to save themselves. This, of

---

[10]"La Popa" would be the correct Spanish name; but we shall in all cases follow the French
forms given on the map.

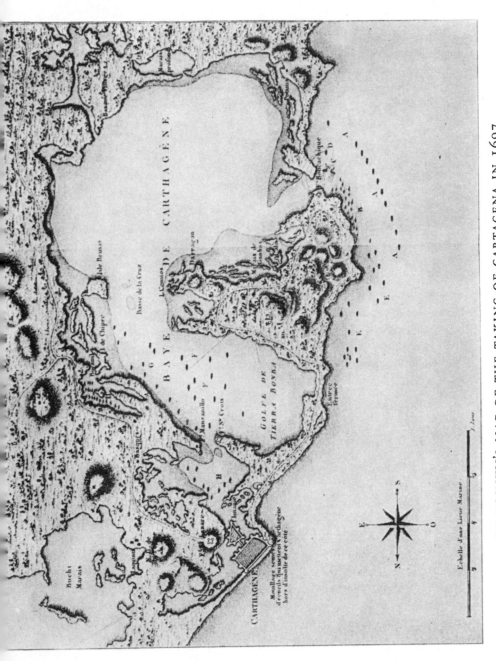

DE POINTIS'S MAP OF THE TAKING OF CARTAGENA IN 1697

course, ended all possibility of making an attack from the east, and De Pointis gave the signal to set sail for an attempt to force the passage at Boucachique.

The reef of rocks that had prevented the landing at Point Hicacos ran westward along the coast and served as a protection to Carthagena, for it kept the French ships from coming in close enough to reach it with their guns. In sailing toward Boucachique, De Pointis had hoped to give the town a taste of what was to come, and he ordered his vessels to close in; but they soon found the water too shallow for safety and were obliged to veer out of range. On reaching the entrance to the harbor the commander anchored a ship close enough to block it and thus prevent any Spanish vessel from leaving it without his permission. The boats were now sent out to take soundings. There was water enough, but the surf was heavy; only near the fort did they discover a small promontory forming a shelter from the sea and at the same time offering a landing party protection from the guns of the fort. Here, on the fifteenth, the commander placed his troops ashore, sending a detachment of Negroes ahead with hatchets to cut a path through the underbrush to the shore of the harbor, where the French were to pitch camp prior to beginning their siege operations, for they were about to attack the fort. The place where they landed was a large peninsula called Tierra Bomba, connected on its eastern side by a very narrow isthmus to the land where Carthagena was situated. To cover the landing operation, two ships and the bomb-galliot kept up a brisk fire on the fort, helped by occasional salvos from the flagship and the mortar on one of the dispatch boats. This the enemy returned in a half-hearted way, doing some damage to the rigging of the attackers. Putting himself at the head of his troops, De Pointis now led the way to the fort. His path lay a short distance from the shore and presently brought him to a rise of ground which offered some protection from the guns of the fort and at the same time enabled him to examine its defenses without exposing himself. Here, amid the ruins of a deserted village, the detachment encamped for the night. The fort was laid out in a square, surrounded by a dry moat eighteen feet deep and about thirty-five wide. It was built on a rocky surface and had walls thirty-two feet high and eight feet thick. These walls were constructed of a stone of granite-like toughness that could withstand the fire of the heaviest artillery. Behind them ramparts forty feet wide were thrown up to form a platform for supporting thirty-three guns.

Under cover of darkness De Pointis's officers made a survey of the place as far as the moat, while the ships landed the guns necessary for the siege. In the morning the soldiers fell to with a will, constructing gabions and fascines and mounting the cannon in place. While busy with this work, they were surprised to see a large boat carrying a number of Spaniards sailing gently through the entrance, in total ignorance of the presence of the French. As the craft closed in, a volley greeted it, killing some fifteen of its occupants, while the rest leaped overboard or hid in the bottom of the boat. She was quickly brought ashore. Among the prisoners De Pointis found two friars, one of whom he selected as a messenger to carry his summons of surrender to the fort. Also, he learned from these men that the galleons were still at Puerto Bello, where they had been for the last six months, and that they were expected at Carthagena any day. In order to impress his messenger with the strength of the French forces, the commander had him examine the artillery and inspect the troops, using the time-honored ruse of moving them from place to place so as to give the friar an exaggerated idea of their numbers. The friar did his best, but the Spanish commander, Don Sancho Ximenes, was not impressed and answered bluntly that he was not yet reduced to the point of capitulating.

News of the French attack had meanwhile reached the Governor of Carthagena, Don Diego Nuñez de los Rios, and early in the afternoon the reinforcements sent by him made their appearance. Anxious to duplicate the feat performed by the soldiers in the morning, when they captured the boat, a group of buccaneers decided to seize the boats carrying these troops. Taking shelter in some of the abandoned houses, they opened fire when the Spaniards neared the fort. The noise of battle attracted the rest of the freebooters, who rushed to the shore to join in the fracas. Here they came within range of the fort and were quickly caught by a deadly musketry fire. They turned and fled.

The buccaneers [says De Pointis, who held these gentry in well-deserved contempt] the buccaneers who are not used to engage where there is any danger, made the most of their heels to bring themselves to shelter: I met them in their way, and finding that words were of no weight with them, I lighted on a cudgel, and with that forced them to return to the post they had abandoned. Du Casse was surprised at this way of carrying men on, yet concealed in silence the vexation he conceived at the action.

Nevertheless, the freebooters had been able to do enough damage to drive the boats back to Carthagena.

De Pointis now thought it time to attack. Leaving the cowardly buccaneers to their own devices, he sent forward two companies of grenadiers and a battalion of regulars to begin the assault. The walls of the fort rested on an escarpment that rose abruptly; by standing close to it the besiegers were in some measure protected from the fire directed at them from above. For scaling these walls, additional battalions were sent in with the required ladders. When they approached the escarpment, they were met by a brisk fire; but in order to hit their marks the defenders were obliged to lean forward in such a manner as to expose themselves to the attackers, who soon drove them back to safer positions, where they could do little damage. The defenders now gave up hope. There were three hundred of them at the most, and one-third of these had already been lost. The encircling forces far outnumbered them; their own reinforcements had been scattered; and now from the ramparts they could see guns and mortars swinging into place. In despair they offered to surrender if they could get favorable terms. De Pointis agreed to be lenient, at the same time threatening to put up his ladders and lead the assault in person if they did not immediately throw down their weapons. Terrified, they complied at once; but owing to the debris they had piled against the gate they could not get it open fast enough to suit De Pointis, and he would not be appeased until they had let down a man from the wall, who assured him that the Spaniards were doing their very best. When at last the obstruction was cleared away and the ponderous doors swung open, the venerable governor of the fort presented the keys to the French commander, saying: "I put into your hands the keys of all the Spanish Indies." Pleased at his success and doubtless touched by the courtly bearing of Don Sancho, De Pointis allowed him to carry away all his possessions and retire with his household and slaves to his estate on the farther side of the Bay of Carthagena. The officers were also given their liberty.

The price which De Pointis paid for the capture of this place was low, only fifty men were sacrificed, and possession of the fort gave him control of the entrance of the harbor. Governor du Casse had, unfortunately, been wounded in the skirmish. The following day, that is, on the seventeenth, the troops which had just landed were reëmbarked and the work of warping the ships into the bay was begun. It was highly important to get the vessels carrying the food and ammunition safely into the harbor, for then De Pointis could lead the bulk of his army to Carthagena by land while the supplies followed by water. His next objective was Fort St. Croix at the entrance to the inner harbor which led to Carthagena iteslf. It was distant about two and one-half leagues. His plan included also the capture of La Poupe, and for this purpose he ordered the buccaneers to embark in boats and start at once. Du Casse was unable to take command of his men, so his duties fell upon Donon de Gallifet, an officer who had but recently come to San Domingo and was therefore looked upon by the freebooters as a comparative stranger and consequently not very well liked. When ordered into the boats, these rascals complied grudgingly; and as soon as De Pointis had turned his back they mutinied. Gallifet seized one recalcitrant by the arm to force him to embark and was jostled in return. He at once appealed to the commander, who promptly had the fellow seized, bound to a tree, and blindfolded. He then called upon a firing squad of his own musketeers to make an example of the mutineer before the crowd. Gallifet, then, in order to win the goodwill of the buccaneers threw himself at the feet of his superior —it was all arranged beforehand—and begged for the culprit's life. De Pointis, after putting on a great show of determination, at last yielded, and magnanimously restored the man to his friends. Having had an example of what might happen to the disobedient, the buccaneers agreed to accept Gallifet as their commander.

During the morning of the eighteenth the fleet entered the bay with little difficulty. When this maneuver had been successfully accomplished, De Pointis set out with his army, leaving 170 men to hold Fort Boucachique. His own forces, that is, those he took with him by land, numbered about 1,700, and besides these he had the 110 colonists, 180 Negroes, and a few others. At noon they reached a ruined castle, half a mile from Fort St. Croix, where they stopped to rest. In the afternoon he continued his march to Carthagena, after sending a detachment under his rear admiral, the Vicomte de Coëtlogon, southward along the peninsula on which the fort was located, for the purpose of selecting a spot, as near it as possible, where a besieging force might encamp. When De Pointis reached the western bastion of Carthagena, the one called San Domingo, a messenger arrived from Coëtlogon saying that the Spaniards had already abandoned the fort, after carrying off the guns and doing what they could to wreck the place.

De Pointis now set out to reconnoiter the ground before him. It was marshy, for here the strip of land on which he had been marching narrowed down to a few yards in breadth. It took but a glance to show that no attack could be launched in this place. When he approached the city, he saw a goodly number of people watching him from the bastion, and this inspired him to send them a summons to surrender, hoping that he had overawed the watchers by the might of his army. To his flag of truce the Governor, be it said to his credit, returned a defiant reply, saying he would defend his city to the utmost whenever the French saw fit to attack. That night a further reconnaissance, carried on under cover of darkness, showed clearly the impossibility of any operations in this locality, the nature of the terrain because of its nearness to the sea was entirely too soft for army maneuvers. Since it was obviously necessary to launch the attack from another direction, De Pointis decided to ferry his men across the inner harbor to some place where he could begin operations by attacking Fort St. Lazare, which guarded the southern approach to the town. He therefore sent Jean de Paty with the colored troops to study the lay of the land and find a suitable place for making a landing. When De Paty returned the following morning, he called in the boats, placed his army on board, and carried them across the little bay to the foot of the hill on which St. Lazare was standing. Here he was joined by Gallifet and his buccaneers, who had found La Poupe deserted and had simply taken it over; also by Coëtlogon who had come from St. Croix, having left twenty men there to hold it.

The next problem before the French was the capture of St. Lazare, for the garrison of this fort had no intention of abandoning it without putting up at least a show of resistance, as it was the key to Carthagena. Furthermore, it covered all the avenues of approach, and unless it was captured it would be impossible to take the city. A brief survey convinced the French commander that it would be a lengthy task to force its surrender if it were besieged in the usual way by heavy artillery, for the hill on which it was located was defended by a natural glacis, covered with shrubs, which ran up to the very foot of the wall. Fortunately he had with him a number of natives, captured at Boucachique, who were willing to act as guides. With the aid of one of these, a scout made his way to the foot of the wall and found it unprotected by any moat or ditch. Following up this bit of information, De Pointis and Coëtlogon ascended a nearby rise of ground and discovered that the fort did not take up the entire hill, but left a good-size space to the right of it where the French could make their way to the foot of the wall unseen, for the ground was covered by a thick forest growth.

With so favorable a situation before him, De Pointis resolved to carry the place by assault. The call to arms was sounded, the army was brought together, and a detachment of slaves was sent on ahead to cut a path through the undergrowth. Following in their footsteps, the troops marched half way up the hill, then divided so as to encircle the fort. The task of approach proved an easy one, and as soon as they were in place they opened up a deadly musketry fire, at the same time bringing up ladders, with the idea of terrifying the garrison rather than of actually using them. The idea had its effect, for the Spaniards quickly took to their heels. When the invaders approached the side farthest from the city, the garrison managed to slip quietly through a gate in the wall nearest the city and rush headlong to the town, while the French piled in at the other end. It was easier than even the most sanguine had expected. The capture of St. Lazare cost hardly a dozen lives on either side; but no sooner had the French entered the fort, than the outposts of Carthagena opened up a terrific fire with their long-range guns and caused them to retire with a loss of sixty men to the farther side of the hill.

Between St. Lazare and Carthagena lay the town of Imanie, a suburb of the city, reached from St. Lazare by a causeway and bridge, known later as the Puente Media Luna, which spanned the arm of the bay separating the town from the land south of it. It was protected on the land, or southern, side by a stout wall. For several days the French worked energetically, preparing to open the siege in the grand manner. A few of the smaller ships were brought into the inner harbor, anchored, and ordered to open fire; but the distance was too great for the mortars they had on board, and they were soon driven back, badly crippled by the guns of the city. The sea attack having proved ineffective for the purpose of supporting the troops who were to attack by land, an elaborate arrangement was made to enable the land forces to carry the place by themselves. Fascines and gabions were erected at the bridge-head by the soldiers, while the sailors landed the artillery from the larger vessels, dragged the guns to their emplacements, with the help of the Negroes, and set them in position. As for the buc-caneers, they behaved as they had done since the beginning of the campaign: they refused to do any hard work, an attitude bitterly resented afterward by the regular forces. The job proceeded with difficulty, the soldiers being obliged to labor with their muskets close at hand, ready to spring to arms at a moment's notice. Despite these handicaps, the entire business was completed in six days. Twenty-seven guns, six of which were of the largest caliber, and five mortars were put ashore and placed in position. The six big fellows were mounted opposite the gate of Imanie at a distance of 120 yards, while five others in charge of Coëtlogon were placed at the foot of the St. Lazare hill, and seven were put in the fort itself. The mortars were placed between the batteries. While these preparations were being made, the enemy kept up a desultory fire, causing considerable damage to the French. Unfortunately a breast-work designed by De Pointis to protect the batteries was not finished in time, and he was painfully wounded while supervising the work. Unable to walk, he had himself carried about in a litter and was thus able to see that his orders were carried out. To ease his burden and make for greater efficiency, he placed his vice-admiral, M. de Lévis-Mirepoix, in charge of the work he could not inspect personally, a duty which the latter discharged with rare skill. Preparations were also made to use the navy in the attack, and for this purpose the sixty-gun "Vermandois" was moved in near enough to join in the bombardment, but since she got more than she could give she was quickly sent back out of danger.

On the twenty-eighth, with every gun in place, the batteries opened fire, assisted by the flagship "Sceptre," which had been ordered to join in the battle. The firing lasted all day and through the night, and when the sun rose the besiegers had the pleasure of seeing the result of their bombardment. Still the enemy's walls were not sufficiently weakened, so De Pointis kept up his pounding until, when evening came, the front of the rampart was in ruins. Anxious to finish the business, De Lévis urged an immediate assault through the breach thus made. But the commander had no desire to move too hastily; he preferred to wait until nightfall, when a complete survey could be undertaken. Thus he was able to learn that the wall, though badly damaged, could not be scaled without the use of ladders. The captain of the engineers now reported that the bridge, which the enemy had tried to destroy by setting off a boatload of powder under it, could still be used, though the gate at the other end, which the French thought they had destroyed by gunfire, had a mound of earth piled up inside it to prevent access to the town through its portals. The only way to get in, he pointed out, was by making a breach in the walls. Moreover, the gabions and facines erected by the French were badly shattered by the enemy's fire, and it was necessary to bring from the harbor a supply of sacks used in the construction of these fascines and fill them with earth to replace those destroyed; also, there were two of the enemy's flanks still in good condition and well armed, and these could bring their guns to bear on the attackers. For these reasons the assault was put off until the men had had time to finish blasting the breach in the wall and building up their own defenses.

The assault was now set for the thirtieth. The order of attack was as follows: first, a sergeant with ten grenadiers, followed by a company of the same; second, the main body of grenadiers; third, 150 workmen with sappers tools; and last, a similar number of buccaneers and Negroes. At this time a curious incident took place. A Negro, apparently on his own initiative, advanced to the foot of the breach with a flag of truce. He was a native of Carthagena, captured and taken to San Domingo sometime earlier, and was merely attempting to learn some news of his family. When the

Spaniards allowed him to approach, he made known his wants and suggested to his former fellow citizens that they might better yield than wait for an attack, since the French would give no quarter. Governor du Casse, who had now sufficiently recovered to rejoin his command, became curious as to what was going on and strode forward to see for himself. He paid little attention to the colored man's actions, but made a careful survey of the condition of the breach in the walls, which he found sufficiently weakened to be carried by assault. Hurrying back to De Pointis, he advised him to lose no time in attacking.

On the morning of the thirtieth the call to arms was sounded. De Lévis took command of the van, and the column started for the breach. The order of march, so carefully planned, was quickly disregarded, the officers rushing ahead sword in hand to see who could be first to attack the enemy. In this manner they entered the breach alone, where they were exposed to a galling fire, which killed and wounded many of them, despite De Lévis's effort to hurry forward men to their support. When the grenadiers finally arrived, they managed to drive back the Spaniards, who rallied at the end of the village streets and counterattacked. De Pointis followed valiantly, in spite of his injuries, accompanied by a score of his own men, who rendered excellent service in clearing the rampart of the sharpshooters who were firing on the troops that were crossing the bridge. In this manner the enemy were driven from pillar to post, until they finally piled up on the causeway leading from Imanie to Carthagena in the vain hope of escaping into the city. The Governor, however, would have none of it. He wisely kept the doors closed, fearing the French might rush in on the heels of the mob. He said plainly enough that he would not let his Spaniards in until they had made an attempt to stem the enemy's advance. Thus, having no choice in the matter, the panicky troops were obliged to make a stand. Their losses—about eight hundred men—gave them a sort of courage born of desperation, aided and abetted by a quantity of wine they had managed to obtain. Herding together, they charged down the causeway and up the main street leading to it, driving the French before them. The French, however, soon rallied and went after their foes with such vigor that 150 were found dead the next day, transfixed with bayonets. This time the Governor was more lenient, or perhaps he felt it would be well to have as many troops as possible within the city, for he opened the gate to his fleeing Spaniards. M. de Coët-logon was fatally wounded in the engagement; the French losses were about sixty.

After the retreat of the Spaniards, the French rested for the remainder of the day, a few busying themselves with repairing the bridge to permit the passage of the guns now needed for battering down the gate. The following morning, the first of May, everything was ready for the final attack. The "Sceptre," the "Vermandois," and the "Saint-Louis" were brought close to shore to help silence a bastion that was causing trouble. Next day they began their work at about three o'clock in the afternoon and continued until six, when white flags were raised over the walls of the city; then the bombardment ceased until the besieged could make their wants known. To the surprise of all, the Spaniards had had enough and were willing to discuss terms of capitulation. De Pointis demanded hostages, though he himself offered none in return; this condition was so promptly accepted that he saw they had no more stomach for a fight. Scarcely had this transaction been completed, when an Indian runner brought the French commander the startling news that reinforcements to the number of more than one thousand were advancing from the south to the relief of Carthagena.

The news seemed at the time to be authentic, for De Pointis maintained that he received it simultaneously from two separate sources. Besides the Indian runner, a messenger arrived from the officer in command of Fort Boucachique, who had led a foraging expedition that took him to the estate of Don Sanchoz Ximenes. Here he had come in contact with troops on the march to Carthagena, from whom he had learned that they were on the way to relieve the place and were planning to approach it by a series of by-ways, which would take them around a group of little lakes, and to enter the town by coming along the seashore. When he heard this, De Pointis landed from his vessels a detachment of seamen known as "scythemen" because they were armed with small scythes attached to long poles, and placing them with as many regular sailors as could be spared he put the entire group in charge of the batteries. At the same time he sent Du Casse with five hundred buccaneers and three hundred soldiers to head off the enemy. Du Casse distributed his troops among the little lakes where he believed the Spaniards intended to pass, and the following day Gallifet was dispatched to help him with additional men. In the end all these preparations proved useless, for the Spaniards did not put in an appearance. Whether there were any reinforcements coming to the aid of Carthagena is an open question; for De Pointis realized that after he had captured the city the buccaneers would be sure to cause trouble by their violence and brutality if they were allowed to enter its walls before he had properly secured the booty, and it is possible, as Charlevoix suggests, that he may have concocted the story in order to get them out of the way for the time being.

Negotiations now began concerning the terms of surrender. Du Casse at that time appeared as an advocate for the Spaniards, for he was continually urging lenient terms for them. After several conversations an agreement was drawn up in six articles that at least saved Spanish honor, though of course De Pointis had to think of his backers when it came to the question of taking over the loot. Don Diego was permitted to leave the city with whatever troops cared to accompany him, taking all his personal belongings. He was also allowed to march out with the honors of war, drums beating, flags flying, matches lighted, and two pieces of artillery. In arranging for the looting of the town the French commander bound himself to respect convents and all places of worship. The Governor agreed to hand over to the French all guns, treasure, and property belonging to the King of Spain, while the merchants were to surrender their inventory books, together with all silver and merchandise which they might be carrying for their customers. Each citizen was free to leave the city, taking with him only personal effects and enough money for his immediate needs, as well as enough slaves to serve him in the style to which he had been accustomed. Those who wished to remain would be permitted to enjoy the privileges of French subjects—that is, after they had paid the tribute about to be levied on all Spaniards—while those who elected to leave must surrender all their property. De Pointis planned to allow the citizens to retain all their possessions save gold, silver, and precious stones, for after all he could not be burdened with household furniture or real estate; and to expedite matters he would permit them to retain half their previous metals and stones if they would provide him with a true inventory of their property. Confiscation of everything was, of course, the penalty for making false returns. The entire transaction, despite its buccaneering character, resembled a drastic levy of tribute more than an attempt to plunder a conquered town. No matter how much he was to steal, De Pointis was determined to steal it in an orderly and decent manner.

The articles of capitulation signed—and they were signed at once—the French entered the city and took immediate possession of the strategic points, Du Casse being designated as governor of the place by M. De Pointis. It was not long, however, before Du Casse ran afoul of his superior. In order to collect the indemnity in a proper manner, the commander had given orders that no one be permitted to leave the town before handing in a complete inventory of his property. For some reason Du Casse issued passes to certain Spaniards, which were honored by the guards at the city gates, thus permitting them to circumvent De Pointis's carefully-worked-out plan. Such a violation of military etiquette was, to put it mildly, bitterly resented by the commander-in-chief, who visited a well-merited rebuke on his subordinate, a rebuke which the latter bitterly resented. He showed his irritation by betaking himself to the suburb of Imanie, where his buccaneers had been stationed. As for De Pointis, he devoted himself to the business of carrying out the terms of the agreement in a conscientious manner; he even ordered the execution of one of his men who had entered a house contrary to orders to do a little plundering on his own hook.

Once the French had taken possession of Carthagena, the Spanish governor proceeded to evacuate the place with his garrison. At the head of 2,800 men, he marched out through the main gate between a double row of French soldiers and sailors, drawn up along the line of march in order to prevent the removal of too many valuables rather than to do honor to a valiant foe. The Spanish troops having gone, De Pointis turned his attention to the difficult problem of collecting his booty. There was plenty of gold and silver in Carthagena, so he believed, but the question was how to get hold of it in the most expeditious manner. The city was a large one; the number of his officers was not great enough to search the place thoroughly in less than six months; while the rank and file were hardly to be trusted with such a task without adequate supervision. To solve the problem expeditiously, he hit upon the plan of permitting each citizen to retain 10 percent of the confiscated portion of his property if he would surrender it promptly, while each citizen would receive 10 percent of any property whose owner he detected making a false declaration to the officials and attempting to withhold a portion of what was due. Since the capitulation provided that everyone was to declare the entire amount of precious metals and stones in his possession, of which he would be allowed to retain half, the present arrangement permitted him to retain, in addition 10 percent of the half he was obliged to surrender. The concession was made in order to expedite the collection of the plunder, for it was hoped that the inhabitants, or at least most of them, would be willing to play fair with the French if they could save more of their property by doing so. The scheme, strange to say, worked better than expected. The Spaniards had evidently expected to lose all and were pleased to learn that they could save a good share.

On the other hand, some difficulty was experienced with the convents. The articles had specified that they should be left undisturbed, in full possession of their property, and under this agreement they claimed exemption for all their own money and also for the sums entrusted to them by private persons. The French commander, of course, did not see it in this light. The clause, he argued, obligated him to respect the convent buildings, but did not cover their contents, otherwise the entire wealth of the city might be given to the religious orders for safe keeping. A controversy arose which was not settled until De Pointis let into the city a few buccaneers, who, as he says, "have a particular talent at discovering hidden treasures." Alarmed at this, the friars, for they well knew how these "particular talents" would be exercised, agreed to disgorge their hidden wealth; but when the pirates had left, the friars again relapsed into silence. Irritated by their refusal and somewhat embarrassed by the necessity for using force on the clergy, De Pointis finally solved the problem by assigning

as searchers officers whom he could trust, with orders to take everything save the sacred vessels used in the sacrifice of the Mass. The
amount of booty gathered in Carthagena was estimated at eight
million crowns. Though great, it might well have been greater,
for Don Diego had received warning in advance that the French
were coming and had sent to a safe place inland the nuns and ladies
of quality, accompanied by 120 mules laden with gold.

The booty collected, De Pointis turned his attention to the buccaneers, for they had been a veritable problem. He had tried honestly to carry out the terms of the capitulation, and he well knew
what disorder these marauders would have caused in the city had
they been present while the gold and silver were being gathered.
When they returned from their wild-goose chase after the forces
that may or may not have been advancing to the relief of the city
and saw that De Pointis had closed the gate against them, they
became more vociferous than ever, even though he tempered this
action by explaining that their exclusion was only temporary.
When at last, after the booty had all been collected and stored
away, he felt obliged to open the gate to them, their conduct
toward the citizens was just what he had feared. To appease them,
some inhabitants employed a few to guard what was left of their
property. In some cases the scheme worked fairly well, but often
the guards became the robbers. The outraged citizens appealed to
De Pointis, pointing out that this was in violation of the terms of
surrender. He listened to their complaints with considerable sympathy, offering to punish the guilty if they were pointed out to
him; but the thieving buccaneers took care to move away from the
scenes of their robberies as soon as they had taken their fill and
to lose themselves in some other part of the city, where they could
not be identified.

The rift between Du Casse and De Pointis now began to widen.
Angered at the treatment handed out to him, the former had left
Carthagena to take up his residence in Imanie, fully determined
to have nothing to do with his commander's management of the
business. Here he busied himself with looking after the interests
of his freebooters, for they suffered greatly from lack of food, so
he said, though De Pointis had agreed to furnish them with provisions. He complained to the commander that his men were re-

duced to eating dogs, cats, and horses, only to be met with the cold
reply that there was nothing to worry about, for pirates were
probably used to such a diet. Du Casse pointed out further that his
contingent at Imanie was so depleted by the recent admission of
many buccaneers to Carthagena that the suburb might be destroyed
by a sudden attack of the enemy, though whence that enemy
might come he did not venture to say. To quiet him, De Pointis
was willing—doubtless he was also eager—to allow most of the
buccaneers to depart, and suggested to the irate governor that he
take three-quarters of his men (all the inhabitants of San Domingo
and a large part of the Negroes) and leave the expedition. Somewhat startled by this order of dismissal, Du Casse changed his
tactics, for what really interested him and his followers was the
distribution of the booty. The gold by this time had been packed
in chests and placed by De Pointis's orders on board his own ships.
Suspecting some trick, Du Casse sent Gallifet with a request that
some of his representatives might be admitted to the hall where
the plunder was stored in order to supervise its handling. This was
met with a prompt refusal, accompanied by a suggestion that
Gallifet for his own good had better not make any further propo-
sitions of this nature, for the commander felt that such a suggestion
was a reflection on his integrity. He was only trying, he said, to
gather the booty in the most efficient way and had no intention of
defrauding the members of the expedition. A suitable distribution
would be made, he assured Gallifet, as soon as the inventory was
complete. Though De Casse was satisfied with this explanation,
his followers were not. On seeing the chests of gold carried on
board the ships they vowed they would use violence to prevent its
being all taken away before the commander had given them their
share, and they swarmed down to the shore ready to make good
their threat. Du Casse, however, was too good an officer to countenance any such breach of discipline. He thrust himself before them
and pleaded with them to show the King and his officials the respect due them and added that they would capture the gold only
over his dead body. His influence was enough to quell this incipient riot, and to show his appreciation De Pointis promised to
make a concession. He did not wish to use violence or inflict severe
punishments, for he might yet need some of the brothers of the

coast on his ships to replace those who had died or fallen in battle. He accordingly arranged a scale of bonuses, giving certain sums to the maimed and wounded, for, as he ironically remarked, there were so few buccaneers in this category that it would make but a small dent in the amount of treasure collected. He also paid out sums to the captains and to those who had distinguished themselves by conspicuous services.

It was now time for the French to depart. De Pointis had originally hoped to leave a garrison in Carthagena to hold the place for France, but in a very short time the weather had undergone an abrupt change and he found himself suddenly plunged into the season most unfavorable to anyone not accustomed to the climate. In less than six days eight hundred men "were seized with a contagious distemper," which caused the death of the majority. This epidemic did not affect Du Casse's command to any extent, for his buccaneers and colonists were well acclimated; it was confined almost entirely to the Europeans and was sufficiently severe to cause De Pointis to abandon any thought of holding Carthagena.

All ideas of triumphs and treasures [he wrote] were effaced by those of sickness and mortality. In short, if the distemper had continued with this rigor, I must have beheld my inevitable ruin in the fairest port of the world, and no enemy near me; not only have lost the fruits of all our labors, but likewise the squadron entrusted to me.

The problem of embarking all the apparatus used for the siege was difficult and also the guns from the ramparts of the city must be taken away. Handicapped by the loss of so many men, De Pointis turned to the buccaneers for assistance, only to be met with the reply that they would work only when they had received their share of the plunder. Undeterred by this De Pointis distributed enough money among a few of them to secure their help, so that by the twenty-fifth of May the artillery and siege machinery were all on board and the fleet was ready to sail. Since some of the fortifications had been destroyed during the siege, the commander determined to make a thorough job of it and blew up the bastions that remained. The same was also done at Boucachique, although the buccaneers had hoped the place might be turned over to them. Someone had suggested leaving Gallifet in charge of the place with a small garrison of freebooters and soldiers, a plan which he had welcomed with enthusiasm, even offering to hold Carthagena if he were given a hundred additional men. De Pointis toyed with the idea, telling the officer who had made the suggestion that if Du Casse would supply the men he (De Pointis) would leave the artillery in the fortifications, since he could not spare a single man from his sadly depleted forces. Gallifet volunteered to guarantee his superior's readiness to do his part if (and here the question came up again) the pirates received their share of the booty. To this the commander made no answer, but quietly gave orders to destroy Boucachique. When this was done, he informed the buccaneers they might take any merchandise in Carthagena that belonged to Spaniards who had abandoned the place, warning them at the same time that if they plundered certain houses he had marked he would at once open fire on their frigates.

This arrangement, however, did not settle the matter; for when they began to divide the gold and precious stones Du Casse was astonished to learn that the written agreement he had made with De Pointis at San Domingo, covering the distribution of the spoils was based on a misunderstanding. The agreement, it will be recalled, allowed the buccaneers to share in the profits of the enterprise as man to man with the seamen of His Majesty's fleet, each according to his corresponding rank. Since the men from San Domingo numbered about a quarter of the total force they should therefore receive about two million crowns as their share. It now transpired that an arrangement made between the commander and the government greatly altered this easy method of computation and reduced the buccaneers' portion to a mere fraction of this sum. When De Pointis took charge of the expedition, he did so with the understanding that his men would receive for their services only a tenth part of the first million and a thirtieth of any additional millions, the lion's share going to the backers of the enterprise. It was this fraction that was now to be divided man for man; and when De Pointis had completed his inventory and had made his calculations, there were only forty thousand crowns for Du Casse's men. The Governor's rage on hearing the announcement may well be imagined. To justify himself, the commander pointed out that those who had furnished the ships, put up the money, and taken the financial risk expected to reap a handsome profit from their investment if the expedition proved successful and could not be expected to hand over a quarter of the gross to the contingent from San Domingo. He emphasized this point by referring to his instructions from the King, which ordered the entire fighting strength of the colony to join the expedition under pain of being treated as rebels. There was one point, however, which he missed: the people of San Domingo had furnished their own vessels and were entitled to some return for this as well as for their services in the field. For this reason their share should be larger man for man than that of the soldiers and sailors of the fleet. Eventually the government upheld this view.[11]

If Du Casse was angry, the attitude of his officers was far worse; at least they determined to do something about it. They held a meeting to discuss a plan of action, and though at first restrained by the presence of the Governor, who they knew would countenance no departure from legal measures to obtain redress, they decided to sack what was left of Carthagena. No sooner said than done, and the entire pirate fleet closed in on the city. Du Casse became alarmed, for here was open mutiny. Without losing a moment, he sent Gallifet to warn M. de Pointis and dispatched Le Page to head off the buccaneers. Gallifet was unable to see the commander, who had just been stricken with illness, nor was he able to obtain from one of the lieutenants a contingent of one hundred men to stop the mutineers. Le Page fared no better. He attempted in vain to stem the tide of rising indignation by reading a proclamation in which De Casse warned his men to respect the authority of the King, promising at the same time to go to France and plead their cause in person before the Court. It was no use. The freebooters figured—and probably quite rightly—that a bird in Carthagena was worth two at Versailles and that they had better help themselves to what they could get than wait for Heaven knows how long for a verdict from France, which might not be favorable when, if ever, it did reach them. Nor was there anything De Pointis could do to restrain them, because of the serious losses his crews had suffered. Thus for a second time within a few days were the citizens of Carthagena obliged to submit to the depredations of a conquerer. The commander did not stay to wit-

[11]For detailed account of the controversy see Du Casse, *L'Amiral du Casse*, pp. 189-236.

ness these disgraceful proceedings; he ordered his fleet to sail first to Cape Tiburon, then to France, without touching at Petit-Goave, where, he understood, the climate was no better than at Carthagena.

On entering the town the buccaneers began operations by locking up all the male inhabitants in the principal church and presenting them with an ultimatum demanding the immediate payment of five million crowns under threat of penalties so dire that they were left to the imagination of the prisoners. To this demand there could be only one answer, and the terrified citizens set themselves to raise this monstrous sum. The first effort fell far short of the amount demanded, and the pirates turned deaf ears to assurances that this was all that was left after De Pointis had levied the first indemity. It was useless for the inhabitants to argue; they were promptly sent back to their work. A thorough search of the houses was now made; churches were looted, graves were robbed, yet the required amount was not forthcoming. Various ruses were now employed to terrify the people into disclosing the whereabouts of their wealth, though to the credit of Du Casse's men, be it said, outright cruelty was discouraged. About one million crowns' worth of plunder was secured in four days; then the buccaneers, believing they had squeezed the place dry, decided to leave. After dividing the gold and silver, they set sail, nine ships in all, for the island of Avache, where they intended to divide the slaves and the merchandise they had taken. [12]

When news arrived in England of the preparations being made for De Pointis's fleet, the Admiralty thought it high time to take steps to protect the colonies of their ally, the King of Spain, and incidentally their own possessions, should De Pointis chance to attack them. Vice-Admiral John Neville had just sailed (November, 1696) to assume command of the Mediterranean station and was already on his way to Cadiz. On arriving there he was overtaken by a messenger who brought him orders to proceed to the

---

[12]There are a number of accounts of the siege of Carthagena. The ones we have consulted are: Pointis, *A Genuine and Particular Account of the Taking of Carthagena; Principal Objects of the Present War in the West Indies.* In the latter work there is a brief account of the siege given in the description of Carthagena, Section III. Both the above narratives may be found in *Historical Tracts, Colonial,* Vol. II. Charlevoix, *Histoire de l'isle espagnole,* IV, 92–164. Oexmelin, *Histoire des avanturiers flibustiers,* Part VI, ch. iii. For modern treatises see Hart, *Admirals of Caribbean*; Rodgers, "A Study of Attacks upon Fortified Harbors," in Proceedings of U. S. Naval Institute, XXX (1904), 537–44; Du Casse, *L'Amiral du Casse,* pp. 159–236.

Madeira Islands, where he would be joined by a fleet under Rear-Admiral George Mees, which he was to take with him to Barbados, there to formulate a plan to destroy De Pointis's armada. Neville obeyed at once. After considerable delay he managed to reach Bridgetown on the twenty-seventh of April, where he was given an enthusiastic welcome. Here several Dutch vessels joined his command. His next stop was Antigua, where he held a consultation with Governor Codrington, from whom he learned that the French squadron was at Petit-Goave and might possibly attack Spanish San Domingo; for there was a report abroad that for many months Du Casse had been using his slaves to clear a path through the jungle for the passage of an expeditionary force.[13] A council of war was called, at which it was decided to sail for Puerto Rico. To carry out this plan, Neville left for that island with his fleet; but while on the way he learned from a captured French privateer that De Pointis had left Petit-Goave some time before, destination unspecified. Fearing that the Frenchman might attack the nearest English possession, which would be Jamaica, Neville altered his plan and steered for Port Royal. On reaching the eastern end of Jamaica he obtained the information from some prowler of the sea that De Pointis had gone to Carthagena. There was now no question about where Neville should go or what he should do; though for some strange reason or other he did not act at once. He went first to Port Royal for a supply of water and remained there for ten days, perhaps because of contrary winds, then, favored by a half-gale from off shore, he cleared the shoals and set out for Carthagena on the fourth of June with a fleet now numbering nearly thirty ships.[14] Thirteen of these came from England in the original squadron; three had been picked up at Barbados; eight were Dutch vessels which had joined the armada as allies. This made twenty-four men-of-war, and to these must be added four fire ships and a ketch.

By the time he got under way the French had finished their work of destruction and were on their way back—De Pointis leading the King's fleet, Du Casse following in a separate division with his

[13]*C.S.P.*, *America & West Indies, 1696–97*, No. 990.
[14]The principal ships were: "Bristol," "Princess Ann," "Hollander," "Trident," "Gosport," "Newcastle," "Monmouth," "Warwick," "Rupert," "Sunderland," "Colchester," "Pembroke," "Virgin," "Lightning."

buccaneers. Fearing the English would be lying in wait for him at
Cape Tiburon, the French commander had altered his course and
was sailing for the Bahama Strait, when Neville came suddenly
upon him. The French first descried the signal lights of the enemy
during the early hours of the seventh of June; when daylight
broke they found themselves within gunshot of the foe with only
ten ships to oppose a fleet outnumbering them three to one. There
was little desire for battle on the part of the French. Illness, to
say nothing of the losses sustained in action, had so decimated
their crews that they were short-handed; besides, they were loaded
down with booty. Anxious to escape as quickly as possible, the
French turned tail and fled, at the same time making ready to
fight in case they should be overtaken. Those not too ill to move
about took their places at the battle stations, while a signal from
the flagship brought all ships into line. When the English came
within range, the "Warwick," being in the van, opened fire on
the nearest French ship. Fortunately for her, she was a good sailer
and soon pulled away from her attacker. The latter promptly
pounced upon a flyboat, which it captured with a valuable cargo
of plate, eight hundred barrels of powder, and one hundred Negroes, the total worth about twenty thousand pounds. Neville
evidently thought the French would make for the Bahama Strait,
since he did not rush to the attack, but attempted rather to head
them off. On seeing this maneuver De Pointis gave the order, during the night, to come about and head back to Carthagena. As
luck would have it, an English vessel was close enough to discover the stratagem and signaled the Admiral, who ordered his
fleet to follow the enemy under all press of sail. For several days
the pursuit continued. A strong wind sprang up, increasing to a
gale, and the English ships began to show flaws in their rigging.
Apparently topmasts were the weak spots, and several were sprung
or broken off entirely, a fault due, so it was said, to the fact that
these masts did not overlap the masts below them sufficiently to
give them the necessary strength. The French vessels were better
constructed, and, except the "Fort," suffered no such serious mis-
haps. On the ninth, De Pointis figured his position as twenty
leagues from Carthagena. In the evening he signaled his command
to change the course to due west, and when darkness fell they

obeyed. During the night they covered a distance of more than twenty leagues, and when daylight came they found they had shaken off the pursuers.

After losing the French fleet Neville made his way to Bouca-chique, where he found that the fort was held by a small garrison. Working his way into the harbor, he reached Carthagena and went ashore to inspect the town. It was, of course, deserted; but on seeing the English flag in the harbor Governor de los Rios ventured to return, hoping, no doubt, to get some assistance. He needed, among other things, some ammunition and so informed the English admiral, though he did not go so far as to make a formal request for a supply. Neville took the hint and replied that he would gladly help out if it were possible for him to remain, but that since a favorable wind was rising, he would be obliged to leave. After putting out to sea he steered eastward until he came to the coast off Sambay, where he saw nine ships of the buc-caneer squadron making for San Domingo under the command of Du Casse. Neville detached four of his vessels to attack the little fleet, while he stood off to the north for Cape Tiburon. The free-booters fled in all directions, each for himself, rather than face the English men-of-war, a wise maneuver, for Neville was able to capture only two ships. Fortunately for him, they carried a rich booty. A third vessel was driven back to Carthagena, where she ran aground. Her crew were captured by the Spaniards and put to work repairing the fortifications. A fourth was wrecked on the San Domingo coast; the five remaining vessels reached various ports of this island in safety.

Admiral Neville, his fleet badly damaged by the gale, managed to limp into the harbor of San Domingo. While lying there he received word from Governor Beeston asking him to destroy Petit-Goave, always a source of trouble to the law-abiding Jamaicans. He complied by sending Rear-Admiral Mees with nine ships to attend to the business. On the eighth of July, Mees made a sur-prise attack on the settlement, landing four hundred men a mile or more to the east of it. Then, marching on the town at daybreak, he managed to seize the guardhouse and the batteries. The uproar awoke Governor du Casse, who bounded out of bed, dashed through a window, and scurried off to a safe retreat among the neighboring hills. Here he eventually managed to rally a number of men and attack the enemy—not a very difficult task, for they had already begun to plunder the town and were by this time too much under the influence of liquor to put up a fight, despite the large number of men involved. Unable to control his men, Mees set fire to the settlement, damaging some forty houses; then, sounding a retreat, he hurried off precipitately, leaving all his plunder and fifty men dead on the field. All he had to show for the venture was a handful of slaves and some inconsiderable objects of loot. On his return to San Domingo he accompanied Neville to Havana to look for the Spanish treasure galleons then due there on their way to Spain, for it was part of his duty to protect them on the way home. His offer was refused by the Spaniards, so he sailed for England, touching first at Virginia. Thence the fleet made its way home under a junior commander, for both Neville and Mees succumbed in Virginia to an epidemic that had carried off many of their men.

M. de Pointis had an exciting journey to France. He steered first for Newfoundland, where he stopped for water. Here he found an English fleet in St. Johns Harbor, and for awhile he stood off the entrance, hoping it would come out to do battle; but news of his strength had gone before him, and the British commander decided not to risk his ships in the face of such greatly superior numbers. De Pointis accordingly sailed for France. On nearing the coast he found himself within cannon shot of a squadron which broke out the English colors. It was too late to retreat, much as he would like to have done so, because of his shortage of man power so he gave orders to open fire. The action was a brief one, just enough to save the "honor of His Majesty's arms," and he was not sorry to see the English vessels eventually disappear into the night. On the twenty-ninth of August he anchored in the harbor of Brest.

The enormous amount of plunder brought back by De Pointis assured him a hearty welcome. For the benefit of those who had underwritten the enterprise an accounting was presently made, showing a total of 7,646,948 francs in gold and silver bullion, a collection of emeralds weighing 1,947 *marcs* (1,051 pounds avoirdupois), and 71 amethysts. A madonna in a silver robe strewn with jewels was accompanied by a coffer full of ecclesiastical silverware. Besides these treasures De Pointis had brought home eighty-two guns and thirty-two bells. Seldom if ever had a French expedition yielded such an enormous profit.

Shortly after he arrived in France the Admiral found himself faced with a complaint instituted by Governor du Casse concerning the distribution of the booty at Carthagena. The Governor had dispatched Donon de Gallifet to represent him and his buccaneers in a suit to obtain a more equitable share. Gallifet was successful; the King upheld his contention, for he was well pleased with the outcome of the venture. He decorated Governor du Casse with the Cross of St. Louis and awarded his men the sum of four hundred thousand livres[15] instead of the paltry forty thousand they had received from De Pointis. In the end only a portion of it ever reached San Domingo, for heavy expenses and the dishonesty of officials ate up a large part of it. The entire transaction eventually recoiled on the devoted heads of Du Casse and Gallifet, who lost much of their popularity with the men of San Domingo.[16]

The siege of Carthagena marked the end of the war in the West Indies. Save for an inconsequential and unsuccessful landing on Martinique by English freebooters in the month of October,[17] no attempt was made by either combatant to attack the possessions of the other. The nations engaged in the struggle were now tired and anxious for peace; in fact feelers for a peace of some sort had been sent out from time to time for the past two years. The first inkling came when King Louis offered the Dutch the abolition of the duty placed upon their imports into France, a great boon to the Dutch merchants, yet one not sufficiently strong to counterbalance Louis's refusal to make certain other concessions. Then France signed a treaty with Savoy, thus relieving the pressure on this front and forcing William of England to realize that he might not be able to carry on the war with the loss of this ally. In truth England and also the Netherlands were beginning to feel a financial pressure that might indeed result in total collapse. As the year 1696 drew to a close, it was generally understood that terms of peace would soon be discussed, Sweden acting as mediator. By the

[15]Charlevoix says 1,400,000, but this is obviously an error.

[16]Charlevoix, *Histoire de l'isle espagnole*, IV, 165–73; Burchett, *Memoirs and Transactions at Sea*, pp. 354 ff.; Lediard, *The Naval History of England*, II, 716–20, Pointis, *A Genuine and Particular Account*, pp. 73–86; Charnock, *Biographia navalis*, II, 63–74.

[17]Labat, *Nouveau voyage aux isles de l'Amérique*, Vol. II, chap, iv.

following May, William realized that conditions in his realm made it impossible for him to continue much longer and that the Dutch were not disposed to advance him any money. As for France, her failure to capture Barcelona discouraged her government, and, moreover, her officials had as yet heard nothing from De Pointis's expedition. Hence the two nations were not averse to holding a conference to discuss terms.[18] The meeting was held at Ryswick. The treaty between France and England, the only one of the treaties signed there which interests us, was signed on September 20, 1697. Under article VII His Most Christian Majesty promised to restore to Great Britain all countries, islands, and fortresses which the English possessed before the war; and likewise the King of England was to restore any territories taken from France. These adjustments were all to be made within the next six months. Commissioners were to be appointed to work out the details of the restorations, with particular regard to the situation at Hudson Bay, which was rather complicated. Under this arrangement the English were obliged to return to the French the northern and southern portions of St. Christopher, captured by Governor Codrington during the course of the war, while the other French and English possessions remained as they were. As in the case of the previous war, ended by the Treaty of Breda ten years earlier, the present war accomplished exactly nothing so far as the Anglo-French situation in the West Indies was concerned. Naval expeditions had been sent out, armies landed, battles fought, sieges laid, invasions repulsed; yet when the war was ended at last neither nation retained a foot of the other's territory.

[18]Morgan, *Economic Aspects of the Negotiations at Ryswick, Royal Historical Society Transactions,* Fourth Series, Vol. XIV.

WAR OF THE SPANISH SUCCESSION

ESPITE the noble sentiments expressed in the Treaty of Ryswick, sentiments that promised an era of unbroken peace, the peace proved in fact to be but a short-lived truce; it was ended five years later by the War of the Spanish Succession. In the West Indies there was, however, little confidence in the idea of a permanent cessation of hostilities, for we find many indications during this lustrum pointing to an early renewal of the long-drawn-out conflict.

The first problem confronting the authorities was the reoccupation of the French portion of St. Christopher by its original owners. The King was anxious to see his subjects reinstated in their rightful possessions, and to further this end he appointed the Comte Jean-Baptiste de Gennes governor of the island and remitted certain imposts for a period of five years in order to make it easier for them to get on their feet. Furthermore, he lost no time in telling his ambassador in London to obtain the necessary orders from the British government for the surrender of French St. Christopher so that the vessel he expected to send out in January (1698) with his own orders might also carry those of King William.[1] Yet the Lords of Trade were in no hurry to yield the island, and even made an effort, albeit a somewhat feeble one, to induce their sovereign to retain the island *in toto* and to give in exchange some other possession, an arrangement which they said was quite within the scope of the powers given the commissioners by the Treaty of Ryswick.[2] Their eagerness to hold French St. Christopher was due to the policy adopted by Governor Codrington after his return from the expedition against Guadeloupe in 1691 according

[1] *C.S.P., America & West Indies, 1697–98*, No. 109.   [2] *Ibid.*, No. 124.

to which he had encouraged colonists from the other islands to settle there by giving them French plantations. To be sure, they had accepted these properties with the understanding that they might lose them at the end of the war. The Governor himself had invested heavily in Kittefonian real estate, and he declared he stood to lose £20,000 by the peace. Nevertheless the King was determined to abide by the terms of Ryswick. He issued peremptory orders to the Lords of Trade for the restoration of the island, at the same time sending similar instructions to Governor Codrington, which he accompanied by a letter authorizing him to claim the time-honored right of the English to gather salt from the salt ponds in French territory.[3]

On receiving these orders Codrington had no choice but to obey, and this he proceeded to do at once, though he did not interpret these instructions as covering the islands of St. Martin and St. Bartholomew, since the King had not specifically mentioned them. These he kept until further orders. As for St. Christopher, he immediately issued instructions to his colonists to vacate the French portions of the island and betake themselves to the English sector. The Governor's commands were received with bitterness. These people had been angered by the terms of the treaty, which took away from them what they thought was theirs by right of conquest, and they determined to even matters up by carrying off everything they could. When they captured the territory at the beginning of the war, they had destroyed most of the buildings in revenge for the property destroyed by the French when the latter had seized their lands; they had left standing only the church and a few houses at Basseterre, expecting that this sector would be theirs at the end of the war. When they learned the terms of the treaty, they saw what was coming and promptly pulled down every house, loaded the lumber on wagons, and carried it off to their own territory.[4]

As might be expected, the French were indignant when they learned of this act of vandalism. An agreement had been drawn up by the two monarchs to cover just such a situation, and in it were four stipulations: 1. The quarters formerly occupied by the French and the dwellings they owned in English territory should be re-

[3]*Ibid.*, No. 147.   [4]*Ibid.*, No. 408.

turned to them in the same condition as they were in 1690; 2. Damages done by the English since the peace should be repaired; 3. Any property sold by the French to the English should be returned in exchange for the purchase price; 4. The French should get back their slaves if the latter should wish to return to them.[5] In the face of this agreement the English, after the signing of the treaty, had indulged in this inexcusable destruction of property. The French commissioners, when they heard of it, at once complained to their King.

It is necessary to interrupt the narrative at this point to say that Governor Codrington died on July 30, 1698. His death put an end to the career of one of England's most energetic West Indian governors. The ten years of his tenure of office had been a period of war, and during this war he had always been on the aggressive. It was he who urged the continuation of the action at Guadeloupe when Captain Wright decided to retire; it was he, also, who later urged renewal of the attack at St. Pierre, when the council of war voted to withdraw. During this stormy period the Leeward Islands had need of a warrior-administrator, and Christopher Codrington filled the bill. For his successor the King appointed on May 23, 1699, the Governor's son, Christopher junior, a scholarly young man who held office for the brief period of four years. He did not leave for his post until August of the following year, because of the difficulties he experienced in collecting his father's back salary, a piece of business he found more to his liking than the duties of governorship. During the interim the President and the Council of Nevis took over the government of the Leeward Islands until the appointment of Edward Fox as governor *pro tempore*.

It was now time for the French to ask for a restitution of their property. Armed with the agreement between the two governments, the Marquis d'Amblimont, now Governor-General of the French islands, wrote the Council of Nevis on December 14, 1698, and enclosed copies of letters he had received from his King ordering him to take over St. Christopher; he said he would start for that island as soon as his messenger returned from Nevis. The Council replied that they would be ready to surrender the colony in

[5] Dessalles, *Histoire générale des Antilles*, II, 216.

ten days. To prepare for this event, they wrote James Norton, then lieutenant-governor of St. Christopher, telling him to have his people evacuate the French quarter at once. [6]

On January 22, 1699, the Marquis d'Amblimont accompanied by the Intendant-General, François-Roger Robert, anchored his little fleet of four ships off Basseterre, where he was received by Governor Norton. The colony was surrendered to the Marquis the following day, with the proper ceremonies, and the French delegation sat down to compose a list of demands for the English commissioners to consider. They requested the restoration of the old boundaries of 1690 between the French and the English territories (which was quickly granted); the surrender of all French cannon taken by the English; restoration of property in the English section originally belonging to French owners and proper reparations for damages done to such property since the signing of the treaty; return of free Negroes taken from the French plantations during the war; renewal of the treaties of 1655 and 1671;[7] destruction of the great fort on Brimstone Hill; and joint use of all sulphur mines, salt ponds, and highways. To all this the English commissioners replied at great length, but raised objections to everything except the first demand. In truth, they believed, or preferred to believe, that they did not have the authority to make any concessions, their business having been concluded with the surrender of the colony. The French, therefore, appealed to Pontchartrain, for they had no intention of letting any of these matters go by default, especially the inexcusable destruction of property since the signing of the treaty, for the damage to the houses alone was estimated at 135,000 livres. The Minister of Marine in turn requested the British government to give Governor Codrington the necessary powers to settle these grievances on his arrival; but nothing definite was ever done, for the intrigues leading up to the coming war soon broke off friendly relations between the two kingdoms. [8] Convinced that nothing more could be accomplished at this time, M. d'Amblimont returned to Martinique, leaving the Comte de Gennes in charge of St. Christopher.

At this time there occurred in Europe the event that led to the

[6]*C.S.P.*, *America & West Indies, 1697–98*, No. 1054.
[7]Treaties affirming partition of St. Christopher.   [8]*Ibid.*, Nos. 74, 264.

rupture of the uneasy peace the world had enjoyed since Ryswick. King Charles II of Spain died in November, 1700. Being childless he had no direct heir to the throne, and the nearest claimants were the Archduke Charles of Austria and Philip of Anjou, grandson of Louis XIV. Charles II left a will bequeathing the crown to Philip, and all Europe stood breathlessly by, waiting to see if Louis would authorize Philip to accept it. The King did not keep the world long in suspense. On receipt of the news of his brother-sovereign's death he presented the young man to his court as Philip V, the future King of Spain. There was no doubt in the mind of all Europe as to what would happen. An alliance between France and Spain would be too powerful a combination for the other powers, who would now bend every effort to prevent Philip from taking the Spanish throne. Preparations were at once begun for the coming conflict.

As a matter of fact, preparations had been started in the West Indies before the death of King Charles, for his health was poor and his end was expected at any time. Louis, in the summer of 1699, sent Sieur Renaud, a skilled engineer, to make a complete inspection of the fortifications. Renaud landed at Guadeloupe, destined to be the scene of the principal conflict of the war, where he drew up plans for the fortification of Basseterre, which had been so easily captured by Governor Codrington ten years before. A portion of this town Renaud planned to surround with a stout wall, joining the district to the fort and leaving the neighboring town of St. François open. In this manner the entire population of the two places could take refuge within its walls. This was the plan already outlined by Governor Auger,[9] who during the campaign of 1691 saw how much harm had been done when the inhabitants retreated through the back of the town to the foothills of the Soufrière, leaving the entire settlement unprotected, save by the garrison of the fort. Thus shortly after this disaster Auger had issued an edict forbidding the inhabitants to withdraw their families in time of invasion under penalty of being abandoned to whatever fate was in store for them. For troops, Auger had at his disposal 1,418 men, divided into a large number of small companies and located in various parts of the island. The total white

[9]Labat, *Nouveau voyage aux isles de l'Amérique*, II, 127.

population was 4,028, to which must be added 7,600 Negroes, slaves for the most part, who were able to furnish a few men to serve in the army. The island of Martinique boasted a far larger population, 19,581, of which 12,900 were slaves and 1,751 were men capable of bearing arms. It was also, as we have seen, strongly fortified and now, for all intents and purposes, practically impregnable.

In the Leeward Islands, Governor Codrington (we refer, of course, to Codrington, junior) was doing his best to prepare for the coming conflict. Nevis, he felt ,was strong enough to fend for itself; Montserrat, despite the questionable loyalty of its Irish population, might come through; Antigua had too large an area for its small population and might need assistance; but St. Christopher was the weak spot in the line of defense and needed all his attention. Its fate would be quickly decided at the outbreak of war, for the two nationalities were at this time fairly well matched, and victory would go to whichever got the jump on the other.[10] Codrington therefore devoted most of his time to St. Christopher. He went there as soon as he felt trouble might break out, for at the first rumor of war the Kittefonians prepared to evacuate the place. He assured these anxious people that he would do everything in his power to bring them help. Upon investigation he learned that he had as many men there as the French, although they were not nearly so well equipped. There was no powder, for one thing, Governor Norton having exhausted the available supply in pyrotechnic displays during his many drinking bouts; but Codrington was fortunately able to send twenty barrels from Antigua and ten from Nevis, with a promise of more from Barbados. He bemoaned his lack of authority to compel the colonists—scattered as they were throughout the two separate parts of the island—to unite for defense, especially as De Gennes had gathered all his men together at Basseterre and was prepared to strike. The French governor had also sent for the men of St. Martin and St. Bartholomew.

After six weeks of untiring effort Codrington returned to Antigua, comforted by the thought that he had accomplished much and was ready to cope with De Gennes. He had been fairly successful, though he failed to persuade the Governor of Barbados to

[10]*C.S.P., America & West Indies, 1701*, No. 784.

send him assistance, for in Barbados, unfortunately, the old feeling of jealousy on the part of the sugar planters still held sway. The bad effect of this attitude on the Leeward Islanders was more to be feared than anything else, for it made the various colonies unwilling to part with any of their men to defend a weaker neighbor. Already there was grumbling in Antigua over the three companies Codrington had proposed to lend St. Christopher. Yet the Governor was not disheartened; he was determined, on the contrary, to strike first.

If war break out [he wrote the Lords of Trade] the title [to St. Christopher] shall be soon decided, and in the meantime I do the public busines-better than if I were there myself. I stayed there six weeks and put the militia in good order. . . And if I hear of war at midnight I shall visit M. de Gennes by break of day.[11]

The situation now came quickly to a head. In May, 1702, the Dutch and the English governments declared war on France and Spain, and the latter replied with a declaration the following July. Just before England took the fatal step King William, who had outlived his wife, Mary, died, and his sister-in-law, the Princess Anne, succeeded him to the throne. News of the accession of this sovereign reached the West Indies during the month of May, and two months later word came of the formal declaration of war by England and the Netherlands. When Governor Codrington received this news, he at once proceeded to make good his threat. Though stricken with fever, he rose from his bed and started for St. Christopher. "The cause must be decided," he said, "and our people won't go where I don't lead." The actual command of the expedition was intrusted to Colonel Walter Hamilton.

In French St. Christopher, Governor de Gennes was anxiously waiting for the English to strike the first blow. The activities of Codrington had changed the balance of power, and the French now no longer felt the confidence they had enjoyed a short time before; indeed, when war was declared they sent their women, children, and slaves to Martinique. De Gennes's forces consisted of four companies of the Marine, numbering 160 men all told, which he used to garrison Basseterre, and some 240 at Pointe de Sable, on the northern side of the English sector, the latter com-

[11]*Ibid.*, No. 997.

manded by Sieur de Courpon. De Gennes had thrown up en-
trenchments around Basseterre and also at the Ravine Guillon,
just south of the frontier line; but these fortifications, he well
knew, were too weak to offer serious resistance. To make matters
worse, one of the King's lieutenants insisted on going to Martinique at this late hour to ask for reinforcements in spite of all that
De Gennes could do to restrain him, thus depriving the little army
of one of its principal leaders. For some reason or other he showed
no eagerness to reach the capital, once he had started, but loafed
along the way, stopping for several days in Guadeloupe instead
of hurrying forward to deliver his message.

To the four hundred French, the English were able to oppose
thirteen hundred men, and on the fourteenth of July, Codrington
and Hamilton brought twelve hundred more from Antigua and
Nevis. These men were landed south of Basseterre for the purpose
of attacking the town from that side while the resident troops
assaulted the outposts on the Ravine Guillon. The latter made a
preliminary attack on the Guillon, which was easily repulsed.
The following day Hamilton sent a flag of truce to the Comte de
Gennes, asking to meet him at the frontier to discuss the situation.
De Gennes complied. He was taken to the meeting place, where
Hamilton coolly informed him that war had been officially declared and that Codrington had been ordered by the Queen to
demand the surrender of the French territory. Two hours were
given the Frenchman to reach a decision. De Gennes at first replied
manfully that he would do his duty, but on returning to his headquarters he called a council of his officers to put the matter up to
them. The situation, it must be admitted, looked none too good,
with only four hundred men—more than half of whom were at
Pointe de Sable—to oppose six times that number, and besides
when the officers were conferring four English vessels accompanied
by twenty barks came over from Nevis and anchored off Basseterre.
It was suggested that they should abandon Basseterre and retreat
to the northern district by following the route taken years before
by Governor de Sales and should there join forces with the troops
of Sieur de Courpon. De Gennes rejected this plan, for reasons
which he said he would explain later to the King. No other solution being offered, a resolution to surrender was placed before the

council and adopted by a vote of twelve to five. Articles of capitulation were drawn up, submitted to Colonel Hamilton, and accepted by him with certain reservations. The French were permitted
to surrender the colony with the honors of war; officers were to
retain their baggage and a limited number of servants; the clergy
were to be respected; and the families of officers and planters were
to be transported to Martinique, as well as those of the Irish
people living in French territory.[12]

On learning that these terms had been accepted De Gennes was
somewhat displeased, for Hamilton had made certain reservations
in the form of marginal notes that the French governor had not
been given an opportunity to endorse. He made much of this point,
saying he would rather remain a prisoner of war with his garrison
than submit to the terms approved by the British commander.
His chief grievance was the surrender of the Ravine Guillon. He
probably felt—and in this he was right—that he would later be
called to account for his easy surrender of St. Christopher, and he
wished that some action would be taken by his subordinates to
justify him. To ease him out of an embarrassing position a group
of officers, both military and civil, together with the leaders of
the clergy, presented him with a signed petition urging him to
approve Colonel Hamilton's reservations in order to save the colony
from total ruin and the colonists from the rigors of conquest.
Satisfied with this, De Gennes raised no further objections, and the
English entered into possession of the French territory.

There was now no further resistance. Sieur de Courpon at Pointe
de Sable had learned from a spy of Hamilton's arrival and had
started south with his little army to join in the general scheme
of defense; he arrived just in time to find Basseterre in the hands
of the enemy and was obliged to surrender without striking a
blow. Once masters of the situation, the British made preparations
to transport the French to their other colonies. Governor de
Gennes was retained as a hostage for the safe return of the ships
furnished by the victors for this purpose. The unfortunate colonists were stripped of most of their possessions and forced into ships
that were to take them to San Domingo, where their conquerors
felt they would be less troublesome than at Martinique or Guade-

[12]*C.S.P., America & West Indies, 1702*, No. 968, sec. i.

loupe, all despite the guarantees in the terms of capitulation. Fortunately, in most cases the deportees, as soon as they were out of sight of St. Christopher, managed to persuade the captains, either by reason or by force, to shape their courses for the nearby French islands instead of steering for far away San Domingo. In this manner did the English strike the first blow of the war and capture St. Christopher, which henceforth was to form a permanent part of the British West Indian empire.

The surrender of St. Christopher had an embarrassing aftermath for the unfortunate Comte de Gennes. Among his own soldiers there were many who did not relish the idea of surrendering without striking a blow, and they vented their wrath against him by storming his house. In Martinique, Acting-Governor de Guitaud and Intendant Robert wrote angry letters to the Minister of Marine, giving an account of the surrender that reflected no credit on De Gennes. All this the unfortunate Governor of St. Christopher had time to ponder over while he was an unwilling hostage in the hands of his captors. When at last the ships bearing the refugees returned and he was released, he chartered a vessel to take him to an estate he owned in Cayenne rather than face the welcome he knew awaited him at Martinique. On the way to Cayenne he was captured by a Dutch buccaneer, who took him to St. Thomas. In some manner he arrived at Martinique a year later, where he was promptly thrown into prison at Fort St. Pierre. By order of the newly appointed Governor-General de Machault de Bellemont acting on instructions from the Court, he was brought to trial for his surrender of the colony. On the whole, says Father Labat, public opinion in Martinique was for him; but the King, who had heard only one side of the story, was furious over the tame surrender of his colony and demanded the immediate trial of the Governor.

The conduct of M. de Gennes on this occasion [wrote Pontchartrain to Machault] has so displeased His Majesty and has seemed to him so dishonorable for the nation that he has ordered me to write you that he wishes that as soon as you arrive in Martinique you will bring him to trial and have him judged by a council of war, so that if he is guilty of any understanding with the enemy, or of the outright cowardice that appears in his action he shall receive the punishment he deserves according to the articles of war.[13]

[13]Dessalles, *Histoire générale des Antilles*, II, 263.

In the face of such bias it was impossible for De Gennes to obtain a fair hearing. He did what he could, convicted three of the King's witnesses of perjury, challenged the competency of some of his judges and even of Machault himself; yet the case went slowly against him. At last he was transferred to Fort Royal, where judgment was pronounced in August, 1704. He was attainted of treason, declared guilty of flagrant cowardice, and for punishment was degraded from his rank of nobility and sentenced to lose his Cross of St. Louis and all the positions he held. He appealed to the King. Shortly after this he sailed for France, but was captured *en route* by the English and taken to Plymouth, where he died shortly after his arrival. His widow took up the case, and in due course of time Louis set aside the verdict of the court at Martinique and rehabilitated the Count by granting her and her children all the honors and emoluments due them as the widow and orphans of a Chevalier of St. Louis and a captain in the Royal Navy.[14]

Before the outbreak of war the alarm which the English felt at the paucity of British ships of war in the West Indies caused them to send a small fleet to look after their colonies. For this purpose the government dispatched Vice-Admiral John Benbow with a squadron of ten vessels. He set sail in September, 1701, arriving at Barbados in November. After a brief stay he proceeded in a leisurely manner to Jamaica, sailing slowly along the coast of Martinique, where he saw plenty of merchantmen but no men-of-war. He was, in fact, a little early; had he come later, he would have encountered the huge armament sent out by the King of France.

This great armada, one of the most powerful ever sent to the West Indies by the French government, consisted of thirty-five vessels, classified as twenty-eight warships (mounting 1,688 guns), five fire ships, and two flutes. These vessels carried all told 12,560 sailors and soldiers.[15] The fleet was commanded by Comte de Château-Renault,[16] who hoisted his flag on the "Merveilleux,"

[14]For an account of the capture of St. Christopher and the trial of De Gennes see Labat, *Nouveau voyage aux isles de l'Amérique*, II, 329–42.

[15]For particulars of the fleet see Calmon-Maison, *Le Maréchal Château-Renault*, Appendix XV.

[16]*François-Louis de Rousselet de Château-Renault*.

a ninety-eight gun ship-of-the-line. Late in November he had sailed from Cadiz with a commission from the King of Spain,[17] but with instructions from Pontchartrain as to what he should do. Since war was imminent, the French government had already sent out a smaller fleet under the Comte Alain-Emmanuel de Coëtlogon (an uncle of the Chevalier de Coëtlogon who served under De Pointis) to convoy home the Spanish treasure fleet. Since this fleet was believed to have already sailed, fears were entertained that it might fall into Benbow's hands. To forestall this, Pontchartrain had sent out a frigate to look for Benbow's squadron, and this ship was to meet Château-Renault at Maderia and report to him. If the English fleet were sighted, the French admiral was to rush at once to cover the Spanish galleons, otherwise he was to proceed to Martinique. The frigate, it so happened, failed to discover any trace of Benbow's command, and as a result Château-Renault laid his course for Fort Royal, where he arrived on January 2, 1702. Here he learned to his surprise that Benbow was already at Jamaica. At Martinique the French commander decided to rest his crews and repair his vessels, confident that Benbow, with his very inferior fleet, would not venture to cause him any trouble. Three weeks later, however, he was startled out of his complacency by the receipt of instructions from Pontchartrain that demanded his immediate attention. He was ordered to attack Barbados, capture it if possible, and keep an eye open for a squadron under Rear-Admiral William Whetstone that was being equipped in England to sail for West Indian service.

When Château-Renault received his orders, he hesitated, for the capture of such a strong post as Barbados, he felt, was beyond his ability. Of some twelve thousand men under his command only twenty-two hundred were landing troops, and even though he raised this number to three thousand by drawing on the garrisons of Martinique and Gaudeloupe he would not have enough to face the five or six thousand white men, reinforced by an equal number of Negroes, who would rush to the defense of their colony. To solve

[17]Since the accession of Philip V to the throne of Spain made a member of the French royal family king, a French officer could accept a Spanish commission without impairing his standing.

the problem Château-Renault called a council on board his flag-ship, made up of his captains and some officers from the capital, whose knowledge of local conditions would be valuable. To this gathering he put the question whether he should obey orders or not. After a full discussion of the subject the council decided unanimously against an attack on Barbados. The success of the enterprise, they felt, was more than doubtful, and also provisions were running low and there would not be enough for the return journey to France even if they should succeed. Furthermore, there was always the possibility that Benbow and his fleet might fall upon them from the rear.

This question decided, Château-Renault cast about for something to do. The possibilities of a descent upon Jamaica were con-sidered and dismissed for the same reasons that had caused him to abandon the project against Barbados. He was speculating on the advisability of attacking one of the Leeward group instead, when news reached him that Coëtlogon, wearied of waiting for the Span-iards to make up their minds about accepting his services as convoy, had returned to France, leaving the galleons at Vera Cruz. Since this left the Spanish treasure fleet at the mercy of Benbow should war be declared, Château-Renault at last realized exactly what he should do, for the safety of the fleet bearing the wealth of France's ally was of far more importance than the capture of one of the Carribbees.

There was no need, of course, for so great a fleet as Château-Renault's to act as convoy. It would be cumbersome; and also the difficulties of feeding so large a number of men were beginning to make themselves felt. For these reasons the Admiral decided to divide his command and send back to Brest a division composed chiefly of his larger vessels and those in poor condition, leaving his own squadron reduced to eighteen ships-of-the-line, two frig-ates, and ten smaller craft, some of which he had picked up at Martinique. Transferring his flag to the "Fort," he gave orders that the two divisions should sail together as far as the passage between Puerto Rico and San Domingo; then they were to separate and the Admiral was to take his squadron to Havana. Here he planned to leave it while he went in person with two or three ships to get the galleons at Vera Cruz.

On the twenty-second of February the fleet set sail from Martinique, to the great relief of the colonists, who had found themselves hard pressed to furnish the huge armada with food and supplies; the crews were also glad to go, for they had lost many men through illness. Ten days later Château-Renault reached the western end of Puerto Rico, where he hoisted the signal that sped the homeward-bound squadron on its way. With his own fleet he then proceeded to Leogane, where he anchored the following evening. Here he remained for about a month, making arrangements for picking up the Spanish ships at Vera Cruz, and during this time he was fortunate enough to get a line on Benbow's fleet from various sea rovers who chanced to come into port. Benbow's command had been increased considerably since his arrival by the addition of a number of vessels already in West Indian waters, so that it now numbered twenty ships, mounting 682 guns. Yet disease had played havoc with the personnel, as it had with Château-Renault's men. Benbow also had his reports on the French fleet, which he quickly realized was too powerful for him to attack, even after the French admiral had sent a part of his squadron home. The situation, then, favored Château-Renault's plans. He had already sent a messenger from Martinique to the Spanish Admiral to tell him what he proposed to do, and he now sent a second one with the news that he was on his way to Havana and with an urgent request to the Spaniards to use all possible dispatch, since his supplies were not sufficient to permit him to wait very long and it would be a pity for the galleons to miss their convoy again. After this he got under way, and he reached Havana on the ninth of April.

At Havana, Château-Renault met the messenger he had sent from Martinique to Vera Cruz. This envoy brought him letters from the governor and the archbishop of that city assuring him that the galleons would be ready to sail on his arrival. Château-Renault, however, discounted these promises, for his messenger informed him that the cargoes, consisting largely of silver ingots, were still in the warehouses, little effort having been made to place them on board the ships. Nevertheless, he felt it advisable to go there, hoping his presence would speed up the work. Since the harbor of Vera Cruz was already crowded with the Spanish vessels, he left the greater part of his fleet at Havana and set out with a few of his lighter ships. He also left instructions that he should be advised at once if Benbow should arrive. On reaching Vera Cruz he found his worst fears realized. Little had been done to fill the holds of the galleons, and he was now informed that they must wait for the arrival of the King's personal treasure, which had to be weighed, counted, and packed in a leisurely manner before it could be delivered on board officially. The French commander arrived on the fifth of May and set the twentieth as the date of departure, hoping this might hurry forward the work; but the fleet was not ready to sail until the tenth of June.

On his return to Havana, Château-Renault found the fleet he had left there a mere shadow of the gallant armada he had brought from France. Death, disease, and desertion had taken their toll of his officers and men. Benbow had not troubled them, for he too had suffered from the same evils. There was therefore only one thing for the French admiral to do, that is, to flee from this pestilential country as quickly as possible; but since he was obliged to wait for the ships he had promised to convoy for the Havana merchants he did not put to sea until the twenty-third of July. When at last he did get under way, he found himself in command of a fleet of eighteen warships, six frigates, and six smaller vessels, convoying twenty-seven merchantmen. He made the crossing without mishap, though war had just been declared, and two months later he brought his fleet safely into Vigo Bay.[18]

At this time the situation in the West Indies was enlivened by the reappearance of Governor du Casse. This gallant official had been in France engaged in some negotiations in connection with the Guinea Company, when the government decided to send him back to San Domingo at the head of a squadron ordered to act as convoy for the Duke of Albuquerque, Viceroy of New Spain. Du Casse, at the head of a fleet consisting of the "Heureux," a sixty-eight gun vessel, a flagship and five lesser ships, arrived at Coruna on the eighth of June, where he took on board the Duke and Duchess of Albuquerque, 117 duennas, and an assortment of monks and friars. There were also eight transports, containing two thou-

[18]An excellent account of Château-Renault's cruise is given in Calmon-Maison, *Le Maréchal Chateau-Renault*, pp. 205–49; see also *C.S.P., America & West Indies, 1702*, No. 163.

sand soldiers. Two months later he arrived in Puerto Rico, where he detailed two vessels from his fleet to convey the Duke and Duchess with their retinue to their destination; ke kept the transports which he intended to convoy himself. These two ships were to accompany him as far as the eastern point of San Domingo and then veer off northward to Cap François to pick up a pilot, while he with the bulk of the fleet, was to make for the Spanish town of San Domingo, where the recently appointed Governor of Carthagena was waiting to take passage for that city. For the purpose, then, of landing this gentleman and of convoying the Spanish troops to their destination Du Casse proposed to visit Santa Marta, Carthagena, and Puerto Bello.

Some time before the French fleet entered the Caribbean, Admiral Benbow got wind of its coming and took steps to intercept it. Having been reinforced in the early part of May by the arrival of William Whetstone and his squadron,[19] he now felt himself a good match for Du Casse, though he could not cope with Château-Renault's huge armada. Early in July a report reached him that Du Casse was soon due at Port Louis (now Aux Cayes), on the southern shore of San Domingo near Ile Avache, and to check the Frenchman's advance he sent Whetstone with six ships to cruise in that locality. Benbow himself proposed to go the following week to Carthagena to find Du Casse in case Whetstone did not come in contact with him.[20] Since there was also the problem of intercepting some victualing ships bound from Petit-Goave to Havana, Benbow sent a third squadron to cruise in the passage between San Domingo and Cuba. Thus his entire command was divided into three separate and independent squadrons. When Benbow was ready to sail, word came that Du Casse was now heading for Leogane, and he accordingly changed his plans and left Port Royal on the twenty-first to head him off. On reaching Leogane, Benbow saw that he had been deceived as to the whereabouts of his enemy, so he improved his time by driving ashore a forty-six gun warhsip, setting fire to two great merchantmen, capturing two others, together with a brigantine and a sloop, and making a general

[19]Several French authors, notably Calmon-Maison, believe that Whetstone had joined Benbow before Château-Renault's arrival, but the English documents clearly show that Whetstone did not arrive until May.

[20]*Ibid.*, No. 560.

nuisance of himself. When thus engaged he received word that Du Casse was *en route* for Carthagena. At last the opportunity had come, and Benbow knew where his enemy could be found. He accordingly set out in pursuit.

Admiral Benbow left Leogane on the twentieth of August in the flagship "Bredah," accompanied by the "Defiance," the "Ruby," the "Greenwich," the "Pendennis," the "Windsor," and the "Falmouth," totaling 398 guns. On the morning of the twenty-ninth he saw off the coast of Santa Marta ten vessels to the eastward. Heading for them, he found he had overtaken Du Casse's squadron, which consisted of the flagship "Heureux," the "Agreeable," the "Phenix," and the "Apollon" (228 guns in all), accompanied by six smaller craft. Now there occurred one of the strangest incidents in all British naval history: a fleet of the Royal Navy was held at bay and driven off by a fleet decidedly inferior in capital ships and weight of metal, solely because of the downright cowardice of at least two of its captains. This, we are bound to say, does not in the least detract from the skill and courage of the French, who during the six days' running fight kept up a continual fire on the enemy's vessels when the latter came close enough to them, until at last Admiral Benbow, despairing of ever getting his ships into a decisive action, was forced to draw away.

About noon the squadrons were close enough to join battle. The English advanced on the foe, the "Defiance" leading the line, with the flagship in the center. It was at this point that Benbow got his first taste of what was to come, for the "Defiance," Captain Richard Kirkby, and the "Windsor," Captain John Constable, showed no eagerness to close in. To get action out of his leading ship, the Admiral was obliged to send a messenger by boat to order Kirkby to set more sail. At four o'clock it was possible to open fire, but after discharging three half-hearted broadsides Kirkby and Constable luffed out of line and out of range, leaving the rest to bear the brunt of battle. The French served their guns smartly, the two rear ships giving the British that came within range some heavy punishment. During the night the two squadrons steered westward, and Benbow took advantage of the lull to reform his line, placing his flagship in the lead and at the same time giving strict orders to his captains to keep in a direct line behind him, half a cable's length from the ship in front. When daylight came Benbow found himself within gunshot of the enemy and only the "Ruby" with him, the rest being three or four miles astern. In the afternoon the two exchanged shots with the French, keeping this up until nightfall. Next day it was again the "Bredah" and the "Ruby" that bore the brunt, the latter taking such a beating in the early morning that it was found necessary to tow her out of range. Kirkby and Constable were close enough to join in the action, but did not fire a shot. The former paid no attention to the Admiral's instructions to deliver a broadside, even when ordered peremptorily to do so. At eight in the morning a gale sprang up. The French put on what sail they could carry and scudded along, closely followed by Benbow, his fleet at last in satisfactory battle formation, all save the sadly battered "Ruby," which had fallen astern. In the afternoon the "Bredah" had reached the two rear ships, and in the exchange of shots that followed for the next two hours she was severely handled, two or three of her guns being dismounted, to say nothing of the damage to the rigging.

On the first of September, when daylight broke, Benbow saw his fleet badly shattered, the two principal stragglers being the "Defiance" and the "Greenwich," which had fallen three or four miles astern. So disgusted was the captain of the "Falmouth" with the conduct of his fellow officers that he sent his lieutenant to the flagship, offering to stand by the Admiral throughout any engagement. Nothing much happened during the day, but the following morning, as soon as it was light, the Admiral and the faithful "Falmouth" started after the French; by ten o'clock they were abreast of them. Broadsides were exchanged, and though no great damage was done, the English managed to capture a galley named the "Ann," which the French had taken some time earlier off Lisbon. At this point Benbow ordered the "Ruby," now almost totally disabled by the punishment she had taken, back to Port Royal, thus scoring first blood for the French. The following day (the third of the month), when the "Bredah" closed in on a Frenchman, a chain shot struck Benbow in the leg. Although badly wounded, he managed to remain at his post, directing the fight until it was finished. The action now became hotter, and soon the

"Bredah" had disabled her opponent, the "Heureux," flagship of Governor du Casse. With the help of the "Falmouth" she had shot away the enemy's main- and fore-topsail yards, wrecked her mizzenmast, and knocked several holes in her sides. At this point the gallant Kirkby brought his ship into action, closely followed by his companions, fired a dozen shots at the "Heureux", and then turned tail and ran "from the poor, disabled ship, the rest following his example, though they had but eight men killed on board them all." Seeing this maneuver, three French men-of-war closed in to save their flagship. Sailing between her and the "Bredah," they took her in tow at the same time pouring their broadsides into the Englishman. In no way daunted, Benbow sent orders to his captains to engage the enemy.

It was at this point that Kirkby took the stand that finally broke the long-suffering Admiral's patience. Boarding the flagship, he protested vigorously against the proposed attack. Surprised at such faintheartedness, Benbow decided to get the opinions of all his captains in writing and signaled them to come on board. In some way or other Kirkby managed to persuade them all, including the captain of the "Falmouth," to sign a statement giving reasons why they thought it inadvisable to continue the fight. They asserted that there was a lack of men and of ammunition; they said that their spars and rigging had been sadly damaged by the six days' fight, so that now the French were superior to them. To all of this the Admiral acidly replied that with the exception of the "Bredah," the "Ruby," and the "Falmouth" the ships represented by these men had not tasted enough action to harm them; but he saw the uselessness of trying to win a battle with this collection of poltroons for his aides (the captain of the "Falmouth" of course excepted), and reluctantly gave the order to return to Port Royal. Even Du Casse saw the true character of the captains, for he presently wrote Benbow: "I had little hopes, on Monday last, but to have supped in your cabin; but it pleased God to order it otherwise. I am thankful for it. As for those cowardly captains who deserted you, hang them up; for, by God, they deserve it."

On his return to Port Royal, Admiral Benbow promptly brought his captains to trial. A court martial was held on board the "Bredah" under the presidency of Admiral Whetstone. Benbow appeared, of course, as chief witness. Much testimony was taken, and the accused was given every opportunity to defend themselves. The signing of the paper in which the captains advised against going into battle was not in itself considered worthy of drastic punishment, since all had signed it, but the conduct of the captains during the six days of battle was thoroughly examined. As a result, the court imposed a death penalty on Richard Kirkby and Cooper Wade, captain of the "Greenwich," while John Constable was sentenced to dismissal. All were sent back to England, where the Admiralty upheld the decision of the court martial, and the unfortunate Kirkby and Wade were executed the following year. Admiral Benbow's wound did not heal, and he died the following November.[21]

[21]Accounts of this battle and the details of the famous court martial are to be found in C.S.P., *America & West Indies, 1702*, Nos. 936, 1063, and in *1702-3*, No. 123. There are also good secondary accounts in Lediard, *Naval History*, pp. 741-44; Clowes, *The Royal Navy*, pp. 368-73; La Roncière, *Histoire de la marine française*, VI, 474-78; Du Casse, *L'Amiral du Casse*, pp. 250-66. George Bernard Shaw, in his comedy *Getting Married*, has one of his characters say that Kirkby and Wade were the first martyrs to British naval snobbery, as they refused to take orders from Admiral Benbow, a promoted cabin boy. Benbow was a rough sort of a man, who ordered his subordinates about in an unpleasant manner. This may explain, but does not justify, their conduct.

❧ X ❧

SIEGE OF GUADELOUPE

WHEN ST CHRISTOPHER had fallen, the officials at Guadeloupe realized that their turn would come next. This
feeling was also shared by the Martinicans, though they
were not so apprehensive, since their fortifications were far stronger
and their militia far greater in numbers. Even before the official
declaration of war, Charles Auger, governor of the former island,
had been active in building up the defenses of Basseterre, hoping
to prevent a repetition of the debacle of ten years earlier. To help
solve the problem of obtaining the necessary labor for this purpose,
he sent for Father Labat, missionary, historian, and amateur
engineer of considerable ability. The father soon found the solution. It had been the custom, he learned, to construct public works
by means of *corveés* to which all, save the clergy, were obliged to
contribute. These *corveés* were under the direction of the captains
of militia, with the result that much favoritism crept in. The
captains granted exemptions to their relatives and friends, while
those who were expected to contribute the labor of their slaves
were frequently remiss in their duties, doubtless with the connivance of the authorities. With war in the offing, such irregu-
larities were fraught with danger to the public welfare, and Father
Labat devised a system that would correct the situation. He
allotted specific jobs to the various militia companies, according
to the number of slaves in the district of a particular company,
and held that company responsible for the work. In this way the
business was pushed through. More than twelve thousand yards
of trenches were thrown up around Basseterre, the redoubts at the
Dos d'Ane, a hill back of the town, and at Trois Rivières, a settlement on the shore on the opposite side of the southern tip of the

island, were put in condition. The walls of Fort St. Charles were strengthened and repaired; a drawbridge was constructed; an open ditch was dug; and a breastwork was thrown up, cutting the fort in two, so that the garrison could retreat within a second line of defense and hold out should the enemy take the outer wall. New batteries were also erected in various places.

Governor Auger planned to erect fortified towers along the shore, joined by trenches, for he felt that a dozen men in such a tower were worth a couple of hundred behind a simple breastwork and that one hundred behind a palisade with a tower on each end could offer enough resistance to check a landing in a particular sector, for with cannon mounted on these towers the gunners could do more damage to the ships than the ships could do to them. Due to lack of time, only one was built, and that was the one at the mouth of the Rivière des Pères. This the Governor wished to have placed on the east bank of the river; but Labat insisted on the west side, on the land belonging to the Dominican Fathers, where the tower would serve to protect their property in case of invasion. It was about forty-five feet in diameter at its foundation, narrowing down to thirty-six feet at the top. The wall was nine feet thick to a height of twelve feet, where it shrank to six. Since there was not enough time for him to finish this redoubt, as he wished, Father Labat filled it with rubble, thus forming a sort of platform on which he mounted a gun. The result was rather unsatisfactory from the military point of view, but it was the best that could be done in a hurry. It was known as the Tour du Père Labat.

Governor Auger had a special census made of all the men in Guadeloupe capable of bearing arms, with special reference to the possibility of using colored troops. It showed that 1,418 men were under arms, including those in the Grande Terre section of the island and those in the Saints. They were divided into companies averaging fifty to sixty men each. The second-in-command to the Governor was the Lieutenant of the King, Hemon Coinard de la Malmaison. An inventory was taken of all available arms and munitions. The colonists were ordered to plant manioc, peas, and other vegetables and to deposit quantities of manioc flour in Fort St. Charles to serve as a reserve in case of necessity. The Governor also established patrols to watch the coast and ordered the colonists living on the shore in the more remote sections to withdraw inland with their families and slaves. Each *quartier* was given mortars with which they could sound an alarm in case of an unexpected invasion. Places were designated for the assembly of troops, and each captain was given instructions as to what he should do under various conditions. The preparations were as complete as ingenuity could make them; nothing was forgotten.[1]

At this time French affairs in Europe, particularly those relating to the West Indies, had taken a turn for the worse. As we have said, Château-Renault's powerful fleet, with its convoy of Spanish galleons, had anchored in Vigo Bay on its return from Havana. In the month of October, 1702, these ships were attacked by the combined English and Dutch fleets, which annihilated the entire armada. Thus, since the squadrons of Benbow and Whetstone were in Jamaica and the French navy was temporarily out of business, a golden opportunity had come for an attack on the French islands. This was just what Codrington desired, and his wishes were echoed in England. It would give him the opportunity to redeem the defeats of his father and the others who had vainly attempted to capture Martinique and Guadeloupe. Moreover, there was another reason for attacking the French. Martinique was impoverished in the way of foodstuffs, a condition due partly to the requisitions levied by Château-Renault and partly to a recent hurricane; thus, when refugees came there from St. Christopher, the shortage compelled many to resort to buccaneering and get their food as best they could wherever they could find it. "The enemy has twenty privateers out," wrote Codrington. "They infest our very harbors every night, take all our vessels, and I can't send a letter from one island to another with orders." A successful attack on Martinique would therefore eliminate this menace.

The home government was not loath to coöperate with Codrington in such a venture. A fleet of six warships, accompanied by ten transports carrying four thousand men, was detached from the main fleet and sent to the West Indies under Commodore Hovenden Walker with orders to touch first at Barbados and then to proceed to the Leeward Islands to join forces with Codrington. At the same

[1]Labat, *Nouveau voyage aux isles de l'Amérique*, II, 323, 345–46.

time the Admiralty was recommending to the Queen the immediate dispatch of a regiment to strengthen Codrington's forces and make possible an energetic attack on the French Islands in order to destroy the colonies and bring the inhabitants to England as prisoners. Fort Royal, it was fondly hoped, would at last fall; when the two islands had been taken, the expedition could proceed to Jamaica, join Benbow, and proceed to capture Placentia Bay in Newfoundland.[2]

Walker arrived at Barbados in January, 1703. Here he remained for six weeks. During this time he lost nearly one quarter of his complement of men through death, disease, and the kind hospitality of the inhabitants, who thought that the best way to make these strangers happy was to murder them with drink. It was early March when he arrived at Antigua. Codrington was greatly disappointed by the delay. Had the fleet come directly to him, he believed he could have captured Martinique, for that island had had a large number of men out privateering a few weeks earlier, but they had now returned to strengthen the defense by their presence. Moreover, Walker would not have lost the thousand or so men now left in Barbados had he come at once to Antigua. As a result of all this, Codrington decided to forego the capture of Martinique and to apply himself to Gaudeloupe instead.[3]

For some time the Governor had been busy recruiting a regiment among his colonists, and to his embarrassment he found a certain "backwardness both in the gentlemen and common people" which retarded the work of enlistment. Yet by the time Walker arrived the Governor had recruited a regiment of twelve companies and two independent companies ro replace the thousand men lost by the Commodore since his departure from England. The fleet assembled off Antigua was large in numbers, though not particularly formidable in fighting strength, since it was composed largely of merchantmen and small vessels picked up to be used as transports. It numbered ten men-of-war,[4] eighteen armed merchantmen, and seventeen other craft collected at random. The fleet carried some four thousand troops. Commodore Walker commanded the squad-

[2]*C.S.P., America & West Indies, 1702-3*, No. 192.   [3]*Ibid.*, No. 362.
[4]"Burford," "Yarmouth," "Cumberland," "Anglesey," "Maidstone," "Chichester," "Boyne," "Sundeland," "Edgar," and "James and Sarah," and "Boyne."

ron from the quarterdeck of the "Boyne"; Governor Codrington was in supreme command.

On the sixteenth of March at five o'clock in the afternoon Walker weighed anchor. He arrived in due time at Mariegalante, where he paused to assemble his ships and receive from Codrington the final orders for the attack. On the nineteenth, at daybreak, he set sail with the entire fleet, save two or three stragglers, and steered westward toward Guadelopue. Vieux Fort was the first to sight them and give the alarm by firing the mortars; the alarm was relayed throughout the island by the artillery stationed in each *quartier*, so that every man rushed to his post. Pausing only for a brief time at the Saints (where a few men tried to land, only to be repulsed by the settlers), the squadron rounded the point and held its course northward to Basseterre. Here the ships veered off, after exchanging a few shots with the shore batteries, for they had no pilots familiar with the coast, and to Walker and his staff it seemed unwise to attempt a landing until the entire land force was together for that purpose. A vessel was accordingly sent off to find the "Anglesey" and the "Maidstone" and bring them to the rendezvous. At this point Father Labat, acting under Governor Auger's orders, took an active hand in the proceedings by rushing on ahead to see that every redoubt and battery was properly manned, ready for the enemy. He suggested that the gunners should fire first with small charges of powder in order to encourage the enemy to come in closer, then give them a full dose. Toward noon the fleet separated into two divisions, the warships heaving to off the Rivière du Baillif, where stood Fort Madeleine, now in a state of disrepair, while the others stood out as if they were to make a landing some two leagues northward.

Governor Auger led his troops along the shore, keeping abreast of the fleet, while he left the Lieutenant of the King at the Rivière des Pères, ready to move to any spot where the English might land. At two in the afternoon the warships closed in, and from the tower that bore his name Father Labat opened fire. His ruse had the desired effect, for the English, seeing that the shot fell short, concluded that the redoubt mounted only small cannon and did not hesitate to approach nearer. Then the French gave them a full charge. Little damage, however, appears to have been done, for the English did not even take the trouble to answer; instead they sent a bark to range along the shore for the purpose of discovering just how the French had arranged their defenses. Fortunately Auger managed to deceive them, for as he proceeded he left a small detachment at various places, thus giving the impression that this entire section of the coast was fully guarded. Having completed its survey, the squadron rejoined the other division and hauled out of range for the night.

Next day the fleet gathered about the Ile à Goyave, their boats filled with men. Auger was puzzled, for such a maneuver might mean a landing at Anse à la Barque, just south of the little island, an excellent harbor, well suited for this purpose. He therefore placed troops on the heights overlooking the harbor, and this it seems proved enough to discourage any attempt at landing, for the enemy, seeing the locality so well protected, soon sailed off. The danger over for the present, Auger returned to Basseterre with La Malmaison, leaving Father Labat with the major, Le Roi de la Poterie, and a sufficient number of men to look after this part of the island.

The sun had not yet risen on the twenty-first when the boats patrolling the shore brought the news that the fleet had again appeared at Goyave. The troops were awakened and quickly sent to the post they had occupied the day before at Anse à la Barque, while a messenger was dispatched to Governor Auger to ask for orders. Auger sent word that they were to guard the Anse and to be particularly careful not to allow any men to be captured, since they might be used as guides by the enemy; above all they were not to venture north of Goyave, for then the English might land at the Anse behind them and cut them off. Meanwhile the inhabitants of this *quartier* were to be sent into the mountains. The fleet now closed in; but seeing that all his feints and ruses did not draw the French out of position Walker decided at three in the afternoon to make a landing. Accordingly he brought his ships nearer the land, just inside the Ile à Goyave, which forms a sort of shelter from the sea, and here he disembarked four or five hundred men. They met with no resistance, for the French could not assemble a sufficient force at this point to oppose them successfully. Emboldened, a body of fifty men scaled a height on which the village of Goyaves was located, and here they found the defenders ready to receive them. The French commander had stationed his men in a well-screened spot at a bend in the path, and they opened fire when the English appeared; but the invaders could not be stopped, and presently they gained the summit, where they took refuge in a stone building hard by the village church. Toward evening the French succeeded in driving them out and down to the shore, where they re-embarked, satisfied that nothing more could be accomplished in this locality. Before leaving they succeeded in destroying the church and the village surrounding it.

This raid showed the futility of any further activities in this region, for the main French army refused to be drawn into a major action so far from Basseterre. Governor Auger, who arrived shortly after the skirmish, was pleased with the result, though he grumbled at the officer who had led the attack, for he had given strict orders to avoid all contact with the enemy in this region. The only person dissatisfied with the turn of events was the local rector, who voiced loud complaints to the Governor over the destruction of his church and house. He also abused Father Labat, whom he accused of having willfully neglected the parish of Goyaves while he busied himself with building up defenses everywhere else. But Labat caught him up by asking him why he had not remained to defend his property instead of running away three days before. With this parting shot the Governor and his clerical aide retired to Fort Madeleine for the night, leaving the troops in charge of La Poterie.

At daybreak the French at Fort Madeleine saw the fleet in the offing. Realizing the impracticability of making any effective landing in the vicinity of Goyave, Codrington had decided to try some place farther south, and for this purpose he selected the section of the coast at the Rivière du Baillif. Auger at once sent La Poterie orders to spread his troops along the shore line from the Rivière des Vieux Habitans to Anse Val de Lorge. The position at Anse à la Barque was abandoned. At the same time the English held a council on board the "Boyne" to draw up a plan for landing. They decided to begin operations that night, or very early the following morning, in order to be able to go into action at daybreak. Meanwhile a frigate got caught in the current when the wind dropped and was forced to anchor not far from Val de Lorge, where she was subjected to a murderous fire from the shore that killed thirty-seven of her crew. To rescue her, several ships closed in, sweeping the shore with their guns. They were successful, for the frigate, after cutting her cables, managed to get away. Eight boat-loads of soldiers now approached the Anse des Vieux Habitans in a preliminary attempt to land, only to be driven off by a brisk fire from La Poterie's men.

During the night there was brought before Governor Auger a slave who said he had been captured by the English off the coast of Brazil from a French ship and assigned to duty on the "Boyne" as a servant. Here he had overheard the plans for the coming at-tack discussed by the council of war; anxious to warn his former masters, the French, for whom he still had great affection, he had slipped overboard unobserved and had swum ashore. According to his story the English would land the following morning at three places: Anse du Gros François, just north of Fort Madeleine, Val de Lorge, and Anse des Vieux Habitans. For credentials the man showed various objects he had carried ashore from the Com-modore's ship.

This story was carefully weighed by Governor Auger and his aides, for it was difficult to believe the enemy would choose these places when there were other good sites much nearer Basseterre. Perhaps this was just a feint to draw off the defenders while the real landing was made at Rivière des Pères. At any rate the Governor thought so, for he changed his arrangements and ordered the three companies at Val de Lorge and points beyond, numbering 185 men, to place themselves under Father Labat along the southern bank of the Rivière du Plessis, which flows into the Gros François. It was the Governor's plan to make a stand along the banks of these rivers against the invaders, who, he believed, would land above them and march southward to Basseterre as the elder Codrington had done twelve years before. The total number of men already at this position was 263, divided into five companies. Auger him-self remained at Fort Madeleine with 317 men, while a company was stationed at Le Baillif, and 600 men were placed along the shore in a line reaching from that point to Basseterre.

These excellent plans for defense did not go through without a hitch. The troops expected from Val de Lorge failed to materialize, and Labat was constrained to send a messenger to advise the Governor of their nonappearance. The trouble, as he soon found out, was due to the fact that Auger's instructions had failed to reach the commanders of the three companies, who refused to stir without written orders. But as the Governor realized full well the importance of the Du Plessis and Gros François position in his scheme of defense, he immediately rushed two of his own companies to Labat, ordering him to send them back when the three from Val de Lorge arrived to take their places.

On board the flagship the Commodore was giving his final instructions. The "Sunderland" and the "Chichester" were to stand in and bombard the batteries at Le Baillif, while the colonial troops were to be sent ashore in boats, which were ordered to return immediately and report at the "Yarmouth", where all the royal troops told off to take part in the attack were assembled. It was at first proposed to send ashore twelve hundred men, but there was delay in getting them to the rendezvous on board the "Yarmouth," and only five hundred took part in the landing. The first detachment landed at Vieux Habitans, seemingly without much opposition, for though the French opened fire on them, not a shot hit one of the boats. Once ashore, they set fire to some houses to notify the fleet of their success. Another detachment was landed at Val de Lorge, while a third, the royal troops, descended in thirty-two boats on the Gros François, where Father Labat was to have erected his line of defense. Here, despite the failure of the three companies to join him, he managed to do a very creditable job. With a gun mounted on one side of the river's mouth, a small detachment of men on the other, and a group of twenty-five stationed on a promontory near by, he was able to drive back the invaders two or three times. From his quarterdeck Walker watched this set-back with growing anxiety, until, at last convinced that something must be done, he sent one of his captains to take command. This officer at once put life into the attack. He drove his men ashore, crushed Labat's opposition, and sent the boats back for fresh troops. As many as fifteen or sixteen hundred men were landed on the spot.

At this critical moment Labat received word that the three

companies he was awaiting had arrived. Getting away to a late
start after Auger had sent a second summons, they had come
southward along the shore from Val de Lorge just when the English detachment was landing. A brief skirmish with the invaders
had held them up momentarily, then, turning inland, they had
gone to the posts on the Rivière du Plessis which they were supposed to occupy according to the original plan of defense. On
hearing of their arrival Labat vaulted onto a horse and rushed forward to meet them. He found them considerably exhausted by
their long march, yet ready to follow him back to the shore where
the enemy had landed and the actual work of defending the island
would take place. Labat started ahead for the purpose of sending
back to the Governor the two companies loaned to him. He found
his men ensconced on the southern bank of the Gros-François, holding at bay four or five hundred invaders lined up on the other side.
At the Anse and on the little promontory the French, he was told,
were holding their own, and he proceeded with the work of replacing the Governor's troops with the new arrivals. At this
moment word was brought him that the position at Gros-François
had been forced. He hurried forward to rally his men, but the
enemy had broken through, and soon the French were in full
retreat all along the line, overwhelmed by superior numbers.

The retreat toward Basseterre was orderly, the French halting
from time to time to check the invaders. Labat hurried on to the
village of Le Baillif, where he found the Governor rallying the
soldiers as fast as they drifted in. He blamed the entire debacle
upon the failure of his messenger to notify the three companies at
Val de Lorge the preceding night, a failure which delayed them
so that they were late in taking up their positions on the river bank,
thus compelling him to weaken his center in order to strengthen
his left, which rested on the shore where the enemy were landing.
Though victorious, the victory was a costly one for the English.
Labat estimates that after landing 350 men were killed and an
equal number wounded, doubtless a gross exaggeration, to which
he adds 200 for the casualties suffered in the boats before the men
set foot on shore. He does not mention French losses at this time.

The fleet now headed southward along the coast. At Le Baillif
the "Chichester" drew in close enough to exchange volleys with

the battery; then her crew took possession of it, only to find the guns carefully spiked. Farther south, Labat with a handful of men entered the redoubt bearing his name and found it deserted. Off the coast was a seventy-gun ship. It was near enough for the sailors on it to exchange words with the French on shore. As Labat's men loaded and fired, they bandied words with the crew who were answering the redoubt with broadsides. After a number of exchanges Labat was advised by Auger to abandon the post, since the neighboring battery of St. Dominic was now in the hands of the English, who would presently open fire on the Tour du Père Labat. Unable to spike his gun, for the spikes had already been carried off by some helpful busybody, Father Labat loaded the cannon with a triple charge of powder and ball to insure its exploding should any one touch it off and then rejoined Governor Auger at Fort Madeleine.

As the day wore on, the French still retreated, and by evening they had crossed the Rivière des Pères and were in the village of St. François. Here Auger called a halt and ordered the trenches on the southern side of the river to be manned. The English were not slow in coming up. They quickly seized the sugar refinery belonging to the Dominicans and, crouching behind it, well protected from the fire of the French, awaited further developments. At this moment Labat received an urgent message from Auger to meet him at once in Basseterre. He hastened thither, making his way carefully along the shore under cover of the trenches, and found the Governor awaiting him in the public square. Auger had a new plan. The troops quartered on the shore and along the Rivière St. Louis (tributary of the Rivière des Pères) were to be called in and placed in trenches in the Bisdary[5] and along the Rivière des Gallions, just south of the fort, because the English, having successfully landed, were now more than a match for the French, thanks to their better discipline and superior numbers. Father Labat demurred; more than that, he opposed the plan vigorously, pointing out that the inhabitants expected to defend the places assigned to them, not to surrender them without a blow. But Auger was firm. He explained that what really troubled him

[5]Just south of the Rivière des Gallions was the Rivière de Sense beyond which lay the section known as the Bisdary.

was the lack of competent leaders. He could not spare La Malmaison, for he needed him at the fort; while his other leader
(he said he had but two)—Lemercier de Maisoncelle, captain of
the first company of the Marine, could not be everywhere. No!
It was better to keep together; concentrate on the fort and hold it
until help came from Martinique. After that it would be a simple
matter to drive out the English, whose numbers in the meantime
would have been lessened by skirmishes and disease. He felt confident of this, for he had learned from prisoners that the English
had only five regiments from England and that they had already
been greatly weakened by yellow fever until they numbered
only 1,500 men. The entire British force, sailors, buccaneers, and
all, numbered in the neighborhood of four thousand. The prisoners
also told of considerable trouble between Codrington and Walker.
Two Irish deserters volunteered at this time the information that
if the French would furnish the transportation back to Europe
one-third of the English forces would take advantage of the offer.

His decision made, Auger with the help of La Malmaison proceeded to carry out the plan, assigning to everyone his post along
the seashore and on the banks of the Rivière des Gallions. Supplies
and ammunition stored outside the fort were brought within its
walls. At this point Father Labat took a hand in the proceedings.
He insisted on two things: first, that the guns of the battery known
as the Carmes should be transported into the fort or, if this was not
possible, should be set up between the fort and the shore, where in
twenty-four hours a well-protected battery could be constructed.
If this were done, the guns would not fall into the enemy's hands,
a calamity to be avoided at all costs, since the spiking of guns was
never more than a temporary measure; the touch holes could be
bored out and the guns turned upon their original owners. In
addition to this, the new battery would cover the town and discourage vessels from approaching. In the second place, Labat insisted that the town should be fired after it had been abandoned.
The enemy always set fire to a town when about to be driven out,
so why not deprive them of whatever use they could make of it
while they were conducting the siege of the fort? La Malmaison
seconded the plan for removing the guns, but he objected to the
burning of Basseterre, for he felt sure that when help came from

Martinique the English would be driven out so fast they would not have the time to set fire to anything. Governor Auger agreed with his subordinate and also vetoed the first suggestion, fearing that if the battery were erected so near the fort the enemy might seize it and thus gain command of the place. He wished to have the guns spiked where they stood. Labat, however, was able to secure permission to burn the carriages and platforms supporting the guns a far more serious damage than merely driving spikes down the touch holes.

At sunset orders were sent La Poterie to retreat to Basseterre, and this he did in an orderly manner. His men had been moved from Val de Lorge to the Rivière du Plessis and thence to the outskirts of Basseterre during the course of the day. The English saw the maneuver and decided to seize the opportunity to attack. When La Poterie approached the Rivière des Pères, the invaders started to cross it at a spot near a local sugar refinery where Auger had posted a company under the command of Le Fèvre le Manchot. The action was spirited; La Poterie's men joined in the battle until the English were obliged to retire and the French companies were able to march into Basseterre unmolested.

Arrangements were now made to withstand a siege. Five companies were sent into the fort, which together with the troops already there made a garrison of 370 men. Three companies were stationed at the Passage de Madame across the Rivière des Gallions, just beyond the fort; the company from Trois Rivières was sent back to that settlement to guard the neighboring harbors and to keep open the road to Capesterre; the men from the Saints were posted at Vieux Fort, Anse de la Croix, and other places in the vicinity; the oldest company held the height at the mouth of the Gallions; and the rest of the troops were placed in the Bisdary, spreading out as far as the hill of that name. The cavalry of Basseterre took over a battery at the Gallions where the Governor had taken his stand, and the cavalry of Capesterre and Grande-Terre, aided and abetted by a company of infantry, guarded the lesser passages of this river. By midnight the orders had been issued and the troops were on their way to take up their positions. It was the end of a long, arduous day, which began at daybreak with the landing of the English army and ended with the enemy at the gates of Basseterre. It was a complete victory for the English. Outnumbered and outfought, the French had been driven back step by step upon their capital; Governor Codrington had succeeded in doing between sunrise and sunset what his father had taken several days to accomplish.

The next day, the twenty-fourth, was a Saturday. Governor Codrington sent a letter to Commodore Walker requesting guns and four days' provisions, for he intended to attack the Dos d'Ane with 1,500 men. If he captured this strategic point, its fall would probably end the campaign. He also asked for the "Angelsey" and the "Chichester" to support him. At ten o'clock in the morning he got under way. When he was near the town he was spotted by a guard, who quickly gave the alarm. The ramparts were manned, two outlying companies were at once brought inside the fort, and the colored troops were placed under the command of Le Fèvre and told to take their stand on the Jesuit estate near by. The English approached in two columns—one along the coast, supported by the ships, the other by a path along the cliff some five hundred paces inland. They met with no resistance, for it was Auger's policy to save his men, and they soon found themselves in St. François, though they did not cross the Rivière aux Herbes separating this town from Basseterre. At this juncture La Fèvre came down from a height of land, from which he had been observing the British advance in order to destroy everything that might be of use to the invaders. He set fire to the sugar cane as far as the Ravine Billau; retracing his steps, he fired all plantations within six hundred paces of the town. A fresh breeze sprang up to fan the flames and spread the fire. Alarmed at the conflagration and thinking it was the prelude to a general attack, the English rushed to arms, took battle positions, and remained on the alert all night, ready for any emergency.

On Sunday, Codrington moved into Basseterre. On Monday he began work on a battery he proposed to erect on the estate belonging to the Jesuit Fathers, selecting for this purpose a spot situated about fourteen hundred feet from the main French battery, which was placed on a sort of mound inside the fort called the cavalier. This proved to be a difficult task, for the French quickly got wind of Codrington's position through a deserter and kept up a galling fire on the men as they hurried forward the work. From Governor Houël's old castle Father Labat could see the enemy's maneuvers and was therefore able to direct the fire from the fort on the soldiers as they strove to place the cannon in position. In spite of all this, the English managed to mount eleven pieces, with which they opened up on the fort on the second of April. The defenders replied with spirit, dismounting two of the enemy's guns during the course of the day and peppering them with musketry fire. The following day the English scored, shattering a French cannon. On the whole, says Labat, the English marksmanship was poor and the battery on the cavalier was never in danger.

Meanwhile Auger received word from Martinique that the new governor-general, M. de Machault, had just arrived at Fort Royal, bringing for Jean Gabaret, then governor of Martinique, a commission naming him lieutenant for all the islands, a position held by the late Comminge de Guitaud and one which placed the new incumbent second only to Machault himself. No sooner had the new governor-general set foot on shore than he began his preparations for sending a relief expedition to Guadeloupe, for he did not intend to lose this, the largest of the French Caribbees, without a struggle. Charles Auger was pleased to receive help, but disgruntled when he heard that Gabaret was to lead the expedition, for Gabaret, though he had had less experience as a governor than Auger, now outranked him, thanks to his recent appointment.[6]

On the third of April came the joyful news of the arrival of the reinforcements at Port Ste. Marie in the Capesterre section. The expedition consisted of two companies of the Marine, four of militia, six of buccaneers, 820 men in all; it was commanded by Governor Gabaret in person. He had as his principal aides MM. de Boisfermé, governor of Mariegalante, Caqueray de Valmenière, and du Parquet,[7] all lieutenants of the King. Twelve vessels escorted by three warships transported the army. Thanks to the foresight of Machault, seconded by the executive ability of the

[6]Both the *Grande encyclopedie* and *Larousse* state that Jean Gabaret died in 1697. Jean and his brother Louis (the latter was killed at Tobago in 1677) both left sons, but they seem to have been ship captains. Jean, we believe, was the man appointed as second-in-command; the date of his death as given must be an error.

[7]Louis-Gaston Caqueray de Valmenière, Jean-Clair Dyel du Parquet.

Intendant Robert, the entire expedition had been got together in six days. Leaving 120 men at Ste. Marie to guard the place and protect the ships should they be attacked from the sea, Gabaret set forth for Fort St. Charles with the main body of his men. He believed it good policy to enter the fort in the grand manner to apprise the besiegers of the arrival of a large body of reinforcements; so with banners flying and trumpets blaring he marched in, taking care to parade his men in full view of the British army.

In the English camp Governor Codrington had been making large scale preparations for storming the Dos d'Ane. He had ordered men, munitions, and even the ships' guns to be brought ashore from the fleet until Commodore Walker felt bound to send him a warning that the vessels were now manned by mere skeleton crews and had scarcely enough powder and shot to protect themselves if attacked. Codrington, in his eagerness to swell the land forces, even went so far as to refuse to return to the "Yarmouth" the sailors he had taken from her even when he ordered her on patrol duty to watch for the fleet which was coming from Martinique. Had this vessel been able to spot the Gabaret expedition, Walker might have led his squadron out in time to intercept it. It was this failure to keep a proper lookout that enabled Gabaret to land his entire force unharmed and to enter the fort in triumph. His arrival was a complete surprise to the English officers.

The day after his arrival Gabaret held a review of the entire garrison in order to present himself as the new commander-in-chief. Realizing the necessity of making arrangements for the accommodation of the reinforcements he had brought, he withdrew half the militia of Gaudeloupe from the fort and replaced them with two of his own companies of the Marine. The following day he led five hundred men out from the northeastern end of the fort to look for a suitable camp site. Arriving at a place about a league from Basseterre, known in modern times as "Camp Jacob," he halted; this, Auger pointed out, would be a good location for an encampment. The men were divided into three groups: one, the largest, was left here under Colonel François de Collart, who had come with Gabaret, and at the place called Camp Martinique; the second, composed of the Guadeloupe militia, was led to a spot nearer the river, called Camp des Gallions, where it was placed under Le

Fèvre le Manchot; the third, a Martinican company under Jean du Buc, occupied a clearing called "the advanced post." M. de Bois-fermé was the immediate commander-in-chief of these three groups, while Gabaret stationed himself on a height from which he could overlook the entire panorama.

The first step in the campaign as planned by Gabaret was to destroy the battery on the Jesuit estate. This was to be done by the encamped troops aided by the garrison, which would make a sally from the fort and join them at the crucial moment; but if the English should advance to the attack, then the French would stand and receive them on their own terrain, which was well suited for the construction of ambuscades and pitfalls. On the sixth of April the battle began. Unfortunately Le Fèvre was a bit hasty. At daybreak he ventured forth without orders at the head of fifty men to ferret out the enemy. He was successful, for he soon came across a detachment of four hundred, who on seeing the weakness of his command, started off in pursuit. Le Fèvre retreated to a position flanked by the river on his left and a ravine on his right where he waited patiently for reinforcements. Boisfermé, the first to grasp the situation, came forward with three hundred men and was soon joined by Du Parquet and Valmenière with their troops. Overwhelmed by superior numbers, the English were driven back to the town, where they were joined by an additional force of seven hundred. The engagement now became general. The English advanced, the French retreated. On reaching the neighborhood of Camp Martinique the British ran into a series of ambuscade, placed there by Collart. Anxious to come to grips with the foes they pressed forward at this point. Met by Collart, they turned, only to find that Du Buc had closed in at the rear, thus trapping them between the two forces. Only the timely arrival of additional troops prevented a complete rout of the English army at this point; after retreating they managed to rally their forces and hold their own against the French. At this time both sides, by mutual agreement, called a halt. It was noon; the sun was high in the heaven; and after a running fight that had been going on since daybreak the men felt themselves entitled to a bite to eat and a midday siesta. During the lull the French gathered up their fallen comrades and found that despite the tremendous firing, marching, and countermarching the casualties so far had been but three killed and ten wounded. Among the former, they were shocked to learn, was their leader, Le Fèvre le Manchot, while Boisfermé was among the latter.

The time now seemed propitious for attacking the English battery, for the invaders had sent a large part of their forces into a battle fought some distance from the sea, thus leaving their right flank wide open. La Malmaison, who had remained at the fort during the morning action, saw that the time had come to lead a sortie and catch the enemy off guard, for the road was open and the French had some four hundred men within the fortifications and stationed along the shore who were eager for action. To obtain permission to make the attack, he sent Father Labat to Gabaret. The commander-in-chief, however, would have none of it. It was too late in the day, he said—though it was only noon—and moreover it would cost too many lives. The latter reason was indeed the true one, for the preservation of the lives of the colonists was to be the basis of his strategy and the one thing on which he insisted during the entire campaign, despite the vehement protests of his officers. Governor Auger, who was with him, protested against such a decision, pointing out that if the English were permitted to continue to use the battery as they had been doing for the past three days the fort would soon be no longer tenable. To all these arguments Gabaret turned a deaf ear. He peremptorily forbade further discussion by saying that he understood his business and needed no advice from his subordinates. Discouraged, Labat returned to the fort to notify La Malmaison of the failure of his mission, while Gabaret ordered the troops facing the enemy to fall back to the trenches near the Passage de Madame. This they did, followed gingerly by the English who feared such an uncalled-for retreat might lead them into a trap.

At the Passage de Madame the French crossed the Rivière des Gallions to take up a strong position in the trenches on the other side. The stream at this point ran between two high banks forming a sort of ravine. On the southern side trenches had been constructed at two levels, but even so the farther bank was high enough to enable the English, when they reached it, to fire down on the upper trench, so that the French in order to find shelter were obliged to crouch down behind the parapet. Still higher up Father Labat had begun a third trench that would have given the French command of the opposite bank, but lack of time had prevented him from completing it. The troops being in position, Labat returned to Auger and found he had assembled some thirty or forty horsemen, which he gave Labat to reinforce the men stationed at the Passage. Labat led them to the place where the third line of trenches was to have been built, and from this advantageous spot, protected as it was by a grove of trees, the little detachment was able to keep up a fire hot enough to drive the enemy to cover as fast as they appeared on the top of the opposite cliff. Encouraged by this the men in the lower trench rushed out from the protection of their parapet, forded the river, clambered up the opposite side, and attacked. In a trice the others joined them, and soon the British were in full retreat, leaving the French masters of the battlefield. A conservative estimate placed the enemy's loss at seventy five killed and the same number wounded, though Labat gives much higher figures; the French losses were only five killed and fifteen wounded. Thus in a way was Gabaret's policy vindicated.

The French had defeated the enemy on the field of battle, but it was a barren victory, for in doing so they had retreated to the other side of the river. They had not even attempted to destroy the battery, which was hammering away at the fort. What was Gabaret's idea? He evidently considered it impossible, or at any rate impracticable, to hold St. Charles for any length of time without great loss of life. His plan, then, was to abandon it and take refuge with his army in the surrounding territory, whither the English would be obliged to pursue them if they expected to hold the island and where the defenders would have an immense advantage, thanks to their thorough familiarity with the terrain. Thus the tables would be turned; the besieged would become the besiegers.

Gabaret's plan met with bitter opposition on the part of the Guadeloupians. Whatever were its merits, it certainly was not an aggressive policy. True, the fort had been damaged and the cavalier had been destroyed, which deprived the defenders of the means of bringing their artillery to play on the English battery; yet the main ramparts held, and it would have been possible for a spirited garrison to repel a general assault, at least so it seemed to everyone else. Nevertheless, Gabaret was inexorable; all the arguments advanced by Auger and La Malmaison had no effect on him; he was determined to blow up the donjon and evacuate the place. When the protestations of their leaders had no effect, the inhabitants took the matter into their own hands. They rushed to Governor Auger who tried to appease them by explaining Gabaret's purpose. They answered that the fort was in as good a condition as ever and that since the English had not attempted to carry it by assault they would not try to do so now. Evacuation of St. Charles, they said, would destroy the morale of the colonists; for if the enemy mastered this citadel, the colonists would be compelled to take refuge in the mountain fastnesses. When word had got around that the Marine companies had no desire to hold the fort, volunteers stepped forward and offered to defend the place to the last man. Unwilling to argue any further, Auger sent the bellicose inhabitants to Gabaret so that he could settle the matter. They repeated their offer. The commander-in-chief was impressed. After all, if they were so eager to fight for their fort why not let them? Yet to replace the Marine companies of Martinique with these men would, as La Poterie pointed out, reflect on the honor of His Majesty's troops; so to satisfy all concerned Gabaret finally ordered both colonists and regulars to defend the fort.

Although out-argued and forced for the time to capitulate, Gabaret, like all men convinced against their will, was still of the same opinion. For several days the garrison remained inactive under the desultory fire of the enemy, expecting an assault which never took place. On the twelfth of April he called a council of war of the officers, councillors, and heads of religious communities. Though not invited, Father Labat was persuaded to attend, for he had just made a survey of the fortifications which convinced him that the damage was not serious and could be easily repaired. Gabaret frowned when he saw the priest enter the room, for he realized he had an adversary who knew what he was talking about. Rising to speak, Labat carefully explained the situation to the gathering. With great detail he sketched the condition of the fort, the technical aspects involved, and the amount of labor necessary to repair the injuries sustained thus far. Then, turning to his superior, he warned him that La Malmaison and nearly all the officers of Gaudeloupe would enter a strong protest should orders be given to abandon the fort.

The time had now come for a showdown. Governor Auger at last felt bound to side with his superior and to cast his vote in favor of evacuation despite the noisy protests of his officers. Since Gabaret was in supreme command, his word was law, and nothing could be done legally to prevent him from abandoning the fort; a refusal to obey him would be equivalent to mutiny. In a last-minute attempt to change the inflexible commander's mind La Malmaison had a personal interview with him. It was time wasted. Returning then to his quarters, he sent Gabaret, as a final gesture, a petition of protest signed by all the officers of the fort. This done, he proceeded to make arrangements for carrying out the wishes of his superiors.

Orders were now issued for the evacuation. Mines were placed in the donjon and under what was left of the cavalier to be exploded after the garrison had left. While these preparations were being completed the "Yarmouth" and the "Sunderland" came in toward the mouth of the river and opened fire on the trenches lining the shore, while the battery on the Jesuit property, which had been silent for several days, joined in the fracas. The French took their places ready to repel the assault, staying well under cover, but the assault never came off. The failure of the garrison to return the fire had caused the invaders to fear some kind of trap, and the bombardment stopped as quickly as it had begun. That night the four Marine companies left the fort, and the following day, the fourteenth of April, the fuses of the mines were lighted and the garrison marched out two hours before daylight. Abandoning the stronghold to the foe, they took up a new position in the trenches on the farther side of the Rivière des Gallions.

A few hours later, after he had assured himself that the mines had exploded, Governor Codrington moved in with his men. He had captured the place in the nick of time, for his ship captains were becoming more and more concerned about the drain of men and supplies to which they were subjected. On entering the fort his first move was to send a detachment to occupy the trenches along the shore; but here his men were met with a stout resistance, and they were obliged to retreat, leaving the French in possession of these fortifications. Blocked in this direction, the Governor hastened to strengthen the walls of the fort facing the river in order to protect his garrison from the French fire.

Governor Auger, after leaving St. Charles, had stationed his men in some trenches on the Savanne de Milet, situated on a rise of ground about eight hundred paces from the sea. As the protection here was inadequate, he set his men to work to strengthen parapets, build gabions, and arrange gun emplacements for a battery which could fire on the fort. It was an excellent position, flanked by the Rivière des Gallions on the right and the Sense on the left. The work was proceeding apace, despite the musketry fire of English marksmen, when word arrived from Gabaret that it must be abandoned at once. For Auger this was the last straw. He could not even protest. The commander was evidently intent upon a full retreat for strategic reasons of his own, so there was nothing to do but to obey. Auger therefore gave orders to cease work and to dismantle the existing fortifications as well as another line of trenches he had started farther up the river. In abandoning these places Boisfermé, acting under Gabaret's orders, set fire to a cluster of buildings owned in part by the Order of Charity and in part by some private persons, reducing them all to ashes, not even sparing the hospital, which was destroyed with the furniture and medicine contained therein. In his haste to get the job done Boisfermé did not even stop to remove the ammunition and foodstuffs stored there. Then Auger led his men inland to the Passage de Madame, where they joined the other forces.

The southern part of the island, in the vicinity of Trois Rivières, was the source of considerable concern to Jean Gabaret, for through this district lay the road to Capesterre and Grande-Terre, sources of French supplies, and to Ste. Marie, the embarkation port for Martinique. Should the English capture Trois Rivières by sea, they would cut the life line of the French and be in a position to attack them in the rear. To forestall this unpleasant eventuality Gabaret sent La Malmaison with 120 men to defend the place. This done, he took measures to fortify the Camp des Gallions according to a plan roughly sketched by Father Labat. A spirit of disunity, unfortunately, held back the work. The Marine companies, in bad odor with the habitans—apparently they were drawn largely from the French jails—and the militia refused to burden themselves with the work of building trenches for their protection. Slaves were called in to do the work, but their owners showed little inclination to force them to labor, for a general discontent with Gabaret's policy had settled on all the inhabitants.

On the twenty-seventh of April an English deserter arrived with the startling news that the previous night a detachment of a thousand men had gone by sea to capture Trois Rivières. Alarmed at this, Gabaret at once dispatched his mounted troops and enough infantry to make up a total of 130 men to support La Malmaison. By a forced march they reached the place just as the English boats were rounding the southern point of the island. By good fortune, however, there was no immediate danger of an attack on a large scale. A fairly heavy sea was running, and the English commander, unable to land his men, gave orders to stand off until more moderate weather prevailed. Meanwhile some of the boats put into Vieux Fort, where they succeeded in getting two hundred men safely landed on the beach. Here they met with little opposition, for the bulk of the troops were stationed on the heights at Trois Rivières, while those guarding Vieux Fort quickly withdrew their meager forces inland where they would be out of harm's way, and allowed the invaders to prowl about the place, burning and looting to their heart's content. Being somewhat careless, these men fell into an ambuscade erected near a ravine by some of the more daring of the local troops and were driven back, leaving some twenty dead on the field before they recovered from their surprise.

On hearing that the route to Capesterre might be cut Gabaret became thoroughly alarmed. If this road fell into enemy hands, he would never be able to rejoin his fleet and return to Martinique. He gave orders with almost indecent haste for his troops to get their supplies and equipment ready for a dash to Ste. Marie, while he set out at once for Capesterre, taking with him his Marine companies, to the great relief of the Guadeloupians. He also ordered the militia and the buccaneers he had brought from Martinique to follow him; but these men, a far better sort than the wretched Marine troops, gave a spirited answer, saying they would not leave the island until the English had gone. The action at Vieux Fort

and the inclement weather now discouraged the invaders from making any further attempts at Trois Rivières, and after their departure
Gabaret plucked up enough courage to abandon his plan of returning to Martinique.

The tide of the campaign was now turning gradually in favor
of the French, though they had abandoned the fort without a
struggle. In the light of the final outcome Gabaret's strategy seems
to have been justified. He had irritated the Gaudeloupians no end
by his lack of aggressiveness, his readiness to fall back when he
might at least have held his ground, and his seeming unwillingness to come to grips with the enemy. Yet there was a real plan
behind all this: he wished, as we have pointed out, to spare the
lives of the colonists as much as possible, and for this purpose he
adopted a truly Fabian policy. He knew, thanks to the deserters
who came to his camp, just how much the English had in the way
of supplies and ammunition; hence, if he could keep his army
intact, these supplies would run out. So long as the French army
was in the field, Codrington could never pretend to have taken
Guadeloupe. Fighting on their own ground, the French could take
advantage of every cover and build ambuscades into which the
English would be bound to fall if they left the fort for the open
field.

If we glance at the situation in the English camp and on board
the fleet, we shall see that this policy was rapidly bearing fruit.
Codrington and Walker were already losing heart. Provisions,
especially bread, were running short, and what did remain was
beginning to spoil. Hope of a successful outcome of the expedition
was rapidly dwindling, for sickness was taking a heavy toll of
those who had not been killed in action. At a council of war held
on the fifth of May it was decided to make preparations for an early
departure, for it would take two weeks to reach one of the English
islands, refit the ships, rest the crews, and be in shape for a further
undertaking. To add to the general discouragement, Governor
Codrington had fallen ill and had returned to Nevis, leaving the
command in the hands of a subordinate. Orders were now given
to carry the guns back to the ships, together with shot and ammunition, while the sailors and soldiers to the number of 2,277
were gradually reëmbarked.

At last the time came for the English to leave. They had failed, and there was nothing for them to do but to retire. On the evening of the fifteenth they evacuated the fort and set fire to the town, determined to destroy the colony, or at least to cripple it as severely as possible, since they could not capture it. By the light of the flames the French saw their houses burning and rushed to arms in the vain hope of saving what had not yet been destroyed and of punishing they invaders. It was too late. When the reached the shore they saw the fleet disappearing in the distance. Thus, after a two months' campaign, did the English expedition retreat, having failed to accomplish its object. Commenting on the results, a British officer gained some satisfaction from the amount of damage inflicted on the enemy.

It [Guadeloupe, he wrote] never before suffered so much by any attempt from the English as at this time; all their guns being either carried off, sunk or burst, their fortifications utterly demolished, a great part of their plantations destroyed, and though the inhabitants had for some time found a refuge in inaccessible mountains and impenetrable woods, yet had we had four or five fourth-or fifth-rate frigates to have cruised about the island, to have prevented any intercourse between that and Martinique, together with only 1,000 English soldiers ashore, the inhabitants must in a few months been obliged to have surrendered themselves.

In truth the invaders had inflicted enormous damage. They had destroyed or badly damaged the towns of Bouillante, Vieux-Habitans, Baillif, St. François, Basseterre, and Vieux Fort, to say nothing of eight churches, five convents, and much farm property. Yet though they lost so much in worldly goods the French loss of life, thanks to the policy of M. Gabaret, was trifling. During the entire campaign there were but twenty-seven killed and fifty wounded. Three years later the French took their revenge. [8]

[8]A detailed account of the campaign is given by Labat (*Nouveau voyage aux isles de l'Amérique*, II, 387–442) who himself played an important part in it. He wrote the account several years after the events took place so that it is bound to contain inaccuracies. It is marred by the author's cordial dislike of Gabaret, who, though not an aggressive and inspiring commander, at any rate succeeded in driving out the invaders in spite of the strong opposition to his methods on the part of some of his own officers, The principal English account, Walker's Journal, is sketchy and deals chiefly with the maneuvers of the fleet. *C.S.P.*, *America & West Indies*, *1702–3*, No. 737. A brief though good account may be found in Guët, *Le Colonel François de Collart*, pp. 324–46.

⁓ XI ⁓

IBERVILLE'S EXPEDITION

D URING THE THREE YEARS following the campaign in Guadeloupe there was little activity of a warlike nature in the
West Indies, certainly no major expedition was undertaken by either the French or the English governments. Charles
Auger was relieved of his post and transferred to San Domingo,
where he replaced the famous Jean du Casse as governor of the
island. His place at Guadeloupe was taken by La Malmaison, who
as soon as he had established himself comfortably in office proceeded to expel the English from Mariegalante and reinstate its
governor, M. de Boisfermé. The cause of this lull in belligerency
was due to the tremendous activities of the navies and the armies
in Europe; the campaigns of Marlborough, the siege of Gibraltar,
and the necessity of keeping large fleets in home waters made it
impossible to give much attention to the West Indies or to spare
ships and men for either an attack on the enemy's colonies or the
defense of one's own. The only incident worthy of notice was the
appearance off Martinique of a privateer fleet bent, presumably,
on an attack on Fort Royal. It rounded Pointe d'Arlet one morning
in December, 1704, and stood in toward the fort, a formidable
armada of twenty-two warships, a like number of merchantmen,
seventeen barks, six galliots, and some odds and ends. A general
alarm was sounded, and the Governor prepared himself for the
worst. But the fleet made no attempt on Fort Royal; instead it
stood northward along the coast toward St. Pierre, a few of the
smaller vessels stopping on the way to do a little plundering. At
two in the afternoon it reached St. Pierre, then lazily kept on its
way and disappeared during the night.[1]

[1]Labat, *Nouveau voyage aux isles de l'Amérique*, II, 466.

At this time there came to France a famous Canadian soldier named Pierre le Moyne d'Iberville, scion of a distinguished colonial family, who had made a reputation for himself by fighting the English on land and sea along the shores of Hudson Bay and by leading expeditions to Louisiana. He was a seaman of great ability, and for his services he had been promoted to the rank of captain in the Royal Navy. During the winter of 1702–3 he had evolved a plan for the destruction of the English fleets off Newfoundland and Virginia, thus severing these colonies from the mother country. To win the King over to this project was not difficult, for the government was ready for any undertaking that would cripple the English fleet. Thus, in the spring of 1703 a small squadron consisting of five ships and two flutes was fitted out and placed at Iberville's disposal; but before he could weigh anchor the order was countermanded and the vessels were detailed to serve another purpose. Undaunted, Iberville drew up a second plan, to be carried out with two ships and a small frigate. This expedition, too, was canceled in January of the following year, this time owing to the commander's illness. A year now passed uneventfully enough, for the hardships suffered by the veteran seaman in his many campaigns were beginning to undermine his strength. Summoned to Paris by the Minister of Marine, who was now planning an expedition on a much larger scale than before, Iberville arrived there, only to fall so seriously ill that his wife and brother came at once from La Rochelle. Thanks to their care, he eventually recovered.

Meanwhile important events had taken place which caused the King to undergo a change of heart. His armies had met with reverses, and his ministers were therefore ready to lend an ear to Iberville's proposal to lead a modest fleet of three frigates and two ships to Havana, where he would establish headquarters for a series of raids on North America. Elaborating on this plan, the King issued orders to Iberville, dated August 29, 1705, instructing him to seize Barbados and Jamaica with the aid of buccaneers, to drive the English from Carolina, to threaten New York, and to help Acadia and Newfoundland. In order to carry out this ambitious program, a large fleet was organized—much larger than the one requested by Iberville—and divided into two squadrons: one, under Iberville himself, consisted of the "Juste" (the flagship), the

"Prince," the Aigle," and the "Sphere"; the other, under the Comte Louis-Henri de Chavagnac, was composed of the "Glorieux" (the flagship), the "Apollon," the "Brilliant," the "Fidèle," the "Ludlow," and the "Nymphe."[2] Iberville was, of course, the commander-in-chief. For a fighting force he was given six hundred soldiers, whose wages were to be paid by the King, and he also took with him a small band of his own Canadians. The cost of the expedition was not borne entirely by the government, since Iberville's ships (not Chavagnac's) were outfitted by a private firm. It was also understood that Iberville and his associates should furnish the provisions and allow the King one-fifth of all prizes taken, after deducting the expenses, while one-tenth was to go to the Admiral and the crew.[3] This European contingent was to form the nucleus of the expedition, which was to be expanded after reaching the West Indies by the addition of buccaneers and colonists, who were expected to assist the undertaking financially and to reimburse themselves, if all went well, with the booty captured. It was also hoped that a junction would be made with the fleet under Jean du Casse, then cruising the Caribbean.

To smooth the way for Iberville, Pontchartrain wrote to M. de Machault, informing him that for the success of his expedition the commander counted as much upon the buccaneers and the inhabitants who might care to enlist as on the soldiers the King had given him. Iberville was to proceed to Martinique to discuss the project with the Governor-General, who, meanwhile, was requested to put in readiness all vessels in the harbor of St. Pierre and to keep the freebooters in port under pretext of having received advance information of a proposed attack on the island by English forces. All this was to be done with the greatest secrecy. Machault, however, did not approve of such an undertaking, for he wished to keep his colonists at home ready to repel a possible attack; so he wrote the Minister expressing his sentiments. For this trouble he received a sharp rebuke (which, unfortunately, did not reach him until after Iberville's arrival) pointing out that the English

[2]Lists of these ships do not agree. See La Ronçière, *Historire de la marine française*, VI, 498–99; *C.S.P.*, *America & West Indies*, *1706–8*, No. 168; Ballet, *La Guadeloupe*, (I, Part iii), 355–56. Ballet's list gives several ships which doubtless were added to the fleet after it had reached Martinique.

[3]Guérin, *Histoire maritime de France*, IV, 161.

had previously attacked several French islands and that the time was now propitious for revenge, since there was no powerful English fleet cruising the Leeward Islands. Furthermore, His Majesty expected the colonists and the buccaneers to volunteer— particularly the buccaneers, who, having no agricultural duties to perform, should be ready for any sort of employment that promised plunder. [4]

When the preparations were finally completed, Iberville set sail from Rochefort, early in January, 1706; but scarcely had he cleared the harbor, when a violent storm drove him to seek shelter in nearby La Rochelle. The Comte de Chavagnac had been more fortunate. His squadron was at Brest, where better weather conditions prevailed. Getting under way in mid-December, he crossed the Atlantic and dropped anchor at Martinique toward the end of January. Machault, of course, had made no preparations to assist the expedition, nor does it appear that he had even apprised the inhabitants of the coming campaign; therefore Chavagnac was obliged to set about obtaining recruits himself. With the permission of Machault, given somewhat reluctantly, he wrote Jean du Buc, commander of the colonists, and François de Collart, now leader of the buccaneers, urging them to join him. Lured by promises of booty, these worthies gathered together in the short space of eight days some four hundred colonists and three hundred freebooters, and to them the Governor-General, roused at last from his indifference, added four comapnies of militia.

While Chavagnac was still at Martinique and even before he had reached the West Indies, news of the expedition had been spread abroad among the British possessions, despite the efforts of King Louis to keep the business a secret. The previous December, Governor Johnson, of Antigua, had warned his colleague in Jamaica that thirty French ships were expected in the Caribbean waters. The latter, though he labeled the report a "French gasconnade," informed the home government of his fears, hinting that an English fleet might well be sent over just in case something happened. [5] Later reports verified this rumor—though the number of ships was actually much smaller—and no sooner had Chav-

[4] Dessalles, *Histoire générale des Antilles*, II, 332, 336–37.
[5] *C.S.P., America & West Indies, 1706–8*, No. 24.

agnac reached Martinique than the news was flashed through the archipelago. In St. Christopher the English had been so confident of the inability of the French to dislodge them that they had neglected to maintain their fortifications or to provide for the garrisons in a suitable manner. The Council seem to have had some sense of their responsibility, but they were blocked by a few influential members of the assembly, whose unwillingness to provide suitable quarters for the officers and men led to a threat by the home government to withdraw the troops entirely. As it was, the available fighting force soon dwindled, according to Governor Johnson, to about 150 men capable of bearing arms.[6]

Chavagnac, now that he had his recruits on board, determined to launch an undertaking of his own before his commander-in-chief arrived. He had heard of some two hundred Frenchmen living at St. Christopher who had a supply of arms carefully concealed and of Negroes who had taken to the mountains, where they were carrying on a guerilla warfare against the English. To St. Christopher, then, he would go, capturing Nevis on the way, should it prove possible to do so. Late in the afternoon of the fourth of February he set sail. First he detached the "Nymphe" to look for a possible English squadron off Barbados, then he proceeded with the fleet to Guadeloupe. He anchored off Basseterre and spent several days collecting a force of three hundred militiamen under Major Poullain. On the thirteenth of February he left Guadeloupe with a formidable array, consisting of the five ships he had brought from France, two merchantmen, and twenty-four brigantines—the last named commanded and manned by buccaneers. He had 1,200 men to use in landing parties. Heading northward, he left Montserrat to port and soon came in sight of Antigua. His actions showed that he had considered the possibility of making a landing here, for he sent the smaller vessels to work their way in and take soundings. Then a strong northerly wind sprang up, preventing the fleet from approaching any closer; the boats were recalled and the entire armada set out for Nevis arriving off Charlestown in the evening, where they anchored about a league from Old Road Fort. When on the following day Chavagnac ordered his men into

[6]*C.S.P., America & West Indies*, 1764-5, Nos. 1281, 1346, 1419.

the boats for a landing, the gale was still blowing strong from the north and it was found impossible to land in the heavy surf pounding on the beach. Besides, the shore at this point was well protected by batteries ready to open fire as soon as the landing party came within range. This delay gave Colonel Richard Abbott ample time to collect his forces and to make ready to repel an invasion. That evening, when the wind went down, the boats were again dropped overboard, filled with men, and sent forth to take soundings, at the same time they took good care to keep out of range of the batteries. For five days Chavagnac kept his fleet off Charlestown, trying out the temper of the defense by closing in from time to time and exchanging shots with the forts. When it became evident that the place was impregnable, at least for him, he gave orders to abandon the attack and set sail for St. Christopher, where he hoped he would find things more to his liking.[7]

At St. Christopher the English, blissfully indifferent to the situation, were in no shape to withstand an invasion. Walter Hamilton, the governor, had indeed sensed the danger; but his assembly, as we have said, would do nothing for defense, neglected to build a line of trenches, warmly recommended by him, and refused to believe in the presence of French men-of-war in the islands. Had they taken a more realistic view of the situation and had the officers done their duty in the coming conflict, Hamilton was sure he could have saved the section around Brimstone Hill and Sandy Point. Undaunted, nevertheless, by this lack of coöperation, the Governor went ahead on his own responsibility with his preparations. He sent four men to Frigate Bay, south of Basseterre, where fifteen years before Sir Timothy Thornhill had landed to attack the French. Here they were to keep watch for the invaders. When the enemy appeared, two of these men were to carry the news to Basseterre, while the other two hurried across the island to warn the Capesterre troops assembled at Cayonne. Hamilton did more than protect his own island. When news was first brought him concerning the presence of Chavagnac's fleet at Guadeloupe, he sent a note of warning to Colonel Abbott, offering him assistance in case of need. A few days later, when the squadron appeared off Nevis, he withdrew his troops from Cayonne and placed them in

[7]C.S.P., *America & West Indies*, *1706–8*, Nos. 167, 168.

the Jesuit College at Basseterre. The Queen's troops were posted in Fort Brimstone and in Fort Charles just north of it, while another force was stationed at Palmetto Point. Thus the Governor was not taken entirely by surprise when Chavagnac hove in sight on the afternoon of the twenty-first.

The ships anchored in Basseterre roadstead—all but six, which dropped down to Palmetto Point and opened fire on the fortifications. Just after midnight Chavagnac landed his troops in Frigate Bay, and at dawn they moved along the coast in the direction of the capital; while Major Poullain and his Guadeloupe contingent of three hundred were sent by sea to Pointe de Sable to effect a landing, cross over to the eastern side, and march down to Cayonne, laying waste the countryside as he proceeded. A force of two hundred colonists, [8] however, blocked his passage when he stepped ashore and offered a three hours' resistance, after which he drove them back to Fort Charles, where they dug themselves in. This put a stop to any excursion into the Capesterre region. At the same time Chavagnac was leading his men toward Basseterre. A small group attempted to bar his way. Scattered by Du Buc, they fell back on some three hundred infantry and one hundred cavalrymen, placed in line of battle across the invaders' path. Chavagnac paused a moment, then, placing Jean-Clair du Parquet's men on his right and Collart's along the shore on his left, he advanced straight toward the enemy, who, finding themselves outnumbered, quickly fell back on Basseterre. Here Hamilton at first decided to make a stand. He sent word to Colonel Stephen Payne to bring the Queen's troops from Brimstone to his assistance; but his staff, seeing the strength of the enemy, advised him to retire to a stronger place. For this reason the Governor decided to make his stand at Palmetto Point. At this moment word came that Payne was engaged at Pointe de Sable and was retreating southward. Taking the cavalry with him, Hamilton hurried northward and found Payne backed up against Fort Charles and beating off the attack as best he could.

Confident that the French could be held here, Hamilton ordered

---

[8]This number may seem inconsistent with Johnson's statement that there were only 150 men capable of bearing arms; but he was referring only to the regular soldiers supplied by the government.

Payne to establish himself at Brimstone Hill with two hundred men, a position he should surely be able to hold as well as Fort Charles. On the twenty-third of February Poullain advanced as far south as Goodwin's Gut, leaving the fort and Brimstone Hill unmolested, and took up his headquarters in a house belonging to Governor Codrington. He was interested only in plundering and laying waste the countryside and felt he could spare neither the men nor the time to take the two strongholds. In truth destruction seems to have been Chavagnac's main purpose. For several days Poullain marched his men through the plantations around Brimstone Hill, burning, pillaging, and destroying everything he could and keeping as much as possible out of range of the guns on Brimstone and at Fort Charles. The buccaneers acquitted themselves, as usual, well in this sort of business. They seem to have been good for little else, says Chavagnac, who evidently shared De Pointis's opinion of these gentry. Chavagnac himself, after entering Basseterre, continued along the coast indulging in activities as destructive as those of Poullain; then he joined his subordinate and the two made a thorough job of the work of pillage.

On the twenty-sixth of February General Hamilton received the first encouraging news. From a prisoner he learned that the French could not remain more than eight days in St. Christopher according to the plan as originally worked out in Martinique; neither did they have the necessary artillery for attacking fortified positions. At the same time a rumor was spread abroad to the effect that fifteen English ships had been seen off Martinique and that Chavagnac had been ordered to return. Be this as it may, the French commander gave his expedition orders to leave. His supplies were running low, he said, and he had now accomplished what he had set out to do. Yet his action in retiring appeared precipitate to the English, for he carried off only some three hundred Negroes and left a store of plunder in the shape of copper utensils and mill machinery on the shore. All this caused considerable speculation among the defenders, and Governor Johnson suggested that Chavagnac might have been frightened by a letter—intercepted by the French—which he (Johnson) wrote to Hamilton containing the news that men-of-war were on the way from Barbados to assist St. Christopher, as well as some ships from Antigua and Montserrat. At any rate, Chavagnac decided to leave. He first embarked the buccaneers, ordering them to stand by in their ships until the rest of the forces were ready to leave; then all would return to Martinique. But these worthy brothers of the coast were too intent on dividing their plunder to bother about the regular troops, and they promptly set sail, leaving Chavagnac to return as best he could. Taken as a whole, the expedition was not a great success, at least from the financial point of view; though the damage done was estimated at three million livres, the booty carried away was small and consisted chiefly of the three hundred Negroes. It was a cheap victory; the French losses were only twenty killed or wounded. [9]

Iberville arrived at Martinique on the seventh of March, where he found Chavagnac awaiting him. He now had a formidable force at his disposal, sufficient for any undertaking in the Caribbee Islands. Twelve men-of-war and twice as many buccaneer ships were ready to transport two thousand soldiers and freebooters, of whom eleven hundred were local recruits, for an attack on Nevis. Toward the end of March, Iberville left for Guadeloupe, where he added to his forces a detachment of fifty young men, scions of the leading families. Here he held a review of his cohorts, a motley host, arrayed in plumes and wigs and with wide ribbons of silk and gold around their necks, but minus the more necessary equipment of shoes and stockings.

The English were in no condition to offer much resistance to such a strong contingent—though they might, according to some of their own officials, have made a better showing than they did, since they had the advantage of fortified positions. The preceding year Governor Johnson had made a complete survey of Nevis, repaired its fortifications, and erected new ones in certain places. Charlestown and vicinity were well provided for. Its roadstead was protected by the inevitable Fort Charles upon a cliff called Pelican Point, which overlooked the harbor. There were also similar posts on the windward side of the island. [10] As to fighting forces, Nevis was somewhat depleted. After Chavagnac's attempt in February, Johnson had seen fit to send back to Antigua the 115 men he had

[9] *Ibid.*, Nos. 152, 168, 195, 341; Guët, *Le Colonel François de Collart*, pp. 251–57.
[10] *C.S.P., America & West Indies, 1704–5*, No. 1344.

brought with him and to remove a detachment already at Nevis, leaving but 35 soldiers to defend the place.[11] Fortunately the local militia of 430 officers and men was able to fill the breach. There were also 330 seamen on the twenty-five merchantmen in Charlestown harbor who might have helped; but these worthy fellows rushed ashore when the fighting was over and lent the enemy a helping hand in looting the colonists.

On the last day of March, Iberville weighed anchor. He steered his course, as Chavagnac had done before him, between Antigua and Montserrat, coming so close to the latter that its Governor reported having seen a fleet of fifty sail.[12] After hovering over the island for a few hours he bore away for Nevis. His plan was to attack the place buccaneer fashion, that is, by surprise and a sudden assault rather than by a regular siege. For this purpose he divided his men into three groups: one under Chavagnac; another under M. de Maunières; and a third which he kept for himself. In this way he could attack simultaneously at three separate points during the night, thus compelling the defenders to divide their forces, not knowing where the main assault would be launched. Iberville was to land on the southern side, Chavagnac on the north, and Maunières was to attack Charlestown. During the afternoon of the second of April watchguards on Nevis, scanning the sea in the direction of Antigua, saw the French fleet bearing down on them. When the squadron neared the island, five ships under Iberville, accompanied by some smaller vessels, detached themselves from the rest and fell away to leeward, while the main fleet held its northward course to give the impression that the principal attack would be launched on that part of the island. The ruse succeeded, and when Chavagnac passed through the narrows between St. Christopher and Nevis to anchor off Cades Point, no one paid the slightest attention to Iberville's maneuver; for Colonel Abbott, completely deceived, had sent most of his men to the Capesterre region, where he thought the attack would be made. As for Maunières, he kept on down the western coast, and when darkness came Chavagnac quietly raised his anchors and joined him. Both

[11]C.S.P., *America & West Indies*, *1706–8*, No. 448.

[12]The English records give a much larger number of ships than were recorded by the French. This is also true of the number of men. Perhaps it was but natural to exaggerate the strength of a victorious enemy.

squadrons then steered for Green Bay, just above Charlestown. Here Colonel Abbott had placed men to repel a possible landing, thirty under Colonel William Burt at Long Point and forty under Colonel William Butler at Gaulding's Point. When the French arrived they found that the former had deserted his post, while the latter had failed to keep a proper watch. Unopposed, Chavagnac landed his troops, each man carrying a musket with bayonet attached and a sword or poleax.

Meanwhile Iberville had anchored his squadron in French Bay (as it was later called, in memory of the invasion) at the southern-most extremity of the island, there to await the signal for the attack. At three o'clock in the morning the distant rumble of guns broke the stillness of the night. Hastily landing his men, the com-mander marched rapidly overland to Charlestown, which he cap-tured without a struggle, for the main body of the troops had been drawn to the windward side of the island by Chavagnac's feint of the preceding day. This done, he attacked several small detach-ments which still held firm and drove them inland. He then ad-vanced to a battery Chavagnac was supposed to take, seized it himself, and sent word to his subordinate that it would be un-necessary for him to disembark his troops. Chavagnac, however, not to be outdone, dispatched his men to capture the merchantmen which had just been loaded with goods destined for England and were lying at anchor ready to sail. By sunrise the job was done, and Charlestown had changed hands. To all intents and purposes Iberville was now master of the colony, but he must first compel the surrender of a little band which still held out. On a hill back of Charlestown this detachment engaged the invaders with con-siderable spirit, putting up a stiff fight against the main forces. They were soon overpowered, however, and were obliged to fall back on a fortified position called in the West Indies a "deodand," that is, a sort of fortified retreat built to be used by women, chil-dren, and the infirm in case of invasion. Here the English soldiers joined some of their own forces who preferred the security of a stronghold to the dangers of the open field. Within the walls of the deodand they all might have held out or have made at least a creditable showing; but when Iberville surrounded the place, he stationed his buccaneers in the front line, hoping to terrify the

the defenders so that they would surrender rather than risk an assault at the hands of such ferocious marauders. The English commander took the hint. Realizing the hopelessness of his position, he accepted the terms offered him by Iberville and capitulated on the fourth of April. [13]

By the conditions of surrender, as drawn up by the French commander, the inhabitants were to retain their wearing apparel and to be allowed to keep suitable dwelling places, but the rest of their goods would become the property of the victors. All were to surrender themselves as prisoners of war, Colonel Abbott and his officers being allowed to retain their arms. Although the Negroes were to be delivered to the French as part of the booty, Iberville with a show of magnanimity gave back a few of these blackamoors to the Colonel and certain prominent persons. The inhabitants were to be subsequently set at liberty, provided a like number of French prisoners then languishing in England and in the English possessions were also given their freedom. To insure the performance of these conditions, the English gave four hostages.

The conditions may have been harsh, but the French were there for loot and proposed to take all they could to reimburse themselves for their expenses and to satisfy the buccaneers. Furthermore, the defense put up by the English did not inspire the French with much respect for their foes. They could not but compare the unsoldierly conduct of the British officers with that of the Negroes, who took to the mountains and drove back the invaders time and again by their murderous fire. The surrender of the deodand where the English were securely entrenched without firing a shot had vastly amused the French, who later admitted that they would have granted more favorable terms had the enemy put up a more spirited resistance. These criticisms of British inefficiency are taken from British sources (Colonel Abbott himself made some stinging comments about his subordinates) and may be regarded as evidence that the French forces were greatly overestimated. Surely the colonists did well to put up any resistance if they had only approximately four hundred men to oppose several times that number.

According to English testimony, Iberville apparently broke the

[13]*Ibid.*, Nos. 270, 282, 357, 452; Dessalles, *Histoire générale des Antilles*, II, 340–42.

treaty immediately. He ordered the colonists in the deodand, whom he regarded (and treated) as prisoners of war, to be brought to Charlestown, while he turned his buccaneers loose to loot and burn the dwellings and the sugar-mills. So thoroughly was the job done, that no more than twenty houses remained standing when the French fleet sailed away. In Charlestown the wretched inhabitants were crowded into various buildings—the men being imprisoned in the church and the jail and not provided with food except that which their wives could obtain for them. To add to their misery an epidemic of smallpox broke out. Such treatment naturally led to vigorous protests by these people, who considered themselves protected by the terms of the capitulation; but Iberville bluntly replied that he regarded them as prisoners because they had failed to give up the Negro slaves according to the agreement, and thus far the French had been able to round up only one-half the available supply. There was a certain amount of irony in Iberville's contention, for the slaves had already taken refuge in the mountains, where they were defending themselves with more zeal than their masters had shown. To break the deadlock, Iberville called a meeting of the principal colonists on the seventeenth and made them a fresh proposal. By this new arrangement he was to forego the plunder he had promised himself and refrain fron inflicting further damage on the colony if the inhabitants would agree to deliver fourteen hundred Negroes to Martinique within the next six months, or, in case this number could not be obtained, to pay one hundred pieces-of-eight for each slave short of the quota. The colonists refused to comply with this request, pleading inability to meet its provisions. But Iberville was anxious to bring the matter to a close, perhaps because his cruisers had reported the presence of a hostile fleet off Barbados (it later turned out to be a French squadron), and he at once ordered the most rigorous measures to be taken to bring his captives to a more reasonable frame of mind. Throwing the men into prison on board his warships, he threatened them with transportation to the Spanish colonies. Colonels Abbott, Burt, and Butler and James Bevon, all members of the Council, were incarcerated on the "Juste" and told they would be carried to France unless they immediately put their signatures to the agreement. It was useless to struggle; there was nothing to do but submit; besides, much might happen in six months. On the nineteenth a document was drawn up to which nearly all the principal inhabitants affixed their signatures, promising to supply the fourteen hundred Negroes within the time specified or pay the forfeit. As a reward for signing, Iberville published a curious proclamation to the effect that all the surplus remaining after the delivery of the Negroes and all the sugar-mills, horses, cattle, and similar property should be divided among the signatories in proportion to their wealth and that no others should have a share, a socialistic arrangement promptly vetoed by the British government. Two days later Iberville sailed with his fleet, taking with him four hostages to guarantee the fulfillment of the treaty.

The expedition had been successful. Iberville had carried off 3,187 Negroes, of whom 800 were destined for the buccaneers, the balance for the fleet; besides, there were 1,400 more (or their cash equivalent) to come later. The destruction had been great; the measures taken to extort the plunder severe. According to Colonel Abbott the French acted with great cruelty, burning churches, digging up the dead (probably to find jewelry), defacing tombstones, destroying records, and imprisoning men and women suspected of being wealthy. In fact it was openly stated that Iberville was a less civilized man than Chavagnac. This of course may have been true, for Iberville had learned his trade by fighting Indians in the wilds of North America, where proper consideration for noncombatants in a captured settlement was not well understood. But when we remember that a large number of his forces were buccaneers whose revolting cruelty had long kept the peaceful colonists of the West Indies in terror, we must credit Iberville with exercising a restraining influence on his lawless followers. Admitting all the accusations brought against the invaders by the English to be true, no instance is given of wanton killing, to say nothing of the use of torture to learn the whereabouts of hidden wealth, a practice popular among the freebooters.[14]

Iberville now returned to Martinique, arriving there on the twenty-sixth of April. He was immensely pleased with the results of his campaign and proud of his army. Before leaving Nevis he had dispatched a vessel to France with tidings of his victory, and

[14]*C.S.P., America & West Indies, 1706–8*, Nos. 270, 357.

now he wrote a eulogy of his troops, expressing regret that only the time element prevented his undertaking other expeditions in this locality. "I do not pretend," he said, "to praise here each officer, but I shall say that generally speaking one could not see better conduct or more courage and firmness, which qualities extend to the rank and file." From Martinique, where the greater part of his forces disbanded, he proceeded to San Domingo, hoping to raise a fresh supply of buccaneers for his further undertakings. Those who had gone with him to Nevis had left him, dissatisfied with their share of the plunder. He sent the squadron to Leogane, while he himself took the "Juste" to Cap François, where he obtained a brigantine of fourteen guns. On rejoining his fleet he made inquiries regarding the possibility of raising recruits there and learned to his great joy that fifteen hundred men could be obtained on short notice.

The English throughout America were now thoroughly alarmed. Governor Hamilton of St. Christopher called loudly for help, expecting a recurrence of the unpleasantness he had experienced a month before. Great fears were also entertained that Iberville would form a junction with Du Casse and that a formidable fleet would undertake the reduction of Jamaica. The governor of that island, fully aroused, proclaimed martial law. Sir William Whetstone, commander of the West India station, made an attempt to prevent the junction of the French fleets, but was driven back by contrary winds. Nor was this fear confined to the West Indies. In New York, Governor Cornbury received word that a French merchant had boarded Iberville's ship and had learned of an intended attack on New York. Remembering Iberville's excursion into the harbor a few years back, the colonists began to clamor for better fortifications. Even in Rhode Island measures were quietly taken to construct batteries for the protection of Newport. Truly the successes at Nevis and St. Christopher had resounded throughout British America.

But the blow never fell. Iberville finally left San Domingo and proceeded to Havana, where he could make preparations for his drive to the north. While his flagship lay in the harbor, he was stricken with yellow fever and died on board July 9, 1706. On the same day his body was taken ashore and buried in the cathedral.

Later this building was torn down, and the church erected on its site does not contain the grave of this great Canadian.

Iberville's campaign was the last major expedition for several years to come and may be regarded as the last of any importance during the war. The center of the great conflict was, of course, in Europe, and it was in European waters that the fleets were most busily engaged. Neither France nor England could spare the ships or supply the money to carry on a war in this remote part of the world, where the stakes were but a few scattered islands, while Spain, whose American policy was always defensive, had no desire to take the initiative when her possessions were not invaded. The King of France had suffered too many defeats at home to adopt an aggressive policy in the West Indies. He even feared lest the successes of Chavagnac and Iberville might cause reprisals and wrote his representative in San Domingo to live on the best possible terms with his Spanish neighbors and try to dissuade them from trading with the Dutch at Cuaraçao. He also urged him to remain at Leogane, where he could keep a watchful eye on Jamaica, for it was rumored that a fleet of ten ships was about to sail from England.

In this manner the war dragged on for several years, punctuated by small naval encounters and occasional raids. Just before the Treaty of Utrecht rang down the curtain on the scene a French expedition was launched against Montserrat that deserves a passing glance. In the month of March, 1712, Jacques Cassard, one of the King's most able seamen, was placed at the head of a small squadron of three warships, five frigates, and two ketches,[15] and sent forth "to blow up earthworks, houses, stores, and all other buildings without exception," both Dutch and English. As the condition of the treasury did not permit heavy expenditures, two of the frigates were outfitted by a group of Marseilles merchants for what they could get in the way of plunder. Sailing from Toulon, Cassard paused long enough at the Cape Verde Islands to sack St. Iago, then he proceeded to Martinique. Here he made arrangements to increase the size of his expedition. He approached

[15]"Neptune," "Temeraire," "Rubis," "Parfaite," "Vestale," "Meduse," "Prince de Frise," "Aligre," "Anne," and "Marine."

three colonels, all influential men, our old friends François de
Collart, Jean du Buc, and Louis du Prey, with the suggestion that
each furnish six hundred men—part militia, part buccaneers—
promising to each a share of the booty. The offer was quickly
snapped up, and Cassard called a council of war, made up of these
three and others of lesser rank, to formulate a plan of campaign.
The general trend of opinion was in favor of an attack on Antigua
if twenty-five hundred or even two thousand men could be assembled,
otherwise it should be Montserrat or St. Christopher or both. In
the end they decided they were strong enough to tackle Antigua.
Recruits were speedily raised, and in three days Du Buc and
Collart had six hundred men each, while Du Prey had gathered
more than three hundred. About thirty boats were secured to
transport them.

On the sixteenth of July, Cassard arrived off Antigua and
anchored in Willoughby Bay. That night he attempted a landing,
but a strong wind arose, too strong for the boats carrying the men
ashore, and Cassard was obliged to abandon his plan after he had
lost several boats and a few men. Foiled in this attempt, he steered
for Montserrat. He anchored first in Carr's Bay, then off Plymouth,
where he opened a general attack. It was successful. Landing guns
as well as men, he was able to bring such a fire to bear upon the
town that the inhabitants were only too glad to escape and take
refuge in the deodand they had constructed far inland. This stronghold Du Buc had the good fortune to capture. The amount of booty
was immense; it included the cargoes of four merchantmen seized
in the roadstead and some twelve hundred slaves, a large number for
such a small island. The sum total of the loot was appraised at
£180,000. There was more than enough to satisfy everyone, and
in order to keep the loyalty of the buccaneers Cassard made sure that
they received a large share; he did not want as much trouble
with them as other commanders had experienced. When the French
were dividing the spoils, the Governor of Antigua sent word to
Barbados asking for help; meanwhile he dispatched four ships to
Montserrat carrying six hundred men, to see what could be done
before the Barbadian contingent arrived. Their appearance off
Plymouth caused the French to withdraw to Basseterre, Guade-

loupe, where the plunder was landed and the ships put in condition for the depredations which Cassard now undertook against the Dutch settlements of Guiana, St. Eustatius, and Curaçao.[16]

The war which had lasted for a decade was now drawing rapidly to a close. In the month of April, 1711, the Emperor Joseph I died and was succeeded by his brother the Archduke Charles. This was the archduke who had been the Anglo-Dutch candidate for the Spanish throne in preference to the Bourbon, Philip V. Should the crowns of both Spain and the Empire be placed upon the brow of this prince, the Austro-Spanish Empire of the sixteenth century would be in a measure revived, and the union of two such powerful nations was something the British government did not care to contemplate. As the lesser of the two evils they preferred the union of France and Spain under the same ruling family provided one monarch did not occupy both thrones. Negotiations for a peace were therefore begun and plenipotentiaries were authorized to meet in Utrecht in January, 1712, to open the discussions. In June an armistice was declared.

The sessions at Utrecht were many and long, for the issues were greatly involved and of paramount importance to Europe. Great Britain and her allies had been uniformly victorious, and now they were about to surrender the issue for which the war had been fought, namely, the Bourbon succession to the Spanish throne. France was beaten and exhausted, yet she was about to gain her point: she was therefore prepared to make concessions. It is impossible for us to discuss the Treaty of Utrecht in all its ramifications; we are interested only in the clauses affecting the Western Hemisphere. When the Treaty was finally signed on April 11, 1713, the English had made decisive gains in solidifying their American colonial empire. The King of France surrendered in perpetuity all the regions adjacent to Hudson Bay and Hudson Strait, including the lands watered by the rivers flowing into them. In addition to this he agreed to pay for the damage done to the property of the Hudson's Bay Company by his subjects since the armistice, the amount due to be determined by a commission appointed for this purpose. The commission was also to pass on

[16]Guët, *Le Colonel François de Collart*, pp. 273-79; *C.S.P., America & West Indies, 1712-14*, Nos. 38, 57, 95, 638; La Nicollière-Teijeiro, *Jacques Cassard*, chap. vii.

claims for losses inflicted by the French on English shipping and at Montserrat and, of course, for damages inflicted on the French by the English; in short, for any harm done by either side after the armistice. The King of France also agreed to surrender French St. Christopher, thus ending forever the dual ownership. In North America the French gave up in addition to the Hudson Bay region the province of Acadia and Port Royal in Nova Scotia, retaining only the island of Cape Breton. In like manner was Newfoundland turned over to Great Britain, though the right was retained for French fishermen to land on certain parts of it to dry their fish.[17]

If the Treaty of Utrecht brought nothing else to the French and English colonists, it at least brought them peace—a peace that lasted more than two score years. For the preceding half-century, from 1665 to 1713, the West Indian settlers had suffered a series of wars broken only by occasional truces, the longest of which lasted almost ten years. But now a change for the better had come. The death of aged Louis XIV, which took place shortly after Utrecht, removed that ambitious monarch from the scene, and Europe, exhausted by her struggles, laid aside her arms to enjoy a period of peace. Freed thus from danger, the French were able to turn their attention exclusively to the development of their rich possessions, and the first half of the eighteenth century shows a steady increase in the wealth of their colonies. The buccaneers, long the scourge of the hard-working colonists, now became a thing of the past. During the latter years of the conflict they had deteriorated sadly in quality, as we can see by comparing the courageous if brutal little band that fought under Colonel Morgan at the first capture of St. Christopher with the wretched crews that served under De Pointis at Carthagena. Deprived of any legitimate outlet for their talents by the coming of a permanent peace, the better element among them retired from the sea, while the worse turned pirate and were hunted by the navies of all nations.

It is difficult to say whether either the French or the English colonists emerged from the conflict in a stronger position than before. The result seems to have been a draw. England obtained all St. Christopher, rather a small gain for fifty years of warfare, yet one which in the long run was likely to encourage peace in these

[17]Vast, *Les Grands traités de règne de Louis XIV*, pp. 76–81.

regions; for the dual ownership of the island was an unnatural situation and was always a source of trouble in spite of its inhabitants' well-meaning resolutions to remain on friendly terms. France retained beside her main possessions St. Bartholomew, St. Eustatius, and half of St. Martin (shared with the Dutch), and also claimed Tobago, for whatever such a claim was worth. Dominica and St. Vincent remained practically a no-man's-land, inhabited only by the Caribs. That so many lives had been lost and so much property destroyed with so little permanent result is not surprising when we stop to look at the picture as a whole. The West Indies were never more than so many pawns in the game of world politics played by their rulers, a game in which the balance of power in Europe and the vast territories of North America were the big stakes. Therefore at the end of a war the various captured Caribbee Islands were given back to their original owners in return for concessions elsewhere. Thanks to the peace now established at Utrecht, the eighteenth century saw these islands reach the highest point of their prosperity. It remained for the nineteenth to see their decline.

BIBLIOGRAPHY

BIBLIOGRAPHY

Ballet, Jules, La Guadeloupe. 3 vols. Basseterre, Guadeloupe, 1894–99.

Bourne, Ruth, Queen Anne's Navy in the West Indies. New Haven, 1939.

Bridges, George W., The Annals of Jamaica. 2 vols. London, 1828.

Burchett, Josiah, Memoirs of Transactions at Sea. London, 1703.

Calmon-Maison, Robert, Le Maréchal de Château-Renault (1637–1716). Paris, 1903.

Charlevoix, Pierre François-Xavier de, Histoire de l'isle espagnole ou de S. Domingue, ecrite particulièrement sur des mémoires manuscrits de P.J.B. Le Pers. Amsterdam, 1733.

Charnock, John, Biographia navalis. London, 1794–96.

Chassaigne, Marc, "Un Maître des requêtes lieutenant-général des armées du roi: M. de la Barre aux Antilles," *Revue des études historiques*, LXXXVI (1920), 321–52.

Clément, Pierre, Lettres, instructions, et mémoires de Colbert. 8 vols. Paris, 1861–82.

Clowes, William L., The Royal Navy. London, 1897–1903.

Crouse, Nellis M., French Pioneers in the West Indies, 1624–1664. New York, 1940.

Daney, Sidney, Histoire de la Martinique. 6 vols. Fort Royal, Martinique, 1846.

Desjeans, J. B. L., Baron de Pointis, *see* Pointis, Sieur.

Dessalles, Adrien, Histoire générale des Antilles. 5 vols. Paris, 1847.

Dessalles. Pierre Regis, Histoire legislative des Antilles; ou, Annales du Conseil Souverain de la Martinique. Ed. with notes by Adrien Dessalles and forming the third volume of his *Histoire générale*.

Du Casse, Robert, L'Amiral du Casse. Paris, 1876.

Du Motey, Henri, Renault, Guillaume d'Orange. Paris, 1908.

Du Tertre, Jean-Baptiste, Histoire générale des Antilles, 4 vols. Paris, 1667–1671.

Esquemeling, John, The Buccaneers of America. New York, 1893.

Funck-Brentano, Frantz, Lettres de cachet à Paris. Paris, 1903.

Great Britain, Privy Council, Acts of the Privy Council of England. Colonial Series. London, 1613–80.

——Public Record Office, Calendar of State Papers, Colonial Series, America and West Indies, 1661–1714.

Guérin, Léon, Histoire maritime de France. 6 vols. Paris, 1857–58.

Guët, Isidore, Le Colonel François de Collart. Vannes, 1893.

Haring, Clarence Henry, The Buccaneers in the West Indies in the XVII Century. New York, 1910.

Hart, Francis R., Admirals of the Caribbean. New York, 1935.

Hingham, Charles S. S., The Development of the Leeward Islands under the Restoration. Cambridge, 1921.

La Barre, Joseph-Antoine Le Febvre de, see Le Febvre de la Barre, Joseph-Antoine.

Labat, Jean-Baptiste, Nouveau voyage aux isles de l'Amérique. 2 vols. La Haye, 1724.

La Nicollière-Teijeiro, Stéphane de, Jacques Cassard, capitaine de vaisseau. Vannes, 1890.

La Roncière, Charles G.M.B. de, Histoire de la marine française. 6 vols. Paris, 1899–1932.

Lediard, Thomas, The Naval History of England. London, 1735.

Le Febvre de la Barre, Joseph-Antoine, Relations de ce qui c'est passé dans les isles et terre-ferme de l'Amérique pendant la dernière guerre avec l'Angleterre. Ed. by Jean de Clodoré. Paris, 1671.

Margry, Pierre, Relations et mémoires inedits pour servire à l'histoire de la France dans les pays d'outremer. Paris, 1867.

Mims, Stewart L., Colbert's West India Policy. New Haven, 1912.

Moreau de Saint-Méry, Médéric Louis E., A Topographical and Political Description of the Spanish Part of Saint-Domingo. Trans by W. Cobbett. 2 vols. Philadelphia, 1798.

——Lois et constitutions des colonies françoises de l'Amérique sous le vent. 6 vols. Paris, 1784–90.

Morgan, William T., The British West Indies during King William's War, 1689–97, Journal of Modern History, II (1930), 378–409.

——Economic Aspects of the Negotiations at Ryswick. Royal Historical Transactions, Fourth Series, XIV (1931), 225–49.

Oexmelin, Alexandre-Olivier (John Esquemeling), Histoire des avanturiers flibustiers. 2 vols. 1775.

Pointis, Sieur (J.B.L. Desjeans, Baron de Pointis), A Genuine and Particular Account of the Taking of Carthagena. London, 1740. Reprinted in Sparks, Historical Tracts, Colonial, vol. II.

Ravaisson, François N.N., Archives de la Bastille. 19 vols. Paris, 1866–1904.

Rodgers, W. L., A Study of Attacks upon Fortified Harbors. Proceedings of the U. S. Naval Institute, XXX (1904), 537–44.

Saint-Yves, M. G., Les Campagnes de Jean d'Estrées dans la mer des Antilles (1676–8), Bulletin de géographie historique et descriptive, 1899 pp. 217–46.

Southey, Thomas, Chronological History of the West Indies. 3 vols. London, 1827.

Spencer, Norman, Relation of the Proceedings against the French in the
    Caribbee Islands, 1691, in Harleian Miscellany, Vol. II, London, 1809.

Vaissière, Pierre de (Georges Pierre Charles de), Saint-Domingue, la
    société et la vie créole sous l'ancien régime (1629-1789). Paris, 1909.

Vast, Henri, Les Grands traités du règne de Louis XIV. Paris, 1893-99.

Wimpffen, Alexander Stanislaus, Baron de, A Voyage to Saint Domingo,
    1788-90. Trans. by J. Wright. Paris. 1817.

INDEX

INDEX

Abbott, Richard, 296, 300, 301, 302, 303, 304
Acadia, 98
Albuquerque, Duke and Duchess of, 260
Amblimont, Marquis d', 105, 107, 110, 248, 249
Anguilla, governor of, 149
Anne, Queen of England, 252
Antigua, governors, 17, 149; French expedition against, 48–52, 55; terms of surrender, 52; returned to English, 83, 86
Arbouville, Chevalier d', 154, 161, 172, 179
Arundell, James, 126
Augiers, Chevalier des, 214
Auger, Charles, governor of Mariegalante, 149, 168; during defense of Martinique, 181, 185, 186, 187, 188, 250; preparations for defense of Guadeloupe, 266–68; during siege, 270–87; relieved of post: made governor of San Domingo, 291
Austro-Spanish Empire, 308

Baas-Castlemore, Jean-Charles de, 143; title and commission given by King, 62, 94; expedition expected, 67, 76; countermanded, 83; program of reorganization, 94 ff.; position re restoration of St. Christopher, 99, 101; during war against Dutch, 103–12 passim; creditable administration: death, 112
Barbados, governors, 61, 99, 100, 149; Leeward Islands made independent of, 100; rivals of northern islands: resulting difficulties, 100, 252; consternation caused by Martinique defeat, 189
Barbuda, island, 52
Baron, Captain, 37, 39
Barre, Antoine Le Febvre de la, 36, 39, 49, 94, 95; plan to regain Cayenne, 5; company formed, 6; summoned to conference with West India Company's directors, 43; in command of fleet, 44; conduct concerning destination, 45; powers and title, 46, 94; concessions to planters, 47; conduct of war by, 47–83 passim; calls upon English

to surrender, 51; treaty obtained by, 52; supreme command, 54; friction between Clodoré and, 56, 95; loss of prestige, 62; new commission as reward for services, 63; victory over English, 81; solves problem of supplies for colonists, 85; diplomatic duels over restitution of St. Christopher, 86–92, 98, 99
Barrett, James, 82
Barry, Samuel, 127
Basque, Michel le, 136
Basseterre, towns by name of, 12n
Basseterre, during siege of Guadeloupe, 266, 273–79 passim
Baston (companion of Grandmaison), 48, 50
Beauregard, Sieur de, 190, 193, 194, 196
Beeston, Sir William, efforts in defense of Jamaica, 190–96, 198, 199; desire to continue war, 211; fears caused by rumors of French strength: appeals for British aid, 213 ff., 242
Beckford, Peter, 192, 198
Benbow, John, Vice-Admiral, 256, 259, 268; encounter with fleet of Du Casse, 261–65; brings captains to trial, 264; death, 265
Bernanos, Major, aids defense of San Domingo, 200–208; death, 208
Berry, Captain John, 61–71 passim
Bevon, James, 303
Bibliography, 311–13
Binckes, Jacob, 110–18 passim; death, 119
Blakiston, Nathaniel, 149, 162, 163, 171, 186
Blanc, Julien le Cordelier du, 17–20, 43, 44
Blathwayt, William, 179
Blénac, Charles de la Roche-Courbon-Comte de, 113, 120; appointed governor-general, 118; islands under, and their rulers, 148; authority restricted, 148; expedition against St. Eustatius, 149 ff.; against St. Christopher, 155 f.; criticized by officers, 160; resigns, 161; resumes governor-generalship, 180; defends Martinique, 181–88; hears of Wilmot's arrival, 199